Frederick Chopin as
A Man And Musician
Vol. 1

by

Frederick Niecks

Frederick Chopin as
A Man And Musician
Vol. 1
by Frederick Niecks

ISBN: 978-93-59321-10-3

Published by

DOUBLE 9 BOOKS
2/13-B, Ansari Road
Daryaganj, New Delhi – 110002
info@double9books.com
www.double9books.com
Tel. 011-40042856

ABOUT THE AUTHOR

Frederick Niecks (3 February 1845 – 24 June 1924) was a German musical scholar and author who spent much of his life in Scotland. His most famous works are biographies of Frédéric Chopin and Robert Schumann. Friedrich Maternus Niecks was born in Düsseldorf, the son of a conductor and instructor, and the grandson of a professional musician. His father taught him music, and he later studied violin with Leopold Auer and others, as well as piano and composition with Julius Tausch. He made his debut at the age of 13 with Charles Auguste de Bériot's Violin Concerto No. 2, then joined the Musikverein orchestra, where he remained until the age of 21. In 1868, he expressed a wish to go to the United Kingdom, and Alexander Mackenzie persuaded him to reside in Scotland, where he worked as a violist in Mackenzie's string quartet in Edinburgh and as an organist and teacher in Dumfries. In 1879, he began contributing to The Musical Times on a regular basis. He wrote a Concise Dictionary of Musical Terms in two editions in 1884. Frédéric Chopin as Man and Musician, his magnum work, was released in 1888, with a German version following in 1889. This was Chopin's first full biography.

CONTENTS

PREFACE

While the novelist has absolute freedom to follow his artistic instinct and intelligence, the biographer is fettered by the subject-matter with which he proposes to deal. The former may hopefully pursue an ideal, the latter must rest satisfied with a compromise between the desirable and the necessary. No doubt, it is possible to thoroughly digest all the requisite material, and then present it in a perfect, beautiful form. But this can only be done at a terrible loss, at a sacrifice of truth and trustworthiness. My guiding principle has been to place before the reader the facts collected by me as well as the conclusions at which I arrived. This will enable him to see the subject in all its bearings, with all its pros and cons, and to draw his own conclusions, should mine not obtain his approval. Unless an author proceeds in this way, the reader never knows how far he may trust him, how far the evidence justifies his judgment. For—not to speak of cheats and fools—the best informed are apt to make assertions unsupported or insufficiently supported by facts, and the wisest cannot help seeing things through the coloured spectacles of their individuality. The foregoing remarks are intended to explain my method, not to excuse carelessness of literary workmanship. Whatever the defects of the present volumes may be—and, no doubt, they are both great and many—I have laboured to the full extent of my humble abilities to group and present my material perspicuously, and to avoid diffuseness and rhapsody, those besetting sins of writers on music.

The first work of some length having Chopin for its subject was Liszt's "Frederic Chopin," which, after appearing in 1851 in the Paris journal "La France musicale," came out in book-form, still in French, in 1852 (Leipzig: Breitkopf and Hartel.—Translated into English by M. W. Cook, and published by William Reeves, London, 1877). George Sand describes it as "un peu exuberant de style, mais rempli de bonnes choses et de tres-belles pages." These words, however, do in no way justice to the book: for, on the one hand, the style is excessively, and not merely a little, exuberant; and, on the other hand, the "good things" and "beautiful pages" amount to a psychological study of Chopin, and an aesthetical study of his works, which it is impossible to over-estimate. Still, the book is no biography. It records few dates and events, and these few are for the most part incorrect. When, in 1878, the second edition of F. Chopin was passing through the press, Liszt remarked to me:—

"I have been told that there are wrong dates and other mistakes in my book, and that the dates and facts are correctly given in Karasowski's biography of Chopin [which had in the meantime been published]. But, though I often thought of reading it, I have not yet done so. I got my information from Paris friends on whom I believed I might depend. The Princess Wittgenstein [who then lived in Rome, but in 1850 at Weimar, and is said to have had a share in the production of the book] wished me to make some alterations in the new edition. I tried to please her, but, when she was still dissatisfied, I told her to add and alter whatever she liked."

From this statement it is clear that Liszt had not the stuff of a biographer in him. And, whatever value we may put on the Princess Wittgenstein's additions and alterations, they did not touch the vital faults of the work, which, as a French critic remarked, was a symphonie funebre rather than a biography. The next book we have to notice, M. A. Szulc's Polish Fryderyk Chopin i Utwory jego Muzyczne (Posen, 1873), is little more than a chaotic, unsifted collection of notices, criticisms, anecdotes, &c., from Polish, German, and French books and magazines. In 1877 Moritz Karasowski, a native of Warsaw, and since 1864 a member of the Dresden orchestra, published his Friedrich Chopin: sein Leben, seine Werke und seine Briefe (Dresden: F. Ries.—Translated into English by E. Hill, under the title Frederick Chopin: "His Life, Letters, and Work," and published by William Reeves, London, in 1879). This was the first serious attempt at a biography of Chopin. The author reproduced in the book what had been brought to light in Polish magazines and other publications regarding Chopin's life by various countrymen of the composer, among whom he himself was not the least notable. But the most valuable ingredients are, no doubt, the Chopin letters which the author obtained from the composer's relatives, with whom he was acquainted. While gratefully acknowledging his achievements, I must not omit to indicate his shortcomings—his unchecked partiality for, and boundless admiration of his hero; his uncritical acceptance and fanciful embellishments of anecdotes and hearsays; and the extreme paucity of his information concerning the period of Chopin's life which begins with his settlement in Paris. In 1878 appeared a second edition of the work, distinguished from the first by a few additions and many judicious omissions, the original two volumes being reduced to one. But of more importance than the second German edition is the first Polish edition, "Fryderyk Chopin: Zycie, Listy, Dziela," two volumes (Warsaw: Gebethner and Wolff, 1882), which contains a series of, till then, unpublished letters from Chopin to Fontana. Of Madame A. Audley's short and readable "Frederic Chopin, sa vie et ses oeuvres" (Paris: E. Plon et Cie., 1880), I need only say that for the most part it follows Karasowski, and where it does not is not always correct. Count Wodzinski's "Les trois Romans de Frederic Chopin" (Paris: Calmann Levy, 1886)—according to the title treating only of the composer's love for Constantia Gladkowska, Maria Wodzinska, and George Sand, but in reality having a wider scope—cannot be altogether ignored, though it is more of the nature of a novel than of a biography. Mr. Joseph Bennett, who based his "Frederic Chopin" (one of Novello's Primers of Musical Biography) on Liszt's and Karasowski's works, had in the parts dealing with Great Britain the advantage of notes by Mr. A.J. Hipkins, who inspired also, to some extent at least, Mr. Hueffer in his essay Chopin ("Fortnightly Review," September, 1877; and reprinted in "Musical Studies"—Edinburgh: A. & C. Black, 1880). This ends the list of biographies with any claims to originality. There are, however, many interesting contributions to a biography of Chopin to be found in works of various kinds. These shall be mentioned in the course of my narrative; here I will point out only the two most important ones— namely, George Sand's "Histoire de ma Vie," first published in the Paris newspaper "La Presse" (1854) and subsequently in book-form; and her six volumes of "Correspondance," 1812-1876 (Paris: Calmann Levy, 1882-1884).

My researches had for their object the whole life of Chopin, and his historical, political, artistical, social, and personal surroundings, but they were chiefly directed to the least known and most interesting period of his career—his life in France, and his visits to Germany and Great Britain. My chief sources of information are divisible into two classes—newspapers, magazines, pamphlets, correspondences, and books; and conversations I held with, and letters I received from, Chopin's pupils, friends, and acquaintances. Of his pupils, my warmest thanks are due to Madame Dubois (nee Camille O'Meara), Madame Rubio (nee Vera de Kologrivof), Mdlle. Gavard, Madame Streicher (nee Friederike Muller), Adolph Gutmann, M. Georges Mathias, Brinley Richards, and Lindsay Sloper; of friends and acquaintances, to Liszt, Ferdinand Hiller, Franchomme, Charles Valentin Alkan, Stephen Heller, Edouard Wolff, Mr. Charles Halle, Mr. G. A. Osborne, T. Kwiatkowski, Prof. A. Chodzko, M. Leonard Niedzwiecki (gallice, Nedvetsky), Madame Jenny Lind-Goldschmidt, Mr. A. J. Hipkins, and Dr. and Mrs. Lyschinski. I am likewise greatly indebted to Messrs. Breitkopf and Hartel, Karl Gurckhaus (the late proprietor of the firm of Friedrich Kistner), Julius Schuberth, Friedrich Hofmeister, Edwin Ashdown, Richault & Cie, and others, for information in connection with the publication of

Chopin's works. It is impossible to enumerate all my obligations—many of my informants and many furtherers of my labours will be mentioned in the body of the book; many, however, and by no means the least helpful, will remain unnamed. To all of them I offer the assurance of my deep-felt gratitude. Not a few of my kind helpers, alas! are no longer among the living; more than ten years have gone by since I began my researches, and during that time Death has been reaping a rich harvest.

The Chopin letters will, no doubt, be regarded as a special feature of the present biography. They may, I think, be called numerous, if we consider the master's dislike to letter-writing. Ferdinand Hiller—whose almost unique collection of letters addressed to him by his famous friends in art and literature is now, and will be for years to come, under lock and key among the municipal archives at Cologne—allowed me to copy two letters by Chopin, one of them written conjointly with Liszt. Franchomme, too, granted me the privilege of copying his friend's epistolary communications. Besides a number of letters that have here and there been published, I include, further, a translation of Chopin's letters to Fontana, which in Karasowski's book (i.e., the Polish edition) lose much of their value, owing to his inability to assign approximately correct dates to them.

The space which I give to George Sand is, I think, justified by the part she plays in the life of Chopin. To meet the objections of those who may regard my opinion of her as too harsh, I will confess that I entered upon the study of her character with the impression that she had suffered much undeserved abuse, and that it would be incumbent upon a Chopin biographer to defend her against his predecessors and the friends of the composer. How entirely I changed my mind, the sequel will show.

In conclusion, a few hints as to the pronunciation of Polish words, which otherwise might puzzle the reader uninitiated in the mysteries of that rarely-learned language. Aiming more at simplicity than at accuracy, one may say that the vowels are pronounced somewhat like this: a as in "arm," aL like the nasal French "on," e as in "tell," e/ with an approach to the French "e/" (or to the German "u [umlaut]" and "o [umlaut]"), eL like the nasal French "in," i as in "pick," o as in "not," o/ with an approach to the French "ou," u like the French ou, and y with an approach to the German "i" and "u." The following consonants are pronounced as in English: b, d, f, g (always hard), h, k, I, m, n, p, s, t, and z. The following single and double consonants differ from the English pronunciation: c like "ts," c/ softer than c, j like "y," l/ like "ll" with the tongue pressed against the upper row of teeth, n/ like "ny" (i.e., n softened by i), r sharper than in English, w like "v," z/ softer than z, z. and rz like the French "j," ch like the German guttural "ch" in "lachen" (similar to "ch" in the Scotch "loch"), cz like "ch" in "cherry," and sz like "sh" in "sharp." Mr. W. R. Morfill ("A Simplified Grammar of the Polish Language") elucidates the combination szcz, frequently to be met with, by the English expression "smasht china," where the italicised letters give the pronunciation. Lastly, family names terminating in take a instead of i when applied to women.

April, 1888.

PROEM

POLAND AND THE POLES

THE works of no composer of equal importance bear so striking a national impress as those of Chopin. It would, however, be an error to attribute this simply and solely to the superior force of the Polish musician's patriotism. The same force of patriotism in an Italian, Frenchman, German, or Englishman would not have produced a similar result. Characteristics such as distinguish Chopin's music presuppose a nation as peculiarly endowed, constituted, situated, and conditioned, as the Polish—a nation with a history as brilliant and dark, as fair and hideous, as romantic and tragic. The peculiarities of the peoples of western Europe have been considerably modified, if not entirely levelled, by centuries of international intercourse; the peoples of the eastern part of the Continent, on the other hand, have, until recent times, kept theirs almost intact, foreign influences penetrating to no depth, affecting indeed no more than the aristocratic few, and them only superficially. At any rate, the Slavonic races have not been moulded by the Germanic and Romanic races as these latter have moulded each other: east and west remain still apart—strangers, if not enemies. Seeing how deeply rooted Chopin's music is in the national soil, and considering how little is generally known about Poland and the Poles, the necessity of paying in this case more attention to the land of the artist's birth and the people to which he belongs than is usually done in biographies of artists, will be admitted by all who wish to understand fully and appreciate rightly the poet-musician and his works. But while taking note of what is of national origin in Chopin's music, we must be careful not to ascribe to this origin too much. Indeed, the fact that the personal individuality of Chopin is as markedly differentiated, as exclusively self-contained, as the national individuality of Poland, is oftener overlooked than the master's national descent and its significance with regard to his artistic production. And now, having made the reader acquainted with the raison d'etre of this proem, I shall plunge without further preliminaries in medias res.

The palmy days of Poland came to an end soon after the extinction of the dynasty of the Jagellons in 1572. So early as 1661 King John Casimir warned the nobles, whose insubordination and want of solidity, whose love of outside glitter and tumult, he deplored, that, unless they remedied the existing evils, reformed their pretended free elections, and renounced their personal privileges, the noble kingdom would become the prey of other nations. Nor was this the first warning. The Jesuit Peter Skarga (1536—1612), an indefatigable denunciator of the vices of the ruling classes, told them in 1605 that their dissensions would bring them under the yoke of those who hated them, deprive them of king and country, drive them into exile, and make them despised by those who formerly feared and respected them. But these warnings remained unheeded, and the prophecies were fulfilled to the letter. Elective kingship, pacta conventa, [Footnote: Terms which a candidate for the throne had to subscribe on his election. They were of course dictated by the electors—i.e., by the selfish interest of one class, the szlachta (nobility), or rather the most powerful of them.] liberum veto, [Footnote: The right of any member to stop the proceedings of the Diet by pronouncing the words "Nie pozwalam" (I do not permit), or others of the same import.] degradation of the burgher class, enslavement of the peasantry, and other devices of an ever-encroaching nobility, transformed the once powerful and flourishing commonwealth into one "lying as if broken-backed on the public highway; a nation anarchic every fibre of it, and under the feet and hoofs of travelling neighbours." [Footnote: Thomas Carlyle, Frederick the Great, vol. viii., p. 105.] In the rottenness of the social organism, venality, unprincipled ambition, and religious intolerance found a congenial soil; and favoured by and favouring foreign intrigues and interferences, they bore deadly fruit—confederations, civil wars, Russian occupation of the country and dominion over king, council, and diet, and the beginning of the end, the first partition (1772) by which Poland lost a third of her territory with five millions of inhabitants. Even worse, however, was to come. For the partitioning powers—Russia, Prussia, and Austria—knew how by bribes and threats to induce the Diet not only to sanction the spoliation, but also so to alter the constitution as to enable them to have a permanent influence over the internal affairs of the Republic.

The Pole Francis Grzymala remarks truly that if instead of some thousand individuals swaying the destinies of Poland, the whole nation had enjoyed equal rights, and, instead of being plunged in darkness and ignorance, the people had been free and consequently capable of feeling and thinking, the national cause, imperilled by the indolence and perversity of one part of the citizens, would have been saved by those who now looked on without giving a sign of life. The "some thousands" here spoken of are of course the nobles, who had grasped all the political power and almost all the wealth of the nation, and, imitating the proud language of

Louis XIV, could, without exaggeration, have said: "L'etat c'est nous." As for the king and the commonalty, the one had been deprived of almost all his prerogatives, and the other had become a rightless rabble of wretched peasants, impoverished burghers, and chaffering Jews. Rousseau, in his Considerations sur le gouvernement de Pologne, says pithily that the three orders of which the Republic of Poland was composed were not, as had been so often and illogically stated, the equestrian order, the senate, and the king, but the nobles who were everything, the burghers who were nothing, and the peasants who were less than nothing. The nobility of Poland differed from that of Other countries not only in its supreme political and social position, but also in its numerousness, character, and internal constitution.

[Footnote: The statistics concerning old Poland are provokingly contradictory. One authority calculates that the nobility comprised 120,000 families, or one fourteenth of the population (which, before the first partition, is variously estimated at from fifteen to twenty millions); another counts only 100,000 families; and a third states that between 1788 and 1792 (i.e., after the first partition) there were 38,314 families of nobles.]

All nobles were equal in rank, and as every French soldier was said to carry a marshal's staff in his knapsack, so every Polish noble was born a candidate for the throne. This equality, however, was rather de jure than de facto; legal decrees could not fill the chasm which separated families distinguished by wealth and fame—such as the Sapiehas, Radziwills, Czartoryskis, Zamoyskis, Potockis, and Branickis—from obscure noblemen whose possessions amount to no more than "a few acres of land, a sword, and a pair of moustaches that extend from one ear to the other," or perhaps amounted only to the last two items. With some insignificant exceptions, the land not belonging to the state or the church was in the hands of the nobles, a few of whom had estates of the extent of principalities. Many of the poorer amongst the nobility attached themselves to their better-situated brethren, becoming their dependents and willing tools. The relation of the nobility to the peasantry is well characterised in a passage of Mickiewicz's epic poem Pan Tadeusz, where a peasant, on humbly suggesting that the nobility suffered less from the measures of their foreign rulers than his own class, is told by one of his betters that this is a silly remark, seeing that peasants, like eels, are accustomed to being skinned, whereas the well-born are accustomed to live in liberty.

Nothing illustrates so well the condition of a people as the way in which justice is administered. In Poland a nobleman was on his estate prosecutor as well as judge, and could be arrested only after conviction, or, in the case of high-treason, murder, and robbery, if taken in the act. And whilst the nobleman enjoyed these high privileges, the peasant had, as the law terms it, no facultatem standi in judicio, and his testimony went for nothing in the courts of justice. More than a hundred laws in the statutes of Poland are said to have been unfavourable to these poor wretches. In short, the peasant was quite at the mercy of the privileged class, and his master could do with him pretty much as he liked, whipping and selling not excepted, nor did killing cost more than a fine of a few shillings. The peasants on the state domains and of the clergy were, however, somewhat better off; and the burghers, too, enjoyed some shreds of their old privileges with more or less security. If we look for a true and striking description of the comparative position of the principal classes of the population of Poland, we find it in these words of a writer of the eighteenth century: "Polonia coelum nobilium, paradisus clericorum, infernus rusticorum."

The vast plain of Poland, although in many places boggy and sandy, is on the whole fertile, especially in the flat river valleys, and in the east at the sources of the Dnieper; indeed, it is so much so that it has been called the granary of Europe. But as the pleasure-loving gentlemen had nobler pursuits to attend to, and the miserable peasants, with whom it was a saying that only what they spent in drink was their own, were not very anxious to work more and better than they could help, agriculture was in a very neglected condition. With manufacture and commerce it stood not a whit better. What little there was, was in the hands of the Jews and foreigners, the nobles not being allowed to meddle with such base matters, and the degraded descendants of the industrious and enterprising ancient burghers having neither the means nor the spirit to undertake anything of the sort. Hence the strong contrast of wealth and poverty, luxury and distress, that in every part of Poland, in town and country, struck so forcibly and painfully all foreign travellers. Of the Polish provinces that in 1773 came under Prussian rule we read that—

> the country people hardly knew such a thing as bread, many
> had never in their life tasted such a delicacy; few villages
> had an oven. A weaving-loom was rare; the spinning-wheel
> unknown. The main article of furniture, in this bare scene of
> squalor, was the crucifix and vessel of holy-water under
> it....It was a desolate land without discipline, without law,
> without a master. On 9,000 English square miles lived 500,000
> souls: not 55 to the square mile. [Footnote: Carlyle.
> Frederick the Great, vol. x., p. 40.]

And this poverty and squalor were not to be found only in one part of Poland, they seem to have been general. Abbe de Mably when seeing, in

1771, the misery of the country (campagne) and the bad condition of the roads, imagined himself in Tartary. William Coxe, the English historian and writer of travels, who visited Poland after the first partition, relates, in speaking of the district called Podlachia, that he visited between Bjelsk and Woyszki villages in which there was nothing but the bare walls, and he was told at the table of the — — — that knives, forks, and spoons were conveniences unknown to the peasants. He says he never saw—

> *a road so barren of interesting scenes as that from Cracow to*
> *Warsaw—for the most part level, with little variation of*
> *surface; chiefly overspread with tracts of thick forest;*
> *where open, the distant horizon was always skirted with wood*
> *(chiefly pines and firs, intermixed with beech, birch, and*
> *small oaks). The occasional breaks presented some pasture-*
> *ground, with here and there a few meagre crops of corn. The*
> *natives were poorer, humbler, and more miserable than any*
> *people we had yet observed in the course of our travels:*
> *whenever we stopped they flocked around us in crowds; and,*
> *asking for charity, used the most abject gestures....The*
> *Polish peasants are cringing and servile in their expressions*
> *of respect; they bowed down to the ground; took off their*
> *hats or caps and held them in their hands till we were out of*
> *sight; stopped their carts on the first glimpse of our*
> *carriage; in short, their whole behaviour gave evident*
> *symptoms of the abject servitude under which they groaned.*
> [FOOTNOTE: William Coxe, Travels in Poland, Russia, Sweden,
> and Denmark (1784—90).]

The Jews, to whom I have already more than once alluded, are too important an element in the population of Poland not to be particularly noticed. They are a people within a people, differing in dress as well as in language, which is a jargon of German-Hebrew. Their number before the first partition has been variously estimated at from less than two millions to fully two millions and a half in a population of from fifteen to twenty millions, and in 1860 there were in Russian Poland 612,098 Jews in a population of 4,867,124.

[FOOTNOTE: According to Charles Forster (in Pologne, a volume of the historical series entitled L'univers pittoresque, published by Firmin

Didot freres of Paris), who follows Stanislas Plater, the population of Poland within the boundaries of 1772 amounted to 20,220,000 inhabitants, and was composed of 6,770,000 Poles, 7,520,000 Russians (i.e., White and Red Russians), 2,110,000 Jews, 1,900,000 Lithuanians, 1,640,000 Germans, 180,000 Muscovites (i.e., Great Russians), and 100,000 Wallachians.]

> *They monopolise [says Mr. Coxe] the commerce and trade of the*
> *country, keep inns and taverns, are stewards to the nobility,*
> *and seem to have so much influence that nothing can be bought*
> *or sold without the intervention of a Jew.*

Our never-failing informant was particularly struck with the number and usefulness of the Jews in Lithuania when he visited that part of the Polish Republic in 1781 —

> *If you ask for an interpreter, they bring you a Jew; if you*
> *want post-horses, a Jew procures them and a Jew drives them;*
> *if you wish to purchase, a Jew is your agent; and this*
> *perhaps is the only country in Europe where Jews cultivate*
> *the ground; in passing through Lithuania, we frequently saw*
> *them engaged in sowing, reaping, mowing, and other works of*
> *husbandry.*

Having considered the condition of the lower classes, we will now turn our attention to that of the nobility. The very unequal distribution of wealth among them has already been mentioned. Some idea of their mode of life may be formed from the account of the Starost Krasinski's court in the diary (year 1759) of his daughter, Frances Krasinska. [FOOTNOTE: A starost (starosta) is the possessor of a starosty (starostwo)—i.e., a castle and domains conferred on a nobleman for life by the crown.] Her description of the household seems to justify her belief that there were not many houses in Poland that surpassed theirs in magnificence. In introducing to the reader the various ornaments and appendages of the magnate's court, I shall mention first, giving precedence to the fair sex, that there lived under the supervision of a French governess six young ladies of noble families. The noblemen attached to the lord of the castle were divided into three classes. In the first class were to be found sons of wealthy, or, at least, well-to-do families who served for honour, and came to the court to acquire good manners and as an introduction to a civil or military career. The starost provided the keep of their horses, and also paid weekly wages of two florins to their grooms. Each of these noble-men had besides a groom another servant who waited on his master at table, standing behind his chair and dining on what he left on his plate. Those of the second class were paid for their services and had fixed duties to perform. Their pay amounted to from 300 to 1,000 florins (a florin being about the value of sixpence), in addition to which gratuities and presents were often given. Excepting the chaplain, doctor, and secretary, they did not, like the preceding class, have the honour of sitting with their master at table. With regard to this privilege it is, however, worth noticing that those courtiers who enjoyed it derived materially hardly any advantage from it, for on week-days wine was served only to the family and their guests, and the dishes of roast meat were arranged pyramidally, so that fowl and venison went to those at the head of the table, and those sitting farther down had to content themselves with the coarser kinds of meat—with beef, pork, &c. The duties of the third class of followers, a dozen young men from fifteen to twenty years of age, consisted in accompanying the family on foot or on horseback, and doing their messages, such as carrying presents and letters of invitation. The second and third classes were under the jurisdiction of the house-steward, who, in the case of the young gentlemen, was not sparing in the application of the cat. A strict injunction was laid on all to appear in good clothes. As to the other servants of the castle, the authoress thought she would find it difficult to specify them; indeed, did not know even the number of their musicians, cooks, Heyducs, Cossacks, and serving maids and men. She knew, however, that every day five tables were served, and that from morning to night two persons were occupied in distributing the things necessary for the kitchen. More impressive even than a circumstantial account like this are briefly-stated facts such as the following: that the Palatine Stanislas Jablonowski kept a retinue of 2,300 soldiers and 4,000 courtiers, valets, armed attendants, huntsmen, falconers, fishers, musicians, and actors; and that Janusz, Prince of Ostrog, left at his death a majorat of eighty towns and boroughs, and 2,760 villages, without counting the towns and villages of his starosties. The magnates who distinguished themselves during the reign of Stanislas Augustus (1764—1795) by the brilliance and magnificence of their courts were the Princes Czartoryski and Radziwill, Count Potocki, and Bishop Soltyk of Cracovia. Our often-quoted English traveller informs us that the revenue of Prince Czartoryski amounted to nearly 100,000 pounds per annum, and that his style of living corresponded with this income. The Prince kept an open table at which there rarely sat down less than from twenty to thirty persons. [FOOTNOTE: Another authority informs us that on great occasions the Czartoryskis received at their table more than twenty thousand persons.] The same informant has much to say about the elegance and luxury of the Polish nobility in their houses and villas, in the decoration and furniture of which he found the French and English styles happily blended. He gives a glowing account of the fetes at which he was present, and says that they were exquisitely refined and got up regardless of expense.

Whatever changes the national character of the Poles has undergone in the course of time, certain traits of it have remained unaltered, and among these stands forth predominantly their chivalry. Polish bravery is so universally recognised and admired that it is unnecessary to enlarge upon it. For who has not heard at least of the victorious battle of Czotzim, of the delivery of Vienna, of the no less glorious defeats of Maciejowice and Ostrolenka, and of the brilliant deeds of Napoleon's Polish Legion? And are not the names of Poland's most popular heroes, Sobieski and Kosciuszko, household words all the world over? Moreover, the Poles have proved their chivalry not only by their valour on the battle-field, but also by their devotion to the fair sex. At banquets in the good olden time it was no uncommon occurrence to see a Pole kneel down before his lady, take off one of her shoes, and drink out of it. But the women of Poland seem to be endowed with a peculiar power. Their beauty, grace, and bewitching manner inflame the heart and imagination of all that set their eyes on them. How often have they not conquered the conquerors of their country? [FOOTNOTE: The Emperor Nicholas is credited with the saying: "Je pourrais en finir des Polonais si je venais a bout des Polonaises."] They remind Heine of the tenderest and loveliest flowers that grow on the banks of the Ganges, and he calls for the brush of Raphael, the melodies of Mozart, the language of Calderon, so that he may conjure up before his readers an Aphrodite of the Vistula. Liszt, bolder than Heine, makes the attempt to portray them, and writes like an inspired poet. No Pole can speak on this subject without being transported into a transcendental rapture that illumines his countenance with a blissful radiance, and inspires him with a glowing eloquence which, he thinks, is nevertheless beggared by the matchless reality.

The French of the North—for thus the Poles have been called—are of a very excitable nature; easily moved to anger, and easily appeased; soon warmed into boundless enthusiasm, and soon also manifesting lack of perseverance. They feel happiest in the turmoil of life and in the bustle of society. Retirement and the study of books are little to their taste. Yet, knowing how to make the most of their limited stock of knowledge, they acquit themselves well in conversation. Indeed, they have a natural aptitude for the social arts which insures their success in society, where they move with ease and elegance. Their oriental mellifluousness, hyperbolism, and obsequious politeness of speech have, as well as the Asiatic appearance of their features and dress, been noticed by all travellers in Poland. Love of show is another very striking trait in the character of the Poles. It struggles to manifest itself among the poor, causes the curious mixture of splendour and shabbiness among the better-situated people, and gives rise to the greatest extravagances among the wealthy. If we may believe the chroniclers and poets, the entertainments of the Polish magnates must have often vied with the marvellous feasts of imperial Rome. Of the vastness of the households with which these grands seigneurs surrounded themselves, enough has already been said. Perhaps the chief channel through which this love of show vented itself was the decoration of man and horse. The entrance of Polish ambassadors with their numerous suites has more than once astonished the Parisians, who were certainly accustomed to exhibitions of this kind. The mere description of some of them is enough to dazzle one — the superb horses with their bridles and stirrups of massive silver, and their caparisons and saddles embroidered with golden flowers; and the not less superb men with their rich garments of satin or gold cloth, adorned with rare furs, their bonnets surmounted by bright plumes, and their weapons of artistic workmanship, the silver scabbards inlaid with rubies. We hear also of ambassadors riding through towns on horses loosely shod with gold or silver, so that the horse-shoes lost on their passage might testify to their wealth and grandeur. I shall quote some lines from a Polish poem in which the author describes in detail the costume of an eminent nobleman in the early part of this century: —

He was clad in the uniform of the palatinate: a doublet
embroidered with gold, an overcoat of Tours silk ornamented
with fringes, a belt of brocade from which hung a sword with
a hilt of morocco. At his neck glittered a clasp with
diamonds. His square white cap was surmounted by a
magnificent plume, composed of tufts of herons' feathers. It
is only on festive occasions that such a rich bouquet, of
which each feather costs a ducat, is put on.

The belt above mentioned was one of the most essential parts and the chief ornament of the old Polish national dress, and those manufactured at Sluck had especially a high reputation. A description of a belt of Sluck, "with thick fringes like tufts," glows on another page of the poem from which I took my last quotation: —

On one side it is of gold with purple flowers; on the other
it is of black silk with silver checks. Such a belt can be
worn on either side: the part woven with gold for festive
days; the reverse for days of mourning.

A vivid picture of the Polish character is to be found in Mickiewicz's epic poem, Pan Tadeusz, from which the above quotations are taken.

[FOOTNOTE: I may mention here another interesting book illustrative of Polish character and life, especially in the second half of the eighteenth century, which has been of much use to me—namely, Count Henry Rzewuski's Memoirs of Pan Severin Soplica, translated into German, and furnished with an instructive preface by Philipp Lubenstein.]

He handles his pencil lovingly; proclaiming with just pride the virtues of his countrymen, and revealing with a kindly smile their weaknesses. In this truest, perhaps, of all the portraits that have ever been drawn of the Poles, we see the gallantry and devotion, the generosity and hospitality, the grace and liveliness in social intercourse, but also the excitability and changefulness, the quickly inflamed enthusiasm and sudden depression, the restlessness and turbulence, the love of outward show and of the pleasures of society, the pompous pride, boastfulness, and other little vanities, in short, all the qualities, good and bad, that distinguish his countrymen. Heinrich Heine, not always a trustworthy witness, but in this case so unusually serious that we will take advantage of his acuteness and conciseness, characterises the Polish nobleman by the following precious mosaic of adjectives: "hospitable, proud, courageous, supple, false (this little yellow stone must not be lacking), irritable, enthusiastic, given to gambling, pleasure-loving, generous, and overbearing." Whether Heine was not mistaken as to the presence of the little yellow stone is a question that may have to be discussed in another part of this work. The observer who, in enumerating the most striking qualities of the Polish character, added "MISTRUSTFULNESS and SUSPICIOUSNESS engendered by many misfortunes and often-disappointed hopes," came probably nearer the truth. And this reminds me of a point which ought never to be left out of sight when contemplating any one of these portraits—namely, the time at which it was taken. This, of course, is always an important consideration; but it is so in a higher degree in the case of a nation whose character, like the Polish, has at different epochs of its existence assumed such varied aspects. The first great change came over the national character on the introduction of elective kingship: it was, at least so far as the nobility was concerned, a change for the worse—from simplicity, frugality, and patriotism, to pride, luxury, and selfishness; the second great change was owing to the disasters that befell the nation in the latter half of the last century: it was on the whole a change for the better, purifying and ennobling, calling forth qualities that till then had lain dormant. At the time the events I have to relate take us to Poland, the nation is just at this last turning-point, but it has not yet rounded it. To what an extent the bad qualities had overgrown the good ones, corrupting and deadening them, may be gathered from contemporary witnesses. George Forster, who was appointed professor of natural history at Wilna in 1784, and remained in that position for several years, says that he found in Poland "a medley of fanatical and almost New Zealand barbarity and French super-refinement; a people wholly ignorant and without taste, and nevertheless given to luxury, gambling, fashion, and outward glitter."

Frederick II describes the Poles in language still more harsh; in his opinion they are vain in fortune, cringing in misfortune, capable of anything for the sake of money, spendthrifts, frivolous, without judgment, always ready to join or abandon a party without cause. No doubt there is much exaggeration in these statements; but that there is also much truth in them, is proved by the accounts of many writers, native and foreign, who cannot be accused of being prejudiced against Poland. Rulhiere, and other more or less voluminous authorities, might be quoted; but, not to try the patience of the reader too much, I shall confine myself to transcribing a clenching remark of a Polish nobleman, who told our old friend, the English traveller, that although the name of Poland still remained, the nation no longer existed. "An universal corruption and venality pervades all ranks of the people. Many of the first nobility do not blush to receive pensions from foreign courts: one professes himself publicly an Austrian, a second a Prussian, a third a Frenchman, and a fourth a Russian."

CHAPTER I

FREDERICK CHOPIN'S ANCESTORS.—HIS FATHER NICHOLAS CHOPIN'S BIRTH, YOUTH, ARRIVAL AND EARLY VICISSITUDES IN POLAND, AND MARRIAGE.—BIRTH AND EARLY INFANCY OF FREDERICK CHOPIN.—HIS PARENTS AND SISTERS.

GOETHE playfully describes himself as indebted to his father for his frame and steady guidance of life, to his mother for his happy disposition and love of story-telling, to his grandfather for his devotion to the fair sex, to his grandmother for his love of finery. Schopenhauer reduces the law of heredity to the simple formula that man has his moral nature, his character, his inclinations, and his heart from his father, and the quality and tendency of his intellect from his mother. Buckle, on the other hand, questions hereditary transmission of mental qualities altogether. Though little disposed to doubt with the English historian, yet we may hesitate to assent to the proposition of the German philosopher; the adoption of a more scientific doctrine, one that recognises a process of compensation, neutralisation, and accentuation, would probably bring us nearer the truth. But whatever the complicated working of the law of heredity may be, there can be no doubt that the tracing of a remarkable man's pedigree is always an interesting and rarely an entirely idle occupation. Pursuing such an inquiry with regard to Frederick Chopin, we find ourselves, however, soon at the end of our tether. This is the more annoying, as there are circumstances that particularly incite our curiosity. The "Journal de Rouen" of December 1, 1849, contains an article, probably by Amedee de Mereaux, in which it is stated that Frederick Chopin was descended from the French family Chopin d'Arnouville, of which one member, a victim of the revocation of the Edict of Nantes, had taken refuge in Poland. [Footnote: In scanning the Moniteur of 1835, I came across several prefects and sous-prefects of the name of Choppin d'Arnouville. (There are two communes of the name of Arnouville, both are in the departement of the Seine et Oise—the one in the arrondissement Mantes, the other in the arrondissement Pontoise. This latter is called Arnouville-les-Gonesse.) I noticed also a number of intimations concerning plain Chopins and Choppins who served their country as maires and army officers. Indeed, the name of Chopin is by no means uncommon in France, and more than one individual of that name has illustrated it by his achievements—to wit: The jurist Rene Chopin or Choppin (1537—1606), the litterateur Chopin (born about 1800), and the poet Charles-Auguste Chopin (1811—1844).] Although this confidently-advanced statement is supported by the inscription on the composer's tombstone in Pere Lachaise, which describes his father as a French refugee, both the Catholicism of the latter and contradictory accounts of his extraction caution us not to put too much faith in its authenticity. M. A. Szulc, the author of a Polish book on Chopin and his works, has been told that Nicholas Chopin, the father of Frederick, was the natural son of a Polish nobleman, who, having come with King Stanislas Leszczynski to Lorraine, adopted there the name of Chopin. From Karasowski we learn nothing of Nicholas Chopin's parentage. But as he was a friend of the Chopin family, and from them got much of his information, this silence might with equal force be adduced for and against the correctness of Szulc's story, which in itself is nowise improbable. The only point that could strike one as strange is the change of name. But would not the death of the Polish ruler and the consequent lapse of Lorraine to France afford some inducement for the discarding of an unpronounceable foreign name? It must, however, not be overlooked that this story is but a hearsay, relegated to a modest foot-note, and put forward without mention of the source whence it is derived. [FOOTNOTE: Count Wodzinski, who leaves Nicholas Chopin's descent an open question, mentions a variant of Szulc's story, saying that some biographers pretended that Nicholas Chopin was descended from one of the name of Szop, a soldier, valet, or heyduc (reitre, valet, ou heiduque) in the service of Stanislas Leszczinski, whom he followed to Lorraine.] Indeed, until we get possession of indisputable proofs, it will be advisable to disregard these more or less fabulous reports altogether, and begin with the first well-ascertained fact—namely, Nicholas Chopin's birth, which took place at Nancy, in Lorraine, on the 17th of August, 1770. Of his youth nothing is known except that, like other young men of his country, he conceived a desire to visit Poland. Polish descent would furnish a satisfactory explanation of Nicholas' sentiments in regard to Poland at this time and subsequently, but an equally satisfactory explanation can be found without having recourse to such a hazardous assumption.

In 1735 Stanislas Leszczynski, who had been King of Poland from 1704 to 1709, became Duke of Lorraine and Bar, and reigned over the Duchies till 1766, when an accident—some part of his dress taking fire—put an end to his existence. As Stanislas was a wise, kind-hearted, and benevolent prince, his subjects not only loved him as long as he lived, but also cherished his memory after his death, when their country had been united to France. The young, we may be sure, would often hear their elders speak of the good times of Duke Stanislas, of the Duke (the philosophe bienfaisant) himself, and of the strange land and people he came from. But Stanislas, besides being an excellent prince, was also an amiable, generous gentleman, who, whilst paying due attention to the well-being of his new subjects, remained to the end of his days a true Pole. From this circumstance it may be easily inferred that the Court of Stanislas proved a great attraction to his countrymen, and that Nancy became a chief halting-place of Polish travellers on their way to and from Paris. Of course, not all the Poles that had settled in the Duchies during the Duke's reign left the country after his demise, nor did their friends from the fatherland altogether cease to visit them in their new home. Thus a connection between the two countries was kept up, and the interest taken by the people of the west in the fortunes of the people in the east was not allowed to die. Moreover, were not the Academie de Stanislas founded by the Duke, the monument erected to his memory, and the square named after him, perpetual reminders to the inhabitants of Nancy and the visitors to that town?

Nicholas Chopin came to Warsaw in or about the year 1787. Karasowski relates in the first and the second German edition of his biography of Frederick Chopin that the Staroscina [FOOTNOTE: The wife of a starosta (vide p. 7.)] Laczynska made the acquaintance of the latter's father, and engaged him as tutor to her children; but in the later Polish edition he abandons this account in favour of one given by Count Frederick Skarbek in his Pamietniki (Memoirs). According to this most trustworthy of procurable witnesses (why he is the most trustworthy will be seen presently), Nicholas Chopin's migration to Poland came about in this way. A Frenchman had established in Warsaw a manufactory of tobacco, which, as the taking of snuff was then becoming more and more the fashion, began to flourish in so high a degree that he felt the need of assistance. He proposed, therefore, to his countryman, Nicholas Chopin, to come to him and take in hand the book-keeping, a proposal which was readily accepted.

The first impression of the young Lorrainer on entering the land of his dreams cannot have been altogether of a pleasant nature. For in the summer of 1812, when, we are told, the condition of the people had been infinitely ameliorated by the Prussian and Russian governments, M. de Pradt, Napoleon's ambassador, found the nation in a state of semi-barbarity, agriculture in its infancy, the soil parched like a desert, the animals stunted, the people, although of good stature, in a state of extreme poverty, the towns built of wood, the houses filled with vermin, and the food revolting. This picture will not escape the suspicion of being overdrawn. But J.G. Seume, who was by no means over-squeamish, and whom experience had taught the meaning of "to rough it," asserts, in speaking of Poland in 1805, that, Warsaw and a few other places excepted, the dunghill was in most houses literally and without exaggeration the cleanest spot, and the only one where one could stand without loathing. But if the general aspect of things left much to be desired from a utilitarian point of view, its strangeness and picturesqueness would not fail to compensate an imaginative youth for the want of order and comfort. The strong contrast of wealth and poverty, of luxury and distress, that gave to the whole country so melancholy an appearance, was, as it were, focussed in its capital. Mr. Coxe, who visited Warsaw not long before Nicholas Chopin's arrival there, says: —

> The streets are spacious, but ill-paved; the churches and
>
> public buildings large and magnificent, the palaces of the
>
> nobility are numerous and splendid; but the greatest part of
>
> the houses, especially the suburbs, are mean and ill-
>
> constructed wooden hovels.

What, however, struck a stranger most, was the throngs of humanity that enlivened the streets and squares of Warsaw, the capital of a nation composed of a medley of Poles, Lithuanians, Red and White Russians, Germans, Muscovites, Jews, and Wallachians, and the residence of a numerous temporary and permanent foreign population. How our friend from quiet Nancy—which long ago had been deserted by royalty and its train, and where literary luminaries, such as Voltaire, Madame du Chatelet, Saint Lambert, &c., had ceased to make their fitful appearances—must have opened his eyes when this varied spectacle unfolded itself before him.

> The streets of stately breadth, formed of palaces in the
>
> finest Italian taste and wooden huts which at every moment
>
> threatened to tumble down on the heads of the inmates; in
>
> these buildings Asiatic pomp and Greenland dirt in strange
>
> union, an ever-bustling population, forming, like a
>
> masked procession, the most striking contrasts. Long-bearded
>
> Jews, and monks in all kinds of habits; nuns of the strictest
>
> discipline, entirely veiled and wrapped in meditation; and in
>
> the large squares troops of young Polesses in light-coloured
>
> silk mantles engaged in conversation; venerable old Polish
>
> gentlemen with moustaches, caftan, girdle, sword, and yellow
>
> and red boots; and the new generation in the most incroyable
>
> Parisian fashion. Turks, Greeks, Russians, Italians, and
>
> French in an ever-changing throng; moreover, an exceedingly
>
> tolerant police that interfered nowise with the popular

amusements, so that in squares and streets there moved about incessantly Pulchinella theatres, dancing bears, camels, and monkeys, before which the most elegant carriages as well as porters stopped and stood gaping.

Thus pictures J. E. Hitzig, the biographer of E. Th. A. Hoffmann, and himself a sojourner in Warsaw, the life of the Polish capital in 1807. When Nicholas Chopin saw it first the spectacle in the streets was even more stirring, varied, and brilliant; for then Warsaw was still the capital of an independent state, and the pending and impending political affairs brought to it magnates from all the principal courts of Europe, who vied with each other in the splendour of their carriages and horses, and in the number and equipment of their attendants.

In the introductory part of this work I have spoken of the misfortunes that befel Poland and culminated in the first partition. But the buoyancy of the Polish character helped the nation to recover sooner from this severe blow than could have been expected. Before long patriots began to hope that the national disaster might be turned into a blessing. Many circumstances favoured the realisation of these hopes. Prussia, on discovering that her interests no longer coincided with those of her partners of 1772, changed sides, and by-and-by even went the length of concluding a defensive and offensive alliance with the Polish Republic. She, with England and other governments, backed Poland against Russia and Austria. Russia, moreover, had to turn her attention elsewhere. At the time of Nicholas Chopin's arrival, Poland was dreaming of a renascence of her former greatness, and everyone was looking forward with impatience to the assembly of the Diet which was to meet the following year. Predisposed by sympathy, he was soon drawn into the current of excitement and enthusiasm that was surging around him. Indeed, what young soul possessed of any nobleness could look with indifference on a nation struggling for liberty and independence. As he took a great interest in the debates and transactions of the Diet, he became more and more acquainted with the history, character, condition, and needs of the country, and this stimulated him to apply himself assiduously to the study of the national language, in order to increase, by means of this faithful mirror and interpreter of a people's heart and mind, his knowledge of these things. And now I must ask the reader to bear patiently the infliction of a brief historical summary, which I would most willingly spare him, were I not prevented by two strong reasons. In the first place, the vicissitudes of Nicholas Chopin's early life in Poland are so closely bound up with, or rather so much influenced by, the political events, that an intelligible account of the former cannot be given without referring to the latter; and in the second place, those same political events are such important factors in the moulding of the national character, that, if we wish to understand it, they ought not to be overlooked.

The Diet which assembled at the end of 1788, in order to prevent the use or rather abuse of the liberum veto, soon formed itself into a confederation, abolished in 1789 the obnoxious Permanent Council, and decreed in 1791, after much patriotic oratory and unpatriotic obstruction, the famous constitution of the 3rd of May, regarded by the Poles up to this day with loving pride, and admired and praised at the time by sovereigns and statesmen, Fox and Burke among them. Although confirming most of the privileges of the nobles, the constitution nevertheless bore in it seeds of good promise. Thus, for instance, the crown was to pass after the death of the reigning king to the Elector of Saxony, and become thenceforth hereditary; greater power was given to the king and ministers, confederations and the liberum veto were declared illegal, the administration of justice was ameliorated, and some attention was paid to the rights and wrongs of the third estate and peasantry. But the patriots who already rejoiced in the prospect of a renewal of Polish greatness and prosperity had counted without the proud selfish aristocrats, without Russia, always ready to sow and nurture discord. Hence new troubles—the confederation of Targowica, Russian demands for the repeal of the constitution and unconditional submission to the Empress Catharine II, betrayal by Prussia, invasion, war, desertion of the national cause by their own king and his joining the conspirators of Targowica, and then the second partition of Poland (October 14, 1793), implying a further loss of territory and population. Now, indeed, the events were hastening towards the end of the sad drama, the finis poloniae. After much hypocritical verbiage and cruel coercion and oppression by Russia and Prussia, more especially by the former, outraged Poland rose to free itself from the galling yoke, and fought under the noble Kosciuszko and other gallant generals with a bravery that will for ever live in the memory of men. But however glorious the attempt, it was vain. Having three such powers as Russia, Prussia, and Austria against her, Poland, unsupported by allies and otherwise hampered, was too weak to hold her own. Without inquiring into the causes and the faults committed by her commanders, without dwelling on or even enumerating the vicissitudes of the struggle, I shall pass on to the terrible closing scene of the drama—the siege and fall of Praga, the suburb of Warsaw, and the subsequent massacre. The third partition (October 24, 1795), in which each of the three powers took her share, followed as a natural consequence, and Poland ceased to exist as an independent state. Not, however, for ever; for when in 1807 Napoleon, after crushing Prussia and defeating Russia, recast at Tilsit to a great extent the political conformation of Europe, bullying King Frederick William III and flattering the Emperor Alexander, he created the Grand Duchy of Warsaw, over which he placed as ruler the then King of Saxony.

Now let us see how Nicholas Chopin fared while these whirlwinds passed over Poland. The threatening political situation and the consequent general insecurity made themselves at once felt in trade, indeed soon paralysed it. What more particularly told on the business in which the young Lorrainer was engaged was the King's desertion of the national cause, which induced the great and wealthy to leave Warsaw and betake themselves for shelter to more retired and safer places. Indeed, so disastrous was the effect of these occurrences on the Frenchman's tobacco manufactory that it had to be closed. In these circumstances Nicholas Chopin naturally thought of returning home, but sickness detained him. When he had recovered his health, Poland was rising under Kosciuszko. He then joined the national guard, in which he was before long promoted to the rank of captain. On the 5th of November, 1794, he was on duty at Praga, and had not his company been relieved a few hours before the fall of the suburb, he would certainly have met there his death. Seeing that all was lost he again turned his thoughts homewards, when once more sickness prevented him from executing his intention. For a time he tried to make a living by teaching French, but ere long accepted an engagement as tutor in the family—then living in the country—of the Staroscina Laczynska, who meeting him by chance had been favourably impressed by his manners and accomplishments. In passing we may note that among his four pupils (two girls and two boys) was one, Mary, who afterwards became notorious by her connection with Napoleon I., and by the son that sprang from this connection, Count Walewski, the minister of Napoleon III. At the beginning of this century we find Nicholas Chopin at Zelazowa Wola, near Sochaczew, in the house of the Countess Skarbek, as tutor to her son Frederick. It was there that he made the acquaintance of Justina Krzyzanowska, a young lady of noble but poor family, whom he married in the year 1806, and who became the mother of four children, three daughters and one son, the latter being no other than Frederick Chopin, the subject of this biography. The position of Nicholas Chopin in the house of the Countess must have been a pleasant one, for ever after there seems to have existed a friendly relation between the two families. His pupil, Count Frederick Skarbek, who prosecuted his studies at Warsaw and Paris, distinguished himself subsequently as a poet, man of science, professor at the University of Warsaw, state official, philanthropist, and many-sided author—more especially as a politico—economical writer. When in his Memoirs the Count looks back on his youth, he remembers gratefully and with respect his tutor, speaking of him in highly appreciative terms. In teaching, Nicholas Chopin's chief aim was to form his pupils into useful, patriotic citizens; nothing was farther from his mind than the desire or unconscious tendency to turn them into Frenchmen. And now approaches the time when the principal personage makes his appearance on the stage.

Frederick Chopin, the only son and the third of the four children of Nicholas and Justina Chopin, was born on February 22, 1810,

[FOOTNOTE: See Preface, p. xii. In the earlier editions the date given was March 1,1809, as in the biography by Karasowski, with whom agree the earlier J. Fontana (Preface to Chopin's posthumous works.—1855), C. Sowinski (Les musiciens polonais et slaves.—1857), and the writer of the Chopin article in Mendel's Musikalisches Conversations-Lexikon (1872). According to M. A. Szulc (Fryderyk Chopin.—1873) and the inscription on the memorial (erected in 1880) in the Holy Cross Church at Warsaw, the composer was born on March 2, 1809. The monument in Pere Lachaise, at Paris, bears the date of Chopin's death, but not that of his birth. Felis, in his Biographie universelle des musiciens, differs widely from these authorities. The first edition (1835—1844) has only the year—1810; the second edition (1861—1865) adds month and day—February 8.]

in a mean little house at Zelazowa Wola, a village about twenty-eight English miles from Warsaw belonging to the Countess Skarbek.

[FOOTNOTE: Count Wodzinski, after indicating the general features of Polish villages—the dwor (manor-house) surrounded by a "bouquet of trees"; the barns and stables forming a square with a well in the centre; the roads planted with poplars and bordered with thatched huts; the rye, wheat, rape, and clover fields, &c.—describes the birthplace of Frederick Chopin as follows: "I have seen there the same dwor embosomed in trees, the same outhouses, the same huts, the same plains where here and there a wild pear-tree throws its shadow. Some steps from the mansion I stopped before a little cot with a slated roof, flanked by a little wooden perron. Nothing has been changed for nearly a hundred years. A dark passage traverses it. On the left, in a room illuminated by the reddish flame of slowly-consumed logs, or by the uncertain light of two candles placed at each extremity of the long table, the maid-servants spin as in olden times, and relate to each other a thousand marvellous legends. On the right, in a lodging of three rooms, so low that one can touch the ceiling, a man of some thirty years, brown, with vivacious eyes, the face closely shaven." This man was of course Nicholas Chopin. I need hardly say that Count Wodzinski's description is novelistically tricked out. His accuracy may be judged by the fact that a few pages after the above passage he speaks of the discoloured tiles of the roof which he told his readers before was of slate.]

The son of the latter, Count Frederick Skarbek, Nicholas Chopin's pupil, a young man of seventeen, stood godfather and gave his name to the new-born offspring of his tutor. Little Frederick's residence at the village cannot have been of long duration.

The establishment of the Grand Duchy of Warsaw in 1807 had ushered in a time big with chances for a capable man, and we may be sure that a young husband and father, no doubt already on the look-out for some more lucrative and independent employment, was determined not to miss them. Few peaceful revolutions, if any, can compare in thoroughness with the one that then took place in Poland; a new sovereign ascended the throne, two differently-constituted representative bodies superseded the old Senate and Diet, the French code of laws was introduced, the army and civil service underwent a complete re-organisation, public instruction obtained a long-needed attention, and so forth. To give an idea of the extent of the improvement effected in matters of education, it is enough to mention that the number of schools rose from 140 to 634, and that a commission was formed for the publication of suitable books of instruction in the Polish language. Nicholas Chopin's hopes were not frustrated; for on October 1, 1810, he was appointed professor of the French language at the newly-founded Lyceum in Warsaw, and a little more than a year after, on January 1, 1812, to a similar post at the School of Artillery and Engineering.

The exact date when Nicholas Chopin and his family settled in Warsaw is not known, nor is it of any consequence. We may, however, safely assume that about this time little Frederick was an inhabitant of the Polish metropolis. During the first years of his life the parents may have lived in somewhat straitened circumstances. The salary of the professorship, even if regularly paid, would hardly suffice for a family to live comfortably, and the time was unfavourable for gaining much by private tuition. M. de Pradt, describing Poland in 1812, says:—

> Nothing could exceed the misery of all classes. The army was not paid, the officers were in rags, the best houses were in ruins, the greatest lords were compelled to leave Warsaw from want of money to provide for their tables. No pleasures, no society, no invitations as in Paris and in London. I even saw princesses quit Warsaw from the most extreme distress. The Princess Radziwill had brought two women from England and France, she wished to send them back, but had to keep them because she was unable to pay their salaries and travelling expenses. I saw in Warsaw two French physicians who informed

*me that they could not procure their fees even from the
greatest lords.*

But whatever straits the parents may have been put to, the weak, helpless infant would lack none of the necessaries of life, and enjoy all the reasonable comforts of his age.

When in 1815 peace was restored and a period of quiet followed, the family must have lived in easy circumstances; for besides holding appointments as professor at some public schools (under the Russian government he became also one of the staff of teachers at the Military Preparatory School), Nicholas Chopin kept for a number of years a boarding-school, which was patronised by the best families of the country. The supposed poverty of Chopin's parents has given rise to all sorts of misconceptions and misstatements. A writer in Larousse's "Grand dictionnaire universel du XIXe siecle" even builds on it a theory explanatory of the character of Chopin and his music: "Sa famille d'origine francaise," he writes, "jouissait d'une mediocre fortune; de la, peut-etre, certains froissements dans l'organisation nerveuse et la vive sensibilite de l'enfant, sentiments qui devaient plus tard se refleter dans ses oeuvres, empreintes generalement d'une profonde melancolie." If the writer of the article in question had gone a little farther back, he might have found a sounder basis for his theory in the extremely delicate physical organisation of the man, whose sensitiveness was so acute that in early infancy he could not hear music without crying, and resisted almost all attempts at appeasing him.

The last-mentioned fact, curious and really noteworthy in itself, acquires a certain preciousness by its being the only one transmitted to us of that period of Chopin's existence. But this scantiness of information need not cause us much regret. During the first years of a man's life biography is chiefly concerned with his surroundings, with the agencies that train his faculties and mould his character. A man's acts and opinions are interesting in proportion to the degree of consolidation attained by his individuality. Fortunately our material is abundant enough to enable us to reconstruct in some measure the milieu into which Chopin was born and in which he grew up. We will begin with that first circle which surrounds the child—his family. The negative advantages which our Frederick found there—the absence of the privations and hardships of poverty, with their depressing and often demoralising influence—have already been adverted to; now I must say a few words about the positive advantages with which he was favoured. And it may be at once stated that they cannot be estimated too highly. Frederick enjoyed the greatest of blessings that can be bestowed upon mortal man— viz., that of being born into a virtuous and well-educated family united by the ties of love. I call it the greatest of blessings, because neither catechism and sermons nor schools and colleges can take the place,, or compensate for the want, of this education that does not stop at the outside, but by its subtle, continuous action penetrates to the very heart's core and pervades the whole being. The atmosphere in which Frederick lived was not only moral and social, but also distinctly intellectual.

The father, Nicholas Chopin, seems to have been a man of worth and culture, honest of purpose, charitable in judgment, attentive to duty, and endowed with a good share of prudence and commonsense. In support of this characterisation may be advanced that among his friends he counted many men of distinction in literature, science, and art; that between him and the parents of his pupils as well as the pupils themselves there existed a friendly relation; that he was on intimate terms with several of his colleagues; and that his children not only loved, but also respected him. No one who reads his son's letters, which indeed give us some striking glimpses of the man, can fail to notice this last point. On one occasion, when confessing that he had gone to a certain dinner two hours later than he had been asked, Frederick foresees his father's anger at the disregard for what is owing to others, and especially to one's elders; and on another occasion he makes excuses for his indifference to non-musical matters, which, he thinks, his father will blame. And mark, these letters were written after Chopin had attained manhood. What testifies to Nicholas Chopin's, abilities as a teacher and steadiness as a man, is the unshaken confidence of the government: he continued in his position at the Lyceumtill after the revolution in 1831, when this institution, like many others, was closed; he was then appointed a member of the board for the examination of candidates for situations as schoolmasters, and somewhat later he became professor of the French language at the Academy of the Roman Catholic Clergy.

It is more difficult, or rather it is impossible, to form anything like a clear picture of his wife, Justina Chopin. None of those of her son's letters that are preserved is addressed to her, and in those addressed to the members of the family conjointly, or to friends, nothing occurs that brings her nearer to us, or gives a clue to her character. George Sand said that she was Chopin's only passion. Karasowski describes her as "particularly tender-hearted and rich in all the truly womanly virtues.....For her quietness and homeliness were the greatest happiness." K. W. Wojcicki, in "Cmentarz Powazkowski" (Powazki Cemetery), expresses, himself in the same strain. A Scotch lady, who had seen Justina Chopin in her old age, and conversed with her in French, told me that she was then "a neat, quiet, intelligent old lady, whose activeness contrasted strongly with the languor of her son, who had not a shadow of energy in him." With regard to the latter part of this account, we must not overlook the fact that my informant knew Chopin only in the last year of his life—i.e., when he was in a very suffering state of mind and body. This is all the information I have been able to collect regarding the character of Chopin's mother. Moreover, Karasowski is not an altogether trustworthy informant; as a friend of the Chopin family he sees in its members so many paragons of intellectual and moral perfection. He proceeds on the de mortuis nil nisi bonum principle, which I venture to suggest is a very bad principle. Let us apply this loving tenderness to our living neighbours, and judge the dead according to their merits. Thus the living will be doubly benefited, and no harm be done to the dead. Still, the evidence before us—including that exclamation about his "best of mothers" in one of Chopin's letters, written from Vienna, soon after the outbreak of the Polish insurrection in 1830: "How glad my mamma will be that I did not come back!"—justifies us, I think, in inferring that Justina Chopin was a woman of the most lovable type, one in whom the central principle of existence was the maternal instinct, that bright ray of light which, dispersed in its action, displays itself in the most varied and lovely colours. That this principle, although often all-absorbing, is not incompatible with the wider and higher social and intellectual interests is a proposition that does not stand in need of proof. But who could describe that wondrous blending of loving strength and lovable weakness of a true woman's character? You feel its beauty and sublimity, and if you attempt to give words to your feeling you produce a caricature.

The three sisters of Frederick all manifested more or less a taste for literature. The two elder sisters, Louisa (who married Professor Jedrzejewicz, and died in 1855) and Isabella (who married Anton Barcinski—first inspector of schools, and subsequently director of steam navigation on the Vistula—and died in 1881), wrote together for the improvement of the working classes. The former contributed now and then, also after her marriage, articles to periodicals on the education of the young. Emilia, the youngest sister, who died at the early age of fourteen (in 1827), translated, conjointly with her sister Isabella, the educational tales of the German author Salzmann, and her poetical efforts held out much promise for the future.

CHAPTER II

FREDERICK'S FIRST MUSICAL INSTRUCTION AND MUSIC-MASTER, ADALBERT ZYWNY.—HIS DEBUT AND SUCCESS AS A PIANIST.—HIS EARLY INTRODUCTION INTO ARISTOCRATIC SOCIETY AND CONSTANT INTERCOURSE WITH THE ARISTOCRACY.—HIS FIRST COMPOSITIONS.—HIS STUDIES AND MASTER IN HARMONY, COUNTERPOINT, AND COMPOSITION, JOSEPH ELSNER.

OUR little friend, who, as we have seen, at first took up a hostile attitude towards music—for his passionate utterances, albeit inarticulate, cannot well be interpreted as expressions of satisfaction or approval—came before long under her mighty sway. The pianoforte threw a spell over him, and, attracting him more and more, inspired him with such a fondness as to induce his parents to provide him, notwithstanding his tender age, with an instructor. To lessen the awfulness of the proceeding, it was arranged that one of the elder sisters should join him in his lessons. The first and only pianoforte teacher of him who in the course of time became one of the greatest and most original masters of this instrument, deserves some attention from us. Adalbert Zywny [FOOTNOTE: This is the usual spelling of the name, which, as the reader will see further on, its possessor wrote Ziwny. Liszt calls him Zywna.], a native of Bohemia, born in 1756, came to Poland, according to Albert Sowinski (Les musiciens polonais et slaves), during the reign of Stanislas Augustus Poniatowski (1764—1795), and after staying for some time as pianist at the court of Prince Casimir Sapieha, settled in Warsaw as a teacher of music, and soon got into good practice, "giving his lessons at three florins (eighteen pence) per hour very regularly, and making a fortune." And thus teaching and composing (he is said to have composed much for the pianoforte, but he never published anything), he lived a long and useful life, dying in 1842 at the age of 86 (Karasowski says in 1840). The punctual and, no doubt, also somewhat pedantic music-master who acquired the esteem and goodwill of his patrons, the best families of Warsaw, and a fortune at the same time, is a pleasant figure to contemplate. The honest orderliness and dignified calmness of his life, as I read it, are quite refreshing in this time of rush and gush. Having seen a letter of his, I can imagine the heaps of original MSS., clearly and neatly penned with a firm hand, lying carefully packed up in spacious drawers, or piled up on well-dusted shelves. Of the man Zywny and his relation to the Chopin family we get some glimpses in Frederick's letters. In one of the year 1828, addressed to his friend Titus Woyciechowski, he writes: "With us things are as they used to be; the honest Zywny is the soul of all our amusements." Sowinski informs us that Zywny taught his pupil according to the classical German method—whatever that may mean—at that time in use in Poland. Liszt, who calls him "an enthusiastic student of Bach," speaks likewise of "les errements d'une ecole entierement classique." Now imagine my astonishment when on asking the well-known pianoforte player and composer Edouard Wolff, a native of Warsaw, [Fooynote: He died at Paris on October 16, 1880.] what kind of pianist Zywny was, I received the answer that he was a violinist and not a pianist. That Wolff and Zywny knew each other is proved beyond doubt by the above-mentioned letter of Zywny's, introducing the former to Chopin, then resident in Paris. The solution of the riddle is probably this. Zywny, whether violinist or not, was not a pianoforte virtuoso—at least, was not heard in public in his old age. The mention of a single name, that of Wenzel W. Wurfel, certainly shows that he was not the best pianist in Warsaw. But against any such depreciatory remarks we have to set Chopin's high opinion of Zywny's teaching capability. Zywny's letter, already twice alluded to, is worth quoting. It still further illustrates the relation in which master and pupil stood to each other, and by bringing us in close contact with the former makes us better acquainted with his character. A particularly curious fact about the letter—considering the nationality of the persons concerned—is its being written in German. Only a fac-simile of the original, with its clear, firm, though (owing to the writer's old age) cramped penmanship, and its quaint spelling and capricious use of capital and small initials, could fully reveal the expressiveness of this document. However, even in the translation there may be found some of the man's characteristic old-fashioned formality, grave benevolence, and quiet homeliness. The outside of the sheet on which the letter is written bears the words, "From the old music-master Adalbert Ziwny [at least this I take to be the meaning of the seven letters followed by dots], kindly to be transmitted to my best friend, Mr. Frederick Chopin, in Paris." The letter itself runs as follows:—

DEAREST MR. F. CHOPIN,—Wishing you perfect health I have the

honour to write to you through Mr. Eduard Wolf. [FOOTNOTE:

The language of the first sentence is neither logical nor

otherwise precise. I shall keep throughout as close as

possible to the original, and also retain the peculiar

spelling of proper names.] I recommend him to your esteemed
friendship. Your whole family and I had also the pleasure of
hearing at his concert the Adagio and Rondo from your
Concerto, which called up in our minds the most agreeable
remembrance of you. May God give you every prosperity! We are
all well, and wish so much to see you again. Meanwhile I send
you through Mr. Wolf my heartiest kiss, and recommending
myself to your esteemed friendship, I remain your faithful
friend,

ADALBERT ZIWNY.

Warsaw, the 12th of June, 1835.

N.B. —Mr. Kirkow, the merchant, and his son George, who was
at Mr. Reinschmid's at your farewell party, recommend
themselves to you, and wish you good health. Adieu.

Julius Fontana, the friend and companion of Frederick, after stating (in his preface to Chopin's posthumous works) that Chopin had never another pianoforte teacher than Zywny, observes that the latter taught his pupil only the first principles. "The progress of the child was so extraordinary that his parents and his professor thought they could do no better than abandon him at the age of 12 to his own instincts, and follow instead of directing him." The progress of Frederick must indeed have been considerable, for in Clementina Tanska-Hofmanowa's Pamiatka po dobrej matce (Memorial of a good Mother) [FOOTNOTE: Published in 1819.] the writer relates that she was at a soiree at Gr— —'s, where she found a numerous party assembled, and heard in the course of the evening young Chopin play the piano—"a child not yet eight years old, who, in the opinion of the connoisseurs of the art, promises to replace Mozart." Before the boy had completed his ninth year his talents were already so favourably known that he was invited to take part in a concert which was got up by several persons of high rank for the benefit of the poor. The bearer of the invitation was no less a person than Ursin Niemcewicz, the publicist, poet, dramatist, and statesman, one of the most remarkable and influential men of the Poland of that day. At this concert, which took place on February 24, 1818, the young virtuoso played a concerto by Adalbert Gyrowetz, a composer once celebrated, but now ignominiously shelved—sic transit gloria mundi—and one of Riehl's "divine Philistines." An anecdote shows that at that time Frederick was neither an intellectual prodigy nor a conceited puppy, but a naive, modest child that played the pianoforte, as birds sing, with unconscious art. When he came home after the concert, for which of course he had been arrayed most splendidly and to his own great satisfaction, his mother said to him: "Well, Fred, what did the public like best?"—"Oh, mamma," replied the little innocent, "everybody was looking at my collar."

The debut was a complete success, and our Frederick—Chopinek (diminutive of Chopin) they called him—became more than ever the pet of the aristocracy of Warsaw. He was invited to the houses of the Princes Czartoryski, Sapieha, Czetwertynski, Lubecki, Radziwill, the Counts Skarbek, Wolicki, Pruszak, Hussarzewski, Lempicki, and others. By the Princess Czetwertynska, who, says Liszt, cultivated music with a true feeling of its beauties, and whose salon was one of the most brilliant and select of Warsaw, Frederick was introduced to the Princess Lowicka, the beautiful Polish wife of the Grand Duke Constantine, who, as Countess Johanna Antonia Grudzinska, had so charmed the latter that, in order to obtain the Emperor's consent to his marriage with her, he abdicated his right of succession to the throne. The way in which she exerted her influence over her brutal, eccentric, if not insane, husband, who at once loved and maltreated the Poles, gained her the title of "guardian angel of Poland." In her salon Frederick came of course also in contact with the dreaded Grand Duke, the Napoleon of Belvedere (thus he was nicknamed by Niemcewicz, from the palace where he resided in Warsaw), who on one occasion when the boy was improvising with his eyes turned to the ceiling, as was his wont, asked him why he looked in that direction, if he saw notes up there. With the exalted occupants of Belvedere Frederick had a good deal of intercourse, for little Paul, a boy of his own age, a son or adopted son of the Grand Duke, enjoyed his company, and sometimes came with his tutor, Count de Moriolles, to his house to take him for a drive. On these occasions the neighbours of the Chopin family wondered not a little what business brought the Grand Duke's carriage, drawn by four splendid horses, yoked in the Russian fashion—i.e., all abreast—to their quarter.

Chopin's early introduction into aristocratic society and constant intercourse with the aristocracy is an item of his education which must not be considered as of subordinate importance. More than almost any other of his early disciplines, it formed his tastes, or at least strongly assisted in developing certain inborn traits of his nature, and in doing this influenced his entire moral and artistic character. In the proem I mentioned an English traveller's encomiums on the elegance in the houses, and the exquisite refinement in the entertainments, of the wealthy nobles in the last quarter of the eighteenth century. We may be sure that in these respects the present century was not eclipsed by its predecessors, at least not in the third decade, when the salons of Warsaw shone at their brightest. The influence of French thought and manners, for the importation and spreading of which King Stanislas Leszczinski was so solicitous that he sent at his own expense many young gentlemen to Paris for their education, was subsequently strengthened by literary taste, national sympathies, and the political connection during the first Empire. But although foreign notions and customs caused much of the old barbarous extravagance and also much of the old homely simplicity to disappear, they did not annihilate the national distinctiveness of the class that was affected by them. Suffused with the Slavonic spirit and its tincture of Orientalism, the importation assumed a character of its own. Liszt, who did not speak merely from hearsay, emphasises, in giving expression to his admiration of the elegant and refined manners of the Polish aristocracy, the absence of formalism and stiff artificiality:—

> In these salons [he writes] the rigorously observed
> proprieties were not a kind of ingeniously-constructed
> corsets that served to hide deformed hearts; they only
> necessitated the spiritualisation of all contacts, the
> elevation of all rapports, the aristocratisation of all
> impressions.

But enough of this for the present.

A surer proof of Frederick's ability than the applause and favour of the aristocracy was the impression he made on the celebrated Catalani, who, in January, 1820, gave four concerts in the town-hall of Warsaw, the charge for admission to each of which was, as we may note in passing, no less than thirty Polish florins (fifteen shillings). Hearing much of the musically-gifted boy, she expressed the wish to have him presented to her. On this being done, she was so pleased with him and his playing that she made him a present of a watch, on which were engraved the words: "Donne par Madame Catalani a Frederic Chopin, age de dix ans."

As yet I have said nothing of the boy's first attempts at composition. Little Frederick began to compose soon after the commencement of his pianoforte lessons and before he could handle the pen. His master had to write down what the pupil played, after which the youthful maestro, often dissatisfied with his first conception, would set to work with the critical file, and try to improve it. He composed mazurkas, polonaises, waltzes, &c. At the age of ten he dedicated a march to the Grand Duke Constantine, who had it scored for a military band and played on parade (subsequently it was also published, but without the composer's name), and these productions gave such evident proof of talent that his father deemed it desirable to get his friend Elsner to instruct him in harmony and counterpoint. At this time, however, it was not as yet in contemplation that Frederick should become a professional musician; on the contrary, he was made to understand that his musical studies must not interfere with his other studies, as he was then preparing for his entrance into the Warsaw Lyceum. As we know that this event took place in 1824, we know also the approximate time of the commencement of Elsner's lessons. Fontana says that Chopin began these studies when he was already remarkable as a pianist. Seeing how very little is known concerning the nature and extent of Chopin's studies in composition, it may be as well to exhaust the subject at once. But before I do so I must make the reader acquainted with the musician who, as Zyvny was Chopin's only pianoforte teacher, was his only teacher of composition.

Joseph Elsner, the son of a cabinet and musical instrument maker at Grottkau, in Silesia, was born on June 1, 1769. As his father intended him for the medical profession, he was sent in 1781 to the Latin school at Breslau, and some years later to the University at Vienna. Having already been encouraged by the rector in Grottkau to cultivate his beautiful voice, he became in Breslau a chorister in one of the churches, and after some time was often employed as violinist and singer at the theatre. Here, where he got, if not regular instruction, at least some hints regarding harmony and kindred matters (the authorities are hopelessly at variance on this and on many other points), he made his first attempts at composition, writing dances, songs, duets, trios, nay, venturing even on larger works for chorus and orchestra. The musical studies commenced in Breslau were continued in Vienna; preferring musical scores to medical books, the conversations of musicians to the lectures of professors, he first neglected and at last altogether abandoned the study of the healing art. A. Boguslawski, who wrote a biography of Elsner, tells the story differently and more poetically. When, after a long illness during his sojourn in Breslau, thus runs his version, Elsner went, on the day of the Holy Trinity in the year 1789, for the first time to church, he was so deeply moved by the sounds of the organ that he fainted. On recovering he felt his whole being filled with such ineffable comfort and happiness that he thought he saw in this occurrence the hand of destiny. He, therefore, set out for Vienna, in order that he might draw as it were at the fountain-head the great principles of his art. Be this as it may, in 1791 we hear of Elsner as violinist in Brunn, in 1792 as musical conductor at a theatre in Lemberg—where he is busy composing dramatic and other works—and near the end of the last century as occupant of the same post at the National Theatre in Warsaw, which town became his home for the rest of his life. There was the principal field of his labours; there he died, after a sojourn of sixty-two years in Poland, on April 18, 1854, leaving behind him one of the most honoured names in the history of his adopted country. Of the journeys he undertook, the longest and most important was, no doubt, that to Paris in 1805. On the occasion of this visit some of his compositions were performed, and when Chopin arrived there twenty-five years afterwards, Elsner was still remembered by Lesueur, who said: "Et que fait notre bon Elsner? Racontez-moi de ses nouvelles." Elsner was a very productive composer: besides symphonies, quartets, cantatas, masses, an oratorio, &c., he composed twenty-seven Polish operas. Many of these works were published, some in Warsaw, some in various German towns, some even in Paris. But his activity as a teacher, conductor, and organiser was perhaps even more beneficial to the development of the musical art in Poland than that as a composer. After founding and conducting several musical societies, he became in 1821 director of the then opened Conservatorium, at the head of which he continued to the end of its existence in 1830. To complete the idea of the man, we must not omit to mention his essay In how far is the Polish language suitable for music? As few of his compositions have been heard outside of Poland, and these few long ago, rarely, and in few places, it is difficult to form a satisfactory opinion with regard to his position as a composer. Most accounts, however, agree in stating that he wrote in the style of the modern Italians, that is to say, what were called the modern Italians in the later part of the last and the earlier part of this century. Elsner tried his strength and ability in all genres, from oratorio, opera, and symphony, down to pianoforte variations, rondos, and dances, and in none of them did he fail to be pleasing and intelligible, not even where, as especially in his sacred music, he made use—a sparing use—of contrapuntal devices, imitations, and fugal treatment. The naturalness, fluency, effectiveness, and practicableness which distinguish his writing for voices and instruments show that he possessed a thorough knowledge of their nature and capability. It was, therefore, not an empty rhetorical phrase to speak of him initiating his pupils "a la science du contre-point et aux effets d'une savante instrumentation."

[FOOTNOTE: "The productions of Elsner," says Fetis, "are in the style of Paer and Mayer's music. In his church music there is a little too much of modern and dramatic forms; one finds in them facility and a natural manner of making the parts sing, but little originality and variety in his ideas. Elsner writes with sufficient purity, although he shows in his fugues that his studies have not been severe."]

For the pupils of the Conservatorium he wrote vocal pieces in from one to ten parts, and he composed also a number of canons in four and five parts, which fact seems to demonstrate that he had no ill-will against the scholastic forms. And now I shall quote a passage from an apparently well-informed writer [FOOTNOTE: The writer of the article Elsner in Schilling's Universal-Lexikon der Tonkunst] (to whom I am, moreover, otherwise indebted in this sketch), wherein Elsner is blamed for certain shortcomings with which Chopin has been often reproached in a less charitable spirit. The italics, which are mine, will point out the words in question:—

One forgives him readily [in consideration of the general excellence of his style] THE OFFENCES AGAINST THE LAW OF

HARMONIC CONNECTION THAT OCCUR HERE AND THERE, AND THE

FACILITY WITH WHICH HE SOMETIMES DISREGARDS THE FIXED RULES

OF STRICT PART-WRITING, *especially in the dramatic works, where he makes effect apparently the ultimate aim of his indefatigable endeavours.*

The wealth of melody and technical mastery displayed in "The Passion of our Lord Jesus Christ" incline Karasowski to think that it is the composer's best work. When the people at Breslau praised Elsner's "Echo Variations" for orchestra, Chopin exclaimed: "You must hear his Coronation Mass, then only can you judge of him as a composer." To characterise Elsner in a few words, he was a man of considerable musical aptitude and capacity, full of nobleness of purpose, learning, industry, perseverance, in short, possessing all qualities implied by talent, but lacking those implied by genius.

A musician travelling in 1841 in Poland sent at the time to the Neue Zeitschrift fur Musik a series of "Reiseblatter" (Notes of Travel), which contain so charming and vivid a description of this interesting personality that I cannot resist the temptation to translate and insert it here almost without any abridgment. Two noteworthy opinions of the writer may be fitly prefixed to this quotation—namely, that Elsner was a Pole with all his heart and soul, indeed, a better one than thousands that are natives of the country, and that, like Haydn, he possessed the quality of writing better the older he grew:—

The first musical person of the town [Warsaw] is still the old, youthful Joseph Elsner, a veteran master of our art, who is as amiable as he is truly estimable. In our day one hardly

meets with a notable Polish musician who has not studied
composition under Pan [i.e., Mr.] Elsner; and he loves all
his pupils, and all speak of him with enthusiasm, and,
according to the Polish fashion, kiss the old master's
shoulder, whereupon he never forgets to kiss them heartily on
both cheeks. Even Charles Kurpinski, the pensioned
Capelhneister of the Polish National Theatre, whose hair is
already grey, is, if I am not very much misinformed, also a
pupil of Joseph Elsner's. One is often mistaken with regard
to the outward appearance of a celebrated man; I mean, one
forms often a false idea of him before one has seen him and
knows a portrait of him. I found Elsner almost exactly as I
had imagined him. Wisocki, the pianist, also a pupil of his,
took me to him. Pan Elsner lives in the Dom Pyarow [House of
Piarists]. One has to start early if one wishes to find him
at home; for soon after breakfast he goes out, and rarely
returns to his cell before evening. He inhabits, like a
genuine church composer, two cells of the old Piarist
Monastery in Jesuit Street, and in the dark passages which
lead to his rooms one sees here and there faded laid-aside
pictures of saints lying about, and old church banners
hanging down. The old gentleman was still in bed when we
arrived, and sent his servant to ask us to wait a little in
the anteroom, promising to be with us immediately. All the
walls of this room, or rather cell, were hung to the ceiling
with portraits of musicians, among them some very rare names
and faces. Mr. Elsner has continued this collection down to
the present time; also the portraits of Liszt, Thalberg,
Chopin, and Clara Wieck shine down from the old monastic
walls. I had scarcely looked about me in this large company
for a few minutes, when the door of the adjoining room
opened, and a man of medium height (not to say little),
somewhat stout, with a round, friendly countenance, grey
hair, but very lively eyes, enveloped in a warm fur dressing-

gown, stepped up to us, comfortably but quickly, and bade us
welcome. Wisocki kissed him, according to the Polish fashion,
as a token of respect, on the right shoulder, and introduced
me to him, whereupon the old friendly gentleman shook hands
with me and said some kindly words.

This, then, was Pan Joseph Elsner, the ancestor of modern
Polish music, the teacher of Chopin, the fine connoisseur and
cautious guide of original talents. For he does not do as is
done only too often by other teachers in the arts, who insist
on screwing all pupils to the same turning-lathe on which
they themselves were formed, who always do their utmost to
ingraft their own I on the pupil, so that he may become as
excellent a man as they imagine themselves to be. Joseph
Elsner did not proceed thus. When all the people of Warsaw
thought Frederick Chopin was entering on a wrong path, that
his was not music at all, that he must keep to Himmel and
Hummel, otherwise he would never do anything decent—the
clever Pan Elsner had already very clearly perceived what a
poetic kernel there was in the pale young dreamer, had long
before felt very clearly that he had before him the founder
of a new epoch of pianoforte-playing, and was far from laying
upon him a cavesson, knowing well that such a noble
thoroughbred may indeed be cautiously led, but must not be
trained and fettered in the usual way if he is to conquer.

Of Chopin's studies under this master we do not know much more
than of his studies under Zywny. Both Fontana and Sowinski say that he
went through a complete course of counterpoint and composition. Elsner,
in a letter written to Chopin in 1834, speaks of himself as "your teacher of
harmony and counterpoint, of little merit, but fortunate." Liszt writes:—

Joseph Elsner taught Chopin those things that are most
difficult to learn and most rarely known: to be exacting
to one's self, and to value the advantages that are only
obtained by dint of patience and labour.

What other accounts of the matter under discussion I have got from books and conversations are as general and vague as the foregoing. I therefore shall not weary the reader with them. What Elsner's view of teaching was may be gathered from one of his letters to his pupil. The gist of his remarks lies in this sentence: —

That with which the artist (who learns continually from his surroundings) astonishes his contemporaries, he can only attain by himself and through himself.

Elsner had insight and self-negation (a rare quality with teachers) enough to act up to his theory, and give free play to the natural tendencies of his pupil's powers. That this was really the case is seen from his reply to one who blamed Frederick's disregard of rules and custom: —

Leave him in peace [he said], his is an uncommon way because his gifts are uncommon. He does not strictly adhere to the customary method, but he has one of his own, and he will reveal in his works an originality which in such a degree has not been found in anyone.

The letters of master and pupil testify to their unceasing mutual esteem and love. Those of the master are full of fatherly affection and advice, those of the pupil full of filial devotion and reverence. Allusions to and messages for Elsner are very frequent in Chopin's letters. He seems always anxious that his old master should know how he fared, especially hear of his success. His sentiments regarding Elsner reveal themselves perhaps nowhere more strikingly than in an incidental remark which escapes him when writing to his friend Woyciechowski. Speaking of a new acquaintance he has made, he says, "He is a great friend of Elsner's, which in my estimation means much." No doubt Chopin looked up with more respect and thought himself more indebted to Elsner than to Zywny; but that he had a good opinion of both his masters is evident from his pithy reply to the Viennese gentleman who told him that people were astonished at his having learned all he knew at Warsaw: "From Messrs. Zywny and Elsner even the greatest ass must learn something."

CHAPTER III

FREDERICK ENTERS THE WARSAW LYCEUM.—VARIOUS
EDUCATIONAL INFLUENCES.—HIS FATHER'S FRIENDS.—RISE OF
ROMANTICISM IN POLISH LITERATURE.—FREDERICK'S STAY AT
SZAFARNIA DURING HIS FIRST SCHOOL HOLIDAYS.—HIS TALENT
FOR IMPROVISATION.—HIS DEVELOPMENT AS A COMPOSER AND
PIANIST.—HIS PUBLIC PERFORMANCES.—PUBLICATION OF OP. I.—
EARLY COMPOSITIONS.—HIS PIANOFORTE STYLE.

FREDERICK, who up to the age of fifteen was taught at home along with his father's boarders, became in 1824 a pupil of the Warsaw Lyceum, a kind of high-school, the curriculum of which comprised Latin, Greek, modern languages, mathematics, history, &c. His education was so far advanced that he could at once enter the fourth class, and the liveliness of his parts, combined with application to work, enabled him to distinguish himself in the following years as a student and to carry off twice a prize. Polish history and literature are said to have been his favourite studies.

Liszt relates that Chopin was placed at an early age in one of the first colleges of Warsaw, "thanks to the generous and intelligent protection which Prince Anton Radziwill always bestowed upon the arts and upon young men of talent." This statement, however, has met with a direct denial on the part of the Chopin family, and may, therefore, be considered as disposed of. But even without such a denial the statement would appear suspicious to all but those unacquainted with Nicholas Chopin's position. Surely he must have been able to pay for his son's schooling! Moreover, one would think that, as a professor at the Lyceum, he might even have got it gratis. As to Frederick's musical education in Warsaw, it cannot have cost much. And then, how improbable that the Prince should have paid the comparatively trifling school-fees and left the young man when he went abroad dependent upon the support of his parents! The letters from Vienna (1831) show unmistakably that Chopin applied to his father repeatedly for money, and regretted being such a burden to him. Further, Chopin's correspondence, which throws much light on his relation to Prince Radziwili, contains nothing which would lead one to infer any such indebtedness as Liszt mentions. But in order that the reader may be in possession of the whole evidence and able to judge for himself, I shall place before him Liszt's curiously circumstantial account in its entirety:—

The Prince bestowed upon him the inappreciable gift of a good education, no part of which remained neglected. His elevated mind enabling him to understand the exigencies of an artist's career, he, from the time of his protege's entering the college to the entire completion of his studies, paid the pension through the agency of a friend, M. Antoine Korzuchowski, [FOOTNOTE: Liszt should have called this gentleman Adam Kozuchowski.] who always maintained cordial relations and a constant friendship with Chopin.

Liszt's informant was no doubt Chopin's Paris friend Albert Grzymala, [FOOTNOTE: M. Karasowski calls this Grzymala erroneously Francis. More information about this gentleman will be given in a subsequent chapter.] who seems to have had no connection with the Chopin family in Poland. Karasowski thinks that the only foundation of the story is a letter and present from Prince Radziwill—acknowledgments of the dedication to him of the Trio, Op. 8—which Adam Kozuchowski brought to Chopin in 1833. [FOOTNOTE: M. Karasowski, Fryderyk Chopin, vol. i., p. 65.]

Frederick was much liked by his school-fellows, which, as his manners and disposition were of a nature thoroughly appreciated by boys, is not at all to be wondered at. One of the most striking features in the character of young Chopin was his sprightliness, a sparkling effervescence that manifested itself by all sorts of fun and mischief. He was never weary of playing pranks on his sisters, his comrades, and even on older people, and indulged to the utmost his fondness for caricaturing by pictorial and personal imitations. In the course of a lecture the worthy rector of the Lyceum discovered the scapegrace making free with the face and figure of no less a person than his own rectorial self. Nevertheless the irreverent pupil got off easily, for the master, with as much magnanimity as wisdom, abstained from punishing the culprit, and, in a subscript which he added to the caricature, even praised the execution of it. A German Protestant pastor at Warsaw, who made always sad havoc of the Polish language, in which he had every Sunday to preach one of his sermons, was the prototype of one of the imitations with which Frederick frequently amused his friends. Our hero's talent for changing the expression of his face, of which George Sand, Liszt, Balzac, Hiller, Moscheles, and other personal acquaintances, speak with admiration, seems already at this time to have been extraordinary. Of the theatricals which the young folks were wont to get up at the paternal house, especially on the name-days of their parents and friends, Frederick was the soul and mainstay. With a good delivery he combined a presence of mind that enabled him to be always ready with an improvisation when another player forgot his part. A clever Polish actor, Albert Piasecki, who was stage-manager on these occasions, gave it as his opinion that the lad was born to be a great actor. In after years two distinguished members of the profession in France, M. Bocage and Mdme. Dorval, expressed similar opinions. For their father's name-day in 1824, Frederick and his sister Emilia wrote conjointly a one-act comedy in verse, entitled THE MISTAKE; OR, THE PRETENDED ROGUE, which was acted by a juvenile company. According to Karasowski, the play showed that the authors had a not inconsiderable command of language, but in other respects could not be called a very brilliant achievement. Seeing that fine comedies are not often written at the ages of fifteen and eleven, nobody will be in the least surprised at the result.

These domestic amusements naturally lead us to inquire who were the visitors that frequented the house. Among them there was Dr. Samuel Bogumil Linde, rector of the Lyceum and first librarian of the National Library, a distinguished philologist, who, assisted by the best Slavonic scholars, wrote a valuable and voluminous "Dictionary of the Polish Language," and published many other works on the Slavonic languages. After this oldest of Nicholas Chopin's friends I shall mention Waclaw Alexander Maciejowski, who, like Linde, received his university education in Germany, taught then for a short time at the Lyceum, and became in 1819 a professor at the University of Warsaw. His contributions to various branches of Slavonic history (law, literature, &c.) are very numerous. However, one of the most widely known of those who were occasionally seen at Chopin's home was Casimir Brodzinski, the poet, critic, and champion of romanticism, a prominent figure in Polish literary history, who lived in Warsaw from about 1815 to 1822, in which year he went as professor of literature to the University of Cracow. Nicholas Chopin's pupil, Count Frederick Skarbek, must not be forgotten; he had now become a man of note, being professor of political economy at the university, and author of several books that treat of that science. Besides Elsner and Zywny, who have already been noticed at some length, a third musician has to be numbered among friends of the Chopin family—namely, Joseph Javurek, the esteemed composer and professor at the Conservatorium; further, I must yet make mention of Anton Barcinski, professor at the Polytechnic School, teacher at Nicholas Chopin's institution, and by-and-by his son-in-law; Dr. Jarocki, the zoologist; Julius Kolberg, the engineer; and Brodowski, the painter. These and others, although to us only names, or little more, are nevertheless not without their significance. We may liken them to the supernumeraries on the stage, who, dumb as they are, help to set off and show the position of the principal figure or figures.

The love of literature which we have noticed in the young Chopins, more particularly in the sisters, implanted by an excellent education and fostered by the taste, habits, and encouragement of their father, cannot but have been greatly influenced and strengthened by the characters and conversation of such visitors. And let it not be overlooked that this was the time of Poland's intellectual renascence—a time when the influence of man over man is greater than at other times, he being, as it were, charged with a kind of vivifying electricity. The misfortunes that had passed over Poland had purified and fortified the nation—breathed into it a new and healthier life. The change which the country underwent from the middle of the eighteenth to the earlier part of the nineteenth century was indeed immense. Then Poland, to use Carlyle's drastic phraseology, had ripened into a condition of "beautifully phosphorescent rot-heap"; now, with an improved agriculture, reviving commerce, and rising industry, it was more prosperous than it had been for centuries. As regards intellectual matters, the comparison with the past was even more favourable to the present. The government that took the helm in 1815 followed the direction taken by its predecessors, and schools and universities flourished; but a most hopeful sign was this, that whilst the epoch of Stanislas Augustus was, as Mickiewicz remarked (in Les Slaves), little Slavonic and not even national, now the national spirit pervaded the whole intellectual atmosphere, and incited workers in all branches of science and art to unprecedented efforts. To confine ourselves to one department, we find that the study of the history and literature of Poland had received a vigorous impulse, folk-songs were zealously collected, and a new school of poetry, romanticism, rose victoriously over the fading splendour of an effete classicism. The literature of the time of Stanislas was a court and salon literature, and under the influence of France and ancient Rome. The literature that began to bud about 1815, and whose germs are to be sought for in the preceding revolutionary time, was more of a people's literature, and under the influence of Germany, England, and Russia. The one was a hot-house plant, the other a garden flower, or even a wild flower. The classics swore by the precepts of Horace and Boileau, and held that among the works of Shakespeare there was not one veritable tragedy. The romanticists, on the other hand, showed by their criticisms and works that their sympathies were with Schiller, Goethe, Burger, Byron, Shukovski, &c. Wilna was the chief centre from which this movement issued, and Brodziriski one of the foremost defenders of the new principles and the precursor of Mickiewicz, the appearance of whose ballads, romances, "Dziady" and "Grazyna" (1822), decided the war in favour of romanticism. The names of Anton Malczewski,

Bogdan Zaleski, Severyn Goszczynski, and others, ought to be cited along with that of the more illustrious Mickiewicz, but I will not weary the reader either with a long disquisition or with a dry enumeration. I have said above that Polish poetry had become more of a people's poetry. This, however, must not be understood in the sense of democratic poetry.

The Polish poets [says C. Courriere, to whose "Histoire de la litterature chez les Slaves" I am much indebted] ransacked with avidity the past of their country, which appeared to them so much the more brilliant because it presented a unique spectacle in the history of nations. Instead of breaking with the historic traditions they respected them, and gave them a new lustre, a new life, by representing them under a more beautiful, more animated, and more striking form. In short, if Polish romanticism was an evolution of poetry in the national sense, it did not depart from the tendencies of its elder sister, for it saw in the past only the nobility; it was and remained, except in a few instances, aristocratic.

Now let us keep in mind that this contest of classicism and romanticism, this turning away from a dead formalism to living ideals, was taking place at that period of Frederick Chopin's life when the human mind is most open to new impressions, and most disposed to entertain bold and noble ideas. And, further, let us not undervalue the circumstance that he must have come in close contact with one of the chief actors in this unbloody revolution.

Frederick spent his first school holidays at Szafarnia, in Mazovia, the property of the Dziewanowski family. In a letter written on August 19, 1824, he gives his friend and school-fellow William Kolberg, some account of his doings there—of his strolls and runs in the garden, his walks and drives to the forest, and above all of his horsemanship. He tells his dear Willie that he manages to keep his seat, but would not like to be asked how. Indeed, he confesses that, his equestrian accomplishments amount to no more than to letting the horse go slowly where it lists, and sitting on it, like a monkey, with fear. If he had not yet met with an accident, it was because the horse had so far not felt any inclination to throw him off. In connection with his drives—in britzka and in coach—he does not forget to mention that he is always honoured with a back-seat. Still, life at Szafarnia was not unmixed happiness, although our hero bore the ills with admirable stoicism:—

Very often [he writes] the flies sit on my prominent nose —
this, however, is of no consequence, it is the habit of these
little animals. The mosquitoes bite me—this too, however, is
of no consequence, for they don't bite me in the nose.

The reader sees from this specimen of epistolary writing that Frederick is still a boy, and if I had given the letter in extenso, the boyishness would have been even more apparent, in the loose and careless style as well as in the frolicsome matter.

His letters to his people at home took on this occasion the form of a manuscript newspaper, called, in imitation of the "Kuryer Warszawski" ("Warsaw Courier"), "Kuryer Szafarski" ("Szafarnia Courier"), which the editor, in imitation of the then obtaining press regulation, did not send off until it had been seen and approved of by the censor, Miss Dziewanowska. One of the numbers of the paper contains among other news the report of a musical gathering of "some persons and demi-persons" at which, on July 15, 1824, Mr. Pichon (anagram of Chopin) played a Concerto of Kalkbrenner's and a little song, the latter being received by the youthful audience with more applause than the former.

Two anecdotes that relate to this stay at Szafarnia further exemplify what has already been said of Frederick's love of fun and mischief. Having on one of his visits to the village of Oberow met some Jews who had come to buy grain, he invited them to his room, and there entertained them with music, playing to them "Majufes."

[FOOTNOTE: Karasowski describes "Majufes" as a kind of Jewish wedding march. Ph. Lobenstein says that it means "the beautiful, the pleasing one." With this word opened a Hebrew song which dates from the time of the sojourn of the Jews in Spain, and which the orthodox Polish Jews sing on Saturdays after dinner, and whose often-heard melody the Poles imitate as a parody of Jewish singing.]

His guests were delighted—they began to dance, told him that he played like a born Jew, and urged him to come to the next Jewish wedding and play to them there. The other anecdote would be a very ugly story were it not for the redeeming conclusion. Again we meet with one of the numerous, but by no means well-loved, class of Polish citizens. Frederick, having heard that a certain Jew had bought grain from Mr. Romecki, the proprietor of Oberow, sent this gentleman a letter purporting to be written by the grain-dealer in question, in which he informed him that after reconsidering the matter he would rather not take the grain. The imitation of the jargon in use among the Polish Jews was so good, and the spelling and writing so bad, that Mr. Romecki was taken in. Indeed, he flew at once into such a passion that he sent for the Jew with the intention of administering to him a sound thrashing. Only Frederick's timely confession saved the poor fellow from his undeserved punishment. But enough of Szafarnia, where the young scapegrace paid so long a holiday visit (from his letter to William Kolberg we learn that he would not see his friend for four weeks more), and where, judging from what has already been told, and also from a remark in the same letter, he must have "enjoyed himself pretty well." And now we will return to Warsaw, to Nicholas Chopin's boarding-school.

To take away any bad impression that may be left by the last anecdote, I shall tell another of a more pleasing character, which, indeed, has had the honour of being made the subject of a picture. It was often told, says Karasowski, by Casimir Wodzinski, a boarder of Nicholas Chopin's. One day when the latter was out, Barcinski, the assistant master, could not manage the noisy boys. Seeing this, Frederick, who just then happened to come into the room, said to them that he would improvise a pretty story if they would sit down and be quiet. This quickly restored silence. He thereupon had the lights extinguished, took his seat at the piano, and began as follows:—

Robbers set out to plunder a house. They come nearer and

nearer. Then they halt, and put up the ladders they have

brought with them. But just when they are about to enter

through the windows, they hear a noise within. This gives

them a fright. They run away to the woods. There, amidst the

stillness and darkness of the night, they lie down and

before long fall fast asleep.

When Frederick had got to this part of the story he began to play softer and softer, and ever softer, till his auditors, like the robbers, were fast asleep. Noticing this he stole out of the room, called in the other inmates of the house, who came carrying lights with them, and then with a tremendous, crashing chord disturbed the sweet slumbers of the evil-doers.

Here we have an instance of "la richesse de son improvisation," by which, as Fontana tells us, Chopin, from his earliest youth, astonished all who had the good fortune to hear him. Those who think that there is no salvation outside the pale of absolute music, will no doubt be horror-stricken at the heretical tendency manifested on this occasion by an otherwise so promising musician. Nay, even the less orthodox, those who do not altogether deny the admissibility of programme-music if it conforms to certain conditions and keeps within certain limits, will shake their heads sadly. The duty of an enthusiastic biographer, it would seem, is unmistakable; he ought to justify, or, at least, excuse his hero—if nothing else availed, plead his youth and inexperience. My leaving the poor suspected heretic in the lurch under these circumstances will draw upon me the reproach of remissness; but, as I have what I consider more important business on hand, I must not be deterred from proceeding to it by the fear of censure.

The year 1825 was, in many respects, a memorable one in the life of Chopin. On May 27 and June 10 Joseph Javurek, whom I mentioned a few pages back among the friends of the Chopin family, gave two concerts for charitable purposes in the large hall of the Conservatorium. At one of these Frederick appeared again in public. A Warsaw correspondent of the "Leipzig Allgemeine musikalische Zeitung" says in the course of one of his letters: —

> The Academist Chopin performed the first Allegro of
> Moscheles' Pianoforte Concerto in F [G?] minor, and an
> improvisation on the aeolopantaleon. This instrument,
> invented by the cabinet-maker Dlugosz, of this town, combines
> the aeolomelodicon [FOOTNOTE: An instrument of the organ
> species, invented by Professor Hoffmann, and constructed by
> the mechanician Brunner, of Warsaw.] with the piano-
> forte....Young Chopin distinguished himself in his
> improvisation by wealth of musical ideas, and under his hands
> this instrument, of which he is a thorough master, made a
> great impression.

Unfortunately we learn nothing of Chopin's rendering of the movement from Moscheles' Concerto. Still, this meagre notice, written by a contemporary—an ear-witness, who wrote down his impressions soon after the performance—is very precious, indeed more precious than the most complete and elaborate criticism written fifty years after the occurrence would be. I cannot help thinking that Karasowski somewhat exaggerates when he says that Chopin's pianoforte playing transported the audience into a state of enthusiasm, and that no concert had a brilliant success unless he took part in it. The biographer seems either to trust too much to the fancy-coloured recollections of his informants, or to allow himself to be carried away by his zeal for the exaltation of his hero. At any rate, the tenor of the above-quoted notice, laudatory as it is, and the absence of Chopin's name from other Warsaw letters, do not remove the doubts which such eulogistic superlatives raise in the mind of an unbiassed inquirer. But that Chopin, as a pianist and as a musician generally, had attained a proficiency far beyond his years becomes evident if we examine his compositions of that time, to which I shall presently advert. And that he had risen into notoriety and saw his talents appreciated cannot be doubted for a moment after what has been said. Were further proof needed, we should find it in the fact that he was selected to display the excellences of the aeolomelodicon when the Emperor Alexander I, during his sojourn in Warsaw in 1825, [FOOTNOTE: The Emperor Alexander opened the Diet at Warsaw on May 13, 1825, and closed it on June 13.] expressed the wish to hear this instrument. Chopin's performance is said to have pleased the august auditor, who, at all events, rewarded the young musician with a diamond ring.

A greater event than either the concert or the performance before the Emperor, in fact, THE event of the year 1825, was the publication of Chopin's Opus 1. Only he who has experienced the delicious sensation of seeing himself for the first time in print can realise what our young author felt on this occasion. Before we examine this work, we will give a passing glance at some less important early compositions of the maestro which were published posthumously.

There is first of all a Polonaise in G sharp minor, said to be of the year 1822, [FOOTNOTE: See No. 15 of the Posthumous Works in the Breitkopf and Hartel edition.] but which, on account of the savoir-faire and invention exhibited in it, I hold to be of a considerably later time. Chopin's individuality, it is true, is here still in a rudimentary state, chiefly manifested in the light-winged figuration; the thoughts and the expression, however, are natural and even graceful, bearing thus the divine impress. The echoes of Weber should be noted. Of two mazurkas, in G and B flat major, of the year 1825, the first is, especially in its last part, rather commonplace; the second is more interesting, because more suggestive of better things, which the first is only to an inconsiderable extent. In No. 2 we meet already with harmonic piquancies which charmed musicians and lovers of music so much in the later mazurkas. Critics and students will not overlook the octaves between, treble and bass in the second bar of part two in No. 1. A. Polonaise in B flat minor, superscribed "Farewell to William Kolberg," of the year 1826, has not less naturalness and grace than the Polonaise of 1822, but in addition to these qualities, it has also at least one thought (part 1) which contains something of the sweet ring of Chopinian melancholy. The trio of the Polonaise is headed by the words: "Au revoir! after an aria from 'Gazza ladra'." Two foot-notes accompany this composition in the Breitkopf and Hartel edition (No. 16 of the Posthumous Works). The first says that the Polonaise was composed "at Chopin's departure from [should be 'for'] Reinerz"; and the second, in connection with the trio, that "some days before Chopin's departure the two friends had been present at a performance of Rossini's opera." There is one other early posthumously-published work of Chopin's, whose status, however, differs from the above-mentioned ones in this, that the composer seems to have intended to publish it. The composition in question is the Variations sur un air national allemand.

Szulc says that Oskar Kolberg related that he had still in his possession these Variations on the theme of Der Schweizerbub, which Chopin composed between his twelfth and seventeenth years at the house of General Sowinski's wife in the course of "a few quarter-hours."

The Variations sur un air national allemand were published after the composer's death along with his Sonata, Op. 4, by Haslinger, of Vienna, in 1851. They are, no doubt, the identical composition of which Chopin in a letter from Vienna (December 1, 1830) writes: "Haslinger received me very kindly, but nevertheless would publish neither the Sonata nor the Second Variations." The First Variations were those on La ci darem, Op. 2, the first of his compositions that was published in Germany. Without inquiring too curiously into the exact time of its production and into the exact meaning of "a few quarter-hours," also leaving it an open question whether the composer did or did not revise his first conception of the Variations before sending them to Vienna, I shall regard this unnumbered work—which, by the way, in the Breitkopf and Hartel edition is dated 1824—on account of its greater simplicity and inferior interest, as an earlier composition than the Premier Rondeau (C minor), Op. 1, dedicated to Mdme. de Linde (the wife of his father's friend and colleague, the rector Dr. Linde), a lady with whom Frederick often played duets. What strikes one at once in both of them is the almost total absence of awkwardness and the presence of a rarely-disturbed ease. They have a natural air which is alike free from affected profundity and insipid childishness. And the hand that wrote them betrays so little inexperience in the treatment of the instrument that they can hold their ground without difficulty and honourably among the better class of light drawing-room pieces. Of course, there are weak points: the introduction to the Variations with those interminable sequences of dominant and tonic chords accompanying a stereotyped run, and the want of cohesiveness in the Rondo, the different subjects of which are too loosely strung together, may be instanced. But, although these two compositions leave behind them a pleasurable impression, they can lay only a small claim to originality. Still, there are slight indications of it in the tempo di valse, the concluding portion of the Variations, and more distinct ones in the Rondo, in which it is possible to discover the embryos of forms—chromatic and serpentining progressions, &c.—which subsequently develop most exuberantly. But if on the one hand we must admit that the composer's individuality is as yet weak, on the other hand we cannot accuse him of being the imitator of any one master—such a dominant influence is not perceptible.

[FOOTNOTE: Schumann, who in 1831 became acquainted with Chopin's Op. 2, and conceived an enthusiastic admiration for the composer, must have made inquiries after his Op. 1, and succeeded in getting it. For on January 1832, he wrote to Frederick Wieck: "Chopin's first work (I believe firmly that it is his tenth) is in my hands: a lady would say that it was very pretty, very piquant, almost Moschelesque. But I believe you will make Clara [Wieck's daughter, afterwards Mdme. Schumann] study it; for there is plenty of Geist in it and few difficulties. But I humbly venture to assert that there are between this composition and Op. 2 two years and twenty works"]

All this, however, is changed in another composition, the Rondeau a la Mazur, Op. 5, dedicated to the Comtesse Alexandrine de Moriolles (a daughter of the Comte de Moriolles mentioned in Chapter II), which, like the Rondo, Op. 1, was first published in Warsaw, and made its appearance in Germany some years later. I do not know the exact time of its composition, but I presume it was a year or two after that of the previously mentioned works. Schumann, who reviewed it in 1836, thought it had perhaps been written in the eighteenth year of the composer, but he found in it, some confused passages excepted, no indications of the author's youth. In this Rondeau a la Mazur the individuality of Chopin and with it his nationality begin to reveal themselves unmistakably. Who could fail to recognise him in the peculiar sweet and persuasive flows of sound, and the serpent-like winding of the melodic outline, the wide-spread chords, the chromatic progressions, the dissolving of the harmonies and the linking of their constituent parts! And, as I have said elsewhere in speaking of this work: "The harmonies are often novel, and the matter is more homogeneous and better welded into oneness."

Chopin's pianoforte lessons, as has already been stated, came to an end when he was twelve years old, and thenceforth he was left to his own resources.

> The school of that time [remarks Fontana] could no longer
> suffice him, he aimed higher, and felt himself impelled
> towards an ideal which, at first vague, before long grew into
> greater distinctness. It was then that, in trying his
> strength, he acquired that touch and style, so different from
> those of his predecessors, and that he succeeded in creating
> at last that execution which since then has been the
> admiration of the artistic world.

The first stages of the development of his peculiar style may be traced in the compositions we have just now discussed. In the variations and first Rondo which Chopin wrote at or before the age of fifteen, the treatment of the instrument not only proves that he was already as much in his element on the pianoforte as a fish in the water, but also shows that an as yet vaguely-perceived ideal began to beckon him onward. Karasowski, informed by witnesses of the boy's studies in pianoforte playing, relates that Frederick, being struck with the fine effect of a chord in extended harmony, and unable, on account of the smallness of his hands, to strike the notes simultaneously, set about thinking how this physical obstacle could be overcome. The result of his cogitations was the invention of a contrivance which he put between his fingers and kept there even during the night, by this means endeavouring to increase the extensibility and flexibility of his hands. Who, in reading of this incident in Chopin's life, is not reminded of Schumann and his attempt to strengthen his fingers, an attempt that ended so fatally for his prospects as a virtuoso! And the question, an idle one I admit, suggests itself: Had Chopin been less fortunate than he was, and lost, like Schumann, the command of one of his hands before he had formed his pianoforte style, would he, as a composer, have risen to a higher position than we know him to have attained, or would he have achieved less than he actually did? From the place and wording of Karasowski's account it would appear that this experiment of Chopin's took place at or near the age of ten. Of course it does not matter much whether we know or do not know the year or day of the adoption of the practice, what is really interesting is the fact itself. I may, however, remark that Chopin's love of wide-spread chords and skips, if marked at all, is not strongly marked in the Variations on the German air and the first Rondo. Let the curious examine with regard to this matter the Tempo di Valse of the former work, and bars 38-43 of the Piu lento of the latter. In the Rondeau a la Mazur, the next work in chronological order, this peculiarity begins to show itself distinctly, and it continues to grow in the works that follow. It is not my intention to weary the reader with microscopical criticism, but I thought the first manifestations of Chopin's individuality ought not to be passed over in silence. As to his style, it will be more fully discussed in a subsequent chapter, where also the seeds from which it sprang will be pointed out.

CHAPTER IV

FREDERICK WORKS TOO HARD.—PASSES PART OF HIS HOLIDAYS (1826) IN REINERZ.—STAYS ALSO AT STRZYZEWO, AND PAYS A VISIT TO PRINCE RADZIWILL.—HE TERMINATES HIS STUDIES AT THE LYCEUM (1827). ADOPTION OF MUSIC AS HIS PROFESSION.— EXCURSIONS.—FOLK-MUSIC AND THE POLISH PEASANTRY.— SOME MORE COMPOSITIONS.—PROJECTED TRAVELS FOR HIS IMPROVEMENT.—HIS OUTWARD APPEARANCE AND STATE OF HEALTH.

THE art which had attracted the child took every day a stronger hold of the youth. Frederick was not always in that sportive humour in which we have seen him repeatedly. At times he would wander about silent and solitary, wrapped in his musical meditations. He would sit up late, busy with his beloved music, and often, after lying down, rise from his bed in the middle of the night in order, to strike a few chords or try a short phrase—to the horror of the servants, whose first thought was of ghosts, the second that their dear young master was not quite right in his mind. Indeed, what with his school-work and his musical studies, our young friend exerted himself more than was good for him. When, therefore, in the holidays of 1826 his youngest sister, Emilia, was ordered by the physicians to go to Reinerz, a watering-place in Prussian Silesia, the parents thought it advisable that the too diligent Frederick should accompany her, and drink whey for the benefit of his health. The travelling party consisted of the mother, two sisters, and himself. A letter which he wrote on August 28, 1826, to his friend William Kolberg, furnishes some information about his doings there. It contains, as letters from watering-places usually do, criticisms of the society and accounts of promenadings, excursions, regular meals, and early hours in going to bed and in rising. As the greater part of the contents can be of no interest to us, I shall confine myself to picking up what seems to me worth preserving. He had been drinking whey and the waters for a fortnight and found he was getting somewhat stouter and at the same time lazy. People said he began to look better. He enjoyed the sight of the valleys from the hills which surround Reinerz, but the climbing fatigued him, and he had sometimes to drag himself down on all-fours. One mountain, the rocky Heuscheuer, he and other delicate persons were forbidden to ascend, as the doctor was afraid that the sharp air at the top would do his patients harm. Of course, Frederick tried to make fun of everything and everyone—for instance, of the wretched wind-band, which consisted of about a dozen "caricatures," among whom a lean bassoon-player with a snuffy hook-nose was the most notable. To the manners of the country, which in some respects seem to have displeased him, he got gradually accustomed.

> *At first I was astonished that in Silesia the women work generally more than the men, but as I am doing nothing myself just now I have no difficulty in falling in with this arrangement.*

During his stay at Reinerz he gave also a concert on behalf of two orphans who had come with their sick mother to this watering-place, and at her death were left so poor as to be unable even to pay the funeral expenses and to return home with the servant who took care of them.

From Reinerz Frederick went to Strzyzewo, the property of Madame Wiesiolowska, his godmother, and sister of his godfather, Count Frederick Skarbek. While he was spending here the rest of his holidays, he took advantage of an invitation he had received from Prince Radziwill (governor of the grand duchy of Posen, and, through his wife, a daughter of Prince Ferdinand, related to the royal family of Prussia) to visit him at his country-seat Antonin, which was not very far from Strzyzewo. The Prince, who had many relations in Poland, and paid frequent visits to that country, must on these occasions have heard of and met with the musical prodigy that was the pet of the aristocracy. Moreover, it is on record that he was present at the concert at Warsaw in 1825 at which Frederick played. We have already considered and disposed of the question whether the Prince, as has been averred by Liszt, paid for young Chopin's education. As a dilettante Prince Radziwill occupied a no less exalted position in art and science than as a citizen and functionary in the body politic. To confine ourselves to music, he was not only a good singer and violoncellist, but also a composer; and in composition he did not confine himself to songs, duets, part-songs, and the like, but undertook the ambitious and arduous task of writing music to the first part of Goethe's Faust. By desire of the Court the Berlin Singakademie used to bring this work to a hearing once every year, and they gave a performance of it even as late as 1879. An enthusiastic critic once pronounced it to be among modern works one of those that evince most genius. The vox populi seems to have repealed this judgment, or rather never to have taken cognisance of the case, for outside Berlin the work has not often been heard. Dr. Langhans wrote to me after the Berlin performance in 1879:—

I heard yesterday Radziwill's Faust for the first time, and,
I may add, with much satisfaction; for the old-fashioned
things to be found in it (for instance, the utilisation of
Mozart's C minor Quartet fugue as overture, the strictly
polyphonous treatment of the choruses, &c.) are abundantly
compensated for by numerous traits of genius, and by the
thorough knowledge and the earnest intention with which the
work is conceived and executed. He dares incredible things in
the way of combining speech and song. That this combination
is an inartistic one, on that point we are no doubt at one,
but what he has effected by this means is nevertheless in the
highest degree remarkable....

By-and-by Chopin will pay the Prince a longer visit, and then we shall learn what he thought of Faust, and how he enjoyed himself at this nobleman's house.

Chopin's studies at the Lyceum terminated in the year 1827. Through his final examination, however, he did not pass so brilliantly as through his previous ones; this time he carried off no prize. The cause of this falling-off is not far to seek; indeed, has already been hinted at. Frederick's inclination and his successes as a pianist and composer, and the persuasions of Elsner and other musical friends, could not but lessen and at last altogether dispel any doubts and misgivings the parents may at first have harboured. And whilst in consequence of this change of attitude they became less exacting with their son in the matter of school-work, the latter, feeling the slackening of the reins, would more and more follow his natural bent. The final examination was to him, no doubt, a kind of manumission which freed him from the last remnant of an oppressive bondage. Henceforth, then, Chopin could, unhindered by disagreeable tasks or other obstacles, devote his whole time and strength to the cultivation of his chosen art. First, however, he spent now, as in the preceding year, some weeks with his friends in Strzyzewo, and afterwards travelled to Danzig, where he visited Superintendent von Linde, a brother of the rector of the Warsaw Lyceum.

Chopin was fond of listening to the singing and fiddling of the country people; and everyone acquainted with the national music of Poland as well as with the composer's works knows that he is indebted to it for some of the most piquant rhythmic, melodic, and even harmonic peculiarities of his style. These longer stays in the country would offer him better opportunities for the enjoyment and study of this land of music than the short excursions which he occasionally made with his father into the neighbourhood of Warsaw. His wonder always was who could have composed the quaint and beautiful strains of those mazurkas, polonaises, and krakowiaks, and who had taught these simple men and women to play and sing so truly in tune. The conditions then existing in Poland were very favourable to the study of folk-lore of any kind. Art-music had not yet corrupted folk-music; indeed, it could hardly be said that civilisation had affected the lower strata of society at all. Notwithstanding the emancipation of the peasants in 1807, and the confirmation of this law in 1815—a law which seems to have remained for a long time and in a great measure a dead letter—the writer of an anonymous book, published at Boston in 1834, found that the freedom of the wretched serfs in Russian Poland was much the same as that of their cattle, they being brought up with as little of human cultivation; nay, that the Polish peasant, poor in every part of the country, was of all the living creatures he had met with in this world or seen described in books, the most wretched. From another publication we learn that the improvements in public instruction, however much it may have benefited the upper classes, did not affect the lowest ones: the parish schools were insufficient, and the village schools not numerous enough. But the peasants, although steeped in superstition and ignorance, and too much addicted to brandy-drinking with its consequences—quarrelsomeness and revengefulness—had not altogether lost the happier features of their original character—hospitality, patriotism, good-naturedness, and, above all, cheerfulness and love of song and dance. It has been said that a simple Slavonic peasant can be enticed by his national songs from one end of the world to the other. The delight which the Slavonic nations take in dancing seems to be equally great. No other nation, it has been asserted, can compare with them in ardent devotion to this amusement. Moreover, it is noteworthy that song and dance were in Poland—as they were of course originally everywhere—intimately united. Heine gives a pretty description of the character of the Polish peasant:—

> It cannot be denied [he writes] that the Polish peasant has often more head and heart than the German peasant in some districts. Not infrequently did I find in the meanest Pole that original wit (not Gemuthswitz, humour) which on every occasion bubbles forth with wonderful iridescence, and that dreamy sentimental trait, that brilliant flashing of an Ossianic feeling for nature whose sudden outbreaks on passionate occasions are as involuntary as the rising of the blood into the face.

The student of human nature and its reflex in art will not call these remarks a digression; at least, not one deserving of censure.

We may suppose that Chopin, after his return to Warsaw and during the following winter, and the spring and summer of 1828, continued his studies with undiminished and, had this been possible, with redoubled ardour. Some of his compositions that came into existence at this time were published after his death by his friend Julius Fontana, who was a daily visitor at his parents' house. We have a Polonaise (D minor) and a Nocturne (E minor) of 1827, and another Polonaise (B flat) and the Rondo for two pianos of 1828. The Sonata, Op. 4, and La ci darem la mano, varie for pianoforte, with orchestral accompaniments, belong also to this time. The Trio (Op. 8), although not finished till 1829, was begun and considerably advanced in 1828. Several of the above compositions are referred to in a letter written by him on September 9, 1828, to one of his most intimate friends, Titus Woyciechowski. The Rondo in C had originally a different form and was recast by him for two pianos at Strzyzewo, where he passed the whole summer of 1828. He tried it with Ernemann, a musician living in Warsaw, at the warehouse of the pianoforte-manufacturer Buchholtz, and was pretty well pleased with his work.

> We intend to play it some day at the Ressource. As to my new
> compositions, I have nothing to show except the as yet
> unfinished Trio (G minor), which I began after your
> departure. The first Allegro I have already tried with
> accompaniment. It appears to me that this trio will have the
> same fate as my sonata and the variations. Both works are now
> in Vienna; the first I have, as a pupil of Elsner's,
> dedicated to him, and on the second I have placed (perhaps
> too boldly) your name. I followed in this the impulse of my
> heart and you will not take it unkindly.

The opportunities which Warsaw offered being considered insufficient for the completion of his artistic education, ways and means were discussed as to how his wants could be best provided for. The upshot of the discussions was the project of excursions to Berlin and Vienna. As, however, this plan was not realised till the autumn of 1828, and no noteworthy incidents or interesting particulars concerning the intervening period of his life have become known, I shall utilise this break in the narrative by trying my hand at a slight sketch of that terra incognita, the history of music in Poland, more particularly the history of the musical life in Warsaw, shortly before and in Chopin's time. I am induced to undertake this task by the consideration that a knowledge of the means of culture within the reach of Chopin during his residence in the Polish capital is indispensable if we wish to form a clear and complete idea of the artist's development, and that such a knowledge will at the same time help us to understand better the contents of some of the subsequent portions of this work. Before, however, I begin a new chapter and with it the above-mentioned sketch, I should like to advert to a few other matters.

The reader may perhaps already have asked the question—What was Chopin like in his outward appearance? As I have seen a daguerreotype from a picture painted when he was seventeen, I can give some sort of answer to this question. Chopin's face was clearly and finely cut, especially the nose with its wide nostrils; the forehead was high, the eyebrows delicate, the lips thin, and the lower one somewhat protruding. For those who know A. Bovy's medallion I may add that the early portrait is very like it; only, in the latter, the line formed by the lower jawbone that runs from the chin towards the ear is more rounded, and the whole has a more youthful appearance. As to the expression, it is not only meditative but even melancholy. This last point leads me naturally to another question. The delicate build of Chopin's body, his early death preceded by many years of ill-health, and the character of his music, have led people into the belief that from childhood he was always sickly in body, and for the most part also melancholy in disposition. But as the poverty and melancholy, so also disappears on closer investigation the sickliness of the child and youth. To jump, however, from this to the other extreme, and assert that he enjoyed vigorous health, would be as great a mistake. Karasowski, in his eagerness to controvert Liszt, although not going quite this length, nevertheless overshoots the mark. Besides it is a misrepresentation of Liszt not to say that the passage excerpted from his book, and condemned as not being in accordance with the facts of the case, is a quotation from G. Sand's novel Lucrezia Floriani (of which more will be said by-and-by), in which the authoress is supposed, although this was denied by her, to have portrayed Chopin. Liszt is a poet, not a chronicler; he must be read as such, and not be taken au pied de la lettre. However, even Karasowski, in whom one notices a perhaps unconscious anxiety to keep out of sight anything which might throw doubt on the health and strength of his hero, is obliged to admit that Chopin was "delicate," although he hastens to add, "but nevertheless healthy and pretty strong." It seems to me that Karasowski makes too much of the statement of a friend of Chopin's— namely, that the latter was, up to manhood, only once ill, and then with nothing worse than a cold. Indeed, in Karasowski's narrative there are not wanting indications that the health of Chopin cannot have been very vigorous; nor his strength have amounted to much; for in one place we read that the youth was no friend of long excursions on foot, and preferred to lie down and dream under beautiful trees; in another place, that his parents sent him to Reinerz and some years afterwards to Vienna, because they thought his studies had affected his health, and that rest and change of air and scene would restore his strength. Further, we are told that his mother and sisters never tired of recommending him to wrap up carefully in cold and wet weather, and that, like a good son and brother, he followed their advice. Lastly, he objected to smoking. Some of the items of this evidence are very trivial, but taken collectively they have considerable force. Of greater significance are the following additional items. Chopin's sister Emilia was carried off at the age of fourteen by pulmonary disease, and his father, as a physician informed me, died of a heart and chest complaint. Stephen Heller, who saw Chopin in 1830 in Warsaw, told me that the latter was then in delicate health, thin and with sunken cheeks, and that the people of Warsaw said that he could not live long, but would, like so many geniuses, die young. The real state of the matter seems to me to have been this. Although Chopin in his youth was at no time troubled with any serious illness, he enjoyed but fragile health, and if his frame did not already contain the seeds of the disease to which he later fell a prey, it was a favourable soil for their reception. How easily was an organisation so delicately framed over-excited and disarranged! Indeed, being vivacious, active, and hard-working, as he was, he lived on his capital. The fire of youth overcame much, not, however, without a dangerous waste of strength, the lamentable results of which we shall see before we have gone much farther. This statement of the case we find, I think, confirmed by Chopin's correspondence—the letter written at Reinerz is in this respect noteworthy.

CHAPTER V

MUSIC AND MUSICIANS IN POLAND BEFORE AND IN CHOPIN'S TIME.

THE golden age of Polish music, which coincides with that of Polish literature, is the sixteenth century, the century of the Sigismonds. The most remarkable musician of that time, and probably the greatest that Poland produced previous to the present century, was Nicolas Gomolka, who studied music in Italy, perhaps under Palestrina, in whose style he wrote. Born in or about the beginning of the second half of the sixteenth century, he died on March 5, 1609. During the reigns of the kings of the house of Saxony (1697-1763) instrumental music is said to have made much progress. Be this as it may, there was no lack of opportunities to study good examples. Augustus the Strong (I. of Saxony and II of Poland) established a special Polish band, called, in contradistinction to the Grosse Kammermusik (Great Chamber-band) in Dresden, Kleine Kammermusik (Little Chamber-band), whose business it was to be in attendance when his majesty went to Poland. These visits took place usually once a year, and lasted from, August to December, but sometimes were more frequent, and shorter or longer, just as occasion might call for. Among the members of the Polish band—which consisted of a leader (Premier), four violins, one oboe, two French horns, three bassoons, and one double bass—we meet with such well-known men as Johann Joachim Quanz and Franz Benda. Their conductor was Alberto Ristori, who at the same time held the post of composer to the Italian actors, a company that, besides plays, performed also little operas, serenades, intermezzi, &c. The usual retinue of the King on his visits to Poland included also a part of the French ballet and comedy. These travels of the artistic forces must have been rich in tragic, comic, and tragi-comic incidents, and would furnish splendid material for the pen of a novelist. But such a journey from the Saxon capital to Warsaw, which took about eight days, and cost on an average from 3,000 to 3,500 thalers (450 to 525 pounds), was a mere nothing compared with the migration of a Parisian operatic company in May, 1700. The ninety-three members of which it was composed set out in carriages and drove by Strasburg to Ulm, there they embarked and sailed to Cracow, whence the journey was continued on rafts. [FOOTNOTE: M. Furstenau, Zur Geschichte der Music und des Theaters am Hofe zu Dresden.] So much for artistic tours at the beginning of the eighteenth century. Frederick Augustus (II of Saxony and III of Poland, 1733-1763) dissolved the Polish band, and organised a similar body which was destined solely for Poland, and was to be resident there. It consisted in 1753 of an organist, two singers, twenty instrumentalists (almost all Germans), and a band-servant, their salary amounting to 5,383 thalers, 10 groschen (a little more than 805 pounds). Notwithstanding this new arrangement, the great Dresden band sometimes accompanied the King to Poland, and when it did not, some of its members at least had to be in attendance for the performance of the solos at the chamber concerts and in the operas. Also such singers, male and female, as were required for the operas proposed for representation had to take to the road. Hasse and his wife Faustina came several times to Poland. That the constellation of the Dresden musical establishment, in its vocal as well as instrumental department, was one of the most brilliant imaginable is sufficiently proved by a glance at the names which we meet with in 1719: Lotti, Heinichen, Veracini, Volumier, Senesino, Tesi, Santa Stella Lotti, Durastanti, &c. Rousseau, writing in 1754, calls the Dresden orchestra the first in Europe. And Burney says in 1772 that the instrumental performers had been some time previously of the first class. No wonder, then, if the visits of such artists improved the instrumental music of Poland.

From Sowinski's Les Musiciens Polonais we learn that on great occasions the King's band was reinforced by those of Prince Czartoryski and Count Wielhorski, thus forming a body of 100 executants. This shows that outside the King's band good musicians were to be found in Poland. Indeed, to keep in their service private bands of native and foreign singers and players was an ancient custom among the Polish magnates; it obtained for a long time, and had not yet died out at the beginning of this century. From this circumstance, however, we must not too rashly conclude that these wealthy noblemen were all animated by artistic enthusiasm. Ostentatiousness had, I am afraid, more to do with it than love of art for art's sake. Music was simply one of the indispensable departments of their establishments, in the splendour and vastness of which they tried to outdo each other and vie with sovereign rulers. The promiscuous enumeration of musicians, cooks, footmen, &c., in the lady's description of a nobleman's court which I referred to in the proem, is in this respect very characteristic. Towards the middle of the last century Prince Sanguszko, who lived at Dubno, in Volhynia, had in his service no less than two bands, to which was sometimes joined a third belonging to Prince Lubomirski. But, it will be asked, what music did they play? An author of Memoirs of the reign of Augustus III tells us that, according to the Polish fashion, they had during meal-times to play national airs, polonaises, mazurkas, &c., arranged for wind-instruments, with or without violins. For special occasions the Prince got a new kind of music, then much in favour—viz., a band of mountaineers playing on flutes and drums. And while the guests were sitting at the banquet, horns, trumpets, and fifes sounded fanfares. Besides the ordinary and extraordinary bands, this exalted personage had among his musical retainers a drummer who performed solos on his instrument. One is glad to learn that when the Prince was alone or had little company, he took delight in listening to trios for two violins and bass, it being then the fashion to play such ensemble pieces. Count Ilinski, the father of the composer John Stanislas Ilinski, engaged for his private theatre two companies, one from Germany and one from Italy. The persons employed in the musical department of his household numbered 124. The principal band, conducted by Dobrzyrnski pere, a good violinist and conductor, consisted of four violins, one viola, one violoncello, one double bass, one flute, one oboe, one clarinet, and one bassoon. Villagers were trained by these players to assist them. Then there was yet another band, one of wind instruments, under the direction of Karelli, a pupil of the Russian composer Bartnianski [Footnote: The Russian Palestrina, whose name is oftener met with in the forms of Bortnianski and Bortniansky]. The chorus was composed of twenty four voices, picked from the young people on Count Ilinski's estates. However questionable the taste of many of these noble art patrons may have been, there were not wanting some who cultivated music with a purer spirit. Some of the best bands were those of the Princes D. Radziwill, Adam Czartoryski, F. Sulkowski, Michael Lubomirski, Counts Ilinski, Oginski, and Wielhorski. Our inquiry into the cultivation of music at the courts of the Polish magnates has carried us beyond the point we had reached in our historical survey. Let us now retrace our steps.

The progress of music above spoken of was arrested by the anarchy and the civil and other wars that began to rage in Poland with such fury in the middle of the last century. King Stanislas Poniatowski (1764-1795) is credited with having exercised great influence on the music of Poland; at any rate, he patronised the arts and sciences right royally. The Italian opera at Warsaw cannot have been of mean standing, seeing that artists such as the composers Paisiello and Cimarosa, and the great violinist, composer, and conductor Pugnani, with his pupil Viotti (the latter playing second violin in the orchestra), were members of the company. And the King's band of foreign and native players has been called one of the best in Europe. Still, all this was but the hothouse bloom of exotics. To bring about a natural harvest of home produce something else was wanted than royal patronage, and this something sprang from the series of disasters that befell the nation in the latter half of the last century, and by shaking it to its very heart's core stirred up its nobler self. As in literature, so in music, the national element came now more and more into action and prominence.

Up to 1778 there had been heard in Poland only Italian and French operas; in this year, for the first time, a Polish opera was put on the stage. It is true the beginning was very modest. The early attempts contained few ensemble pieces, no choruses, and no complex finales. But a new art does not rise from the mind of a nation as Minerva is said to have risen from the head of Jupiter. Nay, even the fact that the first three composers of Polish operas (Kamienski, Weynert, and Kajetani) were not Poles, but foreigners endeavouring to write in the Polish style, does not destroy the significance of the movement. The following statistics will, no doubt, take the reader by surprise:—From the foundation of the national Polish opera in 1778 till April 20, 1859, 5,917 performances of 285 different operas with Polish words took place in Poland. Of these 92 were national Polish operas, the remaining 193 by Italian, French, and German composers; 1,075 representations being given of the former, 4,842 of the latter. The libretti of 41 of the 92 Polish operas were originals, the other 51 were translations. And, lastly, the majority of the 16 musicians who composed the 92 Polish operas were not native Poles, but Czechs, Hungarians, and Germans [FOOTNOTE: Ladislas von Trocki, Die Entwickelung der Oper in Polen. (Leipzig, 1867.)]

A step hardly less important than the foundation of a national opera was the formation, in 1805, of a Musical Society, which had for its object the improvement as well as the amusement of its members. The idea, which originated in the head of one of the Prussian officials then in Warsaw, finding approval, and the pecuniary supplies flowing in abundantly, the Oginski Palace was rented and fitted up, two masters were engaged for the teaching of solo and choral singing, and a number of successful concerts were given. The chief promoters seem to have been Count Krasinski and the two Prussian officials Mosqua and E. Th. A. Hoffmann. In the last named the reader will recognise the famous author of fantastic tales and of no less fantastic musical criticisms, the conductor and composer of operas and other works, &c. According to his biographer, J. E. Hitzig, Hoffmann did not take much interest in the proceedings of the Musical Ressource (that was the name of the society) till it bought the Mniszech Palace, a large building, which, having been damaged by fire, had to undergo extensive repairs. Then, indeed, he set to work with a will, planned the arrangement and fitting-up of the rooms, designed and partly painted the decorations—not without freely indulging his disposition for caricature—and when all was ready, on August 3, 1806 (the King of Prussia's birthday), conducted the first concert in the splendid new hall. The activity of the society was great, and must have been beneficial; for we read that they had every Sunday performances of quartets and other kinds of chamber music, that ladies frequently came forward with pianoforte sonatas, and that when the celebrated violinist Moser, of Berlin, visited Warsaw, he made them acquainted with the finest quartets of Mozart and Haydn. Still, I should not have dwelt so long on the doings of the Musical Ressource were it not that it was the germ of, or at least gave the impulse to, even more influential associations and institutions that were subsequently founded with a view to the wider diffusion and better cultivation of the musical art in Poland. After the battle of Jena the French were not long in making their appearance in Warsaw, whereby an end was put to Prussia's rule there, and her officials were sent about, or rather sent out of, their business. Thus the Musical Ressource lost many of its members, Hoffmann and Mosqua among others. Still, it survived, and was reconstructed with more national elements. In Frederick Augustus of Saxony's reign it is said to have been transformed into a school of singing.

The year 1815 brought into existence two musical institutions that deserve to be noticed — society for the cultivation of church music, which met at the College of the Pianists, and had at its head Count Zabiello as president and Elsner as conductor; and an association, organised by the last-named musician, and presided over by the Princess Sophia Zamoyska, which aimed at the advancement of the musical art in Poland, and provided for the education of music teachers for schools, organists for churches, and singers for the stage. Although I try to do my best with the unsatisfactory and often contradictory newspaper reports and dictionary articles from which I have to draw my data, I cannot vouch for the literal correctness of my notes. In making use of Sowinski's work I am constantly reminded of Voltaire's definition of dictionaries: "Immenses archives de mensonges et d'un peu de verite." Happy he who need not consult them! In 1816 Elsner was entrusted by the minister Staszyc with the direction of a school of dramatic singing and recitation; and in 1821, to crown all previous efforts, a conservatorium was opened, the programme of which might almost have satisfied a Berlioz. The department of instrumental music not only comprised sections for the usual keyed, stringed, and wind instruments, but also one for instruments of percussion. Solo and choral singing were to be taught with special regard to dramatic expression. Besides these and the theoretical branches of music, the curriculum included dancing, Polish literature, French, and Italian. After reading the programme it is superfluous to be informed that the institution was chiefly intended for the training of dramatic artists. Elsner, who was appointed director, selected the teaching staff, with one exception, however, that of the first singing-master, for which post the Government engaged the composer Carlo Evasio Soliva, a pupil of Asioli and Frederici.

The musical taste and culture prevailing in Poland about 1819 is pretty accurately described by a German resident at Cracow. So far as music was concerned Poland had hitherto been ignored by the rest of Europe, and indeed could lay no claim to universal notice in this respect. But the improved culture and greater insight which some had acquired in foreign lands were good seeds that began to bear fruit. As yet, however, the greater part of the public took little or no interest in the better class of music, and was easily pleased and satisfied with polonaises, mazurkas, and other trivial things. In fact, the music in Cracow, notwithstanding the many professional musicians and amateurs living there, was decidedly bad, and not comparable to the music in many a small German town. In Warsaw, where the resources were more plentiful, the state of music was of course also more prosperous. Still, as late as 1815 we meet with the complaint that what was chiefly aimed at in concerts was the display of virtuosity, and that grand, serious works were neglected, and complete symphonies rarely performed. To remedy this evil, therefore, 150 amateurs combined and organised in 1818 a concert institution. Their concerts took place once a week, and at every meeting a new and entire symphony, an overture, a concerto, an aria, and a finale, were performed. The names of Beethoven, Haydn, Mozart, Cherubini, Spohr, Mehul, Romberg, &c., were to be found on their programmes. Strange to say, there were no less than seven conductors: Lessel, Lentz, Wurfel, Haase, Javurek, Stolpe, and Peschke, all good musicians. The orchestra consisted in part of amateurs, who were most numerous among the violins, tenors, and violoncellos. The solo department seems to have been well stocked. To confine ourselves to one instrument, they could pride themselves on having four excellent lady pianists, one of whom distinguished herself particularly by the wonderful dexterity with which she played the most difficult compositions of Beethoven, Field, Ries, and Dussek. Another good sign of the improving taste was a series of twenty-four matinees given on Sundays from twelve to two during the winter of 1818-1819 by Carl Arnold, and much patronised by the highest nobility. The concert-giver, a clever pianist and composer, who enjoyed in his day a good reputation in Germany, Russia, and Poland, produced at every matinee a new pianoforte concerto by one of the best composers—sometimes one of his own—and was assisted by the quartet party of Bielawski, a good violinist, leader in the orchestra, and professor at the Conservatorium. Although Arnold's stay was not of long duration, his departure did not leave the town without good pianists. Indeed, it is a mistake to suppose that Warsaw was badly off with regard to musicians. This will be evident to the reader as soon as I have named some of those living there in the time of Chopin. Wenzel W. Wurfel, one of the professors at the Conservatorium, who stayed in Warsaw from 1815 to 1824, and afterwards went to Vienna, where he became conductor at the Karnthnerthor Theater, was an esteemed pianist and composer, and frequently gave concerts, at one of which he played Field's Concerto in C.

[FOOTNOTE: Wenzel Wilhelm Wurfel, in most dictionaries called Wilhelm Wurfel (exceptions are: E. Bernsdorf's "Neues Universal-Lexikon der Tonkunst", and Dr. Hugo Riemann's "Opern-Handbuch"). A Warsaw correspondent of a German musical paper called him Waclaw Wurfel. In Whistling's "Handbuch der musikalischen Literatur" his Christian names are only indicated by initials—W. W.]

If we scan the list of professors at the Conservatorium we find other musicians whose reputation was not confined to the narrow limits of Warsaw or even Poland. There was, for instance, the pianist and composer Franz Lessel, the favourite pupil of Haydn; and, further, that interesting character Heinrich Gerhard Lentz, who, born and educated at Cologne, went in 1784 to Paris, played with success his first concerto at the Concert Spirituel, published some of his compositions and taught in the best families, arrived in London in 1791, lived in friendly intercourse with Clementi and Haydn, and had compositions of his performed at Solomon's concerts, returned to Germany in 1795, stayed with Prince Louis Ferdinand of Prussia till Dussek supplanted him, and so, wandering about, reached Warsaw, where he gave lessons, founded a pianoforte manufactory, became professor of the organ at the Conservatorium, married twice, and died in 1839. The only other professor at the Conservatorium about whom I shall say a few words is C. E. Soliva, whose name and masters I have already mentioned. Of his works the opera "La testa di bronzo" is the best known. I should have said "was," for nobody now knows anything of his. That loud, shallow talker Count Stendhal, or, to give him his real name, Marie Henry Beyle, heard it at Milan in 1816, when it was first produced. He had at first some difficulty in deciding whether Soliva showed himself in that opera a plagiarist of Mozart or a genius. Finally he came to the conclusion that—

> *there is in it a warmth, a dramatic life, and a strength in*
> *all its effects, which are decidedly not in the style of*
> *Mozart. But Soliva, who is a young man and full of the*
> *warmest admiration for Mozart, has imbibed certain tints of*
> *his colouring.*

The rest is too outrageously ridiculous to be quoted. Whatever Beyle's
purely literary merits and his achievements in fiction may be, I quite
agree with Berlioz, who remarks, a propos of this gentleman's Vie de
Rossini, that he writes "les plus irritantes stupidites sur la musique,

dont il croyait avoir le secret." To which cutting dictum may be added
a no less cutting one of M. Lavoix fils, who, although calling Beyle
an *"ecrivain d'esprit,"* applies to him the appellation of *"fanfaron
d'ignorance en musique."* I would go a step farther than either of these
writers. Beyle is an ignorant braggart, not only in music, but in art
generally, and such esprit as his art criticisms exhibit would be even
more common than it unfortunately now is, if he were oftener equalled
in conceit and arrogance. The pillorying of a humbug is so laudable an
object that the reader will excuse the digression, which, moreover, may
show what miserable instruments a poor biographer has sometimes to
make use of. Another informant, unknown to fame, but apparently more
trustworthy, furnishes us with an account of Soliva in Warsaw. The
writer in question disapproves of the Italian master's drill-method in
teaching singing, and says that as a composer his power of invention
was inferior to his power of construction; and, further, that he was
acquainted with the scores of the best musicians of all times, and an
expert in accompanying on the pianoforte. As Elsner, Zywny, and the
pianist and composer Javurek have already been introduced to the reader,
I shall advert only to one other of the older Warsaw musicians — namely,
Charles Kurpinski, the most talented and influential native composer
then living in Poland. To him and Elsner is chiefly due the progress
which Polish music made in the first thirty years of this century.
Kurpinski came to Warsaw in 1810, was appointed second conductor at
the National Opera-house, afterwards rose to the position of first
conductor, was nominated maitre de chapelle de la cour de Varsovie, was
made a Knight of the St. Stanislas Order, &c. He is said to have learnt
composition by diligently studying Mozart's scores, and in 1811 began to
supply the theatre with dramatic works. Besides masses, symphonies,
&c., he composed twenty-four operas, and published also some theoretical
works and a sketch of the history of the Polish opera. Kurpinski was
by nature endowed with fine musical qualities, uniting sensibility and

energy with easy productivity. Chopin did homage to his distinguished
countryman in introducing into his Grande Fantaisie sur des airs
polonais, Op. 13, a theme of Kurpinski's. Two younger men, both born in
1800, must yet be mentioned to compete the picture. One of them, Moritz
Ernemann, a pupil of Mendelssohn's pianoforte-master, L. Berger,
played with success in Poland and Germany, and has been described by
contemporaries as a finished and expressive, but not brilliant, pianist.
His pleasing compositions are of an instructive and mildly-entertaining
character. The other of the two was Joseph Christoph Kessler, a musician
of very different mettle. After studying philosophy in Vienna, and
composing at the house of Count Potocki in Lemberg his celebrated
Etudes, Op. 20 (published at Vienna, reprinted at Paris, recommended
by Kalkbrenner in his Methode, quoted by Fetis and Moscheles in their
Methode des Methodes, and played in part by Liszt at his concerts),
he tried in 1829 his luck in Warsaw. Schumann thought (in 1835) that
Kessler had the stuff in him to do something great, and always looked
forward with expectation to what he would yet accomplish. Kessler's
studies might be dry, but he was assuredly a "Mann von Geist und sogar
poetischem Geist." He dedicated his twenty-four Preludes, Op. 31, to
Chopin, and Chopin his twenty-four Preludes, Op. 28, to him—that is to
say, the German edition.

By this time the reader must have found out that Warsaw was not such a musical desert as he may at first have imagined. Perfect renderings of great orchestral works, it is true, seem to have been as yet unattainable, and the performances of operas failed likewise to satisfy a pure and trained taste. Nay, in 1822 it was even said that the opera was getting worse. But when the fruits of the Conservatorium had had time to ripen and could be gathered in, things would assume a more promising aspect. Church music, which like other things had much deteriorated, received a share of the attention which in this century was given to the art. The best singing was in the Piarist and University churches. In the former the bulk of the performers consisted of amateurs, who, however, were assisted by members of the opera. They sang Haydn's masses best and oftenest. In the other church the executants were students and professors, Elsner being the conductor.

Besides these choirs there existed a number of musical associations in connection with different churches in Warsaw. Indeed, it cannot be doubted that great progress was made in the first thirty years of this century, and had it not been for the unfortunate insurrection of 1830, Poland would have succeeded in producing a national art and taking up an honourable position among the great musical powers of Europe, whereas now it can boast only of individual artists of more or less skill and originality. The musical events to which the death of the Emperor Alexander I. gave occasion in 1826, show to some extent the musical capabilities of Warsaw. On one day a Requiem by Kozlowski (a Polish composer, then living in St. Petersburg; b. 1757, d. 1831), with interpolations of pieces by other composers, was performed in the Cathedral by two hundred singers and players under Soliva. On another day Mozart's Requiem, with additional accompaniments by Kurpinski (piccolos, flutes, oboes, clarinets, and horns to the Dies irae and Sanctus; harps to the Hostias and Benedictus; and a military brass-band to the closing chorus!!!), was given in the same place by two hundred and fifty executants under the last-mentioned musician. And in the Lutheran church took place a performance of Elsner's Requiem for male voices, violoncellos, bassoons, horns, trumpets, trombones, and drums.

Having made the reader acquainted with the musical sphere in which Chopin moved, I shall take up the thread of the narrative where I left it, and the reader may follow without fear of being again detained by so long an interruption.

CHAPTER VI

Fourteen days in Berlin (From September 14 to 28, 1828).—Return by Posen (Prince Radziwill) and Zullichau (anecdotes) to Warsaw.—Chopin's doings there in the following winter and spring.—his home-life, companions, and preparations for a journey to Vienna.

Chopin, leaving his apprenticeship behind him, was now entering on that period of his life which we may call his Wanderjahre (years of travel). This change in his position and circumstances demands a simultaneous change in the manner of the biographical treatment. Hitherto we have been much occupied with the agencies that made and moulded the man, henceforth we shall fix our main attention on his experiences, actions, and utterances. The materials at our disposal become now more abundant and more trustworthy. Foremost in importance among them, up to Chopin's arrival in Paris, are the letters he wrote at that time, the publication of which we owe to Karasowski. As they are, however, valuable only as chronicles of the writer's doings and feelings, and not, like Mendelssohn's and Berlioz's, also as literary productions, I shall, whilst fully availing myself of the information they contain, confine my quotations from them to the characteristic passages.

Chopin's long-projected and much-desired visit to Berlin came about in this way. In 1828 Frederick William III of Prussia requested the Berlin University to invite the most eminent natural philosophers to take part in a congress to be held in that city under the presidency of Alexander von Humboldt. Nicholas Chopin's friend Dr. Jarocki, the zoologist and professor at the Warsaw University, who had studied and obtained his degree at Berlin, was one of those who were honoured with an invitation. The favourable opportunity which thus presented itself to the young musician of visiting in good company one of the centres of civilisation—for the professor intended to comply with the invitation, and was willing to take his friend's son under his wing—was not allowed to slip by, on the contrary, was seized eagerly. With what feelings, with what an infinitude of youthful hopes and expectations, Chopin looked forward to this journey may be gathered from some expressions in a letter of his (September 9, 1828) addressed to Titus Woyciechowski, where he describes himself as being at the time of writing "like a madman," and accounts for his madness by the announcement: "For I am going to-day to Berlin." To appear in public as a pianist or composer was not one of the objects he had in view. His dearest wishes were to make the acquaintance of the musical celebrities of Berlin, and to hear some really good music. From a promised performance of Spontini's Ferdinand Cortez he anticipated great things.

Professor Jarocki and Chopin left Warsaw on the 9th of September, 1828, and after five days' posting arrived in Berlin, where they put up at the Kronprinz. Among the conveniences of this hotel our friend had the pleasant surprise of finding a good grand piano. He played on it every day, and was rewarded for his pains not only by the pleasure it gave him, but also by the admiration of the landlord. Through his travelling companion's friend and teacher, M. H. K. Lichtenstein, professor of zoology and director of the Zoological Museum, who was a member of the Singakademie and on good terms with Zelter, the conductor of that society, he hoped to be made acquainted with the most distinguished musicians of the Prussian capital, and looked to Prince Radziwill for an introduction to the musical autocrat Spontini, with whom Lichtenstein was not on a friendly footing. In these hopes, however, Chopin was disappointed, and had to content himself with looking at the stars from afar. Speaking of a performance of the Singakademie at which he was present, he says:—

> Spontini, Zelter, and Felix Mendelssohn-Bartholdy were also
> there; but I spoke to none of these gentlemen, as I did not
> think it becoming to introduce myself.

It is not difficult to discover the circumstances that in this respect caused matters to turn out so little in accordance with the young man's wishes. Prince Radziwill was not in Berlin when Chopin arrived, and, although he was expected, perhaps never came, or came too late to be of any use. As to Lichtenstein, his time was too much taken up by his duties as secretary to the congress. Had this not been so, the professor could not only have brought the young artist in contact with many of the musical celebrities in Berlin, but also have told him much about his intimate friend Carl Maria von Weber, who had died little more than two years before. Lichtenstein's connection with Weber was probably the cause of his disagreement with Spontini, alluded to by Chopin. The latter relates in an off-hand way that he was introduced to and exchanged a few words with the editor of the Berliner Musikzeitung, without mentioning that this was Marx. The great theorist had of course then still to make his reputation.

One cannot help wondering at the absence from Chopin's Berlin letters of the name of Ludwig Berger, who, no doubt, like Bernhard

Klein, Rungenhagen, the brothers Ganz, and many another composer and virtuoso in Berlin, was included in the collective expression "distinguished musicians." But one would have thought that the personality of the pupil of Clementi, the companion of A. Klengel, the friend of Steibelt, Field, and Crotch, and the teacher of Mendelssohn and Taubert, would have particularly interested a young pianist. Berger's compositions cannot have been unknown to Chopin, who, moreover, must have heard of him from his Warsaw acquaintance Ernemann. However, be this as it may, our friend was more fortunate as regards hearing good music, which certainly was a more important business than interviewing celebrities, often, alas, so refrigerating in its effect on enthusiastic natures. Before his departure from Warsaw Chopin wrote:—"It is much to hear a really good opera, were it only once; it enables one to form an idea of what a perfect performance is like." Although the most famous singers were on leave of absence, he greatly enjoyed the performances of Spontini's "Ferdinand Cortez", Cimarosa's "Die heimliche Eke" ("Il Matrimonio segreto"), Onslow's "Der Hausirer" ("Le colporteur"), and Winter's "Das unterbrochene Opferfest." Still, they gave rise to some "buts," which he thought would be wholly silenced only in Paris; nay, one of the two singers he liked best, Fraulein von Schatzel (Signora Tibaldi was the other), reminded him by her omissions of chromatic scales even of Warsaw. What, however, affected him more than anything else was Handel's "Ode on St. Cecilia's Day," which he heard at the Singakademie; it came nearest, he said, to the ideal of sublime music which he harboured in his soul. A propos of another musical event he writes:—

> To-morrow the "Freischutz" will be performed; this is the
> fulfilment of my most ardent wish. When I hear it I shall be
> able to make a comparison between the singers here and our
> own.

The "Freischutz" made its first appearance on the Warsaw stage in 1826, and therefore was known to Chopin; whereas the other operas were either unknown to him or were not considered decisive tests.

Music and things connected with music, such as music-shops and pianoforte-manufactories, took up Chopin's attention almost exclusively. He declines with thanks the offer of a ticket for the meetings of the congress:—

> I should gain little or nothing for my mind from these
> discussions, because I am too little of a savant; and,
> moreover, the professional gentlemen might perhaps look at
> me, the layman, and think: "How comes Saul among the
> prophets?"

Of the Royal Library, to which he went with Professor Jarocki, he has no more to say than that "it is very large, but contains few musical works"; and when he visits the Zoological Museum, he thinks all the time what a bore it is, and how he would rather be at Schlesinger's, the best music-shop in the town, and an enterprising publishing house. That he neglects many things which educated men generally prize, he feels himself, and expresses the fear that his father will reproach him with one-sidedness. In his excuse he says:—

I have come to Berlin for my musical education, and the library of Schlesinger, consisting of the most interesting works of the composers of all countries and times, must interest me more than any other collections.

The words, he adds, add nothing to the strength of his argument.

It is a comfort to think that I, too, shall yet come to Schlesinger's, and that it is always good for a young man to see much, as from everything something may be learnt.

According to Karasowski, who reports, no doubt faithfully, what he has heard, Chopin was so well versed in all the branches of science, which he cultivated at the Lyceum, that all who knew him were astonished at his attainments, and prognosticated for him a brilliant future. I am afraid the only authorities for this statement were the parents, the sisters, and other equally indiscriminately-admiring connections, who often discover genius where it is hidden from the cold, unfeeling world outside this sympathetic circle. Not that I would blame an amiable weakness without which love, friendship, in short, happiness were well-nigh impossible. Only a biographer who wishes to represent a man as he really was, and not as he appeared to be to one or more individuals, has to be on his guard against it. Let us grant at once that Chopin made a good figure at the Lyceum—indeed, a quick-witted boy who found help and encouragement at home (the secret of almost all successful education) could hardly do otherwise. But from this to a master of all the arts, to an admirable Crichton, is a great step. Where there is genius there is inclination. Now, however well Chopin acquitted himself of his school-tasks—and even therein you will remember a falling-off was noticeable when outward pressure ceased—science and kindred subjects were subsequently treated by him with indifference. The thorough training which he received in general knowledge entirely failed to implant in him the dispositions of a scholar or thinker. His nature was perhaps a soil unfavourable to such growths, and certainly already preoccupied by a vegetation the luxuriance of which excluded, dwarfed, or crushed everything else. The truth of these remarks is proved by Chopin's letters and his friends' accounts of his tastes and conversation. In connection with this I may quote a passage from a letter which Chopin wrote immediately before starting on his Berlin trip. Jedrzejewicz, a gentleman who by-and-by became Chopin's brother-in-law, and was just then staying in Paris, made there the acquaintance of the Polish musician Sowinski. The latter hearing thus of his talented countryman in Warsaw, and being co-editor with Fetis of the "Revue musicale" (so at least we read in the letter in question, but it is more likely that Sowinski was simply a contributor to the paper), applied to him for a description of the state of music in Poland, and biographical notes on the most celebrated executants and composers. Now let us see what Chopin says in reference to this request.

All these are things with which I have no intention to

meddle. I shall write to him from Berlin that this affair is

not in my line, and that, moreover, I cannot yet form a

judgment such as would be worthy of a Parisian journal, which

must contain only mature and competent opinions, &c.

How much of this is self-knowledge, modesty, or disinclination, I leave the reader to decide, who, no doubt, will smile at the young man's innocence in imagining that Parisian, or, indeed, any journals distinguish themselves generally by maturity and competence of judgment.

At the time of the Berlin visit Chopin was a lively, well-educated, and well-mannered youth, who walked through life pleased and amused with its motley garb, but as yet unconscious of the deeper truths, and the immensities of joy and sadness, of love and hate, that lie beneath. Although the extreme youthfulness, nay boyishness, of the letters written by him at that time, and for some time after, makes him appear younger than he really was, the criticisms and witticisms on what is going on around which they contain, show incontestably that he had more than the usual share of clear and quick-sightedness. His power of observation, however, was directed rather to dress, manners, and the peculiarities and eccentricities of outward appearance generally, than to the essentials which are not always indicated and are often hidden by them. As to his wit, it had a decided tendency towards satire and caricature. He notices the pleasing orderliness and cleanliness of the otherwise not well-favoured surroundings of Berlin as he approaches, considers the city itself too much extended for the number of its inhabitants, of whom it could hold twice as many, is favourably impressed by the fine large palace, the spacious well-built streets, the picturesque bridges, and congratulates himself that he and his fellow-traveller did not take lodgings in the broad but rather too quiet Franzosische Strasse. Yes, our friend is fond of life and society. Whether he thought man the proper study of mankind or not, as Pope held, he certainly found it the most attractive. The passengers in the stage-coach were to him so many personages of a comedy. There was an advocate who tried to shine with his dull jokes, an agriculturist to whom travelling had given a certain varnish of civilisation, and a German Sappho who poured forth a stream of pretentious and at the same time ludicrous complaints. The play unwittingly performed by these unpaid actors was enjoyed by our friend with all the zest the feeling of superiority can give. What a tragi-comical arrangement it is that in this world of ours everybody is laughing at everybody else! The scientists of the congress afforded Chopin an almost unlimited scope for the exercise of his wit. Among them he found so many curious and various specimens that he was induced not only to draw but also to classify them. Having already previously sent home some sketches, he concludes one of his letters with the words "the number of caricatures is increasing." Indeed, there seems to have been only one among these learned gentlemen who impressed him with a feeling of respect and admiration—namely, Alexander von Humboldt. As Chopin's remarks on him are the best part of his three Berlin letters, I shall quote them in full. On seeing Von Humboldt at Lichtenstein's he writes:—

He is not above middle height, and his countenance cannot be called beautiful; but the somewhat protruding, broad, and well-moulded forehead, and the deep inquiring eye, announce the all-embracing mind which animates this humane as well as much-travelled savant. Humboldt spoke French, and as well as his mother-tongue.

One of the chief events of Chopin's visit to Berlin was, according to his own account, his second dinner with the natural philosophers, which took place the day before the close of the congress, and was very lively and entertaining:—

Many appropriate songs were sung in which every one joined with more or less energy. Zelter conducted; he had standing before him on a red pedestal as a sign of his exalted musical dignity a large gilt goblet, which seemed to give him much pleasure. On this day the food was much better than usual. People say the natural philosophers had at their meetings been specially occupied with the amelioration of roasts, sauces, soups, and the like.

"The Berliners are such an impertinent race," says Goethe, "that to keep one's self above water one must have Haare auf den Zahnen, and at times be rude." Such a judgment prepares one for much, but not for what Chopin dares to say:—

> Marylski [one of his Warsaw friends] has not the faintest
> shadow of taste if he asserts that the ladies of Berlin dress
> prettily. They deck themselves out, it is true; but it is a
> pity for the fine stuffs which are cut up for such puppets!

What blasphemy!

After a fortnight's stay in the Prussian capital Professor Jarocki and Chopin turned homeward on September 28, 1828. They did not, however, go straight to Warsaw, but broke their journey at Posen, where they remained two days "in gratiam of an invitation from Archbishop Wolicki." A great part of the time he was at Posen he spent at the house of Prince Radziwill, improvising and playing sonatas of Mozart, Beethoven, and Hummel, either alone or with Capellmeister Klingohr. On October 6 the travellers arrived in Warsaw, which Chopin was so impatient to reach that the professor was prevailed upon to take post-horses from Lowicz. Before I have done with this trip to Berlin I must relate an incident which occurred at a stage between Frankfort on the Oder and Posen.

On arriving at Zullichau our travellers were informed by the postmaster that they would have to wait an hour for horses. This announcement opened up an anything but pleasing prospect. The professor and his companion did the best that could be done in these distressing circumstances—namely, took a stroll through the small town, although the latter had no amenities to boast of, and the fact of a battle having been fought there between the Russians and Prussians in 1759 would hardly fire their enthusiasm. Matters, however, became desperate when on their return there was still neither sign nor sound of horses. Dr. Jarocki comforted himself with meat and drink, but Chopin began to look uneasily about him for something to while away the weariness of waiting. His search was not in vain, for in an adjoining room he discovered an old piano of unpromising appearance, which, on being opened and tried, not only turned out to be better than it looked, but even in tune. Of course our artist did not bethink himself long, but sat down at once, and launched out into an improvisation on a Polish air. One of his fellow-passengers, a German, and an inveterate smoker, attracted by the music, stepped in, and was soon so wrapped up in it that he forgot even his pipe. The other passengers, the postmaster, his buxom wife, and their pretty daughters, came dropping in, one after the other. But when this peaceful conventicle had for some time been listening silently, devoutly, and admiringly, lo, they were startled by a stentorian voice bawling into the room the words:—"Gentlemen, the horses are put in." The postmaster, who was indignant at this untimely interruption, begged the musician to continue. But Chopin said that they had already waited too long, it was time to depart. Upon this there was a general commotion; the mistress of the house solicited and cajoled, the young ladies bashfully entreated with their eyes, and all pressed around the artist and supported the request, the postmaster even offering extra horses if Chopin would go on with his playing. Who could resist? Chopin sat down again, and resumed his fantasia. When he had ended, a servant brought in wine, the postmaster proposed as a toast "the favourite of Polyhymnia," and one of the audience, an old musician, gave voice to his feelings by telling the hero that, "if Mozart had heard you, he would have shaken hands with you and exclaimed 'Bravo!' An insignificant man like me dare not do that." After Chopin had played a mazurka as a wind-up, the tall postmaster took him in his arms, carried him to the coach—the pockets of which the ladies had already filled with wine and eatables—and, bidding him farewell, said that as long as he lived he would think with enthusiasm of Frederick Chopin.

We can have no difficulty in believing the statement that in after-life our artist recalled with pleasure this incident at the post-house of Zullichau, and that his success among these unsophisticated people was dearer to him than many a more brilliant one in the great world of art and fashion. But, it may be asked, did all this happen in exactly the same way in which it is told here? Gentle reader, let us not inquire too curiously into this matter. Of course you have heard of myth-making and legend-making. Well, anecdote-making is a process of a similar nature, a process of accumulation and development. The only difference between the process in the first two cases and that in the third is, that the former is carried on by races, the latter by individuals. A seed-corn of fact falls on the generous soil of the poetic imagination, and forthwith it begins to expand, to sprout, and to grow into flower, shrub, or tree. But there are well and ill-shapen plants, and monstrosities too. The above anecdote is a specimen of the first kind. As a specimen of the last kind may be instanced an undated anecdote told by Sikorski and others. It is likewise illustrative of Chopin's power and love of improvisation. The seed-corn of fact in the case seems to be that one Sunday, when playing during divine service in the Wizytek Church, Chopin, taking for his subjects some motives of the part of the Mass that had just been performed, got so absorbed in his improvisation that he entirely forgot all his surroundings, and turned a deaf ear to the priest at the altar, who had already for the second time chanted 'Per omnia saecula saeculurum.' This is a characteristic as well as a pretty artist-story, which, however, is marred, I think, by the additions of a choir that gathers round the organist and without exception forgets like him time and place, and of a mother superior who sends the sacristan to remind those music-enthusiasts in the organ-gallery of the impatiently waiting priest and acolyte, &c. Men willingly allow themselves to be deceived, but care has to be taken that their credulity be not overtaxed. For if the intention is perceived, it fails in its object; as the German poet says:—"So fuehrt man Absicht und man ist verstimmt."

On the 6th of October, as has already been said, Chopin returned to Warsaw. Judging from a letter written by him at the end of the year (December 27, 1828) to his friend Titus Woyciechowski, he was busy composing and going to parties. The "Rondeau a la Krakowiak," Op. 14, was now finished, and the Trio, Op. 8, was nearly so. A day on which he had not been musically productive seems to have been regarded by him as a lost day. The opening phrase of the following quotation reminds one of the famous exclamation of the Emperor Titus:—

During the last week I have composed nothing worthy either of
God or of man. I run from Ananias to Caiaphas; to-night I
shall be at Madame Wizegerod's, from there I shall drive to a
musical soiree at Miss Kicka's. You know how pleasant it is
to be forced to improvise when one is tired! I have not often
such happy thoughts as come sometimes under my fingers when I
am with you. And then the miserable instruments!

In the same letter he relates that his parents are preparing a small room for him:—

A staircase leads from the entrance directly into it; there I
shall have an old writing-desk, and this nook will be my
retreat.

This remark calls up a passage in a letter written two years later from Vienna to his friend John Matuszynski:—

When your former colleagues, for instance, Rostkowski,
Schuch, Freyer, Kyjewski, Hube, &c., are holding merry
converse in my room, then think that I am laughing and
enjoying myself with you.

A charming little genre picture of Chopin's home-life is to be found in one of his letters from Vienna (December 1, 1830) Having received news from Warsaw, he writes:—

The joy was general, for Titus also had letters from home. I
thank Celinski lor the enclosed note; it brought vividly back

to me the time when I was still amongst you: it seemed to me
as if I were sitting at the piano and Celinski standing
opposite me looking at Mr. Zywny, who just then treated
Linowski to a pinch of snuff. Only Matuszynski was wanting to
make the group complete.

Several names in the above extract remind me that I ought to say a few words about the young men with whom Chopin at that time associated. Many of them were no doubt companions in the noblest sense of the word. Of this class may have been Celinski, Hube, Eustachius Marylski, and Francis Maciejowski (a nephew of the previously-mentioned Professor Waclaw Maciejowski), who are more or less frequently mentioned in Chopin's correspondence, but concerning whom I have no information to give. I am as badly informed about Dziewanowski, whom a letter quoted by Karasowski shows to have been a friend of Chopin's. Of two other friends, Stanislas Kozmian and William Kolberg, we know at least that the one was a few years ago still living at Posen and occupied the post of President of the Society of the Friends of Science, and that the other, to whom the earliest letters of Chopin that have come down to us are addressed, became, not to mention lesser offices and titles, a Councillor of State, and died on June 4,1877. Whatever the influence of the friends I have thus far named may have been on the man Chopin, one cannot but feel inclined to think that Stephen Witwicki and Dominic Magnuszewski, especially the former, must have had a greater influence on the artist. At any rate, these two poets, who made their mark in Polish literature, brought the musician in closest contact with the strivings of the literary romanticism of those days. In later years Chopin set several of Witwicki's songs to music. Both Magnuszewski and Witwicki lived afterwards, like Chopin, in Paris, where they continued to associate with him. Of the musical acquaintances we have to notice first and foremost Julius Fontana, who himself said that he was a daily visitor at Chopin's house. The latter writes in the above-mentioned letter (December 27, 1828) to Titus Woyciechowski: —

The Rondo for two pianos, this orphan child, has found a step-
father in Fontana (you may perhaps have seen him at our
house, he attends the university); he studied it for more
than a month, but then he did learn it, and not long ago we
tried how it would sound at Buchholtz's.

Alexander Rembielinski, described as a brilliant pianist and a composer in the style of Fesca, who returned from Paris to Warsaw and died young, is said to have been a friend of Chopin's. Better musicians than Fontana, although less generally known in the western part of Europe, are Joseph Nowakowski and Thomas Nidecki. Chopin, by some years their junior, had intercourse with them during his residence in Poland as well as afterwards abroad. It does not appear that Chopin had what can rightly be called intimate friends among the young Polish musicians. If we may believe the writer of an article in Sowinski's Dictionary, there was one exception. He tells us that the talented Ignaz Felix Dobrzynski was a fellow-pupil of Chopin's, taking like him private lessons from Elsner. Dobrzynski came to Warsaw in 1825, and took altogether thirty lessons.

> *Working together under the same master, having the same*
>
> *manner of seeing and feeling, Frederick Chopin and I.F.*
>
> *Dobrzynski became united in a close friendship. The same*
>
> *aims, the same artistic tendency to seek the UNKNOWN,*
>
> *characterised their efforts. They communicated to each other*
>
> *their ideas and impressions, followed different routes to*
>
> *arrive at the same goal.*

This unison of kindred minds is so beautiful that one cannot but wish it to have been a fact. Still, I must not hide the circumstance that neither Liszt nor Karasowski mentions Dobrzynski as one of Chopin's friends, and the even more significant circumstance that he is only mentioned twice and en passant in Chopin's letters. All this, however, does not necessarily nullify the lexicographer's statements, and until contradictory evidence is forthcoming we may hold fast by so pleasing and ennobling a creed.

The most intimate of Chopin's early friends, indeed, of all his friends— perhaps the only ones that can be called his bosom friends—have still to be named, Titus Woyciechowski and John Matuszynski. It was to them that Chopin wrote his most interesting and self-revealing letters. We shall meet them and hear of them often in the course of this narrative, for their friendship with the musician was severed only by death. It will therefore suffice to say here that Titus Woyciechowski, who had been Chopin's school-fellow, lived, at the period of the latter's life we have now reached, on his family estates, and that John Matuszynski was then studying medicine in Warsaw.

In his letter of December 27, 1828, Chopin makes some allusions to the Warsaw theatres. The French company had played Rataplan, and at the National Theatre they had performed a comedy of Fredro's, Weber's Preciosa, and Auber's Macon. A musical event whichmust have interested Chopin much more than the performances of the two last-mentioned works took place in the first half of the year 1829—namely, Hummel's appearance in Warsaw. He and Field were, no doubt, those pianists who through the style of their compositions most influenced Chopin. For Hummel's works Chopin had indeed a life-long admiration and love. It is therefore to be regretted that he left in his letters no record of the impression which Hummel, one of the four most distinguished representatives of pianoforte-playing of that time, made upon him. It is hardly necessary to say that the other three representatives—of different generations and schools let it be understood—were Field, Kalkbrenner, and Moscheles. The only thing we learn about this visit of Hummel's to Warsaw is that he and the young Polish pianist made a good impression upon each other. As far as the latter is concerned this is a mere surmise, or rather an inference from indirect proofs, for, strange to say, although Chopin mentions Hummel frequently in his letters, he does not write a syllable that gives a clue to his sentiments regarding him. The older master, on the other hand, shows by his inquiries after his younger brother in art and the visits he pays him that he had a real regard and affection for him.

It is also to be regretted that Chopin says in his letters nothing of Paganini's appearance in Warsaw. The great Italian violinist, who made so deep an impression on, and exercised so great an influence over, Liszt, cannot have passed by without producing some effect on Chopin. That the latter had a high opinion of Paganini may be gathered from later utterances, but what one would like is a description of his feelings and thoughts when he first heard him. Paganini came to Warsaw in 1829, after his visit to Berlin. In the Polish capital he was worshipped with the same ardour as elsewhere, and also received the customary tributes of applause, gold, and gifts. From Oreste Bruni's Niccolo Paganini, celebre violinista Genovese, we learn that his Warsaw worshippers presented him with a gold snuff-box, which bore the following inscription:—Al Cav. Niccolo Paganini. Gli ammiratori del suo talento. Varsovia 19 Luglio 1829.

Some months after this break in what he, no doubt, considered the monotonous routine of Warsaw life, our friend made another excursion, one of far greater importance in more than one respect than that to Berlin. Vienna had long attracted him like a powerful magnet, the obstacles to his going thither were now removed, and he was to see that glorious art-city in which Gluck, Haydn, Mozart, Beethoven, Schubert, and many lesser but still illustrious men had lived and worked.

CHAPTER VII

CHOPIN JOURNEYS TO VIENNA BY WAY OF CRACOW AND OJCOW.—STAYS THERE FOR SOME WEEKS, PLAYING TWICE IN PUBLIC.—RETURNS TO WARSAW BY WAY OF PRAGUE, DRESDEN, AND BRESLAU.

IT was about the middle of July, 1829, that Chopin, accompanied by his friends Celinski, Hube, and Francis Maciejowski, set out on his journey to Vienna. They made a week's halt at the ancient capital of the Polish Republic, the many-towered Cracow, which rises picturesquely in a landscape of great loveliness. There they explored the town and its neighbourhood, both of which are rich in secular and ecclesiastical buildings, venerable by age and historical associations, not a few of them remarkable also as fine specimens of architecture. Although we have no detailed account of Chopin's proceedings, we may be sure that our patriotic friend did not neglect to look for and contemplate the vestiges of his nation's past power and greatness: the noble royal palace, degraded, alas, into barracks for the Austrian soldiery; the grand, impressive cathedral, in which the tombs of the kings present an epitome of Polish history; the town-hall, a building of the 14th century; the turreted St. Florian's gate; and the monumental hillock, erected on the mountain Bronislawa in memory of Kosciuszko by the hands of his grateful countrymen, of which a Frenchman said:—"Void une eloquence touts nouvelle: un peuple qui ne peut s'exprimer par la parole ou par les livres, et qui parle par des montagnes." On a Sunday afternoon, probably on the 24th of July, the friends left Cracow, and in a rustic vehicle drove briskly to Ojcow. They were going to put up not in the place itself, but at a house much patronised by tourists, lying some miles distant from it and the highway. This circumstance led to something like a romantic incident, for as the driver was unacquainted with the bye-roads, they got into a small brook, "as clear and silvery bright as brooks in fairytales," and having walls of rock on the right and left, they were unable to extricate themselves "from this labyrinth." Fortunately they met towards nine o'clock in the evening two peasants who conducted them to their destination, the inn of Mr. Indyk, in which also the Polish authoress Clementina Tanska, who has described this district in one of her works, had lodged—a fact duly reported by Chopin to his sister Isabella and friend Titus. Arriving not only tired but also wet to above the knees, his first business was to guard against taking a cold. He bought a Cracow double-woven woollen night-cap, which he cut in two pieces and wrapped round his feet. Then he sat down by the fire, drank a glass of red wine, and, after talking for a little while longer, betook himself to bed, and slept the sleep of the just. Thus ended the adventure of that day, and, to all appearance, without the dreaded consequences of a cold. The natural beauties of the part of the country where Chopin now was have gained for it the name of Polish Switzerland. The principal sights are the Black Cave, in which during the bloody wars with the Turks and Tartars the women and children used to hide themselves; the Royal Cave, in which, about the year 1300, King Wladyslaw Lokietek sought refuge when he was hardly pressed by the usurper Wenceslas of Bohemia; and the beautifully-situated ruins of Ojcow Castle, once embowered in thick forests. Having enjoyed to the full the beauties of Polish Switzerland, Chopin continued his journey merrily and in favourable weather through the picturesque countries of Galicia, Upper Silesia, and Moravia, arriving in Vienna on July 31.

Chopin's letters tell us very little of his sight-seeing in the Austrian capital, but a great deal of matters that interest us far more deeply. He brought, of course, a number of letters of introduction with him. Among the first which he delivered was one from Elsner to the publisher Hashnger, to whom Chopin had sent a considerable time before some of his compositions, which, however, still remained in manuscript. Haslinger treated Elsner's pupil with an almost embarrassing politeness, and, without being reminded of the MSS. in question, informed his visitor that one of them, the variations on La ci darem la mano, would before long appear in the Odeon series. "A great honour for me, is it not?" writes the happy composer to his friend Titus. The amiable publisher, however, thought that Chopin would do well to show the people of Vienna what his difficult and by no means easily comprehensible composition was like. But the composer was not readily persuaded. The thought of playing in the city where Mozart and Beethoven had been heard frightened him, and then he had not touched a piano for a whole fortnight. Not even when Count Gallenberg entered and Haslinger presented Chopin to him as a coward who dare not play in public was the young virtuoso put on his mettle. In fact, he even declined with thanks the theatre which was placed at his disposal by Count Gallenberg, who was then lessee of the Karnthnerthor Theatre, and in whom the reader has no doubt recognised the once celebrated composer of ballets, or at least the husband of Beethoven's passionately-loved Countess Giulia Guicciardi. Haslinger and Gallenberg were not the only persons who urged him to give the Viennese an opportunity to hear him. Dining at the house of Count Hussarzewski, a worthy old gentleman who admired his young countryman's playing very much, Chopin was advised by everybody present—and the guests belonged to the best society of Vienna—to give a concert. The journalist Blahetka, best known as the father of his daughter, was not sparing in words of encouragement; and Capellmeister Wurfel, who had been kind to Chopin in Warsaw, told him plainly that it would be a disgrace to himself, his parents, and his teachers not to make a public appearance, which, he added, was, moreover, a politic move for this reason, that no one who has composed anything new and wishes to make a noise in the world can do so unless he performs his works himself. In fact, everybody with whom he got acquainted was of the same opinion, and assured him that the newspapers would say nothing but what was flattering. At last Chopin allowed himself to be persuaded, Wurfel took upon him the care of making the necessary arrangements, and already the next morning the bills announced the coming event to the public of Vienna. In a long postscript of a long and confused letter to his people he writes: "I have made up my mind. Blahetka asserts that I shall create a furore, 'being,' as he expressed it, 'an artist of the first rank, and occupying an honourable place by the side of Moscheles, Herz, and Kalkbrenner.'" To all appearance our friend was not disposed to question the correctness of this opinion; indeed, we shall see that although he had his moments of doubting, he was perfectly conscious of his worth. No blame, however, attaches to him on this account; self-respect and self-confidence are not only irreprehensible but even indispensable—that is, indispensable for the successful exercise of any talent. That our friend had his little weaknesses shall not be denied nor concealed. I am afraid he cannot escape the suspicion of having possessed a considerable share of harmless vanity. "All journalists," he writes to his parents and sisters, "open their eyes wide at me, and the members of the orchestra greet me deferentially because I walk with the director of the Italian opera arm-in-arm." Two pianoforte-manufacturers—in one place Chopin says three—offered to send him instruments, but he declined, partly because he had not room enough, partly because he did not think it worth while to begin to practise two days before the concert. Both Stein and Graff were very obliging; as, however, he preferred the latter's instruments, he chose one of this maker's for the concert, and tried to prevent the other from taking offence by speaking him fair.

Chopin made his first public appearance in Vienna at the Karnthnerthor Theatre on August 11, 1829. The programme comprised the following items: Beethoven's Overture to Prometheus; arias of Rossini's and Vaccaj's, sung by Mdlle. Veltheim, singer to the Saxon Court; Chopin's variations on La ci darem la mano and Krakowiak, rondeau de concert (both for pianoforte and orchestra), for the latter of which the composer substituted an improvisation; and a short ballet. Chopin, in a letter to his people dated August 12, 1829, describes the proceedings thus:—

> *Yesterday—i.e., Tuesday, at 7 p.m., I made my debut in the*
> *Imperial Opera-house before the public of Vienna. These*
> *evening concerts in the theatre are called here "musical*
> *academies." As I claimed no honorarium, Count Gallenberg*
> *hastened on my appearance.*

In a letter to Titus Woyciechowski, dated September 12, 1829, he says:—

> *The sight of the Viennese public did not at all excite me,*
> *and I sat down, pale as I was, at a wonderful instrument of*
> *Graff's, at the time perhaps the best in Vienna. Beside me I*
> *had a painted young man, who turned the leaves for me in the*
> *Variations, and who prided himself on having rendered the*
> *same service to Moscheles, Hummel, and Herz. Believe me when*
> *I say that I played in a desperate mood; nevertheless, the*
> *Variations produced so much effect that I was called back*
> *several times. Mdlle. Veltheim sang very beautifully. Of my*
> *improvisation I know only that it was followed by stormy*
> *applause and many recalls.*

To the cause of the paleness and the desperate mood I shall advert anon. Chopin was satisfied, nay, delighted with his success; he had a friendly greeting of "Bravo!" on entering, and this "pleasant word" the audience repeated after each Variation so impetuously that he could not hear the tuttis of the orchestra. At the end of the piece he was called back twice. The improvisation on a theme from La Dame blanche and the Polish tune Chmiel, which he substituted for the Krakowiak, although it did not satisfy himself, pleased, or as Chopin has it, "electrified" the audience. Count Gallenberg commended his compositions, and Count Dietrichstein, who was much with the Emperor, came to him on the stage, conversed with him a long time in French, complimented him on his performance, and asked him to prolong his stay in Vienna. The only adverse criticism which his friends, who had posted themselves in different parts of the theatre, heard, was that of a lady who remarked, "Pity the lad has not a better tournure." However, the affair did not pass off altogether without unpleasant incidents:—

> *The members of the orchestra [Chopin writes to his friend*
> *Titus Woyciechowski] showed me sour faces at the rehearsal;*

what vexed them most was that I wished to make my debut with
a new composition. I began with the Variations which are
dedicated to you; they were to be followed by the Rondo
Krakowiak. We got through the Variations well, the Rondo, on
the other hand, went so badly that we had to begin twice from
the beginning; the cause of this was said to be the bad
writing. I ought to have placed the figures above and not
below the rests (that being the way to which the Viennese
musicians are accustomed). Enough, these gentlemen made such
faces that I already felt inclined to send word in the
evening that I was ill. Demar, the manager, noticed the bad
disposition of the members of the orchestra, who also don't
like Wurfel. The latter wished to conduct himself, but the
orchestra refused (I don't know for what reason) to play
under his direction. Mr. Demar advised me to improvise, at
which proposal the orchestra looked surprised. I was so
irritated by what had happened that in my desperation I
agreed to it; and who knows if my bad humour and strange mood
were not the causes of the great success which my playing
obtained.

Although Chopin passes off lightly the grumbling and grimacing of
the members of the orchestra respecting the bad writing of his music, they
seem to have had more serious reasons for complaint than he alleges in
the above quotation. Indeed, he relates himself that after the occurrence
his countryman Nidecki, who was very friendly to him and rejoiced at his
success, looked over the orchestral parts of the Rondo and corrected them.
The correction of MSS. was at no time of his life a strong point of Chopin's.
That the orchestra was not hostile to him appears from another allusion of
his to this affair:—

The orchestra cursed my badly-written music, and was not at
all favourably inclined towards me until I began the
improvisation; but then it joined in the applause of the
public. From this I saw that it had a good opinion of me.
Whether the other artists had so too I did not know as yet;
but why should they be against me? They must see that I do

not play for the sake of material advantages.

After such a success nothing was more natural than that Chopin should allow himself to be easily persuaded to play again—il n'y a que le premier pas qui coute—but he said he would not play a third time. Accordingly, on August 18, he appeared once more on the stage of the Karnthnerthor Theatre. Also this time he received no payment, but played to oblige Count Gallenberg, who, indeed, was in anything but flourishing circumstances. On this occasion Chopin succeeded in producing the Krakowiak, and repeated, by desire of the ladies, the Variations. Two other items of the programme were Lindpaintner's Overture to Der Bergkonig and a polonaise of Mayseder's played by the violinist Joseph Khayl, a very young pupil of Jansa's.

> *The rendering of the Rondo especially [Chopin writes] gave me*
> *pleasure, because Gyrowetz, Lachner, and other masters, nay,*
> *even the orchestra, were so charmed—excuse the expression—*
> *that they called me back twice.*

In another letter he is more loquacious on the subject:—

> *If the public received me kindly on my first appearance, it*
> *was yesterday still more hearty. When I appeared on the stage*
> *I was greeted with a twice-repeated, long-sustained "Bravo!"*
> *The public had gathered in greater numbers than at the first*
> *concert. The financier of the theatre, Baron—I do not*
> *remember his name—thanked me for the recette and said that*
> *if the attendance was great, it was not on account of the*
> *ballet, which had already been often performed. With my Rondo*
> *I have won the good opinion of all professional musicians—*
> *from Capellmeister Lachner to the pianoforte-tuner, all*
> *praise my composition.*

The press showed itself not less favourable than the public. The fullest account of our artist's playing and compositions, and the impression they produced on this occasion, I found on looking over the pages of the Wiener Theaterzeitung. Chopin refers to it prospectively in a letter to his parents, written on August 19. He had called on Bauerle, the editor of the paper, and had been told that a critique of the concert would soon appear. To satisfy his own curiosity and to show his people that he had said no more than what was the truth in speaking of his success, he became a subscriber to the Wiener Theaterzeitung, and had it sent to Warsaw. The criticism is somewhat long, but as this first step into the great world of art was an event of superlative importance to Chopin, and is one of more than ordinary interest to us, I do not hesitate to transcribe it in full so far as it relates to our artist. Well, what we read in the Wiener Theaterzeitung of August 20, 1829, is this:—

> [Chopin] surprised people, because they discovered in him not only a fine, but a really very eminent talent; on account of the originality of his playing and compositions one might almost attribute to him already some genius, at least, in so far as unconventional forms and pronounced individuality are concerned. His playing, like his compositions—of which we heard on this occasion only variations—has a certain character of modesty which seems to indicate that to shine is not the aim of this young man, although his execution conquered difficulties the overcoming of which even here, in the home of pianoforte virtuosos, could not fail to cause astonishment; nay, with almost ironical naivete he takes it into his head to entertain a large audience with music as music. And lo, he succeeded in this. The unprejudiced public rewarded him with lavish applause. His touch, although neat and sure, has little of that brilliance by which our virtuosos announce themselves as such in the first bars; he emphasised but little, like one conversing in a company of clever people, not with that rhetorical aplomb which is considered by virtuosos as indispensable. He plays very quietly, without the daring elan which generally at once distinguishes the artist from the amateur. Nevertheless, our fine-feeling and acute-judging public recognised at once in this youth, who is a stranger and as yet unknown to fame, a true artist; and this evening afforded the unprejudiced observer the pleasing spectacle of a public which, considered as a moral person, showed itself a true connoisseur and a virtuoso in the comprehension and appreciation of an artistic performance which, in no wise grandiose, was nevertheless gratifying.

There were defects noticeable in the young man's playing,
among which are perhaps especially to be mentioned the non-
observance of the indication by accent of the commencement of
musical phrases. Nevertheless, he was recognised as an artist
of whom the best may be expected as soon as he has heard
more....As in his playing he was like a beautiful young tree
that stands free and full of fragrant blossoms and ripening
fruits, so he manifested as much estimable individuality in
his compositions, where new figures, new passages, new forms
unfolded themselves in the introduction, in the first,
second, and fourth Variations, and in the concluding
metamorphosis of Mozart's theme into a polacca.

Such is the ingenuousness of the young virtuoso that he
undertook to come forward at the close of the concert with a
free fantasia before a public in whose eyes few improvisers,
with the exception of Beethoven and Hummel, have as yet found
favour. If the young man by a manifold change of his themes
aimed especially at amusement, the calm flow of his thoughts
and their firm connection and chaste development were
nevertheless a sufficient proof of his capability as regards
this rare gift. Mr. Chopin gave to-day so much pleasure to a
small audience that one cannot help wishing he may at another
performance play before a larger one....

Although the critic of the Wiener Theaterzeitung is more succinct
in his report (September 1, 1829) of the second concert, he is not less
complimentary. Chopin as a composer as well as an executant justified on
this occasion the opinion previously expressed about him.

He is a young man who goes his own way, and knows how to
please in this way, although his style of playing and writing
differs greatly from that of other virtuosos; and, indeed
chiefly in this, that the desire to make good music
predominates noticeably in his case over the desire to
please. Also to-day Mr. Chopin gave general satisfaction.

These expressions of praise are so enthusiastic that a suspicion might possibly arise as to their trustworthiness. But this is not the only laudatory account to be found in the Vienna papers. Der Sammler, for instance, remarked: "In Mr. Chopin we made the acquaintance of one of the most excellent pianists, full of delicacy and deepest feeling." The Wiener Zeitschrift fur Kunst, Literatur, Theater und Mode, too, had appreciative notices of the concerts.

> He executes the greatest difficulties with accuracy and
> precision, and renders all passages with neatness. The
> tribute of applause which the public paid to this clever
> artist was very great; the concert-piece with orchestra (the
> Variations) especially pleased.

This was written after the first concert, and printed on August 22, 1829. From the criticism on the second concert, which appeared in the same paper a week later (August 29), I cull the following sentences:—

> Chopin performed a new Rondo for pianoforte and orchestra of
> his own composition. This piece is written throughout in the
> chromatic style, rarely rises to geniality, but has passages
> which are distinguished by depth and thoughtful working-out.
> On the whole, however, he seems to be somewhat lacking in
> variety. The master showed in it his dexterity as a pianist
> to perfection, and conquered the greatest difficulties with
> felicity. A longer stay in Vienna might be to the advantage
> of his touch as well as of his ensemble playing with the
> orchestra. He received much applause, and was repeatedly
> called back....At the close Mr. Chopin played to-day the
> Variations on a theme of Mozart's, which he had already
> performed with so much bravura and felicity at his first
> concert. The pleasing and yet substantial variety of this
> composition as well as the fine, successful playing obtained
> also to-day loud applause for the pianist. Connoisseurs and
> amateurs manifested joyously and loudly their recognition of
> his clever playing. This young man...shows in his
> compositions a serious striving to interweave by interesting
> combinations the orchestra with the pianoforte.

In conclusion, let me quote one other journal, this time a purely musical one—namely, the Allgemeine musikalische Zeitung (No. 46, November 18, 1829). The notice, probably written by that debauched genius F.A. Kanne, runs thus:—

Mr. Chopin, a pianist from Warsaw, according to report a
pupil of Wurfel's [which report was of course baseless], came
before us a master of the first rank. The exquisite delicacy
of his touch, his indescribable mechanical dexterity, his
finished shading and portamento, which reflect the deepest
feeling; the lucidity of his interpretation, and his
compositions, which bear the stamp of great genius—
variazioni di bravura, rondo, free fantasia—reveal a
virtuoso most liberally endowed by nature, who, without
previous blasts of trumpets, appears on the horizon like one
of the most brilliant meteors.

Still, the sweets of success were not altogether without some admixture of bitterness, as we may perceive from the following remarks of Chopin's:—

I know that I have pleased the ladies and the musicians.
Gyrowetz, who sat beside Celinski, made a terrible noise, and
shouted "Bravo." Only the out-and-out Germans seem not to
have been quite satisfied.

And this, after having a few days before attributed the applause to the Germans, who "could appreciate improvisations." Tantae animis coelestibus irae? But what was the reason of this indignation? Simply this: a gentleman, who after the second concert came into the coffee-room of the hotel where Chopin was staying, on being asked by some of the guests how he liked the performance, answered laconically, "the ballet was very pretty"; and, although they put some further questions, he would say no more, having no doubt noticed a certain person. And hinc illae lacrimae. Our sensitive friend was indeed so much ruffled at this that he left the room in a pet and went to bed, so as not to hinder, as he explains, the outpouring of the gentleman's feelings. The principal stricture passed on the virtuoso was that he played too softly, or, rather, too delicately. Chopin himself says that on that point all were unanimous. But the touchy artist, in true artist fashion— or shall we be quite just and say "in true human fashion"? adds:—

They are accustomed to the drumming of the native pianoforte
virtuosos. I fear that the newspapers will reproach me with

the same thing, especially as the daughter of an editor is
said to drum frightfully. However, it does not matter; as
this cannot be helped, I would rather that people say I play
too delicately than too roughly.

When Count Moritz Lichnowski, to whom Chopin was introduced by Wurfel, learned after the first concert that the young virtuoso was going to play again, he offered to lend him his own piano for the occasion, for he thought Chopin's feebleness of tone was owing to the instrument he had used. But Chopin knew perfectly the real state of the matter: "This is my manner of playing, which pleases the ladies so very much." Chopin was already then, and remained all his life, nay, even became more and more, the ladies' pianist par excellence. By which, however, I do not mean that he did not please the men, but only that no other pianist was equally successful in touching the most tender and intimate chords of the female heart. Indeed, a high degree of refinement in thought and feeling combined with a poetic disposition are indispensable requisites for an adequate appreciation of Chopin's compositions and style of playing. His remark, therefore, that he had captivated the learned and the poetic natures, was no doubt strictly correct with regard to his success in Vienna; but at the same time it may be accepted as a significant foreshadowing of his whole artistic career. Enough has now been said of these performances, and, indeed, too much, were it not that to ascertain the stage of development reached by an original master, and the effect which his efforts produced on his artistically-cultivated contemporaries, are objects not undeserving a few pages of discussion.

During the twenty days which Chopin spent in Vienna he displayed great activity. He was always busy, and had not a moment to spare. His own public performances did not make him neglect those of others. He heard the violinist Mayseder twice, and went to representations of Boieldieu's "La Dame blanche," Rossini's "Cenerentola," Meyerbeer's "Crociato in Egitto," and other operas. He also visited the picture gallery and the museum of antiquities, delivered letters of introduction, made acquaintances, dined and drank tea with counts and countesses, &c. Wherever Chopin goes we are sure to see him soon in aristocratic and in Polish society.

Everybody says that I have pleased the nobility here
exceedingly The Schwarzenbergs, Wrbnas, &c., were quite
enraptured by the delicacy and elegance of my playing. As a
further proof I may mention the visit which Count
Dietrichstein paid me on the stage.

Chopin called repeatedly on the "worthy old gentleman" Count Hussarzewski and his "worthy lady," with whom he dined once, and who wished him to stay for dinner when he made his farewell call. With the Countess Lichnowska and her daughter he took tea two days after the first concert. They were inexpressibly delighted to hear that he was going to give a second, asked him to visit them on his way through Vienna to Paris, and promised him a letter of introduction to a sister of the Count's. This Count Lichnowski was Count Moritz Lichnowski, the friend of Beethoven, to whom the great master dedicated the Variations, Op. 35, and the Sonata, Op. 90, in which are depicted the woes and joys of the Count's love for the singer Mdlle. Strammer, who afterwards became his wife, and, in fact, was the Countess Lichnowska with whom Chopin became acquainted.

[Footnote: Count Moritz Lichnowski must not be confounded with his elder brother Prince Carl Lichnowski, the pupil and friend of Mozart, and the friend and patron of Beethoven, to whom the latter dedicated his Op. 1, and who died in 1814.]

Among the letters of introduction which Chopin brought with him there was also one for Schuppanzigh, whose name is in musical history indissolubly connected with those of Beethoven and Lichnowski. The eminent quartet leader, although his quartet evenings were over, held out to Chopin hopes of getting up another during his visitor's stay in Vienna — he would do so, he said, if possible. To no one, however, either professional or amateur, was Chopin so much indebted for guidance and furtherance as to his old obliging friend Wurfel, who introduced him not only to Count Gallenberg, Count Lichnowski, and Capellmeister Seyfried, but to every one of his acquaintances who either was a man of influence or took an interest in musical matters. Musicians whose personal acquaintance Chopin said he was glad to make were: Gyrowetz, the author of the concerto with which little Frederick made his debut in Warsaw at the age of nine, an estimable artist, as already stated, who had the sad misfortune to outlive his popularity; Capellmeister Seyfried, a prolific but qualitatively poor composer, best known to our generation as the editor of Albrechtsberger's theoretical works and Beethoven's studies; Conradin Kreutzer, who had already distinguished himself as a virtuoso on the clarinet and pianoforte, and as a conductor and composer, but had not yet produced his "Nachtlager"; Franz Lachner, the friend of Franz Schubert, then a young active conductor and rising composer, now one of the most honoured veterans of his art. With Schuppanzigh's pupil Mayseder, the prince of the Viennese violinists of that day, and indeed one of the neatest, most graceful, and elegant, although somewhat cold, players of his instrument, Chopin had a long conversation. The only critical comments to be found in Chopin's letters on the musicians he came in contact with in the Austrian capital refer to Czerny, with whom he got well acquainted and often played duets for two pianos. Of him the young Polish musician said, "He is a good man, but nothing more." And after having bidden him farewell, he says, "Czerny was warmer than all his compositions." However, it must not be supposed that Chopin's musical acquaintances were confined to the male sex; among them there was at least one belonging to the better and fairer half of humanity—a pianist-composer, a maiden still in her teens, and clever and pretty to boot, who reciprocated the interest he took in her. According to our friend's rather conceited statement I ought to have said—but it would have been very ungallant to do so—he reciprocated the interest she took in him. The reader has no doubt already guessed that I am speaking of Leopoldine Blahetka.

On the whole, Chopin passed his time in Vienna both pleasantly and profitably, as is well shown by his exclamation on the last day of his stay: "It goes crescendo with my popularity here, and this gives me much pleasure." The preceding day Schuppanzigh had said to him that as he left so soon he ought not to be long in coming back. And when Chopin replied that he would like to return to perfect himself, the by-standers told him he need not come for that purpose as he had no longer anything to learn. Although the young musician remarks that these were compliments, he cannot help confessing that he likes to hear them; and of course one who likes to hear them does not wholly disbelieve them, but considers them something more than a mere flatus vocis. "Nobody here," Chopin writes exultingly, "will regard me as a pupil." Indeed, such was the reception he met with that it took him by surprise. "People wonder at me," he remarked soon after his arrival in Vienna, "and I wonder at them for wondering at me." It was incomprehensible to him that the artists and amateurs of the famous musical city should consider it a loss if he departed without giving a concert. The unexpected compliments and applause that everywhere fell upon his ear, together with the many events, experiences, and thoughts that came crowding upon him, would have caused giddiness in any young artist; Chopin they made drunk with excitement and pleasure. The day after the second concert he writes home: "I really intended to have written about something else, but I can't get yesterday out of my head." His head was indeed brimful, or rather full to overflowing, of whirling memories and expectations which he poured into the news—budgets destined for his parents, regardless of logical sequence, just as they came uppermost. The clear, succinct accounts of his visit which he gives to his friend Titus after his return to Warsaw contrast curiously with the confused interminable letters of shreds and patches he writes from Vienna. These latter, however, have a value of their own; they present one with a striking picture of the state of his mind at that time. The reader may consider this part of the biography as an annotated digest of Chopin's letters, of those addressed to his parents as well as of those to his friend Woyciechowski.

At last came the 19th of August, the day of our travelling-party's departure. Chopin passed the whole forenoon in making valedictory visits, and when in the afternoon he had done packing and writing, he called once more on Haslinger—who promised to publish the Variations in about five weeks—and then went to the cafe opposite the theatre, where he was to meet Gyrowetz, Lachner, Kreutzer, and others. The rest shall be told in Chopin's own words:—

> *After a touching parting—it was really a touching parting*
> *when Miss Blahetka gave me as a souvenir her compositions*
> *bearing her own signature, and her father sent his*
> *compliments to you [Chopin's father] and dear mother,*
> *congratulating you on having such a son; when young Stein*
> *[one of the well-known family of pianoforte-manufacturers and*
> *musicians] wept, and Schuppanzigh, Gyrowetz, in one word, all*
> *the other artists, were much moved—well then, after this*
> *touching parting and having promised to return soon, I*
> *stepped into the stage-coach.*

This was at nine o'clock in the evening, and Chopin and his fellow-travellers, accompanied for half-an-hour by Nidecki and some other Poles, leaving behind Vienna and Vienna friends, proceeded on their way to Bohemia.

Prague was reached by our travellers on August 21. The interesting old town did not display its beauties in vain, for Chopin writes admiringly of the fine views from the castle hill, of the castle itself, of "the majestic cathedral with a silver statue of St. John, the beautiful chapel of St. Wenceslas, inlaid with amethysts and other precious stones," and promises to give a fuller and more detailed description of what he has seen by word of mouth. His friend Maciejowski had a letter of introduction to Waclaw Hanka, the celebrated philologist and librarian of the National Museum, to whom Chopin introduced himself as the godson of Count Skarbek. On visiting the museum they were asked, like all on whom the librarian bestowed his special attention, to write their names in the visitors' book. Maciejowski wrote also four mazurka strophes eulogising Hanka's scientific achievements, and Chopin set them to music. The latter brought with him from Vienna six letters of introduction—one from Blahetka and five from

Wurfel—which were respectively addressed to Pixis, to the manager of the theatre, and to other musical big-wigs. The distinguished violin-virtuoso, professor at the Conservatorium, and conductor at the theatre, Frederick Pixis (1786—1842), received Chopin very kindly, gave up some lessons that he might keep him longer and talk with him, and invited him to come again in the afternoon, when he would meet August Alexander Klengel, of Dresden, whose card Chopin had noticed on the table. For this esteemed pianist and famous contrapuntist he had also a letter of introduction, and he was glad to meet him in Prague, as he otherwise would have missed seeing him, Klengel being on his way to Vienna and Italy. They made each other's acquaintance on the stairs leading to Pixis' apartments.

> I heard him play his fugues for two hours; I did not play, as
> they did not ask me to do so. Klengel's rendering pleased me,
> but I must confess I had expected something better (but I beg
> of you not to mention this remark of mine to others).

Elsewhere he writes:—

> Of all the artists whose acquaintance I have made, Klengel
> pleased me most. He played me his fugues (one may say that
> they are a continuation of those of Bach. There are forty-
> eight of them, and the same number of canons). What a
> difference between him and Czerny!

Klengel's opus magnum, the "Canons et Fugues dans tons les tons majeurs et mineurs pour le piano, en deux parties," did not appear till 1854, two years after his death, although it had been completed some decades previously. He carried it about with him on all his travels, unceasingly improving and perfecting it, and may be said to have worked at it for the space of half his life. The two artists who met at Pixis' house got on well together, unlike as they were in their characters and aims. Chopin called on Klengel before the latter's departure from Prague, and spent two hours with him in conversation, neither of them being for a moment at a loss for material to talk about. Klengel gave Chopin a letter of introduction to Morlacchi, the address of which ran: Al ornatissimo Signore Cavaliere Morlacchi, primo maestro della capella Reale, and in which he asked this gentleman to make the bearer acquainted with the musical life of Dresden. How favourably Klengel had impressed his younger brother in art may be gathered from the above-quoted and the following remarks: "He was to me a very agreeable acquaintance, whom I esteem more highly than Czerny, but of this also don't speak, my beloved ones."

[FOOTNOTE: Their disparity of character would have revealed itself unpleasantly to both parties if the grand seigneur Chopin had, like Moritz Hauptmann, been the travelling-companion of the meanly parsimonious Klengel, who to save a few bajocchi left the hotels with uncleaned boots, and calculated the worth of the few things he cared for by scudi.—See Moritz Hauptmann's account of his "canonic" travelling-companion's ways and procedures in the letters to Franz Hauser, vol. i., p. 64, and passim.]

The reader will no doubt notice and admire the caution of our young friend. Remembering that not even Paganini had escaped being censured in Prague, Chopin felt no inclination to give a concert, as he was advised to do. A letter in which he describes his Prague experiences reveals to us one of his weaknesses—one, however, which he has in common with many men of genius. A propos of his bursting into a wrong bedroom he says: "I am absent-minded, you know."

After three pleasant days at Prague the quatrefoil of friends betook themselves again to the road, and wended their way to Teplitz, where they arrived the same evening, and stopped two nights and one day. Here they fell in with many Poles, by one of whom, Louis Lempicki, Chopin was introduced to Prince Clary and his family, in whose castle he spent an evening in very aristocratic society. Among the guests were an Austrian prince, an Austrian and a Saxon general, a captain of the English navy, and several dandies whom Chopin suspected to be Austrian princes or counts. After tea he was asked by the mother of the Princess Clary, Countess Chotek, to play something. Chopin at once went to the piano, and invited those present to give him a theme to improvise upon.

> Hereupon [he relates] I heard the ladies, who had taken seats
> near a table, whisper to each other: "Un theme, un theme."
> Three young princesses consulted together and at last turned
> to Mr. Fritsche, the tutor of Prince Clary's only son, who,
> with the approbation of all present, said to me: "The
> principal theme of Rossini's 'Moses'." I improvised, and, it
> appears, very successfully, for General Leiser [this was the
> Saxon general] afterwards conversed with me for a long time,
> and when he heard that I intended to go to Dresden he wrote
> at once to Baron von Friesen as follows: "Monsieur Frederic
> Chopin est recommande de la part du General Leiser a Monsieur

le Baron de Friesen, Maitre de Ceremonie de S.M. le Roi de
Saxe, pour lui etre utile pendant son sejour a Dresde et de
lui procurer la connaissance de plusieurs de nos artistes."
And he added, in German: "Herr Chopin is himself one of the
most excellent pianists whom I know."

In short, Chopin was made much of; had to play four times, received an invitation to dine at the castle the following day, &c., &c. That our friend, in spite of all these charming prospects, leaving behind him three lovely princesses, and who knows what other aristocratic amenities, rolled off the very next morning at five o'clock in a vehicle hired at the low price of two thalers—i.e., six shillings—must be called either a feat of superhuman heroism or an instance of barbarous insensibility—let the reader decide which. Chopin's visit to Teplitz was not part of his original plan, but the state of his finances was so good that he could allow himself some extravagances. Everything delighted him at Teplitz, and, short as his stay was, he did the sight-seeing thoroughly—we have his own word for it that he saw everything worth seeing, among the rest Dux, the castle of the Waldsteins, with relics of their ancestor Albrecht Waldstein, or Wallenstein.

Leaving Teplitz on the morning of August 26, he arrived in the evening of the same day in Dresden in good health and good humour. About this visit to Dresden little is to be said. Chopin had no intention of playing in public, and did nothing but look about him, admiring nature in Saxon Switzerland, and art in the "magnificent" gallery. He went to the theatre where Goethe's Faust (the first part), adapted by Tieck, was for the first time produced on the stage, Carl Devrient impersonating the principal part. "An awful but grand imagination! In the entr'actes portions from Spohr's opera "Faust" were performed. They celebrated today Goethe's eightieth birthday." It must be admitted that the master-work is dealt with rather laconically, but Chopin never indulges in long aesthetical discussions. On the following Saturday Meyerbeer's "Il Crociato" was to be performed by the Italian Opera—for at that time there was still an Italian Opera in Dresden. Chopin, however, did not stay long enough to hear it, nor did he very much regret missing it, having heard the work already in Vienna. Although Baron von Friesen received our friend most politely, he seems to have been of no assistance to him. Chopin fared better with his letter of introduction to Capellmeister Morlacchi, who returned the visit paid him and made himself serviceable. And now mark this touch of boyish vanity: "Tomorrow morning I expect Morlacchi, and I shall go with him to Miss

Pechwell's. That is to say, I do not go to him, but he comes to me. Yes, yes, yes!" Miss Pechwell was a pupil of Klengel's, and the latter had asked Morlacchi to introduce Chopin to her. She seems to have been not only a technically skilful, fine-feeling, and thoughtful musician, but also in other respects a highly-cultivated person. Klengel called her the best pianist in Dresden. She died young, at the age of 35, having some time previously changed her maiden name for that of Madame Pesadori. We shall meet her again in the course of this biography.

Of the rest of Chopin's journey nothing is known except that it led him to Breslau, but when he reached and left it, and what he did there, are open questions, and not worth troubling about. So much, however, is certain, that on September 12, 1829, he was settled again in his native city, as is proved by a letter bearing that date.

CHAPTER VIII

THE WORKS OF CHOPIN'S FIRST PERIOD.

The only works of Chopin we have as yet discussed are—if we leave out of account the compositions which the master neither published himself nor wished to be published by anybody else—the "Premier Rondeau," Op. 1, the "Rondeau a la Mazur," Op. 5, and "Variations sur un air allemand" (see Chapter III). We must retrace our steps as far back as 1827, and briefly survey the composer's achievements up to the spring of 1829, when a new element enters into his life and influences his artistic work. It will be best to begin with a chronological enumeration of those of Chopin's compositions of the time indicated that have come down to us. In 1827 came into existence or were finished: a Mazurka (Op. 68, No. 2), a Polonaise (Op. 71, No. 1), and a Nocturne (Op. 72); in 1828, "La ci darem la mano, varie" for piano and orchestra (Op. 2), a Polonaise (Op. 71, No. 2), a Rondo for two pianos (Op. 73), a Sonata (Op. 4), a Fantasia on Polish airs for piano and orchestra (Op. 13), a Krakowiak, "Grand Rondeau de Concert," likewise for piano and orchestra (Op. 14), and a Trio for piano, violin, and violoncello (Op. 8); in 1829, a Polonaise (Op. 71, No. 3), a Waltz (Op. 69, No. 2), another Waltz (in E major, without opus number), and a Funeral March (Op. 726). I will not too confidently assert that every one of the last four works was composed in the spring or early summer of 1829; but whether they were or were not, they may be properly ranged with those previously mentioned of 1827 and 1828. The works that bear a higher opus number than 65 were published after the composer's death by Fontana. The Waltz without opus number and the Sonata, Op. 4, are likewise posthumous publications.

The works enumerated above may be divided into three groups, the first of which comprises the Sonata, the Trio, and the Rondo for two pianos.

The Sonata (in C minor) for piano, Op. 4, of which Chopin wrote as early as September 9, 1828, that it had been for some time in the hands of Haslinger at Vienna, was kept by this publisher in manuscript till after the composer's death, being published only in July, 1851. "As a pupil of his I dedicated it to Elsner," says Chopin. It is indeed a pupil's work—an exercise, and not a very successful one. The exigencies of the form overburdened the composer and crushed all individuality out of him. Nowhere is Chopin so little himself, we may even say so unlike himself. The distribution of keys and the character of the themes show that the importance of contrast in the construction of larger works was still unsuspected by him. The two middle movements, a Menuetto and a Larghetto—although in the latter the self-imposed fetters of the 5-4 time prevent the composer from feeling quite at his ease—are more attractive than the rest. In them are discernible an approach to freedom and something like a breath of life, whereas in the first and the last movement there is almost nothing but painful labour and dull monotony. The most curious thing, however, about this work is the lumbering passage-writing of our graceful, light-winged Chopin.

Infinitely superior to the Sonata is the Trio for piano, violin, and violoncello, Op. 8, dedicated to Prince Anton Radziwill, which was published in March, 1833. It was begun early in 1828, was "not yet finished" on September 9, and "not yet quite finished" on December 27 of that year. Chopin tried the first movement in the summer of 1828, and we may assume that, a few details and improvements excepted, the whole was completed at the beginning of 1829. A considerable time, however, elapsed before the composer declared it ready for the press. On August 31, 1830, he writes:—

I tried the Trio last Sunday and was satisfied with it,

perhaps because I had not heard it for a long time. I suppose

you will say, "What a happy man!" Something occurred to me on

hearing it—namely, that it would be better to employ a viola

instead of the violin, for with the violin the E string

dominates most, whilst in my Trio it is hardly ever used. The

viola would stand in a more proper relation to the

violoncello. Then the Trio will be ready for the press.

The composer did not make the intended alteration, and in this he was well advised. For his remarks betray little insight; what preciousness they possess they owe for the most part to the scarcity of similar discussions of craftsmanship in his letters. From the above dates we see that the composer bestowed much time, care, and thought upon the work. Indeed, there can be no doubt that as regards conventional handling of the sonata-form Chopin has in no instance been more successful. Were we to look upon this work as an exercise, we should have to pronounce it a most excellent one. But the ideal content, which is always estimable and often truly beautiful as well as original, raises it high above the status of an exercise. The fundamental fault of the Trio lies in this, that the composer tried to fill a given form with ideas, and to some extent failed to do so—the working-out sections especially testify to the correctness of this opinion. That the notion of regarding

form as a vessel—a notion oftener acted upon than openly professe, mischievous one will hardly be denied, and if it were denied, we cou here discuss so wide a question as that of "What is form?" The comparat ineffective treatment of the violin and violoncello also lays the comp open to censure. Notwithstanding its weaknesses the work was recei with favour by the critics, the most pronounced conservatives not except That the latter gave more praise to it than to Chopin's previously-publish compositions is a significant fact, and may be easily accounted for by th less vigorous originality and less exclusive individuality of the Trio, which although superior in these respects to the Sonata, Op. 4, does not equa the composer's works written in simpler forms. Even the most hostile of Chopin's critics, Rellstab, the editor of the Berlin musical journal Iris, admits—after censuring the composer's excessive striving after originality, and the unnecessarily difficult pianoforte passages with their progressions of intervals alike repellent to hand and ear—that this is "on the whole a praiseworthy work, which, in spite of some excursions into deviating bye-paths, strikes out in a better direction than the usual productions of the modern composers" (1833, No. 21). The editor of the Leipzig "Allgemeine musikalische Zeitung," a journal which Schumann characterises as "a sleepy place," is as eulogistic as the most rabid Chopin admirer could wish. Having spoken of the "talented young man" as being on the one hand under the influence of Field, and on the other under that of Beethoven, he remarks:—

> In the Trio everything is new: the school, which is the neo-
> romantic; the art of pianoforte-playing, the individuality,
> the originality, or rather the genius—which, in the
> expression of a passion, unites, mingles, and alternates so
> strangely with that amiable tenderness [Innigkeit] that the
> shifting image of the passion hardly leaves the draughtsman
> time to seize it firmly and securely, as he would fain do;
> even the position of the phrases is unusual. All this,
> however, would be ambiguous praise did not the spirit, which
> is both old and new, breathe through the new form and give it
> a soul.

I place these criticisms before the reader as historical documents, not as final decisions and examples of judicial wisdom. In fact, I accept neither the strictures of the one nor the sublimifications of the other, although the confident self-assertion of the former and the mystic vagueness of the latter ought, according to use and wont, to carry the weight of authority with them. Schumann, the Chopin champion par excellence, saw clearer, and,

writing three years later (1836), said that the Trio belonged to Chopin's earlier period when the composer still allowed the virtuoso some privileges. Although I cannot go so far as this too admiring and too indulgent critic, and describe the work as being "as noble as possible, more full of enthusiasm than the work of any other poet [so schwarmerisch wie noch kein Dichter gesungen], original in its smallest details, and, as a whole, every note music and life," I think that it has enough of nobility, enthusiasm, originality, music, and life, to deserve more attention than it has hitherto obtained.

Few classifications can at one and the same time lay claim to the highest possible degree of convenience—the raison d'etre of classifications—and strict accuracy. The third item of my first group, for instance, might more properly be said to stand somewhere between this and the second group, partaking somewhat of the nature of both. The Rondo, Op. 73, was not originally written for two pianos. Chopin wrote on September 9, 1828, that he had thus rearranged it during a stay at Strzyzewo in the summer of that year. At that time he was pretty well pleased with the piece, and a month afterwards talked of playing it with his friend Fontana at the Ressource. Subsequently he must have changed his opinion, for the Rondo did not become known to the world at large till it was published posthumously. Granting certain prettinesses, an unusual dash and vigour, and some points of interest in the working-out, there remains the fact that the stunted melodies signify little and the too luxuriant passage-work signifies less, neither the former nor the latter possessing much of the charm that distinguishes them in the composer's later works. The original in this piece is confined to the passage-work, and has not yet got out of the rudimentary stage. Hence, although the Rondo may not be unworthy of finding occasionally a place in a programme of a social gathering with musical accompaniments and even of a non-classical concert, it will disappoint those who come to it with their expectations raised by Chopin's chefs-d'oeuvre, where all is poetry and exquisiteness of style.

The second group contains Chopin's concert-pieces, all of which have orchestral accompaniments. They are: (1) "La ci darem la mano, varie pour le piano," Op. 2; (2) "Grande Fantaisie sur des airs polonais," Op. 13; (3) "Krakowiak, Grande Rondeau de Concert," Op. 14. Of these three the first, which is dedicated to Titus Woyciechowski, has become the most famous, not, however, on account of its greater intrinsic value, but partly because the orchestral accompaniments can be most easily dispensed with, and more especially because Schumann has immortalised it by—what shall I call it?—a poetic prose rhapsody. As previously stated, the work had already in September, 1828, been for some time at Vienna in the hands of Haslinger; it was probably commenced as far back as 1827, but it did not appear in print

till 1830. [FOOTNOTE: It appeared in a serial publication entitled Odeon, which was described on the title-page as: Ausgewahlte grosse Concertstucke fur verschiedene Instrumente (Selected Grand Concert-Pieces for different instruments).] On April 10 of that year Chopin writes that he expects it impatiently. The appearance of these Variations, the first work of Chopin published outside his own country, created a sensation. Of the impression which he produced with it on the Viennese in 1829 enough has been said in the preceding chapter. The Allgemeine musikalische Zeitung received no less than three reviews of it, two of them—that of Schumann and one by "an old musician"—were accepted and inserted in the same number of the paper (1831, Vol. xxxiii., No. 49); the third, by Friedrich Wieck, which was rejected, found its way in the following year into the musical journal Caecilia. Schumann's enthusiastic effusion was a prophecy rather than a criticism. But although we may fail to distinguish in Chopin's composition the flirting of the grandee Don Juan with the peasant-girl Zerlina, the curses of the duped lover Masetto, and the jeers and laughter of the knavish attendant Leporello, which Schumann thought he recognised, we all obey most readily and reverently his injunction, "Hats off, gentlemen: a genius!" In these words lies, indeed, the merit of Schumann's review as a criticism. Wieck felt and expressed nearly the same, only he felt it less passionately and expressed it in the customary critical style. The "old musician," on the other hand, is pedantically censorious, and the redoubtable Rellstab (in the Iris) mercilessly condemnatory. Still, these two conservative critics, blinded as they were by the force of habit to the excellences of the rising star, saw what their progressive brethren overlooked in the ardour of their admiration—namely, the super-abundance of ornament and figuration. There is a grain of truth in the rather strong statement of Rellstab that the composer "runs down the theme with roulades, and throttles and hangs it with chains of shakes." What, however, Rellstab and the "old musician"— for he, too, exclaims, "nothing but bravura and figuration!"—did not see, but what must be patent to every candid and unprejudiced observer, are the originality, piquancy, and grace of these fioriture, roulades, &c., which, indeed, are unlike anything that was ever heard or seen before Chopin's time. I say "seen," for the configurations in the notation of this piece are so different from those of the works of any other composer that even an unmusical person could distinguish them from all the rest; and there is none of the timid groping, the awkward stumbling of the tyro. On the contrary, the composer presents himself with an ease and boldness which cannot but command admiration. The reader will remember what the Viennese critic said about Chopin's "aim"; that it was not to dazzle by the superficial means of the virtuoso, but to impress by the more legitimate ones of the genuine musician. This is true if we compare the Chopin of that day with his fellow-virtuosos Kalkbrenner, Herz, &c.; but if we compare him with his later self, or with Mozart, Beethoven, Mendelssohn, Schumann, &c., the case is different. Indeed, there can be no doubt but that in this and the other pieces of this group, Chopin's aim was that of the virtuoso, only his nature was too rich, too noble, to sink into the inanity of an insipid, conventional brilliancy. Moreover, whilst maintaining that in the works specified language outruns in youthful exuberance thought and emotion, I hasten to add that there are premonitory signs—for instance, in the Op. 2 under discussion, more especially in the introduction, the fifth variation, and the Finale—of what as yet lies latent in the master's undeveloped creative power.

The Grande Fantaisie sur des airs polonais (A major) for the pianoforte and orchestra, Op. 13, dedicated to J. P. Pixis, and published in April, 1834, and the Krakowiak, Grand Rondeau de Concert (F major) for the pianoforte and orchestra, Op. 14, dedicated to the Princesse Adam Czartoryska, and published in June, 1834, are the most overtly Polish works of Chopin. Of the composition of the former, which, according to Karasowski, was sketched in 1828, the composer's letters give no information; but they contain some remarks concerning the latter. We learn that the score of the Krakowiak was finished by December 27, 1828, and find the introduction described as having "as funny an appearance as himself in his pilot-cloth overcoat." In the Fantasia the composer introduces and variates a Polish popular song (Juz miesiac zaszedl), and an air by the Polish composer Kurpinski, and concludes with a Kujawiak, a dance of the mazurka species, in 3-4 time, which derives its name from the district called Kujawia. In connection with this composition I must not omit to mention that the first variation on the Polish popular song contains the germ of the charming Berceuse (Op. 57). The Rondo, Op. 14, has the character of a Krakowiak, a dance in 2-4 time which originated in Cracovia. In no other compositions of the master do the national elements show themselves in the same degree of crudity; indeed, after this he never incorporates national airs and imitates so closely national dances. Chopin remains a true Pole to the end of his days, and his love of and attachment to everything Polish increase with the time of absence from his native country. But as the composer grows in maturity, he subjects the raw material to a more and more thorough process of refinement and development before he considers it fit for artistic purposes; the popular dances are spiritualised, the national characteristics and their corresponding musical idioms are subtilised and individualised. I do not agree with those critics who think it is owing to the strongly-marked, exclusive Polish national character that these two works have gained so little sympathy in the musical world; there are artistic reasons that account for the neglect, which is indeed so great that I do not remember having heard or read of any virtuoso performing either of these pieces in public till a few years ago, when Chopin's talented countrywoman Mdlle. Janotha ventured on a revival of the Fantasia, without, however, receiving, in spite of her finished rendering, much encouragement. The works, as wholes, are not altogether satisfactory in the matter of form, and appear somewhat patchy. This is especially the case in the Fantasia, where the connection of parts is anything but masterly. Then the arabesk-element predominates again quite unduly. Rellstab discusses the Fantasia with his usual obtuseness, but points out correctly that Chopin gives only here and there a few bars of melody, and never a longer melodic strain. The best parts of the works, those that contain the greatest amount of music, are certainly the exceedingly spirited Kujawiak and Krakowiak. The unrestrained merriment that reigns in the latter justifies, or, if it does not justify, disposes us to forgive much. Indeed, the Rondo may be said to overflow with joyousness; now the notes run at random hither and thither, now tumble about head over heels, now surge in bold arpeggios, now skip from octave to octave, now trip along in chromatics, now vent their gamesomeness in the most extravagant capers.

The orchestral accompaniments, which in the Variations, Op. 2, are of very little account, show in every one of the three works of this group an inaptitude in writing for any other instrument than the piano that is quite surprising considering the great musical endowments of Chopin in other respects. I shall not dwell on this subject now, as we shall have to consider it when we come to the composer's concertos.

The fundamental characteristics of Chopin's style—the loose-textured, wide-meshed chords and arpeggios, the serpentine movements, the bold leaps—are exaggerated in the works of this group, and in their exaggeration become grotesque, and not unfrequently ineffective. These works show us, indeed, the composer's style in a state of fermentation; it has still to pass through a clearing process, in which some of its elements will be secreted and others undergo a greater or less change. We, who judge Chopin by his best works, are apt to condemn too precipitately the adverse critics of his early compositions. But the consideration of the luxuriance and extravagance of the passage-work which distinguish them from the master's maturer creations ought to caution us and moderate our wrath. Nay more, it may even lead us to acknowledge, however reluctantly, that amidst the loud braying of Rellstab there occurred occasionally utterances that were by no means devoid of articulation and sense. Take, for instance, this—I do not remember just now a propos of which composition, but it is very appropriate to those we are now discussing:—"The whole striving of the composer must be regarded as an aberration, based on decided talent, we admit, but nevertheless an aberration." You see the most hostile of Chopin's critics does not deny his talent; indeed, Rellstab sometimes, especially subsequently, speaks quite patronisingly about him. I shall take this opportunity to contradict the current notion that Chopin had just cause to complain of backwardness in the recognition of his genius, and even of malicious attacks on his rising reputation. The truth of this is already partly disproved by the foregoing, and it will be fully so by the sequel.

The pieces which I have formed into a third group show us the composer free from the fetters that ambition and other preoccupations impose. Besides Chopin's peculiar handling we find in them more of his peculiar sentiment. If the works of the first group were interesting as illustrating the development of the student, those of the second group that of the virtuoso, and those of both that of the craftsman, the works of the third group furnish us most valuable documents for the history of the man and poet. The foremost in importance of the pieces comprised in this group are no doubt the three polonaises, composed respectively in the years 1827, 1828, and 1829. The bravura character is still prominent, but, instead of ruling supreme, it becomes in every successive work more and more subordinate to thought and emotion. These polonaises, although thoroughly Chopinesque, nevertheless differ very much from his later ones, those published by himself, which are generally more compact and fuller of poetry. Moreover, I imagine I can see in several passages the influence of Weber, whose Polonaise in E flat minor, Polacca in E major, Sonata in A flat major, and Invitation a la Valse (to mention a few apposite instances), respectively published in 1810, 1819, 1816, and 1821, may be supposed to have been known to Chopin. These reminiscences, if such they are, do not detract much from the originality of the compositions; indeed, that a youth of eighteen should have attained such a strongly-developed individuality as the D minor Polonaise exhibits, is truly wonderful.

The Nocturne of the year 1827 (Op. 72, No. 1, E minor) is probably the poorest of the early compositions, but excites one's curiosity as the first specimen of the kind by the incomparable composer of nocturnes. Do not misunderstand me, however, and imagine that I wish to exalt Chopin at the expense of another great musician. Field has the glory not only of having originated the genre, but also of having produced examples that have as yet lost nothing, or very little, of their vitality. His nocturnes are, indeed, a rich treasure, which, undeservedly neglected by the present generation, cannot be superseded by those of his illustrious, and now favoured successor. On the other hand, although Field's priority and influence on Chopin must be admitted, the unprejudiced cannot but perceive that the latter is no imitator. Even where, as for instance in Op. 9, Nos. 1 and 2, the mejody or the form of the accompaniment shows a distinct reminiscence of Field, such is the case only for a few notes, and the next moment Chopin is what nobody else could be. To watch a great man's growth, to trace a master's noble achievements from their humble beginnings, has a charm for most minds. I, therefore, need not fear the reader's displeasure if I direct his attention to some points, notable on this account—in this case to the wide-meshed chords and light-winged flights of notes, and the foreshadowing of the Coda of Op. 9.

Of 1827 we have also a Mazurka in A minor, Op. 68, No. 2. It is simple and rustic, and at the same time graceful. The trio (poco piu mosso), the more original portion of the Mazurka, reappears in a slightly altered form in later mazurkas. It is these foreshadowings of future beauties, that make these early works so interesting. The above-mentioned three polonaises are full of phrases, harmonic, progressions, &c., which are subsequently reutilised in a. purer, more emphatic, more developed, more epigrammatic, or otherwise more perfect form. We notice the same in the waltzes which remain yet to be discussed here.

Whether these Waltzes (in B minor, Op. 69, No. 2; and in E major, without opus number) were really written in the early part of 1829, or later on in the year, need not be too curiously inquired into. As I have already remarked, they may certainly be classed along with the above-discussed works. The first is the more interesting of them. In both we meet with passages that point to more perfect specimens of the kind—for instance, certain rhythmical motives, melodic inflections, and harmonic progressions, to the familiar Waltzes in E flat major (Op. 18) and in A flat major (Op. 34, No. 1); and the D major portion of the Waltz in B minor, to the C major part of the Waltz in A minor (Op. 34, No. 2). This concludes our survey of the compositions of Chopin's first period.

In the legacy of a less rich man, the Funeral March in C minor, Op. 72b, composed (according to Fontana) in 1829, [FOOTNOTE: In Breitkopf and Hartel's Gesammtausgabe of Chopin's works will be found 1826 instead of 1829. This, however, is a misprint, not a correction.]would be a notable item; in that of Chopin it counts for little. Whatever the shortcomings of this composition are, the quiet simplicity and sweet melancholy which pervade it must touch the hearer. But the master stands in his own. light; the famous Funeral March in B flat minor, from the Sonata in B flat minor, Op. 35, composed about ten years later, eclipses the more modest one in C minor. Beside the former, with its sublime force and fervency of passion and imposing mastery of the resources of the art, the latter sinks into weak insignificance, indeed, appears a mere puerility. Let us note in the earlier work the anticipation, (bar 12) of a motive of the chef-d'ceuvre (bar 7), and reminiscences of the Funeral March from Beethoven's. Sonata in A flat major, Op. 26.

CHAPTER IX

CHOPIN'S FIRST LOVE.—FRIENDSHIP WITH TITUS WOYCIECHOWSKI.—
LIFE IN WARSAW AFTER RETURNING FROM VIENNA.—VISIT TO PRINCE
RADZIWILL AT ANTONIN (OCTOBER, 1829).— NEW COMPOSITIONS.— GIVES
TWO CONCERTS.

IN the preceding chapter I alluded to a new element that entered into the life of Chopin and influenced his artistic work. The following words, addressed by the young composer on October 3, 1829, to his friend Titus Woyciechowski, will explain what kind of element it was and when it began to make itself felt:—

Do not imagine that [when I speak of the advantages and desirability of a stay in Vienna] I am thinking of Miss Blahetka, of whom I have written to you; I have—perhaps to my misfortune—already found my ideal, which I worship faithfully and sincerely. Six months have elapsed, and I have not yet exchanged a syllable with her of whom I dream every night. Whilst my thoughts were with her I composed the Adagio of my Concerto, and early this morning she inspired the Waltz which I send along with this letter.

The influence of the tender passion on the development of heart and mind cannot be rated too highly; it is in nine out of ten, if not in ninety-nine out of a hundred cases that which transforms the rhymer into a poet, the artificer into an artist. Chopin confesses his indebtedness to Constantia, Schumann his to Clara. But who could recount all the happy and hapless loves that have made poets? Countless is the number of those recorded in histories, biographies, and anecdotes; greater still the number of those buried in literature and art, the graves whence they rise again as flowers, matchless in beauty, unfading, and of sweetest perfume. Love is indeed the sun that by its warmth unfolds the multitudinous possibilities that lie hidden, often unsuspected, in the depths of the human soul. It was, then, according to Chopin, about April, 1829, that the mighty power began to stir within him; and the correspondence of the following two years shows us most strikingly how it takes hold of him with an ever-increasing firmness of grasp, and shakes the whole fabric of his delicate organisation with fearful violence. The object of Chopin's passion, the being whom he worshipped and in whom he saw the realisation of his ideal of womanhood, was Constantia Gladkowska, a pupil at the Warsaw Conservatorium, of whom the reader will learn more in the course of this and the next chapter.

What reveals perhaps more distinctly than anything else Chopin's idiosyncrasy is his friendship for Titus Woyciechowski. At any rate, it is no exaggeration to say that a knowledge of the nature of Chopin's two passions, his love and his friendship—for this, too, was a passion with him—gives into our hands a key that unlocks all the secrets of his character, of his life, and of their outcome—his artistic work. Nay more, with a full comprehension of, and insight into, these passions we can foresee the sufferings and disappointments which he is fated to endure. Chopin's friendship was not a common one; it was truly and in the highest degree romantic. To the sturdy Briton and gay Frenchman it must be incomprehensible, and the German of four or five generations ago would have understood it better than his descendant of to-day is likely to do. If we look for examples of such friendship in literature, we find the type nowhere so perfect as in the works of Jean Paul Richter. Indeed, there are many passages in the letters of the Polish composer that read like extracts from the German author: they remind us of the sentimental and other transcendentalisms of Siebenkas, Leibgeber, Walt, Vult, and others. There was somethine in Chopin's warm, tender, effusive friendship that may be best characterised by the word "feminine." Moreover, it was so exacting, or rather so covetous and jealous, that he had often occasion to chide, gently of course, the less caressing and enthusiastic Titus. Let me give some instances.

> *December 27th, 1828.—If I scribble to-day again so much*
> *nonsense, I do so only in order to remind you that you are as*
> *much locked in my heart as ever, and that I am the same Fred*
> *I was. You do not like to be kissed; but to-day you must*
> *permit me to do so.*

The question of kissing is frequently brought up.

> *September 12th, 1829.—I embrace you heartily, and kiss you*
> *on your lips if you will permit me.*

> *October 20th, 1829.—I embrace you heartily—many a one*
> *writes this at the end ol his letter, but most people do so*

with little thought of what they are writing. But you may
believe me, my dearest friend, that I do so sincerely, as
truly as my name is Fred.

September 4th, 1830.—Time passes, I must wash myself...do
not kiss me now...but you would not kiss me in any case—even
if I anointed myself with Byzantine oils—unless I forced you
to do so by magnetic means.

Did we not know the writer and the person addressed, one might imagine that the two next extracts were written by a lover to his mistress or vice versa.

November 14th, 1829.—You, my dearest one, do not require my
portrait. Believe me I am always with you, and shall not
forget you till the end of my life.

May 15th, 1830.—You have no idea how much I love you! If I
only could prove it to you! What would I not give if I could
once again right heartily embrace you!

One day he expresses the wish that he and his friend should travel together. But this was too commonplace a sentiment not to be refined upon. Accordingly we read in a subsequent letter as follows:—

September 18th, 1830.—I should not like to travel with you,
for I look forward with the greatest delight to the moment
when we shall meet abroad and embrace each other; it will be
worth more than a thousand monotonous days passed with you
on
the journey.

From another passage in one of these letters we get a good idea of the
influence Titus Woyciechowski exercised on his friend.

April 10, 1830.—Your advice is good. I have already refused
some invitations for the evening, as if I had had a
presentiment of it—for I think of you in almost everything I
undertake. I do not know whether it comes from my having

learned from you how to feel and perceive; but when I compose
anything I should much like to know whether it pleases you;
and I believe that my second Concerto (E minor) will have no
value for me until you have heard it and approved of it.

I quoted the above passage to show how Chopin felt that this friendship had been a kind of education to him, and how he valued his friend's opinion of his compositions—he is always anxious to make Titus acquainted with anything new he may have composed. But in this passage there is another very characteristic touch, and it may easily be overlooked, or at least may not receive the attention which it deserves—I allude to what Chopin says of having had "a presentiment." In superstitiousness he is a true child of his country, and all the enlightenment of France did not succeed in weaning him from his belief in dreams, presentiments, good and evil days, lucky and unlucky numbers, &c. This is another romantic feature in the character of the composer; a dangerous one in the pursuit of science, but advantageous rather than otherwise in the pursuit of art. Later on I shall have to return to this subject and relate some anecdotes, here I shall confine myself to quoting a short passage from one of his early letters.

April 17, 1830.—If you are in Warsaw during the sitting of
the Diet, you will come to my concert—I have something like
a presentiment, and when I also dream it, I shall firmly
believe it.

And now, after these introductory explanations, we will begin the chapter in right earnest by taking up the thread of the story where we left it. On his return to Warsaw Chopin was kept in a state of mental excitement by the criticisms on his Vienna performances that appeared in German papers. He does not weary of telling his friend about them, transcribing portions of them, and complaining of Polish papers which had misrepresented the drift and mistranslated the words of them. I do not wonder at the incorrectness of the Polish reports, for some of these criticisms are written in as uncouth, confused, and vague German as I ever had the misfortune to turn into English. One cannot help thinking, in reading what Chopin says with regard to these matters, that he showed far too much concern about the utterances of the press, and far too much sensitiveness under the infliction of even the slightest strictures. That, however, the young composer was soon engaged on new works may be gathered from the passage (Oct. 3, 1829), quoted at the commencement of this chapter, in which he speaks of the Adagio of a concerto, and a waltz, written whilst his thoughts were with his ideal. These compositions were the second movement of the F minor Concerto and the

Waltz, Op. 70, No. 3. But more of this when we come to discuss the works which Chopin produced in the years 1829 and 1830.

One of the most important of the items which made up our friend's musical life at this time was the weekly musical meetings at the house of Kessler, the pianist-composer characterised in Chapter X. There all the best artists of Warsaw assembled, and the executants had to play prima vista whatever was placed before them. Of works performed at two of these Friday evening meetings, we find mentioned Spohr's Octet, described by Chopin as "a wonderful work"; Ries's Concerto in C sharp minor (played with quartet accompaniment), Hummel's Trio in E major, Prince Louis Ferdinand of Prussia's Quartet, and Beethoven's last Trio, which, Chopin says, he could not but admire for its magnificence and grandeur. To Brzezina's music-shop he paid a visit every day, without finding there, however, anything new, except a Concerto by Pixis, which made no great impression upon him. That Chopin was little satisfied with his situation may be gathered from the following remarks of his:—

> You cannot imagine how sad Warsaw is to me; if I did not feel
>
> happy in my home circle I should not like to live here. Oh,
>
> how bitter it is to have no one with whom one can share joy
>
> and sorrow; oh, how dreadful to feel one's heart oppressed
>
> and to be unable to express one's complaints to any human
>
> soul! You know full well what I mean. How often do I tell my
>
> piano all that I should like to impart to you!

Of course the reader, who is in the secret, knows as well as Titus knew, to whom the letter was addressed, that Chopin alludes to his love. Let us mark the words in the concluding sentence about the conversations with his piano. Chopin was continually occupied with plans for going abroad. In October, 1829, he writes that, wherever fate may lead him, he is determined not to spend the winter in Warsaw. Nevertheless, more than a year passed away before he said farewell to his native city. He himself wished to go to Vienna, his father seems to have been in favour of Berlin. Prince Radziwill and his wife had kindly invited him to come to the Prussian capital, and offered him apartments in their palais. But Chopin was unable to see what advantages he could derive from a stay in Berlin. Moreover, unlike his father, he believed that this invitation was no more than "de belles paroles." By the way, these remarks of Chopin's furnish a strong proof that the Prince was not his patron and benefactor, as Liszt and others have maintained. While speaking of his fixed intention to go somewhere, and of the Prince's invitation, Chopin suddenly exclaims with truly Chopinesque indecision and capriciousness: —

> But what is the good of it all? Seeing that I have begun so
> many new works, perhaps the wisest thing I can do is to stay
> here.

Leaving this question undecided, he undertook in October, 1829, a journey to Posen, starting on the 20th of that month. An invitation from Prince Radziwill was the inducement that led him to quit the paternal roof so soon after his return to it. His intention was to remain only a fortnight from home, and to visit his friends, the Wiesiolowskis, on the way to Antonin. Chopin enjoyed himself greatly at the latter place. The wife of the Prince, a courteous and kindly lady, who did not gauge a man's merits by his descent, found the way to the heart of the composer by wishing to hear every day and to possess as soon as possible his Polonaise in F minor (Op. 71, No. 3). The young Princesses, her daughters, had charms besides those of their beauty. One of them played the piano with genuine musical feeling.

> I have written [reports Chopin to his friend Titus on
> November 14, 1829] during my visit at Prince Radziwill's an
> Alla Polacca with violoncello. It is nothing more than a
> brilliant salon piece, such as pleases ladies. I would like
> Princess Wanda to practise it, so that it might be said that
> I had taught her. She is only seventeen years old and
> beautiful; it would be delightful to have the privilege of
> placing her pretty fingers on the keys. But, joking apart,
> her soul is endowed with true musical feeling, and one does
> not need to tell her whether she is to play crescendo, piano,
> or pianissimo.

According to Liszt, Chopin fondly remembered his visits to Antonin, and told many an anecdote in connection with them.

> The Princess Elisa, one of the daughters of Prince Radziwill,
> who died in the first bloom of her life, left him [Chopin]
> the sweet image of an angel exiled for a short period here
> below.

A passage in the letter of Chopin from which I last quoted throws also a little light on his relation to her.

> You wished one of my portraits; if I could only have pilfered

one of Princess Elisa's, I should certainly have sent it; for

she has two portraits of me in her album, and I am told that

these drawings are very good likenesses.

The musical Prince would naturally be attracted by, and take an interest in, the rising genius. What the latter's opinion of his noble friend as a composer was, he tells Titus Woyciechowski at some length. I may here say, once for all, that all the letters from which extracts are given in this chapter are addressed to this latter.

You know how the Prince loves music; he showed me his "Faust"

and I found in it some things that are really beautiful,

indeed, in part even grandly conceived. In confidence, I

should not at all have credited the Namiestnik [governor,

lord-lieutenant] with such music! Among other things I was

struck by a scene in which Mephistopheles allures Margaret to

the window by his singing and guitar-playing, while at the

same time a chorale is heard from the neighbouring church.

This is sure to produce a great effect at a performance. I

mention this only that you may form an idea of his musical

conceptions. He is a great admirer of Gluck. Theatrical music

has, in his opinion, significance only in so far as it

illustrates the situation and emotion; the overture,

therefore, has no close, and leads at once into the

introduction. The orchestra is placed behind the stage and is

always invisible, in order that the attention of the audience

may not be diverted by external, such as the movements of the

conductor and executants.

Chopin enjoyed himself so much at Antonin that if he had consulted only his pleasure he would have stayed till turned out by his host. But, although he was asked to prolong his visit, he left this "Paradise" and the "two Eves" after a sojourn of eight days. It was his occupations, more especially the F minor Concerto, "impatiently waiting for its Finale," that induced him to practise this self-denial. When Chopin had again taken possession of his study, he no doubt made it his first business, or at least one of the first, to compose the wanting movement, the Rondo, of his Concerto; as, however, there is an interval of more than four months in his extant letters, we hear no more about it till he plays it in public. Before his visit to Antonin (October

20, 1829) he writes to his friend that he has composed "a study in his own manner," and after the visit he mentions having composed "some studies."

Chopin seems to have occasionally played at the Ressource. The reader will remember the composer's intention of playing there with Fontana his Rondo for two pianos. On November 14, 1829, Chopin informs his friend Titus that on the preceding Saturday Kessler performed Hummel's E major Concerto at the Ressource, and that on the following Saturday he himself would perhaps play there, and in the case of his doing so choose for his piece his Variations, Op. 2. Thus composing, playing, and all the time suffering from a certain loneliness—"You cannot imagine how everywhere in Warsaw I now find something wanting! I have nobody with whom I can speak, were it only two words, nobody whom I can really trust"—the day came when he gave his first concert in his native city. This great event took place on March 17, 1830, and the programme contained the following pieces:—

PART I

1. Overture to the Opera "Leszek Bialy," by Elsner.

2. Allegro from the Concerto in F minor, composed and played by F. Chopin.

3. Divertissement for the French horn, composed and played by Gorner.

4. Adagio and Rondo from the Concerto in F minor, composed and played by Chopin.

PART II

1. Overture to the Opera "Cecylja Piaseczynska," by Kurpinski.

2. Variations by Paer, sung by Madame Meier.

3. Pot-pourri on national airs, composed and played by Chopin.

Three days before the concert, which took place in the theatre, neither box nor reserved seat was to be had. But Chopin complains that on the whole it did not make the impression he expected. Only the Adagio and Rondo of his Concerto had a decided success. But let us see the concert-giver's own account of the proceedings.

> The first Allegro of the F minor Concerto (not intelligible
> to all) received indeed the reward of a "Bravo," but I
> believe this was given because the public wished to show that
> it understands and knows how to appreciate serious music.
> There are people enough in all countries who like to assume
> the air of connoisseurs! The Adagio and Rondo produced a very
> great effect. After these the applause and the "Bravos" came
> really from the heart; but the Pot-pourri on Polish airs
> missed its object entirely. There was indeed some applause,
> but evidently only to show the player that the audience had
> not been bored.

We now hear again the old complaint that Chopin's playing was too delicate. The opinion of the pit was that he had not played loud enough, whilst those who sat in the gallery or stood in the orchestra seem to have been better satisfied. In one paper, where he got high praise, he was advised to put forth more energy and power in the future; but Chopin thought he knew where this power was to be found, and for the next concert got a Vienna instrument instead of his own Warsaw one. Elsner, too, attributed the indistinctness of the bass passages and the weakness of tone generally to the instrument. The approval of some of the musicians compensated Chopin to some extent for the want of appreciation and intelligence shown by the public at large "Kurpinski thought he discovered that evening new beauties in my Concerto, and Ernemann was fully satisfied with it." Edouard Wolff told me that they had no idea in Warsaw of the real greatness of Chopin. Indeed, how could they? He was too original to be at once fully understood. There are people who imagine that the difficulties of Chopin's music arise from its Polish national characteristics, and that to the Poles themselves it is as easy as their mother-tongue; this, however, is a mistake. In fact, other countries had to teach Poland what is due to Chopin. That the aristocracy of Paris, Polish and native, did not comprehend the whole Chopin, although it may have appreciated and admired his sweetness, elegance, and exquisiteness, has been remarked by Liszt, an eye and ear-witness and an excellent judge. But his testimony is not needed to convince one of the fact. A subtle poet, be he ever so national, has thoughts and corresponding language beyond the ken of the vulgar, who are to be found in all ranks, high and low. Chopin, imbued as he was with the national spirit, did nevertheless not manifest it in a popularly intelligible form, for in passing through his mind it underwent a process of idealisation and individualisation. It has been repeatedly said that the national predominates over the universal in Chopin's music; it is a still less disputable truth that the individual predominates therein over the national. There are artist-natures whose tendency is to expand and to absorb; others again whose tendency is to contract and to exclude. Chopin is one of the most typical instances of the latter; hence, no wonder that he was not at once fully understood by his countrymen. The great success which Chopin's subsequent concerts in Warsaw obtained does not invalidate E. Wolff's statement, which indeed is confirmed by the composer's own remarks on the taste of the public and its reception of his compositions. Moreover, we shall see that those pieces pleased most in which, as in the Fantasia and Krakowiak, the national raw material was merely more or less artistically dressed up, but not yet digested and assimilated; if the Fantasia left the audience cold at the first concert, this was no doubt owing to the inadequacy of the performance.

No sooner was the first concert over than, with his head still full of it, Chopin set about making preparations for a second, which took place within a week after the first. The programme was as follows:—

PART I

1. Symphony by Nowakowski.

2. Allegro from the Concerto in F minor, composed and played by Chopin.

3. Air Varie by De Beriot, played by Bielawski.

4. Adagio and Rondo from the Concerto in F minor, composed and played by Chopin.

PART II

1. Rondo Krakowiak, composed and played by Chopin.

2. Aria from "Elena e Malvina" by Soliva, sung by Madame Meier.

3. Improvisation on national airs.

This time the audience, which Chopin describes as having been more numerous than at any other concert, was satisfied. There was no end to the applause, and when he came forward to bow his acknowledgments there were calls of "Give another concert!" The Krakowiak produced an immense effect, and was followed by four volleys of applause. His improvisation on the Polish national air "W miescie dziwne obyczaje" pleased only the people in the dress-circle, although he did not improvise in the way he had intended to do, which would not have been suitable for the audience that was present. From this and another remark, that few of the haute volee had as yet heard him, it appears that the aristocracy, for the most part living on their estates, was not largely represented at the concert. Thinking as he did of the public, he was surprised that the Adagio had found such general favour, and that he heard everywhere the most flattering remarks. He was also told that "every note sounded like a bell," and that he had "played much better on the second than on the first instrument." But although Elsner held that Chopin could only be judged after the second concert, and Kurpinski and others expressed their regret that he did not play on the Viennese instrument at the first one, he confesses that he would have preferred playing on his own piano. The success of the concerts may be measured by the following facts: A travelling virtuoso and former pupil of the Paris Conservatoire, Dunst by name, offered in his enthusiasm to treat Chopin with champagne; the day after the second concert a bouquet with a poem was sent to him; his fellow-student Orlowski wrote mazurkas and waltzes on the principal theme of the Concerto, and published them in spite of the horrified composer's request that he should not do so; Brzezina, the musicseller, asked him for his portrait, but, frightened at the prospect of seeing his counterfeit used as a wrapper for butter and cheese, Chopin declined to give it to him; the editor of the "Courier" inserted in his paper a sonnet addressed to Chopin. Pecuniarily the concerts were likewise a success, although the concert-giver was of a different opinion. But then he seems to have had quite prima donna notions about receipts, for he writes very coolly: "From the two concerts I had, after deduction of all expenses, not as much as 5,000 florins (about 125 pounds)." Indeed, he treats this part of the business very cavalierly, and declares that money was no object with him. On the utterances of the papers, which, of course, had their say, Chopin makes some sensible and modest comments.

After my concerts there appeared many criticisms; if in them (especially in the "Kuryer Polski") abundant praise was awarded to me, it was nevertheless not too extravagant. The "Official Journal" has also devoted some columns to my praise; one of its numbers contained, among other things, such stupidities — well meant, no doubt — that I was quite desperate till I had read the answer in the "Gazeta Polska," which justly takes away what the other papers had in their exaggeration attributed to me. In this article it is said that the Poles will one day be as proud of me as the Germans are of Mozart, which is palpable nonsense. But that is not

all, the critic says further: "That if I had fallen into the
hands of a pedant or a Rossinist (what a stupid expression!)
I could not have become what I am." Now, although I am as yet
nothing, he is right in so far that my performance would be
still less than it actually is if I had not studied under
Elsner.

Gratifying as the praise of the press no doubt was to Chopin, it became a matter of small account when he thought of his friend's approving sympathy. "One look from you after the concert would have been worth more to me than all the laudations of the critics here." The concerts, however, brought with them annoyances as well as pleasures. While one paper pointed out Chopin's strongly-marked originality, another advised him to hear Rossini, but not to imitate him. Dobrzynski, who expected that his Symphony would be placed on one of the programmes, was angry with Chopin for not doing so; a lady acquaintance took it amiss that a box had not been reserved for her, and so on. What troubled our friend most of all, and put him quite out of spirits, was the publication of the sonnet and of the mazurkas; he was afraid that his enemies would not let this opportunity pass, and attack and ridicule him. "I will no longer read what people may now write about me," he bursts out in a fit of lachrymose querulousness. Although pressed from many sides to give a third concert, Chopin decided to postpone it till shortly before his departure, which, however, was farther off than he imagined. Nevertheless, he had already made up his mind what to play—namely, the new Concerto (some parts of which had yet to be composed) and, by desire, the Fantasia and the Variations.

CHAPTER X

1829-1830.

MUSIC IN THE WARSAW SALONS.—MORE ABOUT CHOPIN'S CAUTION.—MUSICAL VISITORS TO THE POLISH CAPITAL: WORLITZER, MDLLE. DE BELLEVILLE, MDLLE. SONTAG, &c.— SOME OF CHOPIN'S ARTISTIC AND OTHER DOINGS; VISIT TO POTURZYN.—HIS LOVE FOR CONSTANTIA GLADKOWSKA.— INTENDED AND FREQUENTLY-POSTPONED DEPARTURE FOR ABROAD; IRRESOLUTION.—THE E MINOR CONCERTO AND HIS THIRD CONCERT IN WARSAW.—DEPARTS AT LAST.

After the turmoil and agitation of the concerts, Chopin resumed the even tenor of his Warsaw life, that is to say, played, composed, and went to parties. Of the latter we get some glimpses in his letters, and they raise in us the suspicion that the salons of Warsaw were not overzealous in the cultivation of the classics. First we have a grand musical soiree at the house of General Filipeus, [F-ootnote: Or Philippeus] the intendant of the Court of the Grand Duke Constantine. There the Swan of Pesaro was evidently in the ascendant, at any rate, a duet from "Semiramide" and a buffo duet from "Il Turco in Italia" (in this Soliva took a part and Chopin accompanied) were the only items of the musical menu thought worth mentioning by the reporter. A soiree at Lewicki's offers matter of more interest. Chopin, who had drawn up the programme, played Hummel's "La Sentinelle" and his Op. 3, the Polonaise for piano and violoncello composed at Antonin with a subsequently-added introduction; and Prince Galitzin was one of the executants of a quartet of Rode's. Occasionally, however, better works were performed. Some months later, for instance, at the celebration of a gentleman's name-day, Spohr's Quintet for piano, flute, clarinet, horn, and bassoon was played. Chopin's criticism on this work is as usual short:—

> Wonderfully beautiful, but not quite suitable for the piano.
> Everything Spohr has written for the piano is very difficult,
> indeed, sometimes it is impossible to find any fingering for
> his passages.

On Easter-day, the great feasting day of the Poles, Chopin was invited to breakfast by the poet Minasowicz. On this occasion he expected to meet Kurpinski; and as in the articles which had appeared in the papers a propos of his concerts the latter and Elsner had been pitted against each other, he wondered what would be the demeanour of his elder fellow-countryman and fellow-composer towards him. Remembering Chopin's repeated injunctions to his parents not to mention to others his remarks on musicians, we may be sure that in this as in every other case Chopin proceeded warily. Here is another striking example of this characteristic and highly-developed cautiousness. After hearing the young pianist Leskiewicz play at a concert he writes:—

> *It seems to me that he will become a better player than*
> *Krogulski; but I have not yet dared to express this opinion,*
> *although I have been often asked to do so.*

In the first half of April, 1830, Chopin was so intent on finishing the compositions he had begun that, greatly as he wished to pay his friend Titus Woyciechowski a visit at his country-seat Poturzyn, he determined to stick to his work. The Diet, which had not been convoked for five years, was to meet on the 28th of May. That there would be a great concourse of lords and lordlings and their families and retinues followed as a matter of course. Here, then, was an excellent opportunity for giving a concert. Chopin, who remembered that the haute voice had not yet heard him, did not overlook it. But be it that the Concerto was not finished in time, or that the circumstances proved less favourable than he had expected, he did not carry out his plan. Perhaps the virtuosos poured in too plentifully. In those days the age of artistic vagrancy had not yet come to an end, and virtuosity concerts were still flourishing most vigorously. Blahetka of Vienna, too, had a notion of coming with his daughter to Warsaw and giving some concerts there during the sitting of the Diet. He wrote to Chopin to this effect, and asked his advice. The latter told him that many musicians and amateurs had indeed often expressed a desire to hear Miss Blahetka, but that the expenses of a concert and the many distinguished artists who had arrived or were about to arrive made the enterprise rather hazardous.

> *Now [says Chopin, the cautious, to his friend] he [Blahetka]*
> *cannot say that I have not sufficiently informed him of the*
> *state of things here! It is not unlikely that he will come. I*
> *should be glad to see them, and would do what I could to*
> *procure a full house for his daughter. I should most*
> *willingly play with her on two pianos, for you cannot imagine*

how kindly an interest this German [Mr. Blahetka] took in me

at Vienna.

Among the artists who came to Warsaw were: the youthful Worlitzer, who, although only sixteen years of age, was already pianist to the King of Prussia; the clever pianist Mdlle. de Belleville, who afterwards became Madame Oury; the great violinist Lipinski, the Polish Paganini; and the celebrated Henrietta Sontag, one of the brightest stars of the time. Chopin's intercourse with these artists and his remarks on them are worth noting: they throw light on his character as a musician and man as well as on theirs. He relates that Worlitzer, a youth of Jewish extraction, and consequently by nature very talented, had called on him and played to him several things famously, especially Moscheles' "Marche d'Alexandre variée." Notwithstanding the admitted excellence of Worlitzer's playing, Chopin adds—not, however, without a "this remains between us two"—that he as yet lacks much to deserve the title of Kammer-Virtuos. Chopin thought more highly of Mdlle. de Belleville, who, he says, "plays the piano beautifully; very airily, very elegantly, and ten times better than Worlitzer." What, we may be sure, in no wise diminished his good opinion of the lady was that she had performed his Variations in Vienna, and could play one of them by heart. To picture the object of Chopin's artistic admiration a little more clearly, let me recall to the reader's memory Schumann's characterisation of Mdlle. de Belleville and Clara Wieck.

> *They should not be compared. They are different mistresses of*
> *different schools. The playing of the Belleville is*
> *technically the finer of the two; Clara's is more*
> *impassioned. The tone of the Belleville caresses, but does*
> *not penetrate beyond the ear; that of Clara reaches the*
> *heart. The one is a poetess; the other is poetry itself.*

Chopin's warmest admiration and longest comments were, however, reserved for Mdlle. Sontag. Having a little more than a year before her visit to Warsaw secretly married Count Rossi, she made at the time we are speaking of her last artistic tour before retiring, at the zenith of her fame and power, into private life. At least, she thought then it was her last tour; but pecuniary losses and tempting offers induced her in 1849 to reappear in public. In Warsaw she gave a first series of five or six concerts in the course of a week, went then by invitation of the King of Prussia to Fischbach, and from there returned to Warsaw. Her concerts were remarkable for their brevity. She usually sang at them four times, and between her performances the orchestra played some pieces. She dispensed altogether with the assistance of other virtuosos. But Chopin remarks that so great was the impression she made as a vocalist and the interest she inspired as an artist that one required some rest after her singing. Here is what the composer writes to his friend about her (June 5, 1830): —

> ...It is impossible for me to describe to you how great a pleasure the
>
> acquaintance with this "God-sent one" (as some enthusiasts justly call her) has given me. Prince Radziwiłł introduced me to her, for which I feel greatly obliged to him. Unfortunately, I profited little by her eight days' stay with us, and I saw how she was bored by dull visits from senators, woyewods, castellans, ministers, generals, and adjutants, who only sat and stared at her while they were talking about quite indifferent things. She receives them all very kindly, for she is so very good-natured that she cannot be unamiable to anyone. Yesterday, when she was going to put on her bonnet previously to going to the rehearsal, she was obliged to lock the door of her room, because the servant in the ante-room could not keep back the large number of callers. I should not have one to her if she had not sent for me, Radziwill having asked me to write out a song which he has arranged for her. This is an Ukraine popular song ("Dumka") with variations. The theme and finale are beautiful, but the middle section does not please me (and it pleases Mdlle. Sontag even less than me). I have indeed made some alterations, but it is still good for nothing. I am glad she leaves after to-day's concert, because I shall pet rid of this business, and when Radziwill comes at the close of the Diet he may perhaps relinquish his variations.
>
> Mdlle. Sontag is not beautiful, but in the highest degree captivating; she enchants all with her voice, which indeed is not very powerful, but magnificently cultivated. Her diminuendo is the non plus ultra that can be heard; her portamento wonderfully fine; her chromatic scales, especially

toward the upper part of her voice, unrivalled. She sang us
an aria by Mercadante, very, very beautifully; the variations
by Rode, especially the last roulades, more than excellently.
The variations on the Swiss theme pleased so much that, after
having several times bowed her acknowledgments for the
applause, she had to sing them da capo. The same thing
happened to her yesterday with the last of Rode's variations.
She has, moreover, performed the cavatina from "Il Barbiere",
as well as several arias from "La Gazza ladra" and from "Der
Freischutz". Well, you will hear for yourself what a
difference there is between her erformances and those we have
hitherto heard here. On one occasion was with her when Soliva
came with the Misses Gladkowska [the idea!] and Wolkaw, who
had to sing to her his duet which concludes with the words
"barbara sorte" —you may perhaps remember it. Miss Sontag
remarked to me, in confidence, that both voices were really
beautiful, but already somewhat worn, and that these ladies
must change their method of singing entirely if they did not
wish to run the risk of losing their voices within two years.
She said, in my presence, to Miss Wolkow that she possessed
much facility and taste, but had une voix trop aigue. She
invited both ladies in the most friendly manner to visit her
more frequently, promising to do all in her power to show and
teach them her own manner of singing. Is this not a quite
unusual politeness? Nay, I even believe it is coquetry so
great that it made upon me the impression of naturalness and
a certain naivete; for it is hardly to be believed that a
human being can be so natural unless it knows all the
resources of coquetry. In her neglige Miss Sontag is a
hundred times more beautiful and pleasing than in full
evening-dress. Nevertheless, those who have not seen her in
the morning are charmed with her appearance at the concert.
On her return she will give concerts up to the 22nd of the
month; then, as she herself told me, she intends to go to St.

> Petersburg. Therefore, be quick, dear friend, and come at
> once, so that you may not miss more than the five concerts
> she has already given.

From the concluding sentence it would appear that Chopin had talked himself out on the subject; this, however, is not the case, for after imparting some other news he resumes thus:—

> But I have not yet told you all about Miss Sontag. She has in
> her rendering some entirely new broderies, with which she
> produces great effect, but not in the same way as Paganini.
> Perhaps the cause lies in this, that hers is a smaller genre.
> She seems to exhale the perfume of a fresh bouquet of flowers
> over the parterre, and, now caresses, now plays with her
> voice; but she rarely moves to tears. Radziwill, on the other
> hand, thinks that she sings and acts the last scene of
> Desdemona in Othello in such a manner that nobody can refrain
> from weeping. To-day I asked her if she would sing us
> sometime this scene in costume (she is said to be an
> excellent actress); she answered me that it was true that she
> had often seen tears in the eyes of the audience, but that
> acting excited her too much, and she had resolved to appear
> as rarely as possible on the stage. You have but to come here
> if you wish to rest from your rustic cares. Miss Sontag will
> sing you something, and you will awake to life again and will
> gather new strength for your labours.

Mdlle. Sontag was indeed a unique artist. In power and fulness of voice, in impassioned expression, in dazzling virtuosity, and in grandeur of style, she might be inferior to Malibran, Catalani, and Pasta; but in clearness and sweetness of voice, in purity of intonation, in airiness, neatness, and elegance of execution, and in exquisiteness of taste, she was unsurpassed. Now, these were qualities particularly congenial to Chopin; he admired them enthusiastically in the eminent vocalist, and appreciated similar qualities in the pleasing pianist Mdlle. de Belleville. Indeed, we shall see in the sequel that unless an artist possessed these qualities Chopin had but little sympathy to bestow upon him. He was, however, not slow to discover in these distinguished lady artists a shortcoming in a direction where he himself was exceedingly strong—namely, in subtlety and intensity of feeling. Chopin's opinion of Mdlle. Sontag coincides on the whole with those of other contemporaries; nevertheless, his account contributes some details which add a page to her biography, and a few touches to her portraiture. It is to be regretted that the arrival of Titus Woyciechowski in Warsaw put for a time an end to Chopin's correspondence with him, otherwise we should, no doubt, have got some more information about Mdlle. Sontag and other artists.

While so many stars were shining, Chopin's light seems to have been under an eclipse. Not only did he not give a concert, but he was even passed over on the occasion of a soiree musicale at court to which all the most distinguished artists then assembled at Warsaw were invited— Mdlle. Sontag, Mdlle. de Belleville, Worlitzer, Kurpinski, &c. "Many were astonished," writes Chopin, "that I was not invited to play, but *I* was not astonished." When the sittings of the Diet and the entertainments that accompanied them came to a close Chopin paid a visit to his friend Titus at Poturzyn, and on his return thence proceeded with his parents to Zelazowa Wola to stay for some time at the Count of Skarbek's. After leaving Poturzyn the picture of his friend's quiet rural life continually rose up in Chopin's mind. A passage in one of his letters which refers to his sojourn there seems to me characteristic of the writer, suggestive of moods consonant with his nocturnes and many cantilene in his other works:—

I must confess that I look back to it with great pleasure; I feel always a certain longing for your beautiful country-seat. The weeping-willow is always present to my mind; that arbaleta! oh, I remember it so fondly! Well, you have teased me so much about it that I am punished thereby for all my sins.

And has he forgotten his ideal? Oh, no! On the contrary, his passion grows stronger every day. This is proved by his frequent allusions to her whom he never names, and by those words of restless yearning and heart-rending despair that cannot be read without exciting a pitiful sympathy. As before long we shall get better acquainted with the lady and hear more of her—she being on the point of leaving the comparative privacy of the Conservatorium for the boards that represent the world—it may be as well to study the symptoms of our friend's interesting malady.

The first mention of the ideal we find in the letter dated October 3, 1829, wherein he says that he has been dreaming of her every night for the past six months, and nevertheless has not yet spoken to her. In these circumstances he stood in need of one to whom he might confide his joys and sorrows, and as no friend of flesh and blood was at hand, he often addressed himself to the piano. And now let us proceed with our investigation.

March 27, 1830.—At no time have I missed you so much as now. I have nobody to whom I can open my heart.

April 17, 1830.—In my unbearable longing I feel better as soon as I receive a letter from you. To-day this comfort was more necessary than ever. I should like to chase away the thoughts that poison my joyousness; but, in spite of all, it is pleasant to play with them. I don't know myself what I want; perhaps I shall be calmer after writing this letter.

Farther on in the same letter he says:—

How often do I take the night for the day, and the day for the night! How often do I live in a dream and sleep during the day, worse than if I slept, for I feel always the same; and instead of finding refreshment in this stupor, as in sleep, I vex and torment myself so that I cannot gain strength.

It may be easily imagined with what interest one so far gone in love watched the debut of Miss Gladkowska as Agnese in Paer's opera of the same name. Of course he sends a full account of the event to his friend. She looked better on the stage than in the salon; left nothing to be desired in her tragic acting; managed her voice excellently up to the high j sharp and g; shaded in a wonderful manner, and charmed her slave when she sang an aria with harp accompaniment. The success of the lady, however, was not merely in her lover's imagination, it was real; for at the close of the opera the audience overwhelmed her with never-ending applause. Another pupil of the Conservatorium, Miss Wolkow, made her debut about the same time, discussions of the comparative merits of the two ladies, on the choice of the parts in which they were going to appear next, on the intrigues which had been set on foot for or against them, &c., were the order of the day. Chopin discusses all these matters with great earnestness and at considerable length; and, while not at all stingy in his praise of Miss Wolkow, he takes good care that Miss Gladkowska does not come off a loser:—

Ernemann is of our opinion [writes Chopin] that no singer can easily be compared to Miss Gladkowska, especially as regards just intonation and genuine warmth of feeling, which manifests itself fully only on the stage, and carries away

the audience. Miss Wolkow made several times slight mistakes,

whereas Miss Gladkowska, although she has only been heard

twice in Agnese, did not allow the least doubtful note to

pass her lips.

The warmer applause given to Miss Wolkow did not disturb so staunch a partisan; he put it to the account of Rossini's music which she sang.

When Chopin comes to the end of his account of Miss Gladkowska's first appearance on the stage, he abruptly asks the question: "And what shall I do now?" and answers forthwith: "I will leave next month; first, however, I must rehearse my Concerto, for the Rondo is now finished." But this resolve is a mere flash of energy, and before we have proceeded far we shall come on words which contrast strangely with what we have read just now. Chopin has been talking about his going abroad ever so long, more especially since his return from Vienna, and will go on talking about it for a long time yet. First he intends to leave Warsaw in the winter of 1829-1830; next he makes up his mind to start in the summer of 1830, the question being only whether he shall go to Berlin or Vienna; then in May, 1830, Berlin is already given up, but the time of his departure remains still to be fixed. After this he is induced by the consideration that the Italian Opera season at Vienna does not begin till September to stay at home during the hot summer months. How he continues to put off the evil day of parting from home and friends we shall see as we go on. I called Chopin's vigorously-expressed resolve a flash of energy. Here is what he wrote not much more than a week after (on August 31, 1830): —

I am still here; indeed, I do not feel inclined to go abroad.

Next month, however, I shall certainly go. Of course, only to

follow my vocation and reason, which latter would be in a

sorry plight if it were not strong enough to master every

other thing in my head.

But that his reason was in a sorry plight may be gathered from a letter dated September 4, 1830, which, moreover, is noteworthy, as in the confessions which it contains are discoverable the key-notes of the principal parts that make up the symphony of his character.

I tell you my ideas become madder and madder every day. I am

still sitting here, and cannot make up my mind to fix

definitively the day of my departure. I have always a

presentiment that I shall leave Warsaw never to return to it;

I am convinced that I shall say farewell to my home for ever.
Oh, how sad it must be to die in any other place but where
one was born! What a great trial it would be to me to see
beside my death-bed an unconcerned physician and paid servant
instead of the dear faces of my relatives! Believe me, Titus,
I many a time should like to go to you and seek rest for my
oppressed heart; but as this is not possible, I often hurry,
without knowing why, into the street. But there also nothing
allays or diverts my longing. I return home to... long again
indescribably... I have not yet rehearsed my Concerto; in any
case I shall leave all my treasures behind me by Michaelmas.
In Vienna I shall be condemned to sigh and groan! This is the
consequence of having no longer a free heart! You who know
this indescribable power so well, explain to me the strange
feeling which makes men always expect from the following day
something better than the preceding day has bestowed upon
them? "Do not be so foolish!" That is all the answer I can
give myself; if you know a better, tell me, pray, pray....

After saying that his plan for the winter is to stay two months in Vienna and pass the rest of the season in Milan, "if it cannot be helped," he makes some remarks of no particular interest, and then comes back to the old and ever new subject, the cud that humanity has been chewing from the time of Adam and Eve, and will have to chew till the extinction of the race, whether pessimism or optimism be the favoured philosophy.

Since my return I have not yet visited her, and must tell you
openly that I often attribute the cause of my distress to
her; it seems to me as if people shared this view, and that
affords me a certain satisfaction. My father smiles at it;
but if he knew all, he would perhaps weep. Indeed, I am
seemingly quite contented, whilst my heart....

This is one of the occasions, which occur so frequently in Chopin's letters, where he breaks suddenly off in the course of his emotional outpourings, and subsides into effective silence. On such occasions one would like to see him go to the piano and hear him finish the sentence there. "All I can write to you now is indeed stupid stuff; only the thought of leaving Warsaw..." Another musical opportunity! Where words fail, there music begins.

Only wait, the day will come when you will not fare any

better. Man is not always happy; sometimes only a few moments

of happiness are granted to him in this life; therefore why

should we shun this rapture which cannot last long?

After this the darkness of sadness shades gradually into brighter hues:—

As on the one hand I consider intercourse with the outer

world a sacred duty, so, on the other hand, I regard it as a

devilish invention, and it would be better if men... but I

have said enough!...

The reader knows already the rest of the letter; it is the passage in which Chopin's love of fun gets the better of his melancholy, his joyous spirits of his sad heart, and where he warns his friend, as it were with a bright twinkle in his tearful eyes and a smile on his face, not to kiss him at that moment, as he must wash himself. This joking about his friend's dislike to osculation is not without an undercurrent of seriousness; indeed, it is virtually a reproach, but a reproach cast in the most delicate form and attired in feminine coquetry.

On September 18, 1830, Chopin is still in Warsaw. Why he is still there he does not know; but he feels unspeakably happy where he is, and his parents make no objections to this procrastination.

To-morrow I shall hold a rehearsal [of the E minor Concerto]

with quartet, and then drive to—whither? Indeed, I do not

feel inclined to go anywhere; but I shall on no account stay

in Warsaw. If you have, perhaps, a suspicion that something

dear to me retains me here, you are mistaken, like many

others. I assure you I should be ready to make any sacrifice

if only my own self were concerned, and I—although I am in

love—had yet to keep my unfortunate feelings concealed in my

bosom for some years to come.

Is it possible to imagine anything more inconsistent and self-delusive than these ravings of our friend? Farther on in this very lengthy epistle we come first of all once more to the pending question.

I was to start with the Cracow post for Vienna as early as

this day week, but finally I have given up that idea—you

will understand why. You may be quite sure that I am no

egoist, but, as I love you, am also willing to sacrifice

anything for the sake of others. For the sake of others, I say, but not for the sake of outward appearance. For public opinion, which is in high esteem among us, but which, you may be sure, does not influence me, goes even so far as to call it a misfortune if one wears a torn coat, a shabby hat, and the like. If I should fail in my career, and have some day nothing to eat, you must appoint me as clerk at Poturzyn. There, in a room above the stables, I shall be as happy as I was last summer in your castle. As long as I am in vigour and health I shall willingly continue to work all my life. I have often considered the question, whether I am really lazy or whether I could work more without overexerting my strength. Joking apart, I have convinced myself that I am not the worst idler, and that I am able to work twice as much if necessity demands it.

It often happens that he who wishes to better the opinion which others have formed of him makes it worse; but, I think, as regards you, I can make it neither better nor worse, even if I occasionally praise myself. The sympathy which I have for you forces your heart to have the same sympathetic feelings for me. You are not master of your thoughts, but I command mine; when I have once taken one into my head I do not let it be taken from me, just as the trees do not let themselves be robbed of their green garment which gives them the charm of youth. With me it will be green in winter also, that is, only in the head, but—God help me—in the heart the greatest ardour, therefore, no one need wonder that the vegetation is so luxuriant. Enough...yours for ever...Only now I notice that I have talked too much nonsense. You see yesterday's impression [he refers to the name-day festivity already mentioned] has not yet quite passed away, I am still sleepy and tired, because I danced too many mazurkas.

Around your letters I twine a little ribbon which my ideal
once gave me. I am glad the two lifeless things, the letters
and the ribbon, agree so well together, probably because,
although they do not know each other, they yet feel that they
both come from a hand dear to me.

Even the most courteous of mortals, unless he be wholly destitute of veracity, will hesitate to deny the truth of Chopin's confession that he has been talking nonsense. But apart from the vagueness and illogicalness of several of the statements, the foregoing effusion is curious as a whole: the thoughts turn up one does not know where, how, or why—their course is quite unaccountable; and if they passed through his mind in an unbroken connection, he fails to give the slightest indication of it. Still, although Chopin's philosophy of life, poetical rhapsodies, and meditations on love and friendship, may not afford us much light, edification, or pleasure, they help us substantially to realise their author's character, and particularly his temporary mood.

Great as was the magnetic power of the ideal over Chopin, great as was the irresolution of the latter, the long delay of his departure must not be attributed solely to these causes. The disturbed state of Europe after the outbreak of the July revolution in Paris had also something to do with this interminable procrastination. Passports could only be had for Prussia and Austria, and even for these countries not by everyone. In France the excitement had not yet subsided, in Italy it was nearing the boiling point. Nor were Vienna, whither Chopin intended to go first, and the Tyrol, through which he would have to pass on his way to Milan, altogether quiet. Chopin's father himself, therefore, wished the journey to be postponed for a short time. Nevertheless, our friend writes on September 22 that he will start in a few weeks: his first goal is Vienna, where, he says, they still remember him, and where he will forge the iron as long as it is hot. But now to the climax of Chopin's amorous fever.

I regret very much [he writes on September 22, 1830] that I
must write to you when, as to-day, I am unable to collect my
thoughts. When I reflect on myself I get into a sad mood, and
am in danger of losing my reason. When I am lost in my
thoughts—which is often the case with me—horses could
trample upon me, and yesterday this nearly happened in the
street without my noticing it. Struck in the church by a
glance of my ideal, I ran in a moment of pleasant stupor into

the street, and it was not till about a quarter of an hour

afterwards that I regained my full consciousness; I am

sometimes so mad that I am frightened at myself.

The melancholy cast of the letters cited in this chapter must not lead us to think that despondence was the invariable state of Chopin's mind. It is more probable that when his heart was saddest he was most disposed to write to his friend his confessions and complaints, as by this means he was enabled to relieve himself to some extent of the burden that oppressed him. At any rate, the agitations of love did not prevent him from cultivating his art, for even at the time when he felt the tyranny of the passion most potently, he mentions having composed "some insignificant pieces," as he modestly expresses himself, meaning, no doubt, "short pieces." Meanwhile Chopin had also finished a composition which by no means belongs to the category of "insignificant pieces"—namely, the Concerto in E minor, the completion of which he announces on August 21, 1830. A critical examination of this and other works will be found in a special chapter, at present I shall speak only of its performance and the circumstances connected with it.

On September 18, 1830, Chopin writes that a few days previously he rehearsed the Concerto with quartet accompaniment, but that it does not quite satisfy him:—

> *Those who were present at the rehearsal say that the Finale*
> *is the most successful movement (probably because it is*
> *easily intelligible). How it will sound with the orchestra I*
> *cannot tell you till next Wednesday, when I shall play the*
> *Concerto for the first time in this guise. To-morrow I shall*
> *have another rehearsal with quartet.*

To a rehearsal with full orchestra, except trumpets and drums (on September 22, 1830), he invited Kurpinski, Soliva, and the select musical world of Warsaw, in whose judgment, however, he professes to have little confidence. Still, he is curious to know how—

> *the Capellmeister [Kurpinski] will look at the Italian*
> *[Soliva], Czapek at Kessler, Filipeus at Dobrzynski, Molsdorf*
> *at Kaczynski, Ledoux at Count Sohyk, and Mr. P. at us all. It*
> *has never before occurred that all these gentlemen have been*
> *assembled in one place; I alone shall succeed in this, and I*
> *do it only out of curiosity!*

The musicians in this company, among whom are Poles, Czechs, Germans, Italians, &c., give us a good idea of the mixed character of the musical world of Warsaw, which was not unlike what the musical world of London is still in our day. From the above remark we see that Chopin had neither much respect nor affection for his fellow-musicians; indeed, there is not the slightest sign in his letters that an intimacy existed between him and any one of them. The rehearsals of the Concerto keep Chopin pretty busy, and his head is full of the composition. In the same letter from which I quoted last we find the following passage:—

> I heartily beg your pardon for my hasty letter of to-day; I
> have still to run quickly to Elsner in order to make sure
> that he will come to the rehearsal. Then I have also to
> provide the desks and mutes, which I had yesterday totally
> forgotten; without the latter the Adagio would be wholly
> insignificant, and its success doubtful. The Rondo is
> effective, the first Allegro vigorous. Cursed self-love! And
> if it is anyone's fault that I am conceited it is yours,
> egoist; he who associates with such a person becomes like
> him. But in one point I am as yet unlike you. I can never
> make up my mind quickly. But I have the firm will and the
> secret intention actually to depart on Saturday week, without
> pardon, and in spite of lamentations, tears, and complaints.
> My music in the trunk, a certain ribbon on my heart, my soul
> full of anxiety: thus into the post-chaise. To be sure,
> everywhere in the town tears will flow in streams: from
> Copernicus to the fountain, from the bank to the column of
> King Sigismund; but I shall be cold and unfeeling as a stone,
> and laugh at all those who wish to take such a heart-rending
> farewell of me!

After the rehearsal of the Concerto with orchestra, which evidently made a good impression upon the much-despised musical world of Warsaw, Chopin resolved to give, or rather his friends resolved for him that he should give, a concert in the theatre on October 11, 1830. Although he is anxious to know what effect his Concerto will produce on the public, he seems little disposed to play at any concert, which may be easily understood if we remember the state of mind he is in.

*You can hardly imagine [he writes] how everything here makes
me impatient, and bores me, in consequence of the commotion
within me against which I cannot struggle.*

The third and last of his Warsaw concerts was to be of a more perfect
type than the two preceding ones; it was to be one "without those unlucky
clarinet and bassoon solos," at that time still so much in vogue. To make
up for this quantitative loss Chopin requested the Misses Gladkowska and
Wolkow to sing some arias, and obtained, not without much trouble, the
requisite permission for them from their master, Soliva, and the Minister
of Public Instruction, Mostowski. It was necessary to ask the latter's
permission, because the two young ladies were educated as singers at the
expense of the State.

The programme of the concert was as follows: —

PART I

1. *Symphony by Gorner.*

2. *First Allegro from the Concerto in E minor, composed and
played by Chopin.*

3. *Aria with Chorus by Soliva, sung by Miss Wolkow.*

4. *Adagio and Rondo from the Concerto in E minor, composed
and played by Chopin.*

PART II

1. *Overture to "Guillaume Tell" by Rossini.*

2. *Cavatina from "La Donna del lago" by Rossini, sung by Miss
Gladkowska.*

3. *Fantasia on Polish airs, composed and played by Chopin.*

The success of the concert made Chopin forget his sorrows. There is
not one complaint in the letter in which he gives an account of it; in fact,
he seems to have been enjoying real halcyon days. He had a full house, but
played with as little nervousness as if he had been playing at home. The first
Allegro of the Concerto went very smoothly, and the audience rewarded
him with thundering applause. Of the reception of the Adagio and Rondo

we learn nothing except that in the pause between the first and second parts the connoisseurs and amateurs came on the stage, and complimented him in the most flattering terms on his playing. The great success, however, of the evening was his performance of the Fantasia on Polish airs. "This time I understood myself, the orchestra understood me, and the audience understood us." This is quite in the bulletin style of conquerors; it has a ring of "veni, vidi, vici" about it. Especially the mazurka at the end of the piece produced a great effect, and Chopin was called back so enthusiastically that he was obliged to bow his acknowledgments four times. Respecting the bowing he says: "I believe I did it yesterday with a certain grace, for Brandt had taught me how to do it properly." In short, the concert-giver was in the best of spirits, one is every moment expecting him to exclaim: "Seid umschlungen Millionen, diesen Kuss der ganzen Welt." He is pleased with himself and Streicher's piano on which he had played; pleased with Soliva, who kept both soloist and orchestra splendidly in order; pleased with the impression the execution of the overture made; pleased with the blue-robed, fay-like Miss Wolkow; pleased most of all with Miss Gladkowska, who "wore a white dress and roses in her hair, and was charmingly beautiful." He tells his friend that:

> she never sang so well as on that evening (except the aria in
> "Agnese"). You know "O! quante lagrime per te versai." The
> tutto detesto down to the lower b came out so magnificently
> that Zielinski declared this b alone was worth a thousand
> ducats.

In Vienna the score and parts of the Krakowiak had been found to be full of mistakes, it was the same with the Concerto in Warsaw. Chopin himself says that if Soliva had not taken the score with him in order to correct it, he (Chopin) did not know what might have become of the Concerto on the evening of the concert. Carl Mikuli, who, as well as his fellow-pupil Tellefsen, copied many of Chopin's MSS., says that they were full of slips of the pen, such as wrong notes and signatures, omissions of accidentals, dots, and intervals of chords, and incorrect markings of slurs and 8va's.

Although Chopin wrote on October 5, 1830, that eight days after the concert he would certainly be no longer in Warsaw, that his trunk was bought, his whole outfit ready, the scores corrected, the pocket-handkerchiefs hemmed, the new trousers and the new dress-coat tried on, &c., that, in fact, nothing remained to be done but the worst of all, the leave-taking, yet it was not till the 1st of November, 1830, that he actually did take his departure. Elsner and a number of friends accompanied him to Wola, the first village beyond Warsaw. There the pupils of the Conservatorium awaited them, and sang a cantata composed by Elsner for the occasion. After this the friends once more sat down together to a banquet which had been prepared for them. In the course of the repast a silver goblet filled with Polish earth was presented to Chopin in the name of all.

May you never forget your country [said the speaker,

according to Karasowski], wherever you may wander or sojourn,

may you never cease to love it with a warm, faithful heart!

Remember Poland, remember your friends, who call you with

pride their fellow-countryman, who expect great things of

you, whose wishes and prayers accompany you!

How fully Chopin realised their wishes and expectations the sequel will show: how much such loving words must have affected him the reader of this chapter can have no difficulty in understanding. But now came pitilessly the dread hour of parting. A last farewell is taken, the carriage rolls away, and the traveller has left behind him all that is dearest to him— parents, sisters, sweetheart, and friends. "I have always a presentiment that I am leaving Warsaw never to return to it; I am convinced that I shall say an eternal farewell to my native country." Thus, indeed, destiny willed it. Chopin was never to tread again the beloved soil of Poland, never to set eyes again on Warsaw and its Conservatorium, the column of King Sigismund opposite, the neighbouring church of the Bernardines (Constantia's place of worship), and all those things and places associated in his mind with the sweet memories of his youth and early manhood.

CHAPTER XI

CHOPIN IS JOINED AT KALISZ BY TITUS WOYCIECHOWSKI.—FOUR DAYS AT BRESLAU: HIS VISITS TO THE THEATRE; CAPELLMEISTER SCHNABEL; PLAYS AT A CONCERT; ADOLF HESSE.—SECOND VISIT TO DRESDEN: MUSIC AT THEATRE AND CHURCH; GERMAN AND POLISH SOCIETY; MORLACCHI, SIGNORA PALAZZESI, RASTRELLI, ROLLA, DOTZAUER, KUMMER, KLENGEL, AND OTHER MUSICIANS; A CONCERT TALKED ABOUT BUT NOT GIVEN; SIGHT-SEEING.— AFTER A WEEK, BY PRAGUE TO VIENNA.—ARRIVES AT VIENNA TOWARDS THE END OF NOVEMBER, 1830.

Thanks to Chopin's extant letters to his family and friends it is not difficult to give, with the help of some knowledge of the contemporary artists and of the state of music in the towns he visited, a pretty clear account of his experiences and mode of life during the nine or ten months which intervene between his departure from Warsaw and his arrival in Paris. Without the letters this would have been impossible, and for two reasons: one of them is that, although already a notable man, Chopin was not yet a noted man; and the other, that those with whom he then associated have, like himself, passed away from among us.

Chopin, who, as the reader will remember, left Warsaw on November 1, 1830, was joined at Kalisz by Titus Woyciechowski. Thence the two friends travelled together to Vienna. They made their first halt at Breslau, which they reached on November 6. No sooner had Chopin put up at the hotel Zur goldenen Gans, changed his dress, and taken some refreshments, than he rushed off to the theatre. During his stay in Breslau he was present at three performances—at Raimund's fantastical comedy "Der Alpenkonig und der Menschenfeind", Auber's "Maurer und Schlosser (Le Macon)," and Winter's "Das unterbrochene Opferfest", a now superannuated but then still popular opera. The players succeeded better than the singers in gaining the approval of their fastidious auditor, which indeed might have been expected. As both Chopin and Woyciechowski were provided with letters of introduction, and the gentlemen to whom they were addressed did all in their power to make their visitors' sojourn as pleasant as possible, the friends spent in Breslau four happy days. It is characteristic of the German musical life in those days that in the Ressource, a society of that town, they had three weekly concerts at which the greater number of the performers were amateurs. Capellmeister Schnabel, an old acquaintance of Chopin's, had invited the latter to come to a morning rehearsal. When Chopin entered, an amateur, a young barrister, was going to rehearse Moscheles' E flat major Concerto. Schnabel, on seeing the newcomer, asked him to try the piano. Chopin sat down and played some variations which astonished and delighted the Capellmeister, who had not heard him for four years, so much that he overwhelmed him with expressions of admiration. As the poor amateur began to feel nervous, Chopin was pressed on all sides to take that gentleman's place in the evening. Although he had not practised for some weeks he consented, drove to the hotel, fetched the requisite music, rehearsed, and in the evening performed the Romanza and Rondo of his E minor Concerto and an improvisation on a theme from Auber's "La Muette" ("Masaniello"). At the rehearsal the "Germans" admired his playing; some of them he heard whispering "What a light touch he has!" but not a word was said about the composition. The amateurs did not know whether it was good or bad. Titus Woyciechowski heard one of them say "No doubt he can play, but he can't compose." There was, however, one gentleman who praised the novelty of the form, and the composer naively declares that this was the person who understood him best. Speaking of the professional musicians, Chopin remarks that, with the exception of Schnabel, "the Germans" were at a loss what to think of him. The Polish peasants use the word "German" as an invective, believe that the devil speaks German and dresses in the German fashion, and refuse to take medicine because they hold it to be an invention of the Germans and, consequently, unfit for Christians. Although Chopin does not go so far, he is by no means free from this national antipathy. Let his susceptibility be ruffled by Germans, and you may be sure he will remember their nationality. Besides old Schnabel there was among the persons whose acquaintance Chopin made at Breslau only one other who interests us, and interests us more than that respectable composer of church music; and this one was the organist and composer Adolph Frederick Hesse, then a young man of Chopin's age. Before long the latter became better acquainted with him. In his account of his stay and playing in the Silesian capital, he says of him only that "the second local connoisseur, Hesse, who has travelled through the whole of Germany, paid me also compliments."

Chopin continued his journey on November 10, and on November 12 had already plunged into Dresden life. Two features of this, in some respects quite unique, life cannot but have been particularly attractive to our traveller—namely, its Polish colony and the Italian opera. The former owed its origin to the connection of the house of Saxony with the crown of Poland; and the latter, which had been patronised by the Electors and Kings for hundreds of years, was not disbanded till 1832. In 1817, it is true, Weber, who had received a call for that purpose, founded a German opera at Dresden, but the Italian opera retained the favour of the Court and of a great part of the public, in fact, was the spoiled child that looked down upon her younger sister, poor Cinderella. Even a Weber had to fight hard to keep his own, indeed, sometimes failed to do so, in the rivalry with the ornatissimo Signore Cavaliere Morlacchi, primo maestro della capella Reale.

Chopin's first visit was to Miss Pechwell, through whom he got admission to a soiree at the house of Dr. Kreyssig, where she was going to play and the prima donna of the Italian opera to sing. Having carefully dressed, Chopin made his way to Dr. Kreyssig's in a sedan-chair. Being unaccustomed to this kind of conveyance he had a desire to kick out the bottom of the "curious but comfortable box," a temptation which he, however—to his honour be it recorded—resisted. On entering the salon he found there a great number of ladies sitting round eight large tables:—

> No sparkling of diamonds met my eye, but the more modest glitter of a host of steel knitting-needles, which moved ceaselessly in the busy hands of these ladies. The number of ladies and knitting-needles was so large that if the ladies had planned an attack upon the gentlemen that were present, the latter would have been in a sorry plight. Nothing would have been left to them but to make use of their spectacles as weapons, for there was as little lack of eye-glasses as of bald heads.

The clicking of knitting-needles and the rattling of teacups were suddenly interrupted by the overture to the opera "Fra Diavolo," which was being played in an adjoining room. After the overture Signora Palazzesi sang "with a bell-like, magnificent voice, and great bravura." Chopin asked to be introduced to her. He made likewise the acquaintance of the old composer and conductor Vincent Rastrelli, who introduced him to a brother of the celebrated tenor Rubini.

At the Roman Catholic church, the Court Church, Chopin met Morlacchi, and heard a mass by that excellent artist. The Neapolitan sopranists Sassaroli and Tarquinio sang, and the "incomparable Rolla" played the solo violin. On another occasion he heard a clever but dry mass by Baron von Miltitz, which was performed under the direction of Morlacchi, and in which the celebrated violoncello virtuosos Dotzauer and Kummer played their solos beautifully, and the voices of Sassaroli, Muschetti, Babnigg, and Zezi were heard to advantage. The theatre was, as usual, assiduously frequented by Chopin. After the above-mentioned soiree he hastened to hear at least the last act of "Die Stumme von Portici" ("Masaniello"). Of the performance of Rossini's "Tancredi," which he witnessed on another evening, he praised only the wonderful violin playing of Rolla and the singing of Mdlle. Hahnel, a lady from the Vienna Court Theatre. Rossini's "La Donna del lago," in Italian, is mentioned among the operas about to be performed. What a strange anomaly, that in the year 1830 a state of matters such as is indicated by these names and facts could still obtain in Dresden, one of the capitals of musical Germany! It is emphatically a curiosity of history.

Chopin, who came to Rolla with a letter of introduction from Soliva, was received by the Italian violinist with great friendliness. Indeed, kindness was showered upon him from all sides. Rubini promised him a letter of introduction to his brother in Milan, Rolla one to the director of the opera there, and Princess Augusta, the daughter of the late king, and Princess Maximiliana, the sister-in-law of the reigning king, provided him with letters for the Queen of Naples, the Duchess of Lucca, the Vice-Queen of Milan, and Princess Ulasino in Rome. He had met the princesses and played to them at the house of the Countess Dobrzycka, Oberhofmeisterin of the Princess Augusta, daughter of the late king, Frederick Augustus.

The name of the Oberhofmeisterin brings us to the Polish society of Dresden, into which Chopin seems to have found his way at once. Already two days after his arrival he writes of a party of Poles with whom he had dined. At the house of Mdme. Pruszak he made the acquaintance of no less a person than General Kniaziewicz, who took part in the defence of Warsaw, commanded the left wing in the battle of Maciejowice (1794), and joined Napoleon's Polish legion in 1796. Chopin wrote home: "I have pleased him very much; he said that no pianist had made so agreeable an impression on him."

To judge from the tone of Chopin's letters, none of all the people he came in contact with gained his affection in so high a degree as did Klengel, whom he calls "my dear Klengel," and of whom he says that he esteems him very highly, and loves him as if he had known him from his earliest youth. "I like to converse with him, for from him something is to be learned." The great contrapuntist seems to have reciprocated this affection, at any rate he took a great interest in his young friend, wished to see the scores of his concertos, went without Chopin's knowledge to Morlacchi and to the intendant of the theatre to try if a concert could not be arranged within four days, told him that his playing reminded him of Field's, that his touch was of a peculiar kind, and that he had not expected to find him such a virtuoso.

Although Chopin replied, when Klengel advised him to give a concert, that his stay in Dresden was too short to admit of his doing so, and thought himself that he could earn there neither much fame nor much money, he nevertheless was not a little pleased that this excellent artist had taken some trouble in attempting to smooth the way for a concert, and to hear from him that this had been done not for Chopin's but for Dresden's sake; our friend, be it noted, was by no means callous to flattery. Klengel took him also to a soiree at the house of Madame Niesiolawska, a Polish lady, and at supper proposed his health, which was drunk in champagne.

There is a passage in one of Chopin's letters which I must quote; it tells us something of his artistic taste outside his own art: —

> *The Green Vault I saw last time I was here, and once is*
>
> *enough for me; but I revisited with great interest the*
>
> *picture gallery. If I lived here I would go to it every week,*
>
> *for there are pictures in it at the sight of which I imagine*
>
> *I hear music.*

Thus our friend spent a week right pleasantly and not altogether unprofitably in the Saxon Athens, and spent it so busily that what with visits, dinners, soirees, operas, and other amusements, he leaving his hotel early in the morning and returning late at night, it passed away he did not know how.

Chopin, who made also a short stay in Prague—of which visit, however, we have no account—arrived in Vienna in the latter part of November, 1830. His intention was to give some concerts, and to proceed in a month or two to Italy. How the execution of this plan was prevented by various circumstances we shall see presently. Chopin flattered himself with the belief that managers, publishers, artists, and the public in general were impatiently awaiting his coming, and ready to receive him with open arms. This, however, was an illusion. He overrated his success. His playing at the two "Academies" in the dead season must have remained unnoticed by many, and was probably forgotten by not a few who did notice it. To talk, therefore, about forging the iron while it was hot proved a misconception of the actual state of matters. It is true his playing and compositions had made a certain impression, especially upon some of the musicians who had heard him. But artists, even when free from hostile jealousy, are far too much occupied with their own interests to be helpful in pushing on their younger brethren. As to publishers and managers, they care only for marketable articles, and until an article has got a reputation its marketable value is very small. Nine hundred and ninety-nine out of a thousand judge by names and not by intrinsic worth. Suppose a hitherto unknown statue of Phidias, a painting of Raphael, a symphony of Beethoven, were discovered and introduced to the public as the works of unknown living artists, do you think they would receive the same universal admiration as the known works of the immortal masters? Not at all! By a very large majority of the connoisseurs and pretended connoisseurs they would be criticised, depreciated, or ignored. Let, however, the real names of the authors become known, and the whole world will forthwith be thrown into ecstasy, and see in them even more beauties than they really possess. Well, the first business of an artist, then, is to make himself a reputation, and a reputation is not made by one or two successes. A first success, be it ever so great, and achieved under ever so favourable circumstances, is at best but the thin end of the wedge which has been got in, but which has to be driven home with much vigour and perseverance before the work is done. "Art is a fight, not a pleasure-trip," said the French painter Millet, one who had learnt the lesson in the severe school of experience. Unfortunately for Chopin, he had neither the stuff nor the stomach for fighting. He shrank back at the slightest touch like a sensitive plant. He could only thrive in the sunshine of prosperity and protected against all those inimical influences and obstacles that cause hardier natures to put forth their strength, and indeed are necessary for the full unfolding of all their capabilities. Chopin and Titus Woyciechowski put up at the hotel Stadt London, but, finding the charges too high, they decamped and stayed at the hotel Goldenes Lamm till the lodgings which they had taken were evacuated by the English admiral then in possession of them. From Chopin's first letter after his arrival in the Austrian capital his parents had the satisfaction of learning that their son was in excellent spirits, and that his appetite left nothing to be desired, especially when sharpened by good news from home. In his perambulations he took particular note of the charming Viennese girls, and at the Wilde Mann, where he was in the habit of dining, he enjoyed immensely a dish of Strudeln. The only drawback to the blissfulness of his then existence was a swollen nose, caused by the change of air, a circumstance which interfered somewhat with his visiting operations. He was generally well received by those on whom he called with letters of introduction. In one of the two exceptional cases he let it be understood that, having a letter of introduction from the Grand Duke Constantine to the Russian Ambassador, he was not so insignificant a person as to require the patronage of a banker; and in the other case he comforted himself with the thought that a time would come when things would be changed.

In the letter above alluded to (December 1, 1830) Chopin speaks of one of the projected concerts as if it were to take place shortly; that is to say, he is confident that, such being his pleasure, this will be the natural course of events. His Warsaw acquaintance Orlowski, the perpetrator of mazurkas on his concerto themes, was accompanying the violinist Lafont on a concert-tour. Chopin does not envy him the honour: —

> Will the time come [he writes] when Lafont will accompany me?
>
> Does this question sound arrogant? But, God willing, this may
>
> come to pass some day.

Wurfel has conversations with him about the arrangements for a concert, and Graff, the pianoforte-maker, advises him to give it in the Landstandische Saal, the finest and most convenient hall in Vienna. Chopin even asks his people which of his Concertos he should play, the one in F or the one in E minor. But disappointments were not long in coming. One of his first visits was to Haslinger, the publisher of the Variations on "La ci darem la mano," to whom he had sent also a sonata and another set of variations. Haslinger received him very kindly, but would print neither the one nor the other work. No wonder the composer thought the cunning publisher wished to induce him in a polite and artful way to let him have his compositions gratis. For had not Wurfel told him that his Concerto in F minor was better than Hummel's in A flat, which Haslinger had just published, and had not Klengel at Dresden been surprised to hear that he had received no payment for the Variations? But Chopin will make Haslinger repent of it. "Perhaps he thinks that if he treats my compositions somewhat en bagatelle, I shall be glad if only he prints them; but henceforth nothing will be got from me gratis; my motto will be 'Pay, animal!'" But evidently the animal wouldn't pay, and in fact did not print the compositions till after Chopin's death. So, unless the firm of Haslinger mentioned that he will call on him as soon as he has a room wherein he can receive a visit in return, the name of Lachner does not reappear in the correspondence.

In the management of the Karnthnerthor Theatre, Louis Duport had succeeded, on September 1, 1830, Count Gallenberg, whom severe losses obliged to relinquish a ten years' contract after the lapse of less than two years. Chopin was introduced to the new manager by Hummel.

> He (Duport) [writes Chopin on December 21 to his parents] was
>
> formerly a celebrated dancer, and is said to be very
>
> niggardly; however, he received me in an extremely polite
>
> manner, for perhaps he thinks I shall play for him gratis. He
>
> is mistaken there! We entered into a kind of negotiation, but
>
> nothing definite was settled. If Mr. Duport offers me too
>
> little, I shall give my concert in the large Redoutensaal.

But the niggardly manager offered him nothing at all, and Chopin did not give a concert either in the Redoutensaal or elsewhere, at least not for a long time. Chopin's last-quoted remark is difficult to reconcile with what he tells his friend Matuszyriski four days later: "I have no longer any thought of giving a concert." In a letter to Elsner, dated January 26, 1831, he writes:—

I meet now with obstacles on all sides. Not only does a series of the most miserable pianoforte concerts totally ruin all true music and make the public suspicious, but the occurrences in Poland have also acted unfavourably upon my position. Nevertheless, I intend to have during the carnival a performance of my first Concerto, which has met with Wurfel's full approval.

It would, however, be a great mistake to ascribe the failure of Chopin's projects solely to the adverse circumstances pointed out by him. The chief causes lay in himself. They were his want of energy and of decision, constitutional defects which were of course intensified by the disappointment of finding indifference and obstruction where he expected enthusiasm and furtherance, and by the outbreak of the revolution in Poland (November 30, 1830), which made him tremble for the safety of his beloved ones and the future of his country. In the letter from which I have last quoted Chopin, after remarking that he had postponed writing till he should be able to report some definite arrangement, proceeds to say:—

But from the day that I heard of the dreadful occurrences in our fatherland, my thoughts have been occupied only with anxiety and longing for it and my dear ones. Malfatti gives himself useless trouble in trying to convince me that the artist is, or ought to be, a cosmopolitan. And, supposing this were really the case, as an artist I am still in the cradle, but as a Pole already a man. I hope, therefore, that you will not be offended with me for not yet having seriously thought of making arrangements for a concert.

What affected Chopin most and made him feel lonely was the departure of his friend Woyciechowski, who on the first news of the insurrection returned to Poland and joined the insurgents. Chopin wished to do the same, but his parents advised him to stay where he was, telling him that he was not strong enough to bear the fatigues and hardships of a soldier's life. Nevertheless, when Woyciechowski was gone an irresistible homesickness seized him, and, taking post-horses, he tried to overtake his friend and go with him. But after following him for some stages without making up to him, his resolution broke down, and he returned to Vienna. Chopin's characteristic irresolution shows itself again at this time very strikingly, indeed, his letters are full of expressions indicating and even confessing it. On December 21, 1830, he writes to his parents:—

I do not know whether I ought to go soon to Italy or wait a
little longer? Please, dearest papa, let me know your and the
best mother's will in this matter.

And four days afterwards he writes to Matuszynski:—

You know, of course, that 1 have letters from the Royal Court
of Saxony to the Vice-Queen in Milan, but what shall I do? My
parents leave me to choose; I wish they would give me
instructions. Shall I go to Paris? My acquaintances here
advise me to wait a little longer. Shall I return home? Shall
I stay here? Shall I kill myself? Shall I not write to you
any more?

Chopin's dearest wish was to be at home again. "How I should like to be in Warsaw!" he writes. But the fulfilment of this wish was out of the question, being against the desire of his parents, of whom especially the mother seems to have been glad that he did not execute his project of coming home.

I would not like to be a burden to my father; were it not for
this fear I should return home at once. I am often in such a
mood that I curse the moment of my departure from my sweet
home! You will understand my situation, and that since the
departure of Titus too much has fallen upon me all at once.

The question whether he should go to Italy or to France was soon decided for him, for the suppressed but constantly-increasing commotion which had agitated the former country ever since the July revolution at last vented itself in a series of insurrections. Modena began on February 3,1831, Bologna, Ancona, Parma, and Rome followed. While the "where to go" was thus settled, the "when to go" remained an open question for many months to come. Meanwhile let us try to look a little deeper into the inner and outer life which Chopin lived at Vienna.

The biographical details of this period of Chopin's life have to be drawn almost wholly from his letters. These, however, must be judiciously used.

Those addressed to his parents, important as they are, are only valuable with regard to the composer's outward life, and even as vehicles of such facts they are not altogether trustworthy, for it is always his endeavour to make his parents believe that he is well and cheery. Thus he writes, for instance, to his friend Matuszyriski, after pouring forth complaint after complaint:—"Tell my parents that I am very happy, that I am in want of nothing, that I amuse myself famously, and never feel lonely." Indeed, the Spectator's opinion that nothing discovers the true temper of a person so much as his letters, requires a good deal of limitation and qualification. Johnson's ideas on the same subject may be recommended as a corrective. He held that there was no transaction which offered stronger temptations to fallacy and sophistication than epistolary intercourse:—

> In the eagerness of conversation the first emotions of the
> mind burst out before they are considered. In the tumult of
> business, interest and passion have their genuine effect; but
> a friendly letter is a calm and deliberate performance in the
> cool of leisure, in the stillness of solitude, and surely no
> man sits down by design to depreciate his own character.
> Friendship has no tendency to secure veracity; for by whom
> can a man so much wish to be thought better than he is, as by
> him whose kindness he desires to gain or keep?

These one-sided statements are open to much criticism, and would make an excellent theme for an essay. Here, however, we must content ourselves with simply pointing out that letters are not always calm and deliberate performances, but exhibit often the eagerness of conversation and the impulsiveness of passion. In Chopin's correspondence we find this not unfrequently exemplified. But to see it we must not turn to the letters addressed to his parents, to his master, and to his acquaintances—there we find little of the real man and his deeper feelings—but to those addressed to his bosom-friends, and among them there are none in which he shows himself more openly than in the two which he wrote on December 25, 1830, and January 1, 1831, to John Matuszynski. These letters are, indeed, such wonderful revelations of their writer's character that I should fail in my duty as his biographer were I to neglect to place before the reader copious extracts from them, in short, all those passages which throw light on the inner working of this interesting personality.

> Dec. 25, 1830.—I longed indescribably for your letter; you
> know why. How happy news of my angel of peace always makes

me! How I should like to touch all the strings which not only call up stormy feelings, but also awaken again the songs whose half-dying echo is still flitting on the banks of the Danube-songs which the warriors of King John Sobieski sang!

You advised me to choose a poet. But you know I am an undecided being, and succeeded only once in my life in making a good choice.

The many dinners, soirees, concerts, and balls which I have to go to only bore me. I am sad, and feel so lonely and forsaken here. But I cannot live as I would! I must dress, appear with a cheerful countenance in the salons; but when I am again in my room I give vent to my feelings on the piano, to which, as my best friend in Vienna, I disclose all my sufferings. I have not a soul to whom I can fully unbosom myself, and yet I must meet everyone like a friend. There are, indeed, people here who seem to love me, take my portrait, seek my society; but they do not make up for the want of you [his friends and relations]. I lack inward peace, I am at rest only when I read your [his friends' and relations'] letters, and picture to myself the statue of King Sigismund, or gaze at the ring [Constantia's], that dear jewel. Forgive me, dear Johnnie, for complaining so much to you; but my heart grows lighter when I speak to you thus. To you I have indeed always told all that affected me. Did you receive my little note the day before yesterday? Perhaps you don't care much for my scribbling, for you are at home; but I read and read your letters again and again.

Dr. Freyer has called on me several times; he had learned from Schuch that I was in Vienna. He told me a great deal of interesting news, and enjoyed your letter, which I read to him up to a certain passage. This passage has made me very

sad. Is she really so much changed in appearance? Perhaps she
was ill? One could easily fancy her being so, as she has a
very sensitive disposition. Perhaps she only appeared so to
you, or was she afraid of anything? God forbid that she
should suffer in any way on my account. Set her mind at rest,
and tell her that as long as my heart beats I shall not cease
to adore her. Tell her that even after my death my ashes
shall be strewn under her feet. Still, all this is yet too
little, and you might tell her a great deal more.

I shall write to her myself; indeed, I would have done so
long ago to free myself from my torments; but if my letter
should fall into strange hands, might this not hurt her
reputation? Therefore, dear friend, be you the interpreter
of my feelings; speak for me, "et j'en conviendrai." These
French words of yours flashed through me like lightning. A
Viennese gentleman who walked beside me in the street when I
was reading your letter, seized me by the arm, and was hardly
able to hold me. He did not know what had happened to me. I
should have liked to embrace and kiss all the passers-by, and
I felt happier than I had done for a long time, for I had
received the first letter from you. Perhaps I weary you,
Johnnie, with my passionateness; but it is difficult for me
to conceal from you anything that moves my heart.

The day before yesterday I dined at Madame Beyer's, her name
is likewise Constantia. I like her society, her having that
indescribably dear Christian name is sufficient to account
for my partiality; it gives me even pleasure when one of her
pocket-handkerchiefs or napkins marked "Constantia" comes
into my hands.

I walked alone, and slowly, into St. Stephen's. The church
was as yet empty. To view the noble, magnificent edifice in a

truly devout spirit I leant against a pillar in the darkest
corner of this house of God. The grandeur of the arched roof
cannot be described, one must see St. Stephen's with one's
own eyes. Around me reigned the profoundest silence, which
was interrupted only by the echoing footsteps of the
sacristan who came to light the candles. Behind me was a
grave, before me a grave, only above me I saw none. At that
moment I felt my loneliness and isolation. When the lights
were burning and the Cathedral began to fill with people, I
wrapped myself up more closely in my cloak (you know the way
in which I used to walk through the suburb of Cracow), and
hastened to be present at the Mass in the Imperial Court
Chapel. Now, however, I walked no longer alone, but passed
through the beautiful streets of Vienna in merry company to
the Hofburg, where I heard three movements of a mass
performed by sleepy musicians. At one o'clock in the morning
I reached my lodgings. I dreamt of you, of her, and of my
dear children [his sisters].

The first thing I did to-day was to indulge myself in
melancholy fantasias on my piano.

Advise me what to do. Please ask the person who has always
exercised so powerful an influence over me in Warsaw, and let
me know her opinion; according to that I shall act.

Let me hear once more from you before you take the field.
Vienna, poste restante. Go and see my parents and Constantia.
Visit my sisters often, as long as you are still in Warsaw,
so that they may think that you are coming to me, and that I
am in the other room. Sit down beside them that they may
imagine I am there too; in one word, be my substitute in the
house of my parents.

I shall conclude, dear Johnnie, for now it is really time. Embrace all my dear colleagues for me, and believe that I shall not cease to love you until I cease to love those that are dearest to me, my parents and her.

My dearest friend, do write me soon a few lines. You may even show her this letter, if you think fit to do so.

My parents don't know that I write to you. You may tell them of it, but must by no means show them the letter. I cannot yet take leave of my Johnnie; but I shall be off presently, you naughty one! If W...loves you as heartily as I love you, then would Con...No, I cannot complete the name, my hand is too unworthy. Ah! I could tear out my hair when I think that I could be forgotten by her!

My portrait, of which only you and I are to know, is a very good likeness; if you think it would give her pleasure, I would send it to her through Schuch.

January 1, 1831.—There you have what you wanted! Have you received the letter? Have you delivered any of the messages it contained? To-day I still regret what I have done. I was full of sweet hopes, and now am tormented by anxiety and doubts. Perhaps she mocks at me—laughs at me? Perhaps—ah! does she love me? This is what my passionate heart asks. You wicked AEsculapius, you were at the theatre, you eyed her incessantly with your opera-glass; if this is the case a thunderbolt shall...Do not forfeit my confidence; oh, you! if I write to you I do so only for my own sake, for you do not deserve it.

Just now when I am writing I am in a strange state; I feel as if I were with you [with his dear ones], and were only

dreaming what I see and hear here. The voices which I hear
around me, and to which my ear is not accustomed, make upon
me for the most part only an impression like the rattling of
carriages or any other indifferent noise. Only your voice or
that of Titus could to-day wake me out of my torpor. Life and
death are perfectly alike to me. Tell, however, my parents
that I am very happy, that I am in want of nothing, that I
amuse myself famously, and never feel lonely.

If she mocks at me, tell her the same; but if she inquires
kindly for me, shows some concern about me, whisper to her
that she may make her mind easy; but add also that away from
her I feel everywhere lonely and unhappy. I am unwell, but
this I do not write to my parents. Everybody asks what is the
matter with me. I should like to answer that I have lost my
good spirits. However, you know best what troubles me!
Although there is no lack of entertainment and diversion
here, I rarely feel inclined for amusement.

To-day is the first of January. Oh, how sadly this year
begins for me! I love you [his friends] above all things.
Write as soon as possible. Is she at Radom? Have you thrown
up redoubts? My poor parents! How are my friends faring?

I could die for you, for you all! Why am I doomed to be here
so lonely and forsaken? You can at least open your hearts to
each other and comfort each other. Your flute will have
enough to lament! How much more will my piano have to weep!

You write that you and your regiment are going to take the
field; how will you forward the note? Be sure you do not send
it by a messenger; be cautious! The parents might perhaps—
they might perhaps view the matter in a false light.

I embrace you once more. You are going to the war; return as
a colonel. May all pass off well! Why may I not at least be
your drummer?

Forgive the disorder in my letter, I write as if I were
intoxicated.

The disorder of the letters is indeed very striking; it is great in the
foregoing extracts, and of course ten times greater with the interspersed
descriptions, bits of news, and criticisms on music and musicians. I
preferred separating the fundamental and always-recurring thoughts,
the all-absorbing and predominating feelings, from the more superficial
and passing fancies and affections, and all those matters which were to
him, if not of total indifference, at least of comparatively little moment;
because such a separation enables us to gain a clearer and fuller view of
the inner man and to judge henceforth his actions and works with some
degree of certainty, even where his own accounts and comments and
those of trustworthy witnesses fail us. The psychological student need not
be told to take note of the disorder in these two letters and of their length
(written to the same person within less than a week, they fill nearly twelve
printed pages in Karasowski's book), he will not be found neglecting such
important indications of the temporary mood and the character of which it
is a manifestation. And now let us take a glance at Chopin's outward life in
Vienna.

I have already stated that Chopin and Woyciechowski lived together.
Their lodgings, for which they had to pay their landlady, a baroness, fifty
florins, were on the third story of a house in the Kohlmarkt, and consisted
of three elegant rooms. When his friend left, Chopin thought the rent too
high for his purse, and as an English family was willing to pay as much
as eighty florins, he sublet the rooms and removed to the fourth story,
where he found in the Baroness von Lachmanowicz an agreeable young
landlady, and had equally roomy apartments which cost him only twenty
florins and pleased him quite well. The house was favourably situated,
Mechetti being on the right, Artaria on the left, and the opera behind; and
as people were not deterred by the high stairs from visiting him, not even
old Count Hussarzewski, and a good profit would accrue to him from those
eighty florins, he could afford to laugh at theprobable dismay of his friends
picturing him as "a poor devil living in a garret," and could do so the more
heartily as there was in reality another story between him and the roof. He
gives his people a very pretty description of his lodgings and mode of life:—

I live on the fourth story, in a fine street, but I have to
strain my eyes in looking out of the window when I wish to
see what is going on beneath. You will find my room in my new
album when I am at home again. Young Hummel [a son of the
composer] is so kind as to draw it for me. It is large and
has five windows; the bed is opposite to them. My wonderful
piano stands on the right, the sofa on the left; between the
windows there is a mirror, in the middle of the room a fine,
large, round mahogany table; the floor is polished. Hush!
"The gentleman does not receive visitors in the afternoon" —
hence I can be amongst you in my thoughts. Early in the
morning the unbearably-stupid servant wakes me; I rise, get
my coffee, and often drink it cold because I forget my
breakfast over my playing. Punctually at nine o'clock appears
my German master; then I generally write; and after that,
Hummel comes to work at my portrait, while Nidecki studies my
concerto. And all this time I remain in my comfortable
dressing-gown, which I do not take off till twelve o'clock.
At that hour a very worthy German makes his appearance, Herr
Leibenfrost, who works in the law-courts here. If the weather
is fine I take a walk with him on the Glacis, then we dine
together at a restaurant, Zur bohmischen Kochin, which is
frequented by all the university students; and finally we go
(as is the custom here) to one of the best coffee-houses.
After this I make calls, return home in the twilight, throw
myself into evening-dress, and must be off to some soiree: to-
day here, to-morrow there. About eleven or twelve (but never
later) I return home, play, laugh, read, lie down, put out
the light, sleep, and dream of you, my dear ones.

If is evident that there was no occasion to fear that Chopin would kill himself with too hard work. Indeed, the number of friends, or, not to misuse this sacred name, let us rather say acquaintances, he had, did not allow him much time for study and composition. In his letters from Vienna are mentioned more than forty names of families and single individuals with whom he had personal intercourse. I need hardly add that among them there was a considerable sprinkling of Poles. Indeed, the majority of the houses where he was oftenest seen, and where he felt most happy, were those of his countrymen, or those in which there was at least some Polish member, or which had some Polish connection. Already on December 1, 1830, he writes home that he had been several times at Count Hussarzewski's, and purposes to pay a visit at Countess Rosalia Rzewuska's, where he expects to meet Madame Cibbini, the daughter of Leopold Kozeluch and a pupil of Clementi, known as a pianist and composer, to whom Moscheles dedicated a sonata for four hands, and who at that time was first lady-in-waiting to the Empress of Austria. Chopin had likewise called twice at Madame Weyberheim's. This lady, who was a sister of Madame Wolf and the wife of a rich banker, invited him to a soiree "en petit cercle des amateurs," and some weeks later to a soiree dansante, on which occasion he saw "many young people, beautiful, but not antique [that is to say not of the Old Testament kind], "refused to play, although the lady of the house and her beautiful daughters had invited many musical personages, was forced to dance a cotillon, made some rounds, and then went home. In the house of the family Beyer (where the husband was a Pole of Odessa, and the wife, likewise Polish, bore the fascinating Christian name Constantia— the reader will remember her) Chopin felt soon at his ease. There he liked to dine, sup, lounge, chat, play, dance mazurkas, &c. He often met there the violinist Slavik, and the day before Christmas played with him all the morning and evening, another day staying with him there till two o'clock in the morning. We hear also of dinners at the house of his countrywoman Madame Elkan, and at Madame Schaschek's, where (he writes in July, 1831) he usually met several Polish ladies, who by their hearty hopeful words always cheered him, and where he once made his appearance at four instead of the appointed dinner hour, two o'clock. But one of his best friends was the medical celebrity Dr. Malfatti, physician-in-ordinary to the Emperor of Austria, better remembered by the musical reader as the friend of Beethoven, whom he attended in his last illness, forgetting what causes for complaint he might have against the too irritable master. Well, this Dr. Malfatti received Chopin, of whom he had already heard from Wladyslaw Ostrowski, "as heartily as if I had been a relation of his" (Chopin uses here a very bold simile), running up to him and embracing him as soon as he had got sight of his visiting-card. Chopin became a frequent guest at the doctor's house; in his letters we come often on the announcement that he has dined or is going to dine on such or such a day at Dr. Malfatti's.

> December 1, 1830. — On the whole things are going well with
> me, and I hope with God's help, who sent Malfatti to my
> assistance — oh, excellent Malfatti! — that they will go better

still.

December 25, 1830.—I went to dine at Malfatti's. This excellent man thinks of everything; he is even so kind as to set before us dishes prepared in the Polish fashion.

May 14, 1831.—I am very brisk, and feel that good health is the best comfort in misfortune. Perhaps Malfatti's soups have strengthened me so much that I feel better than I ever did. If this is really the case, I must doubly regret that Malfatti has gone with his family into the country. You have no idea how beautiful the villa is in which he lives; this day week I was there with Hummel. After this amiable physician had taken us over his house he showed us also his garden. When we stood at the top of the hill, from which we had a splendid view, we did not wish to go down again. The Court honours Malfatti every year with a visit. He has the Duchess of Anhalt-Cothen as a neighbour; I should not wonder if she envied him his garden. On one side one sees Vienna lying at one's feet, and in such a way that one might believe it was joined to Schoenbrunn; on the other side one sees high mountains picturesquely dotted with convents and villages. Gazing on this romantic panorama one entirely forgets the noisy bustle and proximity of the capital.

This is one of the few descriptive passages to be found in Chopin's letters—men and their ways interested him more than natural scenery. But to return from the villa to its owner, Chopin characterises his relation to the doctor unequivocally in the following statement:—"Malfatti really loves me, and I am not a little proud of it." Indeed, the doctor seems to have been a true friend, ready with act and counsel. He aided him with his influence in various ways; thus, for instance, we read that he promised to introduce him to Madame Tatyszczew, the wife of the Russian Ambassador, and to Baron Dunoi, *the president of the musical society, whom Chopin thought a very useful personage to know. At Malfatti's he made also the acquaintance of some artists whom he would, perhaps, have had no opportunity of meeting elsewhere. One of these was the celebrated tenor Wild. He came to Malfatti's in the afternoon of Christmas-day, and Chopin, who had been dining there, says: "I accompanied by heart the aria from Othello, which he sang in a masterly style. Wild and Miss Heinefetter are the ornaments of the Court Opera." Of a celebration of Malfatti's name-day Chopin gives the following graphic account in a letter to his parents, dated June 25, 1831:— Mechetti, who wished to surprise him [Malfatti], persuaded the Misses Emmering and Lutzer, and the Messrs. Wild,*

> Cicimara, and your Frederick to perform some music at the honoured man's house; almost from beginning to end the performance was deserving of the predicate "parfait." I never heard the quartet from Moses better sung; but Miss Gladkowska sang "O quante lagrime" at my farewell concert at Warsaw with much more expression. Wild was in excellent voice, and I acted in a way as Capellmeister.

To this he adds the note:—

> Cicimara said there was nobody in Vienna who accompanied so well as I. And I thought, "Of that I have been long convinced." A considerable number of people stood on the terrace of the house and listened to our concert. The moon shone with wondrous beauty, the fountains rose like columns of pearls, the air was filled with the fragrance of the orangery; in short, it was an enchanting night, and the surroundings were magnificent! And now I will describe to you the drawing-room in which we were. High windows, open from top to bottom, look out upon the terrace, from which one has a splendid view of the whole of Vienna. The walls are hung with large mirrors; the lights were faint: but so much the greater was the effect of the moonlight which streamed through the windows. The cabinet to the left of the drawing-

room and adjoining it gives, on account of its large

dimensions, an imposing aspect to the whole apartment. The

ingenuousness and courtesy of the host, the elegant and

genial society, the generally-prevailing joviality, and the

excellent supper, kept us long together.

Here Chopin is seen at his best as a letter writer; it would be difficult to find other passages of equal excellence. For, although we meet frequently enough with isolated pretty bits, there is not one single letter which, from beginning to end, as a whole as well as in its parts, has the perfection and charm of Mendelssohn's letters.

CHAPTER XII

VIENNA MUSICAL LIFE.—KARNTHNERTHOR THEATRE.— SABINE HEINEFETTER.—CONCERTS: HESSE, THALBERG, DOHLER, HUMMEL, ALOYS SCHMITT, CHARLES CZERNY, SLAVIK, MERK, BOCKLET, ABBE STABLER, KIESEWETTER, KANDLER.—THE PUBLISHERS HASLINGER, DIABELLI, MECHETTI, AND JOSEPH CZERNY.—LANNER AND STRAUSS.—CHOPIN PLAYS AT A CONCERT OF MADAME GARZIA-VESTRIS AND GIVES ONE HIMSELF.—HIS STUDIES AND COMPOSITIONS OF THAT TIME.—HIS STATE OF BODY AND MIND.—PREPARATIONS FOR AND POSTPONEMENT OF HIS DEPARTURE.—SHORTNESS OF MONEY.—HIS MELANCHOLY.— TWO EXCURSIONS.—LEAVES FOR MUNICH.—HIS CONCERT AT MUNICH.—HIS STAY AT STUTTGART.—PROCEEDS TO PARIS.

The allusions to music and musicians lead us naturally to inquire further after Chopin's musical experiences in Vienna.

> *January 26, 1831.—If I had not made [he writes] the*
> *exceedingly interesting acquaintance of the most talented*
> *artists of this place, such as Slavik, Merk, Bocklet, and so*
> *forth [this "so forth" is tantalising], I should be very*
> *little satisfied with my stay here. The Opera indeed is good:*
> *Wild and Miss Heinefetter fascinate the Viennese; only it is*
> *a pity that Duport brings forward so few new operas, and*
> *thinks more of his pocket than of art.*

What Chopin says here and elsewhere about Duport's stinginess tallies with the contemporary newspaper accounts. No sooner had the new manager taken possession of his post than he began to economise in such a manner that he drove away men like Conradin Kreutzer, Weigl, and Mayseder. During the earlier part of his sojourn in Vienna Chopin remarked that excepting Heinefetter and Wild, the singers were not so excellent as he had expected to find them at the Imperial Opera. Afterwards he seems to have somewhat extended his sympathies, for he writes in July, 1831:—

> *Rossini's "Siege of Corinth" was lately very well performed*
> *here, and I am glad that I had the opportunity of hearing*

> this opera. Miss Heinefetter and Messrs. Wild, Binder, and
> Forti, in short, all the good singers in Vienna, appeared in
> this opera and did their best.

Chopin's most considerable criticism of this time is one on Miss Heinefetter in a letter written on December 25, 1830; it may serve as a pendant to his criticism on Miss Sontag which I quoted in a preceding chapter.

> Miss Heinefetter has a voice such as one seldom hears; she
> sings always in tune; her coloratura is like so many pearls;
> in short, everything is faultless. She looks particularly
> well when dressed as a man. But she is cold: I got my nose
> almost frozen in the stalls. In "Othello" she delighted me
> more than in the "Barber of Seville," where she represents a
> finished coquette instead of a lively, witty girl. As Sextus
> in "Titus" she looks really quite splendid. In a few days she
> is to appear in the "Thieving Magpie" ["La Gazza ladra"]. I
> am anxious to hear it. Miss Woikow pleased me better as
> Rosina in the "Barber"; but, to be sure, she has not such a
> delicious voice as the Heinefetter. I wish I had heard Pasta!

The opera at the Karnthnerthor Theatre with all its shortcomings was nevertheless the most important and most satisfactory musical institution of the city. What else, indeed, had Vienna to offer to the earnest musician? Lanner and Strauss were the heroes of the day, and the majority of other concerts than those given by them were exhibitions of virtuosos. Imagine what a pass the musical world of Vienna must have come to when Stadler, Kiesewetter, Mosel, and Seyfried could be called, as Chopin did call them, its elite! Abbe Stadler might well say to the stranger from Poland that Vienna was no longer what it used to be. Haydn, Mozart, Beethoven, and Schubert had shuffled off their mortal coil, and compared with these suns their surviving contemporaries and successors—Gyrowetz, Weigl, Stadler, Conradin Kreutzer, Lachner, &c.—were but dim and uncertain lights.

With regard to choral and orchestral performances apart from the stage, Vienna had till more recent times very little to boast of. In 1830-1831 the Spirituel-Concerte (Concerts Spirituels) were still in existence under the conductorship of Lannoy; but since 1824 their number had dwindled down from eighteen to four yearly concerts. The programmes were made up of a symphony and some sacred choruses. Beethoven, Mozart, and Haydn predominated among the symphonists; in the choral department preference was given to the Austrian school of church music; but Cherubim also was a great favourite, and choruses from Handel's oratorios, with Mosel's additional accompaniments, were often performed. The name of Beethoven was hardly ever absent from any of the programmes. That the orchestra consisted chiefly of amateurs, and that the performances took place without rehearsals (only difficult new works got a rehearsal, and one only), are facts which speak for themselves. Franz Lachner told Hanslick that the performances of new and in any way difficult compositions were so bad that Schubert once left the hall in the middle of one of his works, and he himself (Lachner) had felt several times inclined to do the same. These are the concerts of which Beethoven spoke as Winkelmusik, and the tickets of which he denominated Abtrittskarten, a word which, as the expression of a man of genius, I do not hesitate to quote, but which I could not venture to translate. Since this damning criticism was uttered, matters had not improved, on the contrary, had gone from bad to worse. Another society of note was the still existing and flourishing Gesellschaft der Musikfreunde. It, too, gave four, or perhaps five yearly concerts, in each of which a symphony, an overture, an aria or duet, an instrumental solo, and a chorus were performed. This society was afflicted with the same evil as the first-named institution. It was a

> *gladdening sight [we are told] to see counts and tradesmen,*
> *superiors and subalterns, professors and students, noble*
> *ladies and simple burghers' daughters side by side*
> *harmoniously exerting themselves for the love of art.*

As far as choral singing is concerned the example deserves to be followed, but the matter stands differently with regard to instrumental music, a branch of the art which demands not only longer and more careful, but also constant, training. Although the early custom of drawing lots, in order to determine who were to sing the solos, what places the players were to occupy in the orchestra, and which of the four conductors was to wield the baton, had already disappeared before 1831, yet in 1841 the performances of the symphonies were still so little "in the spirit of the composers" (a delicate way of stating an ugly fact) that a critic advised the society to imitate the foreign conservatoriums, and reinforce the band with the best musicians of the capital, who, constantly exercising their art, and conversant with the works of the great masters, were better able to do justice to them than amateurs who met only four times a year. What a boon it would be to humanity, what an increase of happiness, if amateurs would allow themselves to be taught by George Eliot, who never spoke truer and wiser words than when she said:—"A little private imitation of what is good is a sort of private devotion to it, and most of us ought to practise art only in the light of private study—preparation to understand and enjoy what the few can do for us." In addition to the above I shall yet mention a third society, the Tonkunstler-Societat, which, as the name implies, was an association of musicians. Its object was the getting-up and keeping-up of a pension fund, and its artistic activity displayed itself in four yearly concerts. Haydn's "Creation" and "Seasons" were the stock pieces of the society's repertoire, but in 1830 and 1831 Handel's "Messiah" and "Solomon" and Lachner's "Die vier Menschenalter" were also performed.

These historical notes will give us an idea of what Chopin may have heard in the way of choral and orchestral music. I say "may have heard," because not a word is to be found in his extant letters about the concerts of these societies. Without exposing ourselves to the reproach of rashness, we may, however, assume that he was present at the concert of the Gesellschaft der Musikfreunde on March 20, 1831, when among the items of the programme were Beethoven's Pastoral Symphony, and the first movement of a concerto composed and played by Thalberg. On seeing the name of one of the most famous pianists contemporary with Chopin, the reader has, no doubt, at once guessed the reason why I assumed the latter's presence at the concert. These two remarkable, but in their characters and aims so dissimilar, men had some friendly intercourse in Vienna. Chopin mentions Thalberg twice in his letters, first on December 25, 1830, and again on May 28, 1831. On the latter occasion he relates that he went with him to an organ recital given by Hesse, the previously-mentioned Adolf Hesse of Breslau, of whom Chopin now remarked that he had talent and knew how to treat his instrument. Hesse and Chopin must have had some personal intercourse, for we learn that the former left with the latter an album leaf. A propos of this circumstance, Chopin confesses in a letter to his people that he is at a loss what to write, that he lacks the requisite wit. But let us return to the brilliant pianist, who, of course, was a more interesting acquaintance in Chopin's, eyes than the great organist. Born in 1812, and consequently three years younger than Chopin, Sigismund Thalberg had already in his fifteenth year played with success in public, and at the age of sixteen published Op. 1, 2, and 3. However, when Chopin made his acquaintance, he had not yet begun to play only his own compositions (about that time he played, for instance, Beethoven's C minor Concerto at one of the Spirituel-Concerte, where since 1830 instrumental solos were occasionally heard), nor had he attained that in its way unique perfection of beauty of tone and elegance of execution which distinguished him afterwards. Indeed, the palmy days of his career cannot be dated farther back than the year 1835, when he and Chopin met again in Paris; but then his success was so enormous that his fame in a short time became universal, and as a virtuoso only one rival was left him—Liszt, the unconquered. That Chopin and Thalberg entertained very high opinions of each other cannot be asserted. Let the reader judge for himself after reading what Chopin says in his letter of December 25, 1830:—

> *Thalberg plays famously, but he is not my man. He is younger*
> *than I, pleases the ladies very much, makes pot-pourris on*
> *"La Muette" ["Masaniello"], plays the forte and piano with*
> *the pedal, but not with the hand, takes tenths as easily as I*
> *do octaves, and wears studs with diamonds. Moscheles does not*
> *at all astonish him; therefore it is no wonder that only the*
> *tuttis of my concerto have pleased him. He, too, writes*
> *concertos.*

Chopin was endowed with a considerable power of sarcasm, and was fond of cultivating and exercising it. This portraiture of his brother-artist is not a bad specimen of its kind, although we shall meet with better ones.

Another, but as yet unfledged, celebrity was at that time living in Vienna, prosecuting his studies under Czerny—namely, Theodor Dohler. Chopin, who went to hear him play some compositions of his master's at the theatre, does not allude to him again after the concert; but if he foresaw what a position as a pianist and composer he himself was destined to occupy, he could not suspect that this lad of seventeen would some day be held up to the Parisian public by a hostile clique as a rival equalling and even surpassing his peculiar excellences. By the way, the notion of anyone playing compositions of Czerny's at a concert cannot but strangely tickle the fancy of a musician who has the privilege of living in the latter part of the nineteenth century.

Besides the young pianists with a great future before them Chopin came also in contact with aging pianists with a great past behind them. Hummel, accompanied by his son, called on him in the latter part of December, 1830, and was extraordinarily polite. In April, 1831, the two pianists, the setting and the rising star, were together at the villa of Dr. Malfatti. Chopin informed his master, Elsner, for whose masses he was in quest of a publisher, that Haslinger was publishing the last mass of Hummel, and added:— For he now lives only by and for Hummel.

> *It is rumoured that*
> *the last compositions of Hummel do not sell well, and yet he*
> *is said to have paid a high price for them. Therefore he now*
> *lays all MSS. aside, and prints only Strauss's waltzes.*

Unfortunately there is not a word which betrays Chopin's opinion of Hummel's playing and compositions. We are more fortunate in the case of another celebrity, one, however, of a much lower order. In one of the prosaic intervals, of the sentimental rhapsody, indited on December 25, 1830, there occur the following remarks:—

The pianist Aloys Schmitt of Frankfort-on-the-Main, famous
for his excellent studies, is at present here; he is a man
above forty. I have made his acquaintance; he promised to
visit me. He intends to give a concert here, and one must
admit that he is a clever musician. I think we shall
understand each other with regard to music.

Having looked at this picture, let the reader look also at this other, dashed off a month later in a letter to Elsner:—

The pianist Aloys Schmitt has been flipped on the nose by the
critics, although he is already over forty years old, and
composes eighty-years-old music.

From the contemporary journals we learn that, at the concert mentioned by Chopin, Schmitt afforded the public of Vienna an opportunity of hearing a number of his own compositions—which were by no means short drawing-room pieces, but a symphony, overture, concerto, concertino, &c.—and that he concluded his concert with an improvisation. One critic, at least, described his style of playing as sound and brilliant. The misfortune of Schmitt was to have come too late into the world—respectable mediocrities like him always do that—he never had any youth. The pianist on whom Chopin called first on arriving in Vienna was Charles Czerny, and he

was, as he is always (and to everybody), very polite, and
asked, "Hat fleissig studirt?" [Have you studied diligently?]
He has again arranged an overture for eight pianos and
sixteen performers, and seems to be very happy over it.

Only in the sense of belonging rather to the outgoing than to the incoming generation can Czerny be reckoned among the aged pianists, for in 1831 he was not above forty years of age and had still an enormous capacity for work in him—hundreds and hundreds of original and transcribed compositions, thousands and thousands of lessons. His name appears in a passage of one of Chopin's letters which deserves to be quoted for various reasons: it shows the writer's dislike to the Jews, his love of Polish music, and his contempt for a kind of composition much cultivated by Czerny. Speaking of the violinist Herz, "an Israelite," who was almost hissed when he made his debut in Warsaw, and whom Chopin was going to hear again in Vienna, he says:—

> At the close of the concert Herz will play his own Variations
> on Polish airs. Poor Polish airs! You do not in the least
> suspect how you will be interlarded with "majufes" [see page
> 49, foot-note], and that the title of "Polish music" is only
> given you to entice the public. If one is so outspoken as to
> discuss the respective merits of genuine Polish music and
> this imitation of it, and to place the former above the
> latter, people declare one to be mad, and do this so much the
> more readily because Czerny, the oracle of Vienna, has
> hitherto in the fabrication of his musical dainties never
> produced Variations on a Polish air.

Chopin had not much sympathy with Czerny the musician, but seems to have had some liking for the man, who indeed was gentle, kind, and courteous in his disposition and deportment.

A much more congenial and intimate connection existed between Chopin, Slavik, and Merk. [FOOTNOTE: Thus the name is spelt in Mendel's Musikalisches Conversations-Lexikon and by E. A. Melis, the Bohemian writer on music. Chopin spells it Slawik. The more usual spelling, however, is Slawjk; and in C.F. Whistling's Handbuch der musikalischen Literatur (Leipzig, 1828) it is Slavjk.] Joseph Slavik had come to Vienna in 1825 and had at once excited a great sensation. He was then a young man of nineteen, but technically already superior to all the violinists that had been heard in the Austrian capital. The celebrated Mayseder called him a second Lipinski. Pixis, his master at the Conservatorium in Prague, on seeing some of this extraordinary pupil's compositions—a concerto, variations, &c.—had wondered how anyone could write down such mad, unplayable stuff. But Slavik before leaving Prague proved at a farewell concert that there was at least one who could play the mad stuff. All this, however, was merely the prelude to what was yet to come. The appearance of Paganini in 1828 revealed to him the, till then, dimly-perceived ideal of his dreams, and the great Italian violinist, who took an interest in this ardent admirer and gave him some hints, became henceforth his model. Having saved a little money, he went for his further improvement to Paris, studying especially under Baillot, but soon returned to accept an engagement in the Imperial Band. When after two years of hard practising he reappeared before the public of Vienna, his style was altogether changed; he mastered the same difficulties as Paganini, or even greater ones, not, however, with the same unfailing certainty, nor with an always irreproachable intonation. Still, there can be no doubt that had not a premature death (in 1833, at the age of twenty-seven) cut short his career, he would have spread his fame all over the world. Chopin, who met him first at Wurfel's, at once felt a liking for him, and when on the following day he heard him play after dinner at Beyer's, he was more pleased with his performance than with that of any other violinist except Paganini. As Chopin's playing was equally sympathetic to Slavik, they formed the project of writing a duet for violin and piano. In a letter to his friend Matuszynski (December 25, 1830) Chopin writes:—

> I have just come from the excellent violinist Slavik. With
> the exception of Paganini, I never heard a violin-player like
> him. Ninety-six staccato notes in one bow! It is almost
> incredible! When I heard him I felt inclined to return to my
> lodgings and sketch variations on an Adagio [which they had
> previously agreed to take for their theme] of Beethoven's.

The sight of the post-office and a letter from his Polish friends put the variations out of his mind, and they seem never to have been written, at least nothing has been heard of them. Some remarks on Slavik in a letter addressed to his parents (May 28, 1831) show Chopin's admiration of and affection for his friend still more distinctly:—

> He is one of the Viennese artists with whom I keep up a
> really friendly and intimate intercourse. He plays like a
> second Paganini, but a rejuvenated one, who will perhaps in
> time surpass the first. I should not believe it myself if I
> had not heard him so often....Slavik fascinates the listener
> and brings tears into his eyes.

Shortly after falling in with Slavik, Chopin met Merk, probably at the house of the publisher Mechetti, and on January 1, 1831, he announces to his friend in Warsaw with unmistakable pride that "Merk, the first violoncellist in Vienna," has promised him a visit. Chopin desired very much to become acquainted with him because he thought that Merk, Slavik, and himself would form a capital trio. The violoncellist was considerably older than either pianist or violinist, being born in 1795. Merk began his musical career as a violinist, but being badly bitten in the arm by a big dog, and disabled thereby to hold the violin in its proper position (this is what Fetis relates), he devoted himself to the violoncello, and with such success as to become the first solo player in Vienna. At the time we are speaking of he was a member of the Imperial Orchestra and a professor at the Conservatorium. He often gave concerts with Mayseder, and was called the Mayseder of the violoncello. Chopin, on hearing him at a soiree of the well-known autograph collector Fuchs, writes home:—

Limmer, one of the better artists here in Vienna, produced

some of his compositions for four violoncelli. Merk, by his

expressive playing, made them, as usual, more beautiful than

they really are. People stayed again till midnight, for Merk

took a fancy to play with me his variations. He told me that

he liked to play with me, and it is always a great treat to

me to play with him. I think we look well together. He is the

first violoncellist whom I really admire.

Of Chopin's intercourse with the third of the "exceedingly interesting acquaintances" whom he mentions by name, we get no particulars in his letters. Still, Carl Maria von Bocklet, for whom Beethoven wrote three letters of recommendation, who was an intimate friend of Schubert's, and whose interpretations of classical works and power of improvisation gave him one of the foremost places among the pianists of the day, cannot have been without influence on Chopin. Bocklet, better than any other pianist then living in Vienna, could bring the young Pole into closer communication with the German masters of the preceding generation; he could, as it were, transmit to him some of the spirit that animated Beethoven, Schubert, and Weber. The absence of allusions to Bocklet in Chopin's letters does not, however, prove that he never made any, for the extant letters are only a small portion of those he actually wrote, many of them having in the perturbed state of Poland never reached their destination, others having been burnt by his parents for fear of the Russian police, and some, no doubt, having been lost through carelessness or indifference.

The list of Chopin's acquaintances is as yet far from being exhausted. He had conversations with old Abbe Stadler, the friend of Haydn and Mozart, whose Psalms, which he saw in MS., he admired. He also speaks of one of the performances of old, sacred, and secular music which took place at Kiesewetter's house as if he were going to it. But a musician of Chopin's nature would not take a very lively interest in the historical aspect of the art; nor would the learned investigator of the music of the Netherlanders, of the music of the Arabs, of the life and works of Guido d'Arezzo, &c., readily perceive the preciousness of the modern composer's originality. At any rate, Chopin had more intercourse with the musico-literary Franz Kandler, who wrote favourable criticisms on his performances as a composer and player, and with whom he went on one occasion to the Imperial Library, where the discovery of a certain MS. surprised him even more than the magnitude and order of the collection, which he could not imagine to be inferior to that of Bologna—the manuscript in question being no other than his Op. 2, which Haslinger had presented to the library. Chopin found another MS. of his, that of the Rondo for two pianos, in Aloys Fuchs's famous collection of autographs, which then comprised 400 numbers, but about the year 1840 had increased to 650 numbers, most of them complete works. He must have understood how to ingratiate himself with the collector, otherwise he would hardly have had the good fortune to be presented with an autograph of Beethoven.

Chopin became also acquainted with almost all the principal publishers in Vienna. Of Haslinger enough has already been said. By Czerny Chopin was introduced to Diabelli, who invited him to an evening party of musicians. With Mechetti he seems to have been on a friendly footing. He dined at his house, met him at Dr. Malfatti's, handed over to him for publication his Polonaise for piano and violoncello (Op. 3), and described him as enterprising and probably persuadable to publish Elsner's masses. Joseph Czerny, no relation of Charles's, was a mere business acquaintance of Chopin's. Being reminded of his promise to publish a quartet of Elsner's, he said he could not undertake to do so just then (about January 26, 1831), as he was publishing the works of Schubert, of which many were still in the press.

Therefore [writes Chopin to his master] I fear your MS. will have to wait. Czerny, I have found out now, is not one of the richest publishers here, and consequently cannot easily risk the publication of a work which is not performed at the Sped or at the Romische Kaiser. Waltzes are here called works; and Lanner and Strauss, who lead the performances, Capellmeister. In saying this, however, I do not mean that all people here are of this opinion; on the contrary, there are many who laugh at it. Still, it is almost only waltzes that are published.

It is hardly possible for us to conceive the enthusiasm and ecstasy into which the waltzes of the two dance composers transported Vienna, which was divided into two camps:—

The Sperl and Volksgarten [says Hanslick] were on the Strauss and Lanner days the favourite and most frequented "concert

localities." In the year 1839 Strauss and Lanner had already
each of them published more than too works. The journals were
thrown into ecstasy by every new set of waltzes; innumerable
articles appeared on Strauss, and Lanner, enthusiastic,
humorous, pathetic, and certainly longer than those that were
devoted to Beethoven and Mozart.

These glimpses of the notabilities and manners of a by-gone generation, caught, as it were, through the chinks of the wall which time is building up between the past and the present, are instructive as well as amusing. It would be a great mistake to regard these details, apparently very loosely connected with the life of Chopin, as superfluous appendages to his biography. A man's sympathies and antipathies are revelations of his nature, and an artist's surroundings make evident his position and merit, the degree of his originality being undeterminable without a knowledge of the time in which he lived. Moreover, let the impatient reader remember that, Chopin's life being somewhat poor in incidents, the narrative cannot be an even-paced march, but must be a series of leaps and pauses, with here and there an intervening amble, and one or two brisk canters.

Having described the social and artistic sphere, or rather spheres, in which Chopin moved, pointed out the persons with whom he most associated, and noted his opinions regarding men and things, almost all that is worth telling of his life in the imperial city is told—almost all, but not all. Indeed, of the latter half of his sojourn there some events have yet to be recorded which in importance, if not in interest, surpass anything that is to be found in the preceding and the foregoing part of the present chapter. I have already indicated that the disappointment of Chopin's hopes and the failure of his plans cannot altogether be laid to the charge of unfavourable circumstances. His parents must have thought so too, and taken him to task about his remissness in the matter of giving a concert, for on May 14, 1831, Chopin writes to them:—"My most fervent wish is to be able to fulfil your wishes; till now, however, I found it impossible to give a concert." But although he had not himself given a concert he had had an opportunity of presenting himself in the best company to the public of Vienna. In the "Theaterzeitung" of April 2, 1831, Madame Garzia-Vestris announced a concert to be held in the Redoutensaal during the morning hours of April 4, in which she was to be assisted by the Misses Sabine and Clara Heinefetter, Messrs. Wild, Chopin, Bohm (violinist), Hellmesberger (violinist, pupil of the former), Merk, and the brothers Lewy (two horn-players). Chopin was distinguished from all the rest, as a homo ignotus et novus, by the parenthetical "pianoforte-player" after his name, no such information being thought necessary in the case of the other artists. The times are changed, now most readers require parenthetical elucidation after each name except that of Chopin. "He has put down the mighty from their seat and has exalted them of low degree!" The above-mentioned exhortation of his parents seems to have had the desired effect, and induced Chopin to make an effort, although now the circumstances were less favourable to his giving a concert than at the time of his arrival. The musical season was over, and many people had left the capital for their summer haunts; the struggle in Poland continued with increasing fierceness, which was not likely to lessen the backwardness of Austrians in patronising a Pole; and in addition to this, cholera had visited the country and put to flight all who were not obliged to stay. I have not been able to ascertain the date and other particulars of this concert. Through Karasowski we learn that it was thinly attended, and that the receipts did not cover the expenses. The "Theaterzeitung," which had given such full criticisms of Chopin's performances in 1829, says not a word either of the matinee or of the concert, not even the advertisement of the latter has come under my notice. No doubt Chopin alludes to criticisms on this concert when he writes in the month of July:—

Louisa [his sister] informs me that Mr. Elsner was very much

pleased with the criticism; I wonder what he will say of the

others, he who was my teacher of composition?

Kandler, the Vienna correspondent of the "Allgemeine musikalische Zeitung," after discussing in that paper (September 21, 1831) the performances of several artists, among others that of the clever Polish violin-virtuoso Serwaczynski, turns to "Chopin, also from the Sarmatian capital, who already during his visit last year proved himself a pianist of the first rank," and remarks:—

The execution of his newest Concerto in E minor, a serious

composition, gave no cause to revoke our former judgment. One

who is so upright in his dealings with genuine art is

deserving our genuine esteem.

All things considered, I do not hesitate to accept Liszt's statement that the young artist did not produce such a sensation as he had a right to expect. In fact, notwithstanding the many pleasant social connections he had, Chopin must have afterwards looked back with regret, probably with bitterness, on his eight months' sojourn in Vienna. Not only did he add nothing to his fame as a pianist and composer by successful concerts and new publications, but he seems even to have been sluggish in his studies and in the production of new works. How he leisurely whiled away the mornings at his lodgings, and passed the rest of the day abroad and in society, he himself has explicitly described. That this was his usual mode of life at Vienna, receives further support from the self-satisfaction with which he on one occasion mentions that he had practised from early morning till two o'clock in the afternoon. In his letters we read only twice of his having finished some new compositions. On December 21, 1830, he writes:—

> I wished to enclose my latest waltz, but the post is about to
>
> depart, and I have no longer time to copy it, therefore I
>
> shall send it another time. The mazurkas, too, I have first
>
> to get copied, but they are not intended for dancing.

And in the month of July, 1831, "I have written a polonaise, which I must leave here for Wurfel." There are two more remarks about compositions, but of compositions which were never finished, perhaps never begun. One of these remarks refers to the variations on a theme of Beethoven's, which he intended to compose conjointly with Slavik, and has already been quoted; the other refers to a grander project. Speaking of Nidecki, who came every morning to his lodgings and practised his (Chopin's) concerto, he says (December 21, 1830):—

> If I succeed in writing a concerto for two pianos so as to
>
> satisfy myself, we intend to appear at once with it in
>
> public; first, however, I wish to play once alone.

What an interesting, but at the same time what a gigantic, subject to write on the history of the unrealised plans of men of genius would be! The above-mentioned waltz, polonaise, and mazurkas do not, of course, represent the whole of Chopin's output as a composer during the time of his stay in Vienna; but we may surmise with some degree of certainty that few works of importance have to be added to it. Indeed, the multiplicity of his social connections and engagements left him little time for himself, and the condition of his fatherland kept him in a constant state of restlessness. Poland and her struggle for independence were always in his mind; now he laments in his letters the death of a friend, now rejoices at a victory, now asks eagerly if such or such a piece of good news that has reached him is true, now expresses the hope that God will be propitious to their cause, now relates that he has vented his patriotism by putting on the studs with the Polish eagles and using the pocket-handkerchief with the Kosynier (scythe-man) depicted on it.

> What is going on at home? [he writes, on May 28, 1831.] I am
>
> always dreaming of you. Is there still no end to the
>
> bloodshed? I know your answer: "Patience!" I, too, always

comfort myself with that.

But good health, he finds, is the best comfort in misfortune, and if his bulletins to his parents could be trusted he was in full enjoyment of it.

Zacharkiewicz of Warsaw called on me; and when his wife saw
me at Szaszek's, she did not know how to sufficiently express
her astonishment at my having become such a sturdy fellow. I
have let my whiskers grow only on the right side, and they
are growing very well; on the left side they are not needed
at all, for one sits always with the right side turned to the
public.

Although his "ideal" is not there to retain him, yet he cannot make up his mind to leave Vienna. On May 28, he writes:—

How quickly this dear time passes! It is already the end of
May, and I am still in Vienna. June will come, and I shall
probably be still here, for Kumelski fell ill and was obliged
to take to bed again.

It was not only June but past the middle of July before Chopin left, and I am afraid he would not always have so good an excuse for prolonging his stay as the sickness of his travelling-companion. On June 25, however, we hear of active preparations being made for departure.

I am in good health, that is the only thing that cheers me,
for it seems as if my departure would never take place. You
all know how irresolute I am, and in addition to this I meet
with obstacles at every step. Day after day I am promised my
passport, and I run from Herod to Pontius Pilate, only to get
back what I deposited at the police office. To-day I heard
even more agreeable news—namely, that my passport has been
mislaid, and that they cannot find it; I have even to send in
an application for a new one. It is curious how now every
imaginable misfortune befalls us poor Poles. Although I am
ready to depart, I am unable to set out.

Chopin had been advised by Mr. Beyer to have London instead of Paris put as a visa in his passport. The police complied with his request that this should be done, but the Russian Ambassador, after keeping the document for two days, gave him only permission to travel as far as Munich. But Chopin did not care so long as he got the signature of the French Ambassador. Although his passport contained the words "passant par Paris a Londres," and he in after years in Paris sometimes remarked, in allusion to these words, "I am here only in passing," he had no intention of going to London. The fine sentiment, therefore, of which a propos of this circumstance some writers have delivered themselves was altogether misplaced. When the difficulty about the passport was overcome, another arose: to enter Bavaria from cholera-stricken Austria a passport of health was required. Thus Chopin had to begin another series of applications, in fact, had to run about for half a day before he obtained this additional document.

Chopin appears to have been rather short of money in the latter part of his stay in Vienna—a state of matters with which the financial failure of the concert may have had something to do. The preparations for his departure brought the pecuniary question still more prominently forward. On June 25, 1831, he writes to his parents:—

I live as economically as possible, and take as much care of
every kreuzer as of that ring in Warsaw [the one given him by
the Emperor Alexander]. You may sell it, I have already cost
you so much.

He must have talked about his shortness of money to some of his friends in Vienna, for he mentions that the pianist-composer Czapek, who calls on him every day and shows him much kindness, has offered him money for the journey should he stand in need of it. One would hardly have credited Chopin with proficiency in an art in which he nevertheless greatly excelled—namely, in the art of writing begging letters. How well he understood how to touch the springs of the parental feelings the following application for funds will prove.

July, 1831.—But I must not forget to mention that I shall
probably be obliged to draw more money from the banker Peter
than my dear father has allowed me. I am very economical;
but, God knows, I cannot help it, for otherwise I should have
to leave with an almost empty purse. God preserve me from
sickness; were, however, anything to happen to me, you might
perhaps reproach me for not having taken more. Pardon me, but
consider that I have already lived on this money during May,
June, and July, and that I have now to pay more for my dinner
than I did in winter. I do not do this only because I myself

feel I ought to do so, but also in consequence of the good

advice of others. I am very sorry that I have to ask you for

it; my papa has already spent more than three groschen for

me; I know also very well how difficult it is to earn money.

Believe me, my dearest ones, it is harder for me to ask than

for you to give. God will not fail to assist us also in the

future, punctum!

Chopin was at this time very subject to melancholy, and did not altogether hide the fact even from his parents. He was perhaps thinking of the "lengthening chain" which he would have to drag at this new remove. He often runs into the street to seek Titus Woyciechowski or John Matuszynski. One day he imagines he sees the former walking before him, but on coming up to the supposed friend is disgusted to find "a d— — Prussian."

I lack nothing [he writes in July, 1831] except more life,

more spirit! I often feel unstrung, but sometimes as merry as

I used to be at home. When I am sad I go to Madame Szaszek's;

there I generally meet several amiable Polish ladies who with

their hearty, hopeful words always cheer me up, so that I

begin at once to imitate the generals here. This is a fresh

joke of mine; but those who saw it almost died with laughing.

But alas, there are days when not two words can be got out of

me, nor can anyone find out what is the matter with me; then,

to divert myself, I generally take a thirty-kreuzer drive to

Hietzing, or somewhere else in the neighbourhood of Vienna.

This is a valuable bit of autobiography; it sets forth clearly Chopin's proneness to melancholy, which, however, easily gave way to his sportiveness. That low spirits and scantiness of money did not prevent Chopin from thoroughly enjoying himself may be gathered from many indications in his letters; of these I shall select his descriptions of two excursions in the neighbourhood of Vienna, which not only make us better acquainted with the writer, but also are interesting in themselves.

June 25, 1831. — The day before yesterday we were with

Kumelski and Czapek...on the Kahlenberg and Leopoldsberg. It

was a magnificent day; I have never had a finer walk. From

the Leopoldsberg one sees all Vienna, Wagram, Aspern,

Pressburg, even Kloster-Neuburg, the castle in which Richard the Lion-hearted lived for a long time as a prisoner. Also the whole of the upper part of the Danube lay before our eyes. After breakfast we ascended the Kahlenberg, where King John Sobieski pitched his camp and caused the rockets to be fired which announced to Count Starhemberg, the commandant of

Vienna, the approach of the Polish army. There is the Camaldolese Monastery in which the King knighted his son James before the attack on the Turks and himself served as acolyte at the Mass. I enclose for Isabella a little leaf from that spot, which is now covered with plants. From there we went in the evening to the Krapfenwald, a beautiful valley, where we saw a comical boys' trick. The little fellows had enveloped themselves from head to foot in leaves and looked like walking bushes. In this costume they crept from one visitor to another. Such a boy covered with leaves and his head adorned with twigs is called a "Pfingstkonig" [Whitsuntide-King]. This drollery is customary here at Whitsuntide.

The second excursion is thus described: —

July, 1831. — The day before yesterday honest Wurfel called on me; Czapek, Kumelski, and many others also came, and we drove together to St. Veil — a beautiful place; I could not say the same of Tivoli, where they have constructed a kind ol caroitsscl, or rather a track with a sledge, which is called Rutsch. It is a childish amusement, but a great number of grown-up people have themselves rolled down the hill in this carriage just for pastime. At first I did not feel inclined to try it, but as there were eight of us, all good friends, we began to vie with each other in sliding down. It was folly, and yet we all laughed heartily. I myself joined in the sport with much satisfaction until it struck me that healthy and strong men could do something better — now, when humanity calls to them for protection and defence. May the devil take this frivolity!

In the same letter Chopin expresses the hope that his use of various, not quite unobjectionable, words beginning with a "d" may not give his parents a bad opinion of the culture he has acquired in Vienna, and removes any possible disquietude on their part by assuring them that he has adopted nothing that is Viennese in its nature, that, in fact, he has not even learnt to play a Tanzwalzer (a dancing waltz). This, then, is the sad result of his sojourn in Vienna.

On July 20, 1831, Chopin, accompanied by his friend Kumelski, left Vienna and travelled by Linz and Salzburg to Munich, where he had to wait some weeks for supplies from home. His stay in the capital of Bavaria, however, was not lost time, for he made there the acquaintance of several clever musicians, and they, charmed by his playing and compositions, induced him to give a concert. Karasowski tells us that Chopin played his E minor Concerto at one of the Philharmonic Society's concerts—which is not quite correct, as we shall see presently—and adds that

> *the audience, carried away by the beauty of the composition*
>
> *and his excellent, poetic rendering, overwhelmed the young*
>
> *virtuoso with loud applause and sincere admiration.*

In writing this the biographer had probably in his mind the following passage from Chopin's letter to Titus Woyciechowski, dated Paris, December 16, 1831:—"I played [to Kalkbrenner, in Paris] the E minor Concerto, which charmed the people of the Bavarian capital so much." The two statements are not synonymous. What the biographer says may be true, and if it is not, ought to be so; but I am afraid the existing documents do not bear it out in its entirety. Among the many local and other journals which I have consulted, I have found only one notice of Chopin's appearance at Munich, and when I expectantly scanned a resume of Munich musical life, from the spring to the end of the year 1831, in the "Allgemeine musikalische Zeitung," I found mention made of Mendelssohn and Lafont, but not of Chopin. Thus, unless we assume that Karasowski—true to his mission as a eulogising biographer, and most vigorous when unfettered by definite data—indulged in exaggeration, we must seek for a reconciliation of the enthusiasm of the audience with the silence of the reporter in certain characteristics of the Munich public. Mendelssohn says of it:—

> *The people here [in Munich] have an extraordinary receptivity*
>
> *for music, which is much cultivated. But it appears to me*
>
> *that everything makes an impression and that the impressions*
>
> *do not last.*

Speaking of Mendelssohn, it is curious to note how he and Chopin were again and again on the point of meeting, and again and again failed to meet. In Berlin Chopin was too bashful and modest to address his already famous young brother-artist, who in 1830 left Vienna shortly before Chopin arrived, and in 1831 arrived in Munich shortly after Chopin had left. The only notice of Chopin's public appearance in Munich I have been able to discover, I found in No. 87 (August 30, 1831) of the periodical "Flora", which contains, under the heading "news," a pretty full account of the "concert of Mr. Chopin of Warsaw." From this account we learn that Chopin was assisted by the singers Madame Pellegrini and Messrs. Bayer, Lenz, and Harm, the clarinet-player Barmann, jun., and Capellmeister Stunz. The singers performed a four-part song, and Barmann took part in a cavatina (sung by Bayer, the first tenor at the opera) with clarinet and pianoforte accompaniment by Schubert (?). What the writer of the account says about Chopin shall be quoted in full:—

On the 28th August, Mr. F. Chopin, of Warsaw, gave a morning concert [Mittags Concert] in the hall of the Philharmonic Society, which was attended by a very select audience. Mr. Chopin performed on the pianoforte a Concerto in E minor of his own composition, and showed an excellent virtuosity in the treatment of his instrument; besides a developed technique, one noticed especially a charming delicacy of execution, and a beautiful and characteristic rendering of the motives. The composition was, on the whole, brilliantly and well written, without surprising, however, by extraordinary novelty or a particular profundity, with the exception of the Rondo, whose principal thought as well as the florid middle sections, through an original combination of a melancholy trait with a capriccio, evolved a peculiar charm, on which account it particularly pleased. The concert-giver performed in conclusion a fantasia on Polish national songs. There is a something in the Slavonic songs which almost never fails in its effect, the cause of which, however, is difficult to trace and explain; for it is not only the rhythm and the quick change from minor to major which produce this charm. No one has probably understood better how to combine the national character of such folk-

songs with a brilliant concert style than Bernhard Romberg
[Footnote: The famous violoncellist], who by his compositions
of this kind, put in a favourable light by his masterly
playing, knew how to exercise a peculiar fascination. Quite
of this style was the fantasia of Mr. Chopin, who gained
unanimous applause.

From Munich Chopin proceeded to Stuttgart, and during his stay there learnt the sad news of the taking of Warsaw by the Russians (September 8, 1831). It is said that this event inspired him to compose the C minor study (No. 12 of Op. 10), with its passionate surging and impetuous ejaculations. Writing from Paris on December 16, 1831, Chopin remarks, in allusion to the traeic denouement of the Polish revolution: "All this has caused me much pain. Who could have foreseen it!"

With his visits to Stuttgart Chopin's artist-life in Germany came to a close, for, although he afterwards repeatedly visited the country, he never played in public or made a lengthened stay there. Now that Chopin is nearing Paris, where, occasional sojourns elsewhere (most of them of short duration) excepted, he will pass the rest of his life, it may interest the reader to learn that this change of country brought with it also a change of name, at least as far as popular pronunciation and spelling went. We may be sure that the Germans did not always give to the final syllable the appropriate nasal sound. And what the Polish pronunciation was is sufficiently indicated by the spelling "Szopen," frequently to be met with. I found it in the Polish illustrated journal "Kiosy," and it is also to be seen in Joseph Sikorski's "Wspomnienie Szopena" ("Reminiscences of Chopin"). Szulc and Karasowski call their books and hero "Fryderyk Chopin."

CHAPTER XIII

CHOPIN'S PRODUCTIONS FROM THE SPRING OF 1829 TO THE END OF 1831.—THE CHIEF INFLUENCES THAT HELPED TO FORM HIS STYLE OF COMPOSITION.

Let us pause for a little in our biographical inquiries and critically examine what Chopin had achieved as a composer since the spring of 1829. At the very first glance it becomes evident that the works of the last two years (1829-1831) are decidedly superior to those he wrote before that time. And this advance was not due merely to the increased power derived from practice; it was real growth, which a Greek philosopher describes as penetration of nourishment into empty places, the nourishment being in Chopin's case experience of life's joys and sorrows. In most of the works of what I call his first period, the composer luxuriates, as it were, in language. He does not regard it solely or chiefly as the interpreter of thoughts and feelings, he loves it for its own sake, just as children, small and tall, prattle for no other reason than the pleasure of prattling. I closed the first period when a new element entered Chopin's life and influenced his artistic work. This element was his first love, his passion for Constantia Gtadkowska. Thenceforth Chopin's compositions had in them more of humanity and poetry, and the improved subject-matter naturally, indeed necessarily, chastened, ennobled, and enriched the means and ways of expression. Of course no hard line can be drawn between the two periods—the distinctive quality of the one period appears sometimes in the work of the other: a work of the earlier period foreshadows the character of the later; one of the later re-echoes that of the earlier.

The compositions which we know to have been written by Chopin between 1829 and 1831 are few in number. This may be partly because Chopin was rather idle from the autumn of 1830 to the end of 1831, partly because no account of the production of other works has come down to us. In fact, I have no doubt that other short pieces besides those mentioned by Chopin in his letters were composed during those years, and subsequently published by him. The compositions oftenest and most explicitly mentioned in the letters are also the most important ones—namely, the concertos. As I wish to discuss them at some length, we will keep them to the last, and see first what allusions to other compositions we can find, and what observations these latter give rise to.

On October 3, 1829, Chopin sends his friend Titus Woyciechowski a waltz which, he says, was, like the Adagio of the F minor Concerto, inspired by his ideal, Constantia Gladkowska:—

Pay attention to the passage marked with a ; nobody, except you, knows of this. How happy would I be if I could play my newest compositions to you! In the fifth bar of the trio the bass melody up to E flat dominates, which, however, I need not tell you, as you are sure to feel it without being told.

The remark about the bass melody up to E flat in the trio gives us a clue to which of Chopin's waltzes this is. It can be no other than the one in D flat which Fontana published among his friend's posthumous works as Op. 70, No. 3. Although by no means equal to any of the waltzes published by Chopin himself, one may admit that it is pretty; but its chief claim to our attention lies in the fact that it contains germs which reappear as fully-developed flowers in other examples of this class of the master's works—the first half of the first part reappears in the opening (from the ninth bar onward) of Op. 42 (Waltz in A flat major); and the third part, in the third part (without counting the introductory bars) of Op. 34, No. 1 (Waltz in A flat major).

On October 20, 1829, Chopin writes:—"During my visit at Prince Radziwill's [at Antonin] I wrote an Alla Polacca. It is nothing more than a brilliant salon piece, such as pleases ladies"; and on April 10, 1830:—

I shall play [at a soiree at the house of Lewicki] Hummel's "La Sentinelle," and at the close my Polonaise with violoncello, for which I have composed an Adagio as an introduction. I have already rehearsed it, and it does not sound badly.

Prince Radziwill, the reader will remember, played the violoncello. It was, however, not to him but to Merk that Chopin dedicated this composition, which, before departing from Vienna to Paris, he left with Mechetti, who eventually published it under the title of "Introduction et Polonaise brillante pour piano et violoncelle," dediees a Mr. Joseph Merk. On the whole we may accept Chopin's criticism of his Op. 3 as correct. The Polonaise is nothing but a brilliant salon piece. Indeed, there is very little in this composition—one or two pianoforte passages, and a finesse here and there excepted—that distinguishes it as Chopin's. The opening theme verges even dangerously to the commonplace. More of the Chopinesque than in the Polonaise may be discovered in the Introduction, which was less of a piece d'occasion. What subdued the composer's individuality was no doubt the violoncello, which, however, is well provided with grateful cantilene.

On two occasions Chopin writes of studies. On October 20, 1829: "I have composed a study in my own manner"; and on November 14, 1829: "I have written some studies; in your presence I would play them well." These studies are probably among the twelve published in the summer of 1833, they may, however, also be among those published in the autumn of 1837. The twelfth of the first sheaf of studies (Op. 10) Chopin composed, as already stated, at Stuttgart, when he was under the excitement caused by the news of the taking of Warsaw by the Russians on September 8, 1831.

The words "I intend to write a Polonaise with orchestra," contained in a letter dated September 18, 1830, give rise to the interesting question: "Did Chopin realise his intention, and has the work come down to us?" I think both questions can be answered in the affirmative. At any rate, I hold that internal evidence seems to indicate that Op. 22, the "Grande Polonaise brillante precedee d'un Andante spianato avec orchestre," which was published in the summer of 1836, is the work in question. Whether the "Andante" was composed at the same time, and what, if any, alterations were subsequently made in the Polonaise, I do not venture to decide. But the Polonaise has so much of Chopin's early showy virtuosic style and so little of his later noble emotional power that my conjecture seems reasonable. Moreover, the fact that the orchestra is employed speaks in favour of my theory, for after the works already discussed in the tenth chapter, and the concertos with which we shall concern ourselves presently, Chopin did not in any other composition (i.e., after 1830) write for the orchestra. His experiences in Warsaw, Vienna, and Paris convinced him, no doubt, that he was not made to contend with masses, either as an executant or as a composer. Query: Is the Polonaise, of which Chopin says in July, 1831, that he has to leave it to Wurfel, Op. 22 or another work?

Two other projects of Chopin, however, seem to have remained unrealised—a Concerto for two pianos which he intended to play in public at Vienna with his countryman Nidecki (letter of December 21, 1830), and Variations for piano and violin on a theme of Beethoven's, to be written conjointly by himself and Slavik (letters of December 21 and 25, 1830). Fragments of the former of these projected works may, however, have been used in the "Allegro de Concert," Op. 46, published in 1842.

In the letter of December 21, 1830, there is also an allusion to a waltz and mazurkas just finished, but whether they are to be found among the master's printed compositions is more than I can tell.

The three "Ecossaises" of the year 1830, which Fontana published as Op. 72, No. 3, are the least individual of Chopin's compositions, and almost the only dances of his which may be described as dance music pure and simple—rhythm and melody without poetry, matter with a minimum of soul.

The posthumous Mazurka (D major) of 1829-30 is unimportant. It contains nothing notable, except perhaps the descending chromatic successions of chords of the sixth. In fact, we can rejoice in its preservation only because a comparison with a remodelling of 1832 allows us to trace a step in Chopin's development.

And now we come to the concertos, the history of which, as far as it is traceable in the composer's letters, I will here place before the reader. If I repeat in this chapter passages already quoted in previous chapters, it is for the sake of completeness and convenience.

> *October 3, 1829.—I have—perhaps to my misfortune—already found my ideal, whom I worship faithfully and sincerely. Six months have elapsed and I have not yet exchanged a syllable with her of whom I dream every night. Whilst my thoughts were with her I composed the Adagio of my Concerto.*

The Adagio here mentioned is that of the F minor Concerto, Op. 21, which he composed before but published after the F. minor Concerto, Op. 11—the former appearing in print in April, 1836, the latter in September, 1833. [Footnote: The slow movements of Chopin's concertos are marked Larglietto, the composer uses here the word Adagio generically—i.e., in the sense of slow movement generally.] Karasowski says mistakingly that the movement referred to is the Adagio of the E minor Concerto. He was perhaps misled by a mistranslation of his own. In the German version of his Chopin biography he gives the concluding words of the above quotation as "of my new Concerto," but there is no new in the Polish text (na ktorego pamiatke skomponowalem Adagio do mojego Koncertu).

> *October 20, 1829.—Elsner has praised the Adagio of the Concerto. He says that there is something new in it. As to the Rondo I do not wish yet to hear a judgment, for I am not yet satisfied with it myself. I am curious whether I shall finish this work when I return [from a visit to Prince Radziwill].*

November 14, 1829. —I received your last letter at Antonin at Radziwill's. I was there a week; you cannot imagine how quickly and pleasantly the time passed to me. I left by the last coach, and had much trouble in getting away. As for me I should have stayed till they had turned me out; but my occupations and, above all things, my Concerto, which is impatiently waiting for its Finale, have compelled me to take leave of this Paradise.

On March 17, 1830, Chopin played the F minor Concerto at the first concert he gave in Warsaw. How it was received by the public and the critics on this occasion and on that of a second concert has been related in the ninth chapter (p.131).

March 27, 1830. —I hope yet to finish before the holidays the first Allegro of my second Concerto [i.e., the one in E minor], and therefore I should in any case wait till after the holidays [to give a third concert], although I am convinced that I should have this time a still larger audience than formerly; for the haute volee has not yet heard me.

On April 10, 1830, Chopin writes that his Concerto is not yet finished; and on May 15, 1830: —

The Rondo for my Concerto is not yet finished, because the right inspired mood has always beep wanting. If I have only the Allegro and the Adagio completely finished I shall be without anxiety about the Finale. The Adagio is in E major, and of a romantic, calm, and partly melancholy character. It is intended to convey the impression which one receives when the eye rests on a beloved landscape that calls up in one's soul beautiful memories —for instance, on a fine, moonlit spring night. I have written violins with mutes as an accompaniment to it. I wonder if that will have a good effect? Well, time will show.

August 21, 1830. —Next month I leave here; first, however, I must rehearse my Concerto, for the Rondo is now finished.

For an account of the rehearsals of the Concerto and its first public performance at Chopin's third Warsaw concert on October u, 1830, the reader is referred to the tenth chapter (p. 150). [FOOTNOTE: In the following remarks on the concertos I shall draw freely from the critical commentary on the Pianoforte Works of Chopin, which I contributed some years ago (1879) to the Monthly Musical Record.]

Chopin, says Liszt, wrote beautiful concertos and fine sonatas, but it is not difficult to perceive in these productions "plus de volonte que d'inspiration." As for his inspiration it was naturally "imperieuse, fantasque, irreflechie; ses allures ne pouvaient etre que libres." Indeed, Liszt believes that Chopin—

> did violence to his genius every time he sought to fetter it
>
> by rules, classifications, and an arrangement that was not
>
> his own, and could not accord with the exigencies of his
>
> spirit, which was one of those whose grace displays itself
>
> when they seem to drift along [alter a la derive]....The
>
> classical attempts of Chopin nevertheless shine by a rare
>
> refinement of style. They contain passages of great interest,
>
> parts of surprising grandeur.

With Chopin writing a concerto or a sonata was an effort, and the effort was always inadequate for the attainment of the object—a perfect work of its kind. He lacked the peculiar qualities, natural and acquired, requisite for a successful cultivation of the larger forms. He could not grasp and hold the threads of thought which he found flitting in his mind, and weave them into a strong, complex web; he snatched them up one by one, tied them together, and either knit them into light fabrics or merely wound them into skeins. In short, Chopin was not a thinker, not a logician—his propositions are generally good, but his arguments are poor and the conclusions often wanting. Liszt speaks sometimes of Chopin's science. In doing this, however, he misapplies the word. There was nothing scientific in Chopin's mode of production, and there is nothing scientific in his works. Substitute "ingenious" (in the sense of quick-witted and possessed of genius, in the sense of the German geistreich) for "scientific," and you come near to what Liszt really meant. If the word is applicable at all to art, it can be applicable only to works which manifest a sustained and dominating intellectual power, such, for instance, as a fugue of Bach's, a symphony of Beethoven's, that is, to works radically different from those of Chopin. Strictly speaking, the word, however, is not applicable to art, for art and science are not coextensive; nay, to some extent, are even inimical to each other. Indeed, to call a work of art purely and simply "scientific," is tantamount to saying that it is dry and uninspired by the muse. In dwelling so long on this point my object was not so much to elucidate Liszt's meaning as Chopin's character as a composer.

Notwithstanding their many shortcomings, the concertos may be said to be the most satisfactory of Chopin's works in the larger forms, or at least those that afford the greatest amount of enjoyment. In some respects the concerto-form was more favourable than the sonata-form for the exercise of Chopin's peculiar talent, in other respects it was less so. The concerto-form admits of a far greater and freer display of the virtuosic capabilities of the pianoforte than the sonata-form, and does not necessitate the same strictness of logical structure, the same thorough working-out of the subject-matter. But, on the other hand, it demands aptitude in writing for the orchestra and appropriately solid material. Now, Chopin lacked such aptitude entirely, and the nature of his material accorded little with the size of the structure and the orchestral frame. And, then, are not these confessions of intimate experiences, these moonlight sentimentalities, these listless dreams, &c., out of place in the gaslight glare of concert-rooms, crowded with audiences brought together to a great extent rather by ennui, vanity, and idle curiosity than by love of art?

The concerto is the least perfect species of the sonata genus; practical, not ideal, reasons have determined its form, which owes its distinctive features to the calculations of the virtuoso, not to the inspiration of the creative artist. Romanticism does not take kindly to it. Since Beethoven the form has been often modified, more especially the long introductory tutti omitted or cut short. Chopin, however, adhered to the orthodox form, taking unmistakably Hummel for his model. Indeed, Hummel's concertos were Chopin's model not only as regards structure, but also to a certain extent as regards the character of the several movements. In the tutti's of the first movement, and in the general complexion of the second (the slow) and the third (Rondo) movement, this discipleship is most apparent. But while noting the resemblance, let us not overlook the difference. If the bones are Hummel's (which no doubt is an exaggeration of the fact), the flesh, blood, and soul are Chopin's. In his case adherence to the orthodox concerto-form was so much the more regrettable as writing for the orchestra was one of his weakest points. Indeed, Chopin's originality is gone as soon as he writes for another instrument than the pianoforte. The commencement of the first solo is like the opening of a beautiful vista after a long walk through dreary scenery, and every new entry of the orchestra precipitates you from the delectable regions of imagination to the joyless deserts of the actual. Chopin's inaptitude in writing for the orchestra is, however, most conspicuous where he employs it conjointly with the pianoforte. Carl

Klindworth and Carl Tausig have rescored the concertos: the former the one in F minor, the latter the one in E minor. Klindworth wrote his arrangement of the F minor Concerto in 1867-1868 in London, and published it ten years later at Moscow (P. Jurgenson).[FOOTNOTE: The title runs: "Second Concerto de Chopin, Op. 21, avec un nouvel accompagnement d'orchestre d'apres la partition originale par Karl Klindworth. Dedie a Franz Lizt." It is now the property of the Berlin publishers Bote and Bock.] A short quotation from the preface will charactise his work:—

> The principal pianoforte part has, notwithstanding the entire
> remodelling of the score, been retained almost unchanged.
> Only in some passages, which the orchestra, in consequence of
> a richer instrumentation, accompanies with greater fulness,
> the pianoforte part had, on that account, to be made more
> effective by an increase of brilliance. By these divergences
> from the original, from the so perfect and beautifully
> effectuating [effectuirenden] pianoforte style of Chopin,
> either the unnecessary doubling of the melody already
> pregnantly represented by the orchestra was avoided, or—in
> keeping with the now fuller harmonic support of the
> accompaniment—some figurations of the solo instrument
> received a more brilliant form.

Of Tausig's labour [FOOTNOTE: "Grosses Concert in E moll. Op. 11." Bearberet von Carl Tausig. Score, pianoforte, and orchestral parts. Berlin: Ries and Erler.] I shall only say that his cutting-down and patching-up of the introductory tutti, to mention only one thing, are not well enough done to excuse the liberty taken with a great composer's work. Moreover, your emendations cannot reach the vital fault, which lies in the conceptions. A musician may have mastered the mechanical trick of instrumentation, and yet his works may not be at heart orchestral. Instrumentation ought to be more than something that at will can be added or withheld; it ought to be the appropriate expression of something that appertains to the thought. The fact is, Chopin could not think for the orchestra, his thoughts took always the form of the pianoforte language; his thinking became paralysed when he made use of another medium of expression. Still, there have been critics who thought differently. The Polish composer Sowinski declared without circumlocution that Chopin "wrote admirably for the orchestra." Other countrymen of his dwelt at greater length, and with no less enthusiasm, on what is generally considered a weak point in the master's equipment.

A Paris correspondent of the Neue Zeitschrift fur Musik (1834) remarked a propos of the F minor Concerto that there was much delicacy in the instrumentation. But what do the opinions of those critics, if they deserve the name, amount to when weighed against that of the rest of the world, nay, even against that of Berlioz alone, who held that "in the compositions of Chopin all the interest is concentrated in the piano part, the orchestra of his concertos is nothing but a cold and almost useless accompaniment"?

All this and much more may be said against Chopin's concertos, yet such is the charm, loveliness, delicacy, elegance, and brilliancy of the details, that one again and again forgives and forgets their shortcomings as wholes. But now let us look at these works a little more closely.

The first-composed and last-published Concerto, the one in F minor, Op. 21 (dedicated to Madame la Comtesse Delphine Potocka), opens with a tutti of about seventy bars. When, after this, the pianoforte interrupts the orchestra impatiently, and then takes up the first subject, it is as if we were transported into another world and breathed a purer atmosphere. First, there are some questions and expostulations, then the composer unfolds a tale full of sweet melancholy in a strain of lovely, tenderly-intertwined melody. With what inimitable grace he winds those delicate garlands around the members of his melodic structure! How light and airy the harmonic base on which it rests! But the contemplation of his grief disturbs his equanimity more and more, and he begins to fret and fume. In the second subject he seems to protest the truthfulness and devotion of his heart, and concludes with a passage half upbraiding, half beseeching, which is quite captivating, nay more, even bewitching in its eloquent persuasiveness. Thus far, from the entrance of the pianoforte, all was irreproachable. How charming if Chopin had allowed himself to drift on the current of his fancy, and had left rules, classifications, &c., to others! But no, he had resolved to write a concerto, and must now put his hand to the rudder, and have done with idle dreaming, at least for the present—unaware, alas, that the idle dreamings of some people are worth more than their serious efforts. Well, what is unpoetically called the working-out section—to call it free fantasia in this instance would be mockery—reminds me of Goethe's "Zauberlehrling," who said to himself in the absence of his master, "I noted his words, works, and procedure, and, with strength of mind, I also shall do wonders." How the apprentice conjured up the spirits, and made them do his bidding; how, afterwards, he found he had forgotten the formula with which to stop and banish them, and what were the consequent sad results, the reader will, no doubt, remember. The customary repetition of the first section of the movement calls for no remark. Liszt cites the second movement (Larghetto, A flat major) of this work as a specimen of the morceaux d'une surprenante grandeur to be found in Chopin's concertos and sonatas, and mentions that the composer had a marked predilection for it, delighting in frequently playing it. And Schumann exclaims: "What are ten editorial crowns compared to one such Adagio as that in the second concerto!" The beautiful deep-toned, love-laden cantilena, which is profusely and exquisitely ornamented in Chopin's characteristic style, is interrupted by a very impressive recitative of some length, after which the cantilena is heard again. But criticism had better be silent, and listen here attentively. And how shall I describe the last movement (Allegro vivace F minor, 3-4)—its feminine softness and rounded contours, its graceful, gyrating, dance-like motions, its sprightliness and frolicsomeness? Unless I quote every part and particle, I feel I cannot do justice to it. The exquisite ease and grace, the subtle spirit that breathes through this movement, defy description, and, more, defy the attempts of most performers to reproduce the original. He who ventures to interpret Chopin ought to have a soul strung with chords which the gentlest breath of feeling sets in vibration, and a body of such a delicate and supple organisation as to echo with equal readiness the music of the soul. As to the listener, he is carried away in this movement from one lovely picture to another, and no time is left him to reflect and make objections with reference to the whole.

The Concerto in E minor, Op. 11, dedicated to Mr. Fred Kalkbrenner, shows more of volonte and less of inspiration than the one in F minor. One can almost read in it the words of the composer, "If I have only the Allegro and the Adagio completely finished, I shall be in no anxiety about the Finale." The elongated form of the first movement—the introductory tutti alone extends to 138 bars—compares disadvantageously with the greater compactness of the corresponding movement in the F minor Concerto, and makes still more sensible the monotony resulting from the key-relation of the constituent parts, the tonic being the same in both subjects. The scheme is this:—First subject in E minor, second subject in E major, working-out section in C major, leading through various keys to the return of the first subject in E minor and of the second subject in G major, followed by a close in E minor. The tonic is not relieved till the commencement of the working-out section. The re-entrance of the second subject brings, at last, something of a contrast. How little Chopin understood the importance or the handling of those powerful levers, key-relation and contrast, may also be observed in the Sonata, Op. 4, where the last movement brings the first subject in C minor and the second in G minor. Here the composer preserves the same mode (minor), there the same tonic, the result being nearly the same in both instances. But, it may be asked, was not this languid monotony which results from the employment of these means just what Chopin intended?

The only reply that can be made to this otherwise unanswerable objection is, so much the worse for the artist's art if he had such intentions. Chopin's description of the Adagio quoted above—remember the beloved landscape, the beautiful memories, the moonlit spring night, and the muted violins—hits off its character admirably. Although Chopin himself designates the first Allegro as "vigorous"—which in some passages, at least from the composer's standpoint, we may admit it to be—the fundamental mood of this movement is one closely allied to that which he says he intended to express in the Adagio. Look at the first movement, and judge whether there are not in it more pale moonlight reveries than fresh morning thoughts. Indeed, the latter, if not wholly absent, are confined to the introductory bars of the first subject and some passage-work. Still, the movement is certainly not without beauty, although the themes appear somewhat bloodless, and the passages are less brilliant and piquant than those in the F minor Concerto. Exquisite softness and tenderness distinguish the melodious parts, and Chopin's peculiar coaxing tone is heard in the semiquaver passage marked tranquillo of the first subject. The least palatable portion of the movement is the working-out section. The pianoforte part therein reminds one too much of a study, without having the beauty of Chopin's compositions thus entitled; and the orchestra amuses itself meanwhile with reminiscences of the principal motives. Chopin's procedure in this and similar cases is pretty much the same (F minor Concerto, Krakowiak, &c.), and recalls to my mind—may the manes of the composer forgive me—a malicious remark of Rellstab's. Speaking of the introduction to the Variations, Op. 2, he says: "The composer pretends to be going to work out the theme." It is curious, and sad at the same time, to behold with what distinction Chopin treats the bassoon, and how he is repaid with mocking ingratitude. But enough of the orchestral rabble. The Adagio is very fine in its way, but such is its cloying sweetness that one longs for something bracing and active. This desire the composer satisfies only partially in the last movement (Rondo vivace, 2-4, E major). Nevertheless, he succeeds in putting us in good humour by his gaiety, pretty ways, and tricksy surprises (for instance, the modulations from E major to E flat major, and back again to E major). We seem, however, rather to look on the play of fantoccini than the doings of men; in short, we feel here what we have felt more or less strongly throughout the whole work—there is less intensity of life and consequently less of human interest in this than in the F minor Concerto.

Almost all my remarks on the concertos run counter to those made by W. von Lenz. The F minor Concerto he holds to be an uninteresting work, immature and fragmentary in plan, and, excepting some delicate ornamentation, without originality. Nay, he goes even so far as to say that the passage-work is of the usual kind met with in the compositions of Hummel and his successors, and that the cantilena in the larghetto is in the jejune style of Hummel; the last movement also receives but scanty and qualified praise. On the other hand, he raves about the E minor Concerto, confining himself, however, to the first movement. The second movement he calls a "tiresome nocturne," the Rondo "a Hummel." A tincture of classical soberness and self-possession in the first movement explains Lenz's admiration of this composition, but I fail to understand the rest of his predilections and critical utterances.

In considering these concertos one cannot help exclaiming—What a pity that Chopin should have set so many beautiful thoughts and fancies in such a frame and thereby marred them! They contain passages which are not surpassed in any of his most perfect compositions, yet among them these concertos cannot be reckoned. It is difficult to determine their rank in concerto literature. The loveliness, brilliancy, and piquancy of the details bribe us to overlook, and by dazzling us even prevent us from seeing, the formal shortcomings of the whole. But be their shortcomings ever so great and many, who would dispense with these works? Therefore, let us be thankful, and enjoy them without much grumbling.

Schumann in writing of the concertos said that Chopin introduced Beethoven spirit [Beethovenischen Geist] into the concert-room, dressing the master's thoughts, as Hummel had done Mozart's, in brilliant, flowing drapery; and also, that Chopin had instruction from the best, from Beethoven, Schubert, and Field—that the first might be supposed to have educated his mind to boldness, the second his heart to tenderness, the third his fingers to dexterity. Although as a rule a wonderfully acute observer, Schumann was not on this occasion very happy in the few critical utterances which he vouchsafed in the course of the general remarks of which his notice mainly consists. Without congeniality there cannot be much influence, at least not in the case of so exclusive and fastidious a nature as Chopin's. Now, what congeniality could there be between the rugged German and the delicate Pole? All accounts agree in that Chopin was far from being a thorough-going worshipper of Beethoven—he objected to much in his matter and manner, and, moreover, could not by any means boast an exhaustive acquaintance with his works. That Chopin assimilated something of Beethoven is of course more likely than not; but, if a fact, it is a latent one. As to Schubert, I think Chopin knew too little of his music to be appreciably influenced by him. At any rate, I fail to perceive how and where the influence reveals itself. Of Field, on the other hand, traces are discoverable, and even more distinct ones of Hummel. The idyllic serenity of the former and the Mozartian sweetness of the latter were truly congenial to him; but no less, if not more, so was Spohr's elegiac morbidezza. Chopin's affection for Spohr is proved by several remarks in his letters: thus on one occasion (October 3, 1829) he calls the master's Octet a wonderful work; and on another occasion (September 18, 1830) he says that the Quintet for pianoforte, flute, clarinet, bassoon, and horn (Op. 52) is a wonderfully beautiful work, but not suitable for the pianoforte. How the gliding cantilena in sixths and thirds of the minuet and the serpentining chromatic passages in the last movement of the last-mentioned work must have flattered his inmost soul! There can be no doubt that Spohr was a composer who made a considerable impression upon Chopin. In his music there is nothing to hurt the most fastidious sensibility, and much to feed on for one who, like Jaques in "As you like it", could "suck melancholy out of a song, as a weasel eggs."

Many other composers, notably the supremely-loved and enthusiastically-admired Mozart and Bach, must have had a share in Chopin's development; but it cannot be said that they left a striking mark on his music, with regard to which, however, it has to be remembered that the degree of external resemblance does not always accurately indicate the degree of internal indebtedness. Bach's influence on Mendelssohn, Schumann, Chopin, and others of their contemporaries, and its various effects on their styles, is one of the curiosities of nineteenth century musical history; a curiosity, however, which is fully disclosed only by subtle analysis. Field and especially Hummel are those musicians who—more, however, as pianists than as composers (i.e., more by their pianoforte language than by their musical thoughts)—set the most distinct impress on Chopin's early virtuosic style, of which we see almost the last in the concertos, where it appears in a chastened and spiritualised form very different from the materialism of the Fantasia (Op. 13) and the Krakowiak (Op. 14). Indeed, we may say of this style that the germ, and much more than the germ, of almost every one of its peculiarities is to be found in the pianoforte works of Hummel and Field; and this statement the concertos of these masters, more especially those of the former, and their shorter pieces, more especially the nocturnes of the latter, bear out in its entirety. The wide-spread broken chords, great skips, wreaths of rhythmically unmeasured ornamental notes, simultaneous combinations of unequal numbers of notes (five or seven against four, for instance), &c., are all to be found in the compositions of the two above-named pianist-composers. Chopin's style, then, was not original? Most decidedly it was. But it is not so much new elements as the development and the different commixture, in degree and kind, of known elements which make an individual style—the absolutely new being, generally speaking, insignificant compared with the acquired and evolved. The opinion that individuality is a spontaneous generation is an error of the same kind as that imagination has nothing to do with memory. Ex nihilo nihil fit. Individuality should rather be regarded as a feminine organisation which conceives and brings forth; or, better still, as a growing thing which feeds on what is germane to it, a thing with self-acting suctorial organs that operate whenever they come in contact with suitable food. A nucleus is of course necessary for the development of an individuality, and this nucleus is the physical and intellectual constitution of the individual. Let us note in passing that the development of the individuality of an artistic style presupposes the development of the individuality of the man's character. But not only natural dispositions, also acquired dexterities affect the development of the individuality of an artistic style. Beethoven is orchestral even in his pianoforte works. Weber rarely ceases to be operatic. Spohr cannot help betraying the violinist, nor Schubert the song-composer. The more Schumann got under his command the orchestral forces, the more he impressed on them the style which he had formed previously by many years of playing and writing for the pianoforte. Bach would have been another Bach if he had not been an organist. Clementi was and remained all his life a pianist. Like Clementi, so was also Chopin under the dominion of his instrument. How the character of the man expressed itself in the style of the artist will become evident when we examine Chopin's masterpieces. Then will also be discussed the influence on his style of the Polish national music.

CHAPTER XIV

PARIS IN 1831.—LIFE IN THE STREETS.—ROMANTICISM AND LIBERALISM.—ROMANTICISM IN LITERATURE.—CHIEF LITERARY PUBLICATIONS OF THE TIME.—THE PICTORIAL ARTS.—MUSIC AND MUSICIANS.—CHOPIN'S OPINION OF THE GALAXY OF SINGERS THEN PERFORMING AT THE VARIOUS OPERA-HOUSES.

Chopin's sensations on plunging, after his long stay in the stagnant pool of Vienna, into the boiling sea of Paris might have been easily imagined, even if he had not left us a record of them. What newcomer from a place less populous and inhabited by a less vivacious race could help wondering at and being entertained by the vastness, variety, and bustle that surrounded him there?

> *Paris offers anything you may wish [writes Chopin]. You can amuse yourself, mope, laugh, weep, in short, do whatever you like; no one notices it, because thousands do the same. Everybody goes his own way....The Parisians are a peculiar people. When evening sets in one hears nothing but the crying of titles of little new books, which consist of from three to four sheets of nonsense. The boys know so well how to recommend their wares that in the end—willing or not—one buys one for a sou. They bear titles such as these:—"L'art de faire, des amours, et de les conserver ensuite"; "Les amours des pretres"; "L'Archeveque de Paris avec Madame la duchesse de Berry"; and a thousand similar absurdities which, however, are often very wittily written. One cannot but be astonished at the means people here make use of to earn a few pence.*

All this and much more may be seen in Paris every day, but in 1831 Paris life was not an everyday life. It was then and there, if at any time and anywhere, that the "roaring loom of Time" might be heard: a new garment was being woven for an age that longed to throw off the wornout, tattered, and ill-fitting one inherited from its predecessors; and discontent and hopefulness were the impulses that set the shuttle so busily flying hither and thither. This movement, a reaction against the conventional formalism and barren, superficial scepticism of the preceding age, had ever since the beginning of the century been growing in strength and breadth. It pervaded all the departments of human knowledge and activity—politics, philosophy, religion, literature, and the arts. The doctrinaire school in politics and the eclectic school in philosophy were as characteristic products of the movement as the romantic school in poetry and art. We recognise the movement in Lamennais' attack on religious indifference, and in the gospel of a "New Christianity" revealed by Saint Simon and preached and developed by Bazard and Enfantin, as well as in the teaching of Cousin, Villemain, and Guizot, and in the works of V. Hugo, Delacroix, and others. Indeed, unless we keep in view as far as possible all the branches into which the broad stream divides itself, we shall not be able to understand the movement aright either as a whole or in its parts. V. Hugo defines the militant—i.e., negative side of romanticism as liberalism in literature. The positive side of the liberalism of the time might, on the other hand, not inaptly be described as romanticism in speculation and practice. This, however, is matter rather for a history of civilisation than for a biography of an artist. Therefore, without further enlarging on it, I shall let Chopin depict the political aspect of Paris in 1831 as he saw it, and then attempt myself a slight outline sketch of the literary and artistic aspect of the French capital, which signifies France.

Louis Philippe had been more than a year on the throne, but the agitation of the country was as yet far from being allayed:—

> There is now in Paris great want and little money in
> circulation. One meets many shabby individuals with wild
> physiognomies, and sometimes one hears an excited, menacing
> discussion on Louis Philippe, who, as well as his ministers,
> hangs only by a single hair. The populace is disgusted with
> the Government, and would like to overthrow it, in order to
> make an end of the misery; but the Government is too well on
> its guard, and the least concourse of people is at once
> dispersed by the mounted police.

Riots and attentats were still the order of the day, and no opportunity for a demonstration was let slip by the parties hostile to the Government. The return of General Ramorino from Poland, where he had taken part in the insurrection, offered such an opportunity. This adventurer, a natural son of Marshal Lannes, who began his military career in the army of Napoleon, and, after fighting wherever fighting was going on, ended it on the Piazza d'Armi at Turin, being condemned by a Piedmontese court-martial to be shot for disobedience to orders, was hardly a worthy recipient of the honours bestowed upon him during his journey through Germany and France. But the personal merit of such popular heroes of a day is a consideration of little moment; they are mere counters, counters representative of ideas and transient whims.

> The enthusiasm of the populace for our general is of course
> known to you [writes Chopin to his friend Woyciechowski].
> Paris would not be behind in this respect. [Footnote: The
> Poles and everything Polish were at that time the rage in
> Paris; thus, for instance, at one of the theatres where
> dramas were generally played, they represented now the whole
> history of the last Polish insurrection, and the house was
> every night crammed with people who wished to see the combats
> and national costumes.] The Ecole de Medecine and the jeune
> France, who wear their beards and cravats according to a
> certain pattern, intend to honour him with a great
> demonstration. Every political party—I speak of course only
> of the ultras—has its peculiar badge: the Carlists have
> green waistcoats, the Republicans and Napoleonists (and these
> form the jeune France) [red], [Footnote: Chopin has omitted
> this word, which seems to be necessary to complete the
> sentence; at least, it is neither in the Polish nor German
> edition of Karasowski's book.] the Saint-Simonians who
> profess a new religion, wear blue, and so forth. Nearly a
> thousand of these young people marched with a tricolour
> through the town in order to give Ramorino an ovation.
> Although he was at home, and notwithstanding the shouting of
> "Vive les Polonais!" he did not show himself, not wishing to
> expose himself to any unpleasantness on the part of the
> Government. His adjutant came out and said that the general
> was sorry he could not receive them and begged them to return
> some other day. But the next day he took other lodgings. When

some days afterwards an immense mass of people — not only young

men, but also rabble that had congregated near the
Pantheon — proceeded to the other side of the Seine to
Ramorino's house, the crowd increased like an avalanche till
it was dispersed by several charges of the mounted police who
had stationed themselves at the Pont Neuf. Although many were
wounded, new masses of people gathered on the Boulevards
under my windows in order to join those who were expected
from the other side of the Seine. The police was now
helpless, the crowd increased more and more, till at last a
body of infantry and a squadron of hussars advanced; the
commandant ordered the municipal guard and the troops to
clear the footpaths and street of the curious and riotous mob
and to arrest the ringleaders. (This is the free nation!) The
panic spread with the swiftness of lightning: the shops were
closed, the populace flocked together at all the corners of
the streets, and the orderlies who galloped through the
streets were hissed. All windows were crowded by spectators,
as on festive occasions with us at home, and the excitement
lasted from eleven o'clock in the morning till eleven o'clock
at night. I thought that the affair would have a bad end; but
towards midnight they sang "Allons enfants de la patrie!" and
went home. I am unable to describe to you the impression
which the horrid voices of this riotous, discontented mob
made upon me! Everyone was afraid that the riot would be
continued next morning, but that was not the case. Only
Grenoble has followed the example of Lyons; however, one
cannot tell what may yet come to pass in the world!

The length and nature of Chopin's account show what a lively interest he took in the occurrences of which he was in part an eye and ear-witness, for he lived on the fourth story of a house (No. 27) on the Boulevard Poissonniere, opposite the Cite Bergere, where General Ramorino lodged. But some of his remarks show also that the interest he felt was by no means a pleasurable one, and probably from this day dates his fear and horror of the mob. And now we will turn from politics, a theme so distasteful to Chopin that he did not like to hear it discussed and could not easily be induced to take part in its discussion, to a theme more congenial, I doubt not, to all of us.

Literary romanticism, of which Chateaubriand and Madame de Stael were the harbingers, owed its existence to a longing for a greater fulness of thought, a greater intenseness of feeling, a greater appropriateness and adequateness of expression, and, above all, a greater truth to life and nature. It was felt that the degenerated classicists were "barren of imagination and invention," offered in their insipid artificialities nothing but "rhetoric, bombast, fleurs de college, and Latin-verse poetry," clothed "borrowed ideas in trumpery imagery," and presented themselves with a "conventional elegance and noblesse than which there was nothing more common." On the other hand, the works of the master-minds of England, Germany, Spain, and Italy, which were more and more translated and read, opened new, undreamt-of vistas. The Bible, Homer, and Shakespeare began now to be considered of all books the most worthy to be studied. And thus it came to pass that in a short time a most complete revolution was accomplished in literature, from abject slavery to unlimited freedom.

> There are neither rules nor models [says V. Hugo, the leader
> of the school, in the preface to his Cromwell (1827)], or
> rather there are no other rules than the general laws of
> nature which encompass the whole art, and the special laws
> which for every composition result from the conditions of
> existence peculiar to each subject. The former are eternal,
> internal, and remain; the latter variable, external, and
> serve only once.

Hence theories, poetics, and systems were to be broken up, and the old plastering which covered the fagade of art was to be pulled down. From rules and theories the romanticists appealed to nature and truth, without forgetting, however, that nature and art are two different things, and that the truth of art can never be absolute reality. The drama, for instance, must be "a concentrating mirror which, so far from enfeebling, collects and condenses the colouring rays and transforms a glimmer into a light, a light into a flame." To pass from form to matter, the attention given by the romanticists to history is particularly to be noted. Pierre Dubois, the director of the philosophical and literary journal "Le Globe," the organ of romanticism (1824-1832), contrasts the poverty of invention in the works of the classicists with the inexhaustible wealth of reality, "the scenes of disorder, of passion, of fanaticism, of hypocrisy, and of intrigue," recorded in history. What the dramatist has to do is to perform the miracle "of reanimating the personages who appear dead on the pages of a chronicle, of discovering by analysis all the shades of the passions which caused these hearts to beat, of recreating their language and costume." It is a significant fact that Sainte-Beuve opened the campaign of romanticism in "Le Globe" with a "Tableau de la poesie francaise au seizieme siecle," the century of the "Pleiade," and of Rabelais and Montaigne. It is a still more significant fact that the members of the "Cenacle," the circle of kindred minds that gathered around Victor Hugo—Alfred de Vigny, Emile Deschamps, Sainte-Beuve, David d'Angers, and others—"studied and felt the real Middle Ages in their architecture, in their chronicles, and in their picturesque vivacity." Nor should we overlook in connection with romanticism Cousin's aesthetic teaching, according to which, God being the source of all beauty as well as of all truth, religion, and morality, "the highest aim of art is to awaken in its own way the feeling of the infinite." Like all reformers the romanticists were stronger in destruction than in construction. Their fundamental doctrines will hardly be questioned by anyone in our day, but the works of art which they reared on them only too often give just cause for objection and even rejection. However, it is not surprising that, with the physical and spiritual world, with time and eternity at their arbitrary disposal, they made themselves sometimes guilty of misrule. To "extract the invariable laws from the general order of things, and the special from the subject under treatment," is no easy matter. V. Hugo tells us that it is only for a man of genius to undertake such a task, but he himself is an example that even a man so gifted is fallible. In a letter written in the French capital on January 14, 1832, Mendelssohn says of the "so-called romantic school" that it has infected all the Parisians, and that on the stage they think of nothing but the plague, the gallows, the devil, childbeds, and the like. Nor were the romances less extravagant than the dramas. The lyrical poetry, too, had its defects and blemishes. But if it had laid itself open to the blame of being "very unequal and very mixed," it also called for the praise of being "rich, richer than any lyrical poetry France had known up to that time." And if the romanticists, as one of them, Sainte-Beuve, remarked, "abandoned themselves without control and without restraint to all the instincts of their nature, and also to all the pretensions of their pride, or even to the silly tricks of their vanity," they had, nevertheless, the supreme merit of having resuscitated what was extinct, and even of having created what never existed in their language. Although a discussion of romanticism without a characterisation of its specific and individual differences is incomplete, I must bring this part of my remarks to a close with a few names and dates illustrative of the literary aspect of Paris in 1831.

I may, however, inform the reader that the subject of romanticism will give rise to further discussion in subsequent chapters.

The most notable literary events of the year 1831 were the publication of Victor Hugo's "Notre Dame de Paris," "Feuilles d'automne," and "Marion Delorme"; Dumas' "Charles VII"; Balzac's "La peau de chagrin"; Eugene Sue's "Ata Gull"; and George Sand's first novel, "Rose et Blanche," written conjointly with Sandeau. Alfred de Musset and Theophile Gautier made their literary debuts in 1830, the one with "Contes d'Espagne et d'Italie," the other with "Poesies." In the course of the third decade of the century Lamartine had given to the world "Meditations poetiques," "Nouvelles Meditations poetiques," and "Harmonies poetiques et religieuses"; Victor Hugo, "Odes et Ballades," "Les Orientales," three novels, and the dramas "Cromwell" and "Hernani"; Dumas, "Henri III et sa Cour," and "Stockholm, Fontainebleau et Rome"; Alfred de Vigny, "Poemes antiques et modernes" and "Cinq-Mars"; Balzac, "Scenes de la vie privee" and "Physiologie du Mariage." Besides the authors just named there were at this time in full activity in one or the other department of literature, Nodier, Beranger, Merimee, Delavigne, Scribe, Sainte-Beuve, Villemain, Cousin, Michelet, Guizot, Thiers, and many other men and women of distinction.

A glance at the Salon of 1831 will suffice to give us an idea of the then state of the pictorial art in France. The pictures which attracted the visitors most were: Delacroix's "Goddess of Liberty on the barricades"; Delaroche's "Richelieu conveying Cinq-Mars and De Thou to Lyons," "Mazarin on his death-bed," "The sons of Edward in the Tower," and "Cromwell beside the coffin of diaries I."; Ary Scheffer's "Faust and Margaret," "Leonore," "Talleyrand," "Henri IV.," and "Louis Philippe"; Robert's "Pifferari," "Burial," and "Mowers"; Horace Vernet's "Judith," "Capture of the Princes Conde," "Conti, and Longueville," "Camille Desmoulins," and "Pius VIII" To enumerate only a few more of the most important exhibitors I shall yet mention Decamps, Lessore, Schnetz, Judin, and Isabey. The dry list will no doubt conjure up in the minds of many of my readers vivid reproductions of the masterpieces mentioned or suggested by the names of the artists.

Romanticism had not invaded music to the same extent as the literary and pictorial arts. Berlioz is the only French composer who can be called in the fullest sense of the word a romanticist, and whose genius entitles him to a position in his art similar to those occupied by V. Hugo and Delacroix in literature and painting. But in 1831 his works were as yet few in number and little known. Having in the preceding year obtained the prix de Rome, he was absent from Paris till the latter part of 1832, when he began to draw upon himself the attention, if not the admiration, of the public by the concerts in which he produced his startlingly original works. Among the foreign musicians residing in the French capital there were many who had adopted the principles of romanticism, but none of them was so thoroughly imbued with its spirit as Liszt—witness his subsequent publications. But although there were few French composers who, strictly speaking, could be designated romanticists, it would be difficult to find among the younger men one who had not more or less been affected by the intellectual atmosphere.

An opera, "La Marquise de Brinvilliers," produced in 1831 at the Opera-Comique, introduces to us no less than nine dramatic composers, the libretto of Scribe and Castil-Blaze being set to music by Cherubini, Auber, Batton, Berton, Boieldieu, Blangini, Carafa, Herold, and Paer. [Footnote: Chopin makes a mistake, leaving out of account Boieldieu, when he says in speaking of "La Marquise de Brinvilliers" that the opera was composed by eight composers.] Cherubini, who towers above all of them, was indeed the high-priest of the art, the grand-master of the craft. Although the Nestor of composers, none equalled him in manly vigour and perennial youth. When seventy-six years of age (in 1836) he composed his fine Requiem in D minor for three-part male chorus, and in the following year a string quartet and quintet. Of his younger colleagues so favourable an account cannot be given. The youngest of them, Batton, a grand prix, who wrote unsuccessful operas, then took to the manufacturing of artificial flowers, and died as inspector at the Conservatoire, need not detain us. Berton, Paer, Blangini, Carafa (respectively born in 1767, 1771, 1781, and 1785), once composers who enjoyed the public's favour, had lost or were losing their popularity at the time we are speaking of; Rossini, Auber, and others having now come into fashion. They present a saddening spectacle, these faded reputations, these dethroned monarchs! What do we know of Blangini, the "Musical Anacreon," and his twenty operas, one hundred and seventy two-part "Notturni," thirty-four "Romances," &c.? Where are Paer's oratorios, operas, and cantatas performed now? Attempts were made in later years to revive some of Carafa's earlier works, but the result was on each occasion a failure. And poor Berton? He could not bear the public's neglect patiently, and vented his rage in two pamphlets, one of them entitled "De la musique mecanique et de la musique philosophique," which neither converted nor harmed anyone. Boieldieu, too, had to deplore the failure of his last opera, "Les deux nuits" (1829), but then his "La Dame blanche," which had appeared in 1825, and his earlier "Jean de Paris" were still as fresh as ever. Herold had only in this year (1831) scored his greatest success with "Zampa." As to Auber, he was at the zenith of his fame. Among the many operas he had already composed, there were three of his best—"Le Macon," "La Muette," and "Fra Diavolo"—and this inimitable master of the genre sautillant had still a long series of charming works in petto. To exhaust the list of prominent men in the dramatic department we have to add only a few names. Of the younger masters I shall mention Halevy, whose most successful work, "La Juive," did not come out till 1835, and Adam, whose best opera, "Le postilion de Longjumeau," saw the foot-lights in 1836. Of the older masters we must not overlook Lesueur, the composer of "Les Bardes," an opera which came out in 1812, and was admired by Napoleon. Lesueur, distinguished as a composer of dramatic and sacred music, and a writer on musical matters, had, however, given up all professional work with the exception of teaching composition at the Conservatoire. In fact, almost all the above-named old gentlemen, although out of fashion as composers, occupied important positions in the musical commonwealth as professors at that institution. Speaking of professors I must not forget to mention old Reicha (born in 1770), the well-known theorist, voluminous composer of instrumental music, and esteemed teacher of counterpoint and composition.

But the young generation did not always look up to these venerable men with the reverence due to their age and merit. Chopin, for instance, writes:—

> *Reicha I know only by sight. You can imagine how curious I am*
> *to make his personal acquaintance. I have already seen some*
> *of his pupils, but from them I have not obtained a favourable*
> *opinion of their teacher. He does not love music, never*
> *frequents the concerts of the Conservatoire, will not speak*
> *with anyone about music, and, when he gives lessons, looks*
> *only at his watch. Cherubini behaves in a similar manner; he*
> *is always speaking of cholera and the revolution. These*
> *gentlemen are mummies; one must content one's self with*
> *respectfully lookingat them from afar, and studying their*
> *works for instruction.*

In these remarks of Chopin the concerts of the Conservatoire are made mention of; they were founded in 1828 by Habeneck and others and intended for the cultivation of the symphonic works of the great masters, more especially of Beethoven. Berlioz tells us in his Memoires, with his usual vivacity and causticity, what impressions the works of Beethoven made upon the old gentlemen above-named. Lesueur considered instrumental music an inferior genre, and although the C minor Symphony quite overwhelmed him, he gave it as his opinion that "one ought not to write such music." Cherubini was profoundly irritated at the success of a master who undermined his dearest theories, but he dared not discharge the bile that was gathering within him. That, however, he had the courage of his opinion may be gathered from what, according to Mendelssohn, he said of Beethoven's later works: "Ca me fait eternuer." Berton looked down with pity on the whole modern German school. Boieldieu, who hardly knew what to think of the matter, manifested "a childish surprise at the simplest harmonic combinations which departed somewhat from the three chords which he had been using all his life." Paer, a cunning Italian, was fond of letting people know that he had known Beethoven, and of telling stories more or less unfavourable to the great man, and flattering to the narrator. The critical young men of the new generation were, however, not altogether fair in their judgments; Cherubini, at least, and Boieldieu too, deserved better treatment at their hands.

In 1830 Auber and Rossini (who, after his last opera "Guillaume Tell," was resting on his laurels) were the idols of the Parisians, and reigned supreme on the operatic stage. But in 1831 Meyerbeer established himself as a third power beside them, for it was in that year that "Robert le Diable" was produced at the Academic Royale de Musique. Let us hear what Chopin says of this event. Speaking of the difficulties with which composers of operas have often to contend he remarks:—

> Even Meyerbeer, who for ten years had been favourably known in the musical world, waited, worked, and paid in Paris for three years in vain before he succeeded in bringing about the performance of his opera "Robert le Diable," which now causes such a furore. Auber had got the start of Meyerbeer with his works, which are very pleasing to the taste of the people, and he did not readily make room for the foreigner at the Grand Opera.

And again:—

> If there was ever a brilliant mise en scene at the Opera-Italien, I cannot believe that it equalled that of Robert le Diable, the new five-act opera of Meyerbeer, who has also written "Il Crociato." "Robert" is a masterpiece of the new school, where the devils sing through speaking-trumpets and the dead rise from their graves, but not as in "Szarlatan" [an opera of Kurpinski's], only from fifty to sixty persons all at once! The stage represents the interior of a convent ruin illuminated by the clear light of the full moon whose

rays fall on the graves of the nuns. In the last act appear
in brilliant candle-light monks with ancense, and from behind
the scene are heard the solemn tones of the organ. Meyerbeer
has made himself immortal by this work; but he had to wait
more than three years before he could get it performed.
People say that he has spent more than 20,000 francs for the
organ and other things made use of in the opera.

[Footnote: This was the current belief at the time, which
Meyerbeer, however, declares to be false in a letter
addressed to Veron, the director of the Opera:—"L'orgue a
ete paye par vous, fourni par vous, comme toutes les choses
que reclamait la mise en scene de Robert, et je dois declarer
que loin de vous tenir au strict neccessaire, vous avez
depasse de bcaucoup les obligations ordinaires d'un directeur
envers les auteurs et le public."]

The creative musicians having received sufficient attention, let us now turn for a moment to the executive ones. Of the pianists we shall hear enough in the next chapter, and therefore will pass them by for the present. Chopin thought that there were in no town more pianists than in Paris, nor anywhere more asses and virtuosos. Of the many excellent virtuosos on stringed and wind-instruments only a few of the most distinguished shall be mentioned. Baillot, the veteran violinist; Franchomme, the young violoncellist; Brod, the oboe-player; and Tulou, the flutist. Beriot and Lafont, although not constant residents like these, may yet be numbered among the Parisian artists. The French capital could boast of at least three first-rate orchestras—that of the Conservatoire, that of the Academic Royale, and that of the Opera-Italien. Chopin, who probably had on December 14 not yet heard the first of these, takes no notice of it, but calls the orchestra of the theatre Feydeau (Opera-Comique) excellent. Cherubini seems to have thought differently, for on being asked why he did not allow his operas to be performed at that institution, he answered:—"Je ne fais pas donner des operas sans choeur, sans orchestre, sans chanteurs, et sans decorations." The Opera-Comique had indeed been suffering from bankruptcy; still, whatever its shortcomings were, it was not altogether without good singers, in proof of which assertion may be named the tenor Chollet, Madame Casimir, and Mdlle. Prevost. But it was at the Italian Opera that a constellation of vocal talent was to be found such as has perhaps at no time been equalled: Malibran-Garcia, Pasta,

Schroder-Devrient, Rubini, Lablache, and Santini. Nor had the Academic, with Nourrit, Levasseur, Derivis, Madame Damoreau-Cinti, and Madame Dorus, to shrink from a comparison. Imagine the treat it must have been to be present at the concert which took place at the Italian Opera on December 25, 1831, and the performers at which comprised artists such as Malibran, Rubini, Lablache, Santini, Madame Raimbaux, Madame Schroder-Devrient, Madame Casadory, Herz, and De Beriot!

Chopin was so full of admiration for what he had heard at the three operatic establishments that he wrote to his master Elsner:—

> It is only here that one can learn what singing is. I believe that not Pasta, but Malibran-Garcia is now the greatest singer in Europe. Prince Valentin Radziwill is quite enraptured by her, and we often wish you were here, for you would be charmed with her singing.

The following extracts from a letter to his friend Woyciechowski contain some more of Chopin's criticism:—

> As regards the opera, I must tell you that I never heard so fine a performance as I did last week, when the "Barber of Seville" was given at the Italian Opera, with Lablache, Rubini, and Malibran-Garcia in the principal parts. Of "Othello" there is likewise an excellent rendering in prospect, further also of "L'Italiana in Algeri." Paris has in this respect never offered so much as now. You can have no idea of Lablache. People say that Pasta's voice has somewhat failed, but I never heard in all my life such heavenly singing as hers. Malibran embraces with her wonderful voice a compass of three octaves; her singing is quite unique in its way, enchanting! Rubini, an excellent tenor, makes endless roulades, often too many colorature, vibrates and trills continually, for which he is rewarded with the greatest applause. His mezza voce is incomparable. A Schroder-Devrient is now making her appearance, but she does not produce such a furore here as in Germany. Signora Malibran personated Othello, Schroder-Devrient Desdemona. Malibran is little, the German lady taller. One thought sometimes that Desdemona was

going to strangle Othello. It was a very expensive
performance; I paid twenty-four francs for my seat, and did
so because I wished to see Malibran play the part of the
Moor, which she did not do particularly well. The orchestra
was excellent, but the mise en scene in the Italian Opera is
nothing compared with that of the French Academie
Royale...Madame Damoreau-Cinti sings also very beautifully; I
prefer her singing to that of Malibran. The latter astonishes
one, but Cinti charms. She sings the chromatic scales and
colorature almost more perfectly than the famous flute-player
Tulou plays them. It is hardly possible to find a more
finished execution. In Nourrit, the first tenor of the Grand
Opera, [Footnote: It may perhaps not be superfluous to point
out that Academie Royale (Imperial, or Nationale, as the case
may be) de Musique, or simply Academie de Musique, and Grand
Opera, or simply Opera, are different names for one and the
same thing—namely, the principal opera-house in France, the
institution whose specialties are grand opera and ballet.]
one admires the warmth of feeling which speaks out of his
singing. Chollet, the first tenor of the Opera-Comique, the
best performer of Fra Diavolo, and excellent in the operas
"Zampa" and "Fiancee," has a manner of his own in conceiving
the parts. He captivates all with his beautiful voice, and is
the favourite of the public.

CHAPTER XV

1831-1832.

ACQUAINTANCES AND FRIENDS: CHERUBINI, BAILLOT, FRANCHOMME, LISZT, MILLER, OSBORNE, MENDELSSOHN.— CHOPIN AND KALKBRENNER.—CHOPIN'S AIMS AS AN ARTIST.— KALKBRENNER'S CHARACTER AS A MAN AND ARTIST.—CHOPIN'S FIRST PARIS CONCERT.—FETIS.—CHOPIN PLAYS AT A CONCERT GIVEN BY THE PRINCE DE LA MOSKOWA.—HIS STATE OF MIND.— LOSS OF HIS POLISH LETTERS.—TEMPORARILY STRAITENED CIRCUMSTANCES AND BRIGHTENING PROSPECTS.—PATRONS AND WELL-WISHERS.—THE "IDEAL."—A LETTER TO HILLER.

Chopin brought only a few letters of introduction with him to Paris: one from Dr. Malfatti to Paer, and some from others to music-publishers. Through Paer he was made acquainted with Cherubini, Rossini, Baillot, and Kalkbrenner. Although Chopin in one of his early Paris letters calls Cherubini a mummy, he seems to have subsequently been more favourably impressed by him. At any rate, Ferdinand Hiller—who may have accompanied the new-comer, if he did not, as he thinks he did, introduce him, which is not reconcilable with his friend's statement that Paer made him acquainted with Cherubini—told me that Chopin conceived a liking for the burbero maestro, of whom Mendelssohn remarked that he composed everything with his head without the help of his heart.

The house of Cherubini [writes Veron in his "Memoires d'un
Bourgeois de Paris"] was open to artists, amateurs, and
people of good society; and every Monday a numerous assembly
thronged his salons. All foreign artists wished to be
presented to Cherubini. During these last years one met often
at his house Hummel, Liszt, Chopin, Moscheles, Madame
Grassini, and Mademoiselle Falcon, then young and brilliant
in talent and beauty; Auber and Halevy, the favourite pupils
of the master; and Meyerbeer and Rossini.

As evidence of the younger master's respect for the older one may be adduced a copy made by Chopin of one of Cherubini's fugues. This manuscript, which I saw in the possession of M. Franchomme, is a miracle of penmanship, and surpasses in neatness and minuteness everything I have seen of Chopin's writing, which is always microscopic.

From Dr. Hiller I learnt also that Chopin went frequently to Baillot's house. It is very probable that he was present at the soirees which Mendelssohn describes with his usual charming ease in his Paris letters. Baillot, though a man of sixty, still knew how to win the admiration of the best musicians by his fine, expressive violin-playing. Chopin writes in a letter to Elsner that Baillot was very amiable towards him, and had promised to take part with him in a quintet of Beethoven's at his concert; and in another letter Chopin calls Baillot "the rival of Paganini."

As far as I can learn there was not much intercourse between Chopin and Rossini. Of Kalkbrenner I shall have presently to speak at some length; first, however, I shall say a few words about some of the most interesting young artists whose acquaintance Chopin made.

One of these young artists was the famous violoncellist Franchomme, who told me that it was Hiller who first spoke to him of the young Pole and his unique compositions and playing. Soon after this conversation, and not long after the new-comer's arrival in Paris, Chopin, Liszt, Hiller, and Franchomme dined together. When the party broke up, Chopin asked Franchomme what he was going to do. Franchomme replied he had no particular engagement. "Then," said Chopin, "come with me and spend an hour or two at my lodgings." "Well," was the answer of Franchomme, "but if I do you will have to play to me." Chopin had no objection, and the two walked off together. Franchomme thought that Chopin was at that time staying at an hotel in the Rue Bergere. Be this as it may, the young Pole played as he had promised, and the young Frenchman understood him at once. This first meeting was the beginning of a life-long friendship, a friendship such as is rarely to be met with among the fashionable musicians of populous cities.

Mendelssohn, who came to Paris early in December, 1831, and stayed there till about the middle of April, 1832, associated a good deal with this set of striving artists. The diminutive "Chopinetto," which he makes use of in his letters to Hiller, indicates not only Chopin's delicate constitution of body and mind and social amiability, but also Mendelssohn's kindly feeling for him. [Footnote: Chopin is not mentioned in any of Mendelssohn's Paris letters. But the following words may refer to him; for although Mendelssohn did not play at Chopin's concert, there may have been some talk of his doing so. January 14, 1832: "Next week a Pole gives a concert; in it I have to play a piece for six performers with Kalkbrenner, Hiller and Co." Osborne related in his "Reminiscences of Frederick Chopin," a paper read before a meeting of the Musical Association (April 5, 1880), that he, Chopin, Hiller, and Mendelssohn, during the latter's stay in Paris, frequently dined together at a restaurant. They ordered and paid the dinner in turn. One evening at dessert they had a very animated conversation about authors and their manuscripts. When they were ready to leave Osborne called the waiter, but instead of asking for la note a payer, he said "Garcon, apportez-moi votre manuscrit." This sally of the mercurial Irishman was received with hearty laughter, Chopin especially being much tickled by the profanation of the word so sacred to authors. From the same source we learn also that Chopin took delight in repeating the criticisms on his performances which he at one time or other had chanced to overhear.

Not the least interesting and significant incident in Chopin's life was his first meeting and early connection with Kalkbrenner, who at that time— when Liszt and Thalberg had not yet taken possession of the commanding positions they afterwards occupied—enjoyed the most brilliant reputation of all the pianists then living. On December 16, 1831, Chopin writes to his friend Woyciechowski:—

> You may easily imagine how curious I was to hear Herz and
> Hiller play; they are ciphers compared with Kalkbrenner.
> Honestly speaking, I play as well as Herz, but I wish I could
> play as well as Kalkbrenner. If Paganini is perfect, so also
> is he, but in quite another way. His repose, his enchanting
> touch, the smoothness of his playing, I cannot describe to
> you, one recognises the master in every note—he is a giant
> who throws all other artists into the shade. When I visited
> him, he begged me to play him something. What was I to do? As
> I had heard Herz, I took courage, seated myself at the
> instrument, and played my E minor Concerto, which charmed the
> people of the Bavarian capital so much. Kalkbrenner was
> astonished, and asked me if I were a pupil of Field's. He
> remarked that I had the style of Cramer, but the touch of
> Field. It amused me that Kalkbrenner, when he played to me,
> made a mistake and did not know how to go on; but it was
> wonderful to hear how he found his way again. Since this

meeting we see each other daily, either he calls on me or I
on him. He proposed to teach me for three years and make a
great artist of me. I told him that I knew very well what I
still lacked; but I will not imitate him, and three years are
too much for me. He has convinced me that I play well only
when I am in the right mood for it, but less well when this
is not the case. This cannot be said of Kalkbrenner, his
playing is always the same. When he had watched me for a long
time, he came to the conclusion that I had no method; that I
was indeed on a very good path, but might easily go astray;
and that when he ceased to play, there would no longer be a
representative of the grand pianoforte school left. I cannot
create a new school, however much I may wish to do so,
because I do not even know the old one; but I know that my
tone-poems have some individuality in them, and that I always
strive to advance.

If you were here, you would say "Learn, young man, as long as
you have an opportunity to do so!" But many dissuade me from
taking lessons, are of opinion that I play as well as
Kalkbrenner, and that it is only vanity that makes him wish
to have me for his pupil. That is nonsense. Whoever knows
anything of music must think highly of Kalkbrenner's talent,
although he is disliked as a man because he will not
associate with everybody. But I assure you there is in him
something higher than in all the virtuosos whom I have as yet
heard. I have said this in a letter to my parents, who quite
understand it. Elsner, however, does not comprehend it, and
regards it as jealousy on Kalkbrenner's part that he not only
praises me, but also wishes that my playing were in some
respects different from what it is. In spite of all this I
may tell you confidentially that I have already a
distinguished name among the artists here.

Elsner expressed his astonishment that Kalkbrenner should require three years to reveal to Chopin the secrets of his art, and advised his former pupil not to confine the exercise of his musical talent to pianoforte-playing and the composition of pianoforte music. Chopin replies to this in a letter written on December 14, 1831, as follows:—

> In the beginning of last year, although I knew what I yet
> lacked, and how very far I still was from equalling the model
> I have in you, I nevertheless ventured to think, "I will
> approach him, and if I cannot produce, a Lokietek ["the
> short," surname of a king of Poland; Elsner had composed an
> opera of that name], I may perhaps give to the world a
> Laskonogi ["the thin-legged," surname of another king of
> Poland]." To-day all such hopes are annihilated; I am forced
> to think of making my way in the world as a pianist. For some
> time I must keep in the background the higher artistic aim of
> which you wrote to me. In order to be a great composer one
> must possess, in addition to creative power, experience and
> the faculty of self-criticism, which, as you have taught me,
> one obtains not only by listening to the works of others, but
> still more by means of a careful critical examination of
> one's own.

After describing the difficulties which lie in the way of the opera composer, he proceeds:—

> It is my conviction that he is the happier man who is able to
> execute his compositions himself. I am known here and there
> in Germany as a pianist; several musical journals have spoken
> highly of my concerts, and expressed the hope of seeing me
> soon take a prominent position among the first pianoforte-
> virtuosos. I had to-day anopportunity or fulfilling the
> promise I had made to myself. Why should I not embrace it?...
> I should not like to learn pianoforte-playing in Germany, for
> there no one could tell me precisely what it was that I
> lacked. I, too, have not seen the beam in my eye. Three
> years' study is far too much. Kalkbrenner, when he had heard
> me repeatedly, came to see that himself. From this you may

see that a true meritorious virtuoso does not know the
feeling of envy. I would certainly make up my mind to study
for three years longer if I were certain that I should then
reach the aim which I have kept in view. So much is clear to
me, I shall never become a copy of Kalkbrenner; he will not
be able to break my perhaps bold but noble resolve—TO CREATE
A NEW ART-ERA. If I now continue my studies, I do so only in
order to stand at some future time on my own feet. It was not
difficult for Ries, who was then already recognised as a
celebrated pianist, to win laurels at Berlin, Frankfort-on-
the-Main, Dresden, &c., by his opera Die Rauberbraut. And how
long was Spohr known as an excellent violinist before he had
written Faust, Jessonda, and other works? I hope you will not
deny me your blessing when you see on what grounds and with
what intentions I struggle onwards.

This is one of the most important letters we have of Chopin; it brings before us, not the sighing lover, the sentimental friend, but the courageous artist. On no other occasion did he write so freely and fully of his views and aims. What heroic self-confidence, noble resolves, vast projects, flattering dreams! And how sad to think that most of them were doomed to end in failure and disappointment! But few are the lives of true artists that can really be called happy! Even the most successful have, in view of the ideally conceived, to deplore the quantitative and qualitative shortcomings of the actually accomplished. But to return to Kalkbrenner. Of him Chopin said truly that he was not a popular man; at any rate, he was not a popular man with the romanticists. Hiller tells us in his "Recollections and Letters of Mendelssohn" how little grateful he and his friends, Mendelssohn included, were for Kalkbrenner's civilities, and what a wicked pleasure they took in worrying him. Sitting one day in front of a cafe on the Boulevard des Italiens, Hiller, Liszt, and Chopin saw the prim master advancing, and knowing how disagreeable it would be to him to meet such a noisy company, they surrounded him in the friendliest manner, and assailed him with such a volley of talk that he was nearly driven to despair, which, adds Hiller, "of course delighted us." It must be confessed that the great Kalkbrenner, as M. Marmontel in his "Pianistes celebres" remarks, had "certaines etroitesses de caractere," and these "narrownesses" were of a kind that particularly provokes the ridicule of unconventional and irreverent minds. Heine is never more biting than when he speaks of Kalkbrenner. He calls him a mummy, and describes him as being dead long ago and having lately also married. This, however, was some years after the time we are speaking of. On another occasion Heine writes that Kalkbrenner is envied

> *for his elegant manners, for his polish and sweetishness, and*
> *for his whole marchpane-like appearance, in which, however,*
> *ihe calm observer discovers a shabby admixture of involuntary*
> *Berlinisms of the lowest class, so that Koreff could say of*
> *the man as wittily as correctly: "He looks like a bon-bon*
> *that has been in the mud."*

A thorough belief in and an unlimited admiration of himself form the centre of gravity upon which the other qualities of Kalkbrenner's character balance themselves. He prided himself on being the pattern of a fine gentleman, and took upon him to teach even his oldest friends how to conduct themselves in society and at table. In his gait he was dignified, in his manners ceremonious, and in his speech excessively polite. He was addicted to boasting of honours offered him by the King, and of his intimacy with the highest aristocracy. That he did not despise popularity with the lower strata of society is evidenced by the anecdote (which the virtuoso is credited with having told himself to his guests) of the fish-wife who, on reading his card, timidly asks him to accept as a homage to the great Kalkbrenner a splendid fish which he had selected for his table. The artist was the counterpart of the man. He considered every success as by right his due, and recognised merit only in those who were formed on his method or at least acknowledged its superiority. His artistic style was a chastened reflex of his social demeanour.

It is difficult to understand how the Kalkbrenner-Chopin affair could be so often misrepresented, especially since we are in possession of Chopin's clear statements of the facts. [FOOTNOTE: Statements which are by no means invalidated by the following statement of Lenz:—"On my asking Chopin 'whether Kalkbrenner had understood much about it' [i.e. the art of pianoforte-playing], followed the answer: 'It was at the beginning of my stay in Paris.'"]. There are no grounds whatever to justify the assumption that Kalkbrenner was actuated by jealousy, artfulness, or the like, when he proposed that the wonderfully-gifted and developed Chopin should become his pupil for three years. His conceit of himself and his method account fully for the strangeness of the proposal. Moreover, three years was the regulation time of Kalkbrenner's course, and it was much that he was willing to shorten it in the case of Chopin. Karasowski, speaking as if he had the gift of reading the inmost thoughts of men, remarks: "Chopin did not suspect what was passing in Kalkbrenner's mind when he was playing to him." After all, I should like to ask, is there anything surprising in the fact that the admired virtuoso and author of a "Methode pour apprendre le Piano a l'aide du Guide-mains; contenant les principes de musique; un systems complet de doigter; des regles sur l'expression," &c., found fault with Chopin's strange fingering and unconventional style? Kalkbrenner could not imagine anything superior to his own method, anything finer than his own style. And this inability to admit the meritoriousness or even the legitimacy of anything that differed from what he was accustomed to, was not at all peculiar to this great pianist; we see it every day in men greatly his inferiors. Kalkbrenner's lament that when he ceased to play there would be no representative left of the grand pianoforte school ought to call forth our sympathy. Surely we cannot blame him for wishing to perpetuate what he held to be unsurpassable! According to Hiller, Chopin went a few times to the class of advanced pupils which Kalkbrenner had advised him to attend, as he wished to see what the thing was like. Mendelssohn, who had a great opinion of Chopin and the reverse of Kalkbrenner, was furious when he heard of this. But were Chopin's friends correct in saying that he played better than Kalkbrenner, and could learn nothing from him? That Chopin played better than Kalkbrenner was no doubt true, if we consider the emotional and intellectual qualities of their playing. But I think it was not correct to say that Chopin could learn nothing from the older master. Chopin was not only a better judge of Kalkbrenner than his friends, who had only sharp eyes for his short-comings, and overlooked or undervalued his good qualities, but he was also a better judge of himself and his own requirements. He had an ideal in his mind, and he thought that Kalkbrenner's teaching would help him to realise it. Then there is also this to be considered: unconnected with any school, at no time guided by a great master of the instrument, and left to his own devices at a very early age, Chopin found himself, as it were, floating free in the air without a base to stand on, without a pillar to lean against. The consequent feeling of isolation inspires at times even the strongest and most independent self-taught man—and Chopin, as a pianist, may almost be called one—with distrust in the adequacy of his self-acquired attainments, and an exaggerated idea of the advantages of a school education. "I cannot create a new school, because I do not even know the old one." This may or may not be bad reasoning, but it shows the attitude of Chopin's mind. It is also possible that he may have felt the inadequacy and inappropriateness of his technique and style for other than his own compositions. And many facts in the history of his career as an executant would seem to confirm the correctness of such a feeling. At any rate, after what we have read we cannot attribute his intention of studying under Kalkbrenner to undue self-depreciation. For did he not consider his own playing as good as that of Herz, and feel that he had in him the stuff to found a new era in music? But what was it then that attracted him to Kalkbrenner, and made him exalt this pianist above all the pianists he had heard? If the reader will recall to mind what I said in speaking of Mdlles. Sontag and Belleville of Chopin's love of beauty of tone, elegance, and neatness, he cannot be surprised at the young pianist's estimate of the virtuoso of whom Riehl says: "The essence of his nature was what the philologists call elegantia—he spoke the purest Ciceronian Latin on the piano." As a knowledge of Kalkbrenner's artistic personality will help to further our acquaintance with Chopin, and as our knowledge of it is for the most part derived from the libels and caricatures of well-intentioned critics, who in their zeal for a nobler and more glorious art overshoot the mark of truth, it will be worth our while to make inquiries regarding it.

Kalkbrenner may not inaptly be called the Delille of pianist-composers, for his nature and fate remind us somewhat of the poet. As to his works, although none of them possessed stamina enough to be long-lived, they would have insured him a fairer reputation if he had not published so many that were written merely for the market. Even Schumann confessed to having in his younger days heard and played Kalkbrenner's music often and with pleasure, and at a maturer age continued to acknowledge not only the master's natural virtuoso amiability and clever manner of writing effectively for fingers and hands, but also the genuinely musical qualities of his better works, of which he held the Concerto in D minor to be the "bloom," and remarks that it shows the "bright sides" of Kalkbrenner's "pleasing talent." We are, however, here more concerned with the pianist than with the composer. One of the best sketches of Kalkbrenner as a pianist is to be found in a passage which I shall presently quote from M. Marmontel's collection of "Silhouettes et Medaillons" of "Les Pianistes celebres." The sketch is valuable on account of its being written by one who is himself a master, one who does not speak from mere hearsay, and who, whilst regarding Kalkbrenner as an exceptional virtuoso, the continuator of Clementi, the founder ("one of the founders" would be more correct) of modern pianoforte-playing, and approving of the leading principle of his method, which aims at the perfect independence of the fingers and their preponderant action, does not hesitate to blame the exclusion of the action of the wrist, forearm, and arm, of which the executant should not deprive himself "dans les accents de legerete, d'expression et de force." But here is what M. Marmontel says:—

The pianoforte assumed under his fingers a marvellous and never harsh sonorousness, for he did not seek forced effects. His playing, smooth, sustained, harmonious, and of a perfect evenness, charmed even more than it astonished; moreover, a

faultless neatness in the most difficult passages, and a left
hand of unparalleled bravura, made Kalkbrenner an
extraordinary virtuoso. Let us add that the perfect
independence of the fingers, the absence of the in our day so
frequent movements of the arms, the tranquillity of the hands
and body, a perfect bearing—all these qualities combined,
and many others which we forget, left the auditor free to
enjoy the pleasure of listening without having his attention
diverted by fatiguing gymnastics. Kalkbrenner's manner of
phrasing was somewhat lacking in expression and communicative
warmth, but the style was always noble, true, and of the
grand school.

We now know what Chopin meant when he described Kalkbrenner as "perfect and possessed of something that raised him above all other virtuosos"; we now know also that Chopin's admiration was characteristic and not misplaced. Nevertheless, nobody will think for a moment of disagreeing with those who advised Chopin not to become a pupil of this master, who always exacted absolute submission to his precepts; for it was to be feared that he would pay too dear for the gain of inferior accomplishments with the loss of his invaluable originality. But, as we have seen, the affair came to nothing, Chopin ceasing to attend the classes after a few visits. What no doubt influenced his final decision more than the advice of his friends was the success which his playing and compositions met with at the concert of which I have now to tell the history. Chopin's desertion as a pupil did not terminate the friendly relation that existed between the two artists. When Chopin published his E minor Concerto he dedicated it to Kalkbrenner, and the latter soon after composed "Variations brillantes (Op. 120) pour le piano sur une Mazourka de Chopin," and often improvised on his young brother-artist's mazurkas. Chopin's friendship with Camille Pleyel helped no doubt to keep up his intercourse with Kalkbrenner, who was a partner of the firm of Pleyel & Co.

The arrangements for his concert gave Chopin much trouble, and had they not been taken in hand by Paer, Kalkbrenner, and especially Norblin, he would not have been able to do anything in Paris, where one required at least two months to get up a concert. This is what Chopin tells Elsner in the letter dated December 14, 1831. Notwithstanding such powerful assistance he did not succeed in giving his concert on the 25th of December, as he at first intended. The difficulty was to find a lady vocalist. Rossini, the director of the Italian Opera, was willing to help him, but Robert, the second director, refused to give permission to any of the singers in his company to perform at the concert, fearing that, if he did so once, there would be no end of applications. As Veron, the director of the Academie Royale likewise refused Chopin's request, the concert had to be put off till the 15th of January, 1832, when, however, on account of Kalkbrenner's illness or for some other reason, it had again to be postponed. At last it came off on February 26, 1832. Chopin writes on December 16, 1831, about the arrangements for the concert:—

> Baillot, the rival of Paganini, and Brod, the celebrated oboe-
> player, will assist me with their talent. I intend to play my
> F minor Concerto and the Variations in B flat...I shall play
> not only the concerto and the variations, but also with
> Kalkbrenner his duet "Marche suivie d'une Polonaise" for two
> pianos, with the accompaniment of four others. Is this not an
> altogether mad idea? One of the grand pianos is very large,
> and is for Kalkbrenner; the other is small (a so-called mono-
> chord), and is for me. On the other large ones, which are as
> loud as an orchestra, Hiller, Osborne, Stamati, and Sowinski
> are to play. Besides these performers, Norblin, Vidal, and
> the celebrated viola-player Urban will take part in the
> concert.

The singers of the evening were Mdlles. Isambert and Tomeoni, and M. Boulanger. I have not been able to discover the programme of the concert. Hiller says that Chopin played his E minor Concerto and some of his mazurkas and nocturnes. Fetis, in the Revue musicale (March 3, 1832), mentions only in a general way that there were performed a concerto by Chopin, a composition for six pianos by Kalkbrenner, some vocal pieces, an oboe solo, and "a quintet for violin [sic], executed with that energy of feeling and that variety of inspiration which distinguish the talent of M. Baillot." The concert, which took place in Pleyel's rooms, was financially a failure; the receipts did not cover the expenses. The audience consisted chiefly of Poles, and most of the French present had free tickets. Hiller says that all the musical celebrities of Paris were there, and that Chopin's performances took everybody by storm. "After this," he adds, "nothing more was heard of want of technique, and Mendelssohn applauded triumphantly." Fetis describes this soiree musicale as one of the most pleasant that had been given that year. His criticism contains such interesting and, on the whole, such excellent remarks that I cannot resist the temptation to quote the more remarkable passages:—

> *Here is a young man who, abandoning himself to his natural impressions and without taking a model, has found, if not a complete renewal of pianoforte music, at least a part of what has been sought in vain for a long time—namely, an abundance of original ideas of which the type is to be found nowhere. We do not mean by this that M. Chopin is endowed with a powerful organisation like that of Beethoven, nor that there are in his music such powerful conceptions as one remarks in that of this great man. Beethoven has composed pianoforte music, but I speak here of pianists' music, and it is by comparison with the latter that I find in M. Chopin's inspirations the indication of a renewal of forms which may exercise in time much influence over this department of the art.*

Of Chopin's concerto Fetis remarks that it:—

> *equally astonished and surprised his audience, as much by the novelty of the melodic ideas as by the figures, modulations, and general disposition of the movements. There is soul in these melodies, fancy in these figures, and originality in everything. Too much luxuriance in the modulations, disorder in the linking of the phrases, so that one seems sometimes to hear an improvisation rather than written music, these are the defects which are mixed with the qualities I have just now pointed out. But these defects belong to the age of the artist; they will disappear when experience comes. If the subsequent works of M. Chopin correspond to his debut, there can be no doubt but that he will acquire a brilliant and merited reputation.*

> *As an executant also the young artist deserves praise. His playing is elegant, easy, graceful, and possesses brilliance and neatness. He brings little tone out of the instrument,*

and resembles in this respect the majority of German
pianists. But the study which he is making of this part of
his art, under the direction of M. Kalkbrenner, cannot fail
to give him an important quality on which the nerf of
execution depends, and without which the accents of the
instrument cannot be modified.

Of course dissentient voices made themselves heard who objected to this and that; but an overwhelming majority, to which belonged the young artists, pronounced in favour of Chopin. Liszt says that he remembers his friend's debut:—

The most vigorous applause seemed not to suffice to our
enthusiasm in the presence of this talented musician, who
revealed a new phase of poetic sentiment combined with such
happy innovations in the form of his art.

The concluding remark of the above-quoted criticism furnishes an additional proof that Chopin went for some time to Kalkbrenner's class. As Fetis and Chopin were acquainted with each other, we may suppose that the former was well informed on this point. In passing, we may take note of Chopin's account of the famous historian and theorist's early struggles:—

Fetis [Chopin writes on December 14, 1831], whom I know, and
from whom one can learn much, lives outside the town, and
comes to Paris only to give his lessons. They say he is
obliged to do this because his debts are greater than the
profits from his "Revue musicale." He is sometimes in danger
of making intimate acquaintance with the debtors' prison. You
must know that according to the law of the country a debtor
can only be arrested in his dwelling. Fetis has, therefore,
left the town and lives in the neighbourhood of Paris, nobody
knows where.

On May 20, 1832, less than three months after his first concert, Chopin made his second public appearance in Paris, at a concert given by the Prince de la Moskowa for the benefit of the poor. Among the works performed was a mass composed by the Prince. Chopin played the first movement of:—

the concerto, which had already been heard at Pleyel's rooms,
and had there obtained a brilliant success. On this occasion
it was not so well received, a fact which, no doubt, must be

attributed to the instrumentation, which is lacking in
lightness, and to the small volume of tone which M. Chopin
draws from the piano. However, it appears to us that the
music of this artist will gain in the public opinion when it
becomes better known. [FOOTNOTE: From the "Revue
musicale."]

The great attraction of the evening was not Chopin, but Brod, who "enraptured" the audience. Indeed, there were few virtuosos who were as great favourites as this oboe-player; his name was absent from the programme of hardly any concert of note.

In passing we will note some other musical events of interest which occurred about the same time that Chopin made his debut. On March 18 Mendelssohn played Beethoven's G major Concerto with great success at one of the Conservatoire concerts, [FOOTNOTE: It was the first performance of this work in Paris.] the younger master's overture to the "Midsummer Night's Dream" had been heard and well received at the same institution in the preceding month, and somewhat later his "Reformation Symphony" was rehearsed, but laid aside. In the middle of March Paganini, who had lately arrived, gave the first of a series of concerts, with what success it is unnecessary to say. Of Chopin's intercourse with Zimmermann, the distinguished pianoforte-professor at the Conservatoire, and his family we learn from M. Marmontel, who was introduced to Chopin and Liszt, and heard them play in 1832 at one of his master's brilliant musical fetes, and gives a charming description of the more social and intimate parties at which Chopin seems to have been occasionally present.

Madame Zimmermann and her daughters did the honours to a
great number of artists. Charades were acted; the forfeits
that were given, and the rebuses that were not guessed, had
to be redeemed by penances varying according to the nature of
the guilty ones. Gautier, Dumas, and Musset were condemned to
recite their last poem. Liszt or Chopin had to improvise on a
given theme, Mesdames Viardot, Falcon, and Euggnie Garcia had
also to discharge their melodic debts, and I myself remember
having paid many a forfeit.

The preceding chapter and the foregoing part of this chapter set forth the most important facts of Chopin's social and artistic life in his early Paris days. The following extract from a letter of his to Titus Woyciechowski, dated December 25, 1831, reveals to us something of his inward life, the gloom of which contrasts violently with the outward brightness:—

Ah, how I should like to have you beside me!... You cannot imagine how sad it is to have nobody to whom I can open my troubled heart. You know how easily I make acquaintances, how I love human society—such acquaintances I make in great numbers—but with no one, no one can I sigh. My heart beats as it were always "in syncopes," therefore I torment myself and seek for a rest—for solitude, so that the whole day nobody may look at me and speak to me. It is too annoying to me when there is a pull at the bell, and a tedious visit is announced while I am writing to you. At the moment when I was going to describe to you the ball, at which a divine being with a rose in her black hair enchanted me, arrives your letter. All the romances of my brain disappear? my thoughts carry me to you, I take your hand and weep...When shall we see each other again?...Perhaps never, because, seriously, my health is very bad. I appear indeed merry, especially when I am among my fellow-countrymen; but inwardly something torments me—a gloomy presentiment, unrest, bad dreams, sleeplessness, yearning, indifference to everything, to the desire to live and the desire to die. It seems to me often as if my mind were benumbed, I feel a heavenly repose in my heart, in my thoughts I see images from which I cannot tear myself away, and this tortures me beyond all measure. In short, it is a combination of feelings that are difficult to describe...Pardon me, dear Titus, for telling you of all this; but now I have said enough...I will dress now and go, or rather drive, to the dinner which our countrymen give to-day to Ramorino and Langermann...Your letter contained much that was news to me; you have written me four pages and thirty-seven lines—in all my life you have never been so liberal to me, and I stood in need of something of the kind, I stood indeed very much in need of it.

*What you write about my artistic career is very true, and I
myself am convinced of it.*

I drive in my own equipage, only the coachman is hired.

*I shall close, because otherwise I should be too late for the
post, for I am everything in one person, master and servant.
Take pity on me and write as often as possible!—Yours unto
death,*

FREDERICK.

In the postscript of this letter Chopin's light fancy gets the better of his heavy heart; in it all is fun and gaiety. First he tells his friend of a pretty neighbour whose husband is out all day and who often invites him to visit and comfort her. But the blandishments of the fair one were of no avail; he had no taste for adventures, and, moreover, was afraid to be caught and beaten by the said husband. A second love-story is told at greater length. The dramatis personae are Chopin, John Peter Pixis, and Francilla Pixis, a beautiful girl of sixteen, a German orphan whom the pianist-composer, then a man of about forty-three, had adopted, and who afterwards became known as a much-admired singer. Chopin made their acquaintance in Stuttgart, and remarks that Pixis said that he intended to marry her. On his return to Paris Pixis invited Chopin to visit him; the latter, who had by this time forgotten pretty Francilla, was in no hurry to call. What follows must be given in Chopin's own words:—

> *Eight days after the second invitation I went to his house,
> and accidentally met his pet on the stairs. She invited me to
> come in, assuring me it did not matter that Mr. Pixis was not
> at home; meanwhile I was to sit down, he would return soon,
> and so on. A strange embarrassment seized both of us. I made
> my excuses—for I knew the old man was very jealous—and said
> I would rather return another time. While we were talking
> familiarly and innocently on the staircase, Pixis came up,
> looking over his spectacles in order to see who was speaking
> above to his bella. He may not have recognised us at once,*

quickened his steps, stopped before us, and said to her
harshly: "Qu'est-ce que vous faites ici?" and gave her a
severe lecture for receiving young men in his absence, and so
on. I addressed Pixis smilingly, and said to her that it was
somewhat imprudent to leave the room in so thin a silk dress.
At last the old man became calm — he took me by the arm and
led me into the drawing-room. He was in such a state of
excitement that he did not know what seat to offer me; for he
was afraid that, if he had offended me, I would make better
use of his absence another time. When I left he accompanied
me down stairs, and seeing me smile (for I could not help
doing so when I found I was thought capable of such a thing),
he went to the concierge and asked how long it was since I
had come. The concierge must have calmed his fears, for since
that time Pixis does not know how to praise my talent
sufficiently to all his acquaintances. What do you think of
this? I, a dangerous seducteur!

The letters which Chopin wrote to his parents from Paris passed, after his mother's death, into the hands of his sister, who preserved them till September 19, 1863. On that day the house in which she lived in Warsaw — a shot having been fired and some bombs thrown from an upper story of it when General Berg and his escort were passing — was sacked by Russian soldiers, who burned or otherwise destroyed all they could lay hands on, among the rest Chopin's letters, his portrait by Ary Scheffer, the Buchholtz piano on which he had made his first studies, and other relics. We have now also exhausted, at least very nearly exhausted, Chopin's extant correspondence with his most intimate Polish friends, Matuszynski and Woyciechowski, only two unimportant letters written in 1849 and addressed to the latter remaining yet to be mentioned. That the confidential correspondence begins to fail us at this period (the last letter is of December 25, 1831) is particularly inopportune; a series of letters like those he wrote from Vienna would have furnished us with the materials for a thoroughly trustworthy history of his settlement in Paris, over which now hangs a mythical haze. Karasowski, who saw the lost letters, says they were tinged with melancholy.

Besides the thought of his unhappy country, a thought constantly kept alive by the Polish refugees with whom Paris was swarming, Chopin had another more prosaic but not less potent cause of disquietude and sadness.

His pecuniary circumstances were by no means brilliant. Economy cannot fill a slender purse, still less can a badly-attended concert do so, and Chopin was loath to be a burden on his parents who, although in easy circumstances, were not wealthy, and whose income must have been considerably lessened by some of the consequences of the insurrection, such as the closing of schools, general scarcity of money, and so forth. Nor was Paris in 1831, when people were so busy with politics, El Dorado for musicians. Of the latter, Mendelssohn wrote at the time that they did not, like other people, wrangle about politics, but lamented over them. "One has lost his place, another his title, and a third his money, and they say this all proceeds from the 'juste milieu.'" As Chopin saw no prospect of success in Paris he began to think, like others of his countrymen, of going to America. His parents, however, were against this project, and advised him either to stay where he was and wait for better things, or to return to Warsaw. Although he might fear annoyances from the Russian government on account of his not renewing his passport before the expiration of the time for which it was granted, he chose the latter alternative. Destiny, however, had decided the matter otherwise.[FOOTNOTE: Karasowski says that Liszt, Hiller, and Sowinski dissuaded him from leaving Paris. Liszt and Hiller both told me, and so did also Franchomme, that they knew nothing of Chopin having had any such intention; and Sowinski does not mention the circumstance in his Musiciens polonais.] One day, or, as some will have it, on the very day when he was preparing for his departure, Chopin met in the street Prince Valentine Radziwill, and, in the course of the conversation which the latter opened, informed him of his intention of leaving Paris. The Prince, thinking, no doubt, of the responsibility he would incur by doing so, did not attempt to dissuade him, but engaged the artist to go with him in the evening to Rothschild's. Chopin, who of course was asked by the hostess to play something, charmed by his wonderful performance, and no doubt also by his refined manners, the brilliant company assembled there to such a degree that he carried off not only a plentiful harvest of praise and compliments, but also some offers of pupils. Supposing the story to be true, we could easily believe that this soiree was the turning-point in Chopin's career, but nevertheless might hesitate to assert that it changed his position "as if by enchantment." I said "supposing the story to be true," because, although it has been reported that Chopin was fond of alluding to this incident, his best friends seem to know nothing of it: Liszt does not mention it, Hiller and Franchomme told me they never heard of it, and notwithstanding Karasowski's contrary statement there is nothing to be found about it in Sowinski's Musiciens polonais. Still, the story may have a substratum of truth, to arrive at which it has only to be shorn of its poetical accessories and exaggerations, of which, however, there is little in my version.

But to whatever extent, or whether to any extent at all, this or any similar soiree may have served Chopin as a favourable introduction to a wider circle of admirers and patrons, and as a stepping-stone to success, his indebtedness to his countrymen, who from the very first befriended and encouraged him, ought not to be forgotten or passed over in silence for the sake of giving point to a pretty anecdote. The great majority of the Polish refugees then living in Paris would of course rather require than be able to afford help and furtherance, but there was also a not inconsiderable minority of persons of noble birth and great wealth whose patronage and influence could not but be of immense advantage to a struggling artist. According to Liszt, Chopin was on intimate terms with the inmates of the Hotel Lambert, where old Prince Adam Czartoryski and his wife and daughter gathered around them "les debris de la Pologne que la derniere guerre avait jetes au loin." Of the family of Count Plater and other compatriots with whom the composer had friendly intercourse we shall speak farther on. Chopin's friends were not remiss in exerting themselves to procure him pupils and good fees at the same time. They told all inquirers that he gave no lesson for less than twenty francs, although he had expressed his willingness to be at first satisfied with more modest terms. Chopin had neither to wait in vain nor to wait long, for in about a year's time he could boast of a goodly number of pupils.

The reader must have noticed with surprise the absence of any mention of the "Ideal" from Chopin's letters to his friend Titus Woyciechowski, to whom the love-sick artist was wont to write so voluminously on this theme. How is this strange silence to be accounted for? Surely this passionate lover could not have forgotten her beneath whose feet he wished his ashes to be spread after his death? But perhaps in the end of 1831 he had already learnt what was going to happen in the following year. The sad fact has to be told: inconstant Constantia Gladkowska married a merchant of the name of Joseph Grabowski, at Warsaw, in 1832; this at least is the information given in Sowinski's biographical dictionary Les musiciens polonais et slaves.[FOOTNOTE: According to Count Wodzinski she married a country gentleman, and subsequently became blind.] As the circumstances of the case and the motives of the parties are unknown to me, and as a biographer ought not to take the same liberties as a novelist, I shall neither expatiate on the fickleness and mercenariness of woman, nor attempt to describe the feelings of our unfortunate hero robbed of his ideal, but leave the reader to make his own reflections and draw his own moral.

On August 2, 1832, Chopin wrote a letter to Hiller, who had gone in the spring of the year to Germany. What the young Pole thought of this German brother-artist may be gathered from some remarks of his in the letter to Titus Woyciechowski dated December 16, 1831:—

The concert of the good Hiller, who is a pupil of Hummel and
a youth of great talent, came off very successfully the day
before yesterday. A symphony of his was received with much
applause. He has taken Beethoven for his model, and his work
is full of poesy and inspiration.

Since then the two had become more intimate, seeing each other almost every day, Chopin, as Osborne relates, being always in good spirits when Hiller was with him. The bearer of the said letter was Mr. Johns, to whom the five Mazurkas, Op. 7, are dedicated, and whom Chopin introduced to Hiller as "a distinguished amateur of New Orleans." After warmly recommending this gentleman, he excuses himself for not having acknowledged the receipt of his friend's letter, which procured him the pleasure of Paul Mendelssohn's acquaintance, and then proceeds:—

Your trios, my dear friend, have been finished for a long
time, and, true to my character of a glutton, I have gulped
down your manuscripts into my repertoire. Your concerto will
be performed this month by Adam's pupils at the examination
of the Conservatoire. Mdlle. Lyon plays it very well. La
Tentation, an opera-ballet by Halevy and Gide, has not
tempted any one of good taste, because it has just as little
interest as your German Diet harmony with the spirit of the
age. Maurice, who has returned from London, whither he had
gone for the mise en scene of Robert (which has not had a
very great success), has assured us that Moscheles and Field
will come to Paris for the winter. This is all the news I
have to give you. Osborne has been in London for the last two
months. Pixis is at Boulogne. Kalkbrenner is at Meudon,
Rossini at Bordeaux. All who know you await you with open
arms. Liszt will add a few words below. Farewell, dear
friend.

Yours most truly,
F. CHOPIN.
Paris, 2/8/32

CHAPTER XVI

1832-1834.

CHOPIN'S SUCCESS IN SOCIETY AND AS A TEACHER.—VARIOUS CONCERTS AT WHICH HE PLAYED.—A LETTER FROM CHOPIN AND LISZTTOHILLER.—SOMEOFHISFRIENDS.—STRANGEBEHAVIOUR.—A LETTER TO FRANCHOMME.—CHOPIN'S RESERVE.—SOME TRAITS OF THE POLISH CHARACTER.—FIELD.—BERLIOZ.—NEO-ROMANTICISM AND CHOPIN'S RELATION TO IT.—WHAT INFLUENCE HAD LISZT ON CHOPIN'S DEVELOPMENT—PUBLICATION OF WORKS.—THE CRITICS.—INCREASING POPULARITY.—JOURNEY IN THE COMPANY OF HILLER TO AIX-LA-CHAPELLE.—A DAY AT DUSSELDORF WITH MENDELSSOHN.

IN the season 1832-1833 Chopin took his place as one of the acknowledged pianistic luminaries of the French capital, and began his activity as a professor par excellence of the aristocracy. "His distinguished manners, his exquisite politeness, his studied and somewhat affected refinement in all things, made Chopin the model professor of the fashionable nobility." Thus Chopin is described by a contemporary. Now he shall describe himself. An undated letter addressed to his friend Dominic Dziewanowski, which, judging from an allusion to the death of the Princess Vaudemont, [FOOTNOTE: In a necrology contained in the Moniteur of January 6, 1833, she is praised for the justesse de son esprit, and described as naive et vraie comme une femme du peuple, genereuse comme une grande dame. There we find it also recorded that she saved M. de Vitrolles pendant les Cent-jours, et M. de Lavalette sous la Restoration.] must have been written about the second week of January, 1833, gives much interesting information concerning the writer's tastes and manners, the degree of success he had obtained, and the kind of life he was leading. After some jocular remarks on his long silence—remarks in which he alludes to recollections of Szafarnia and the sincerity of their friendship, and which he concludes with the statement that he is so much in demand on all sides as to betorn to pieces—Chopin proceeds thus:—

I move in the highest society—among ambassadors, princes,

and ministers; and I don't know how I got there, for I did

not thrust myself forward at all. But for me this is at
present an absolute necessity, for thence comes, as it were,
good taste. You are at once credited with more talent if you
are heard at a soiree of the English or Austrian
Ambassador's. Your playing is finer if the Princess Vaudemont
patronises you. "Patronises" I cannot properly say, for the
good old woman died a week ago. She was a lady who reminded
me of the late Kasztelanowa Polaniecka, received at her house
the whole Court, was very charitable, and gave refuge to many
aristocrats in the days of terror of the first revolution.
She was the first who presented herself after the days of
July at the Court of Louis Philippe, although she belonged to
the Montmorency family (the elder branch), whose last
descendant she was. She had always a number of black and
white pet dogs, canaries, and parrots about her; and
possessed also a very droll little monkey, which was
permitted even to... bite countesses and princesses.

Among the Paris artists I enjoy general esteem and
friendship, although I have been here only a year. A proof of
this is that men of great reputation dedicate their
compositions to me, and do so even before I have paid them
the same compliment—for instance, Pixis his last Variations
for orchestra. He is now even composing variations on a theme
of mine. Kalkbrenner improvises frequently on my mazurkas.
Pupils of the Conservatoire, nay, even private pupils of
Moscheles, Herz, and Kalkbrenner (consequently clever
artists), still take lessons from me, and regard me as the
equal of Field. Really, if I were somewhat more silly than I
am, I might imagine myself already a finished artist;
nevertheless, I feel daily how much I have still to learn,
and become the more conscious of it through my intercourse
with the first artists here, and my perception of what every
one, even of them, is lacking in. But I am quite ashamed of

myself for what I have written just now, having praised
myself like a child. I would erase it, but I have no time to
write another letter. Moreover, you will remember my
character as it formerly was; indeed, I have remained quite
the same, only with this one difference, that I have now
whiskers on one side—unfortunately they won't grow at all on
the other side. To-day I have to give five lessons; you will
imagine that I must soon have made a fortune, but the
cabriolet and the white gloves eat the earnings almost up,
and without these things people would deny my bon ton. I love
the Carlists, hate the Philippists, and am myself a
revolutionist; therefore I don't care for money, but only for
friendship, for the preservation of which I earnestly entreat
you.

This letter, and still more the letters which I shall presently transcribe, afford irrefragable evidence of the baselessness of the often-heard statement that Chopin's intercourse was in the first years of his settlement in Paris confined to the Polish salons. The simple unexaggerated truth is that Chopin had always a predilection for, and felt more at home among, his compatriots.

In the winter 1832-1833 Chopin was heard frequently in public. At a concert of Killer's (December 15, 1832) he performed with Liszt and the concert-giver a movement of Bach's Concerto for three pianos, the three artists rendering the piece "avec une intelligence de son caractere et une delicatesse parfaite." Soon after Chopin and Liszt played between the acts of a dramatic performance got up for the benefit of Miss Smithson, the English actress and bankrupt manager, Berlioz's flame, heroine of his "Episode de la vie d'un artiste," and before long his wife. On April 3, 1833, Chopin assisted at a concert given by the brothers Herz, taking part along with them and Liszt in a quartet for eight hands on two pianos. M. Marmontel, in his silhouette of the pianist and critic Amedee de Mereaux, mentions that in 1832 this artist twice played with Chopin a duo of his own on "Le Pre aux Clercs," but leaves us in uncertainty as to whether they performed it at public concerts or private parties. M. Franchomme told me that he remembered something about a concert given by Chopin in 1833 at the house of one of his aristocratic friends, perhaps at Madame la Marechale de Lannes's! In summing up, as it were, Chopin's activity as a virtuoso, I may make use of the words of the Paris correspondent of the "Allgemeine musikalische

Zeitung," who reports in April, 1833, that "Chopin and Osborne, as well as the other celebrated masters, delight the public frequently." In short, Chopin was becoming more and more of a favourite, not, however, of the democracy of large concert-halls, but of the aristocracy of select salons.

The following letter addressed to Hiller, written by Chopin and Liszt, and signed by them and Franchomme, brings together Chopin's most intimate artist friends, and spreads out before us a vivid picture of their good fellowship and the society in which they moved. I have put the portions written by Liszt within brackets [within parentheses in this e-text]. Thus the reader will see what belongs to each of the two writers, and how they took the pen out of each other's hand in the middle of a phrase and even of a word. With regard to this letter I have further to remark that Hiller, who was again in Germany, had lately lost his father: —

{This is at least the twentieth time that we have made arrangements to meet, sometimes at my house, sometimes here, [Footnote: At Chopin's lodgings mentioned farther on.] with the intention of writing to you, and some visit, or other unexpected hindrance, has always prevented us from doing so!...I don't know whether Chopin will be able to make any excuses to you; as regards myself it seems to me that we have been so excessively rude and impertinent that excuses are no longer either admissible or possible.

We have sympathised deeply with you in your sorrow, and longed to be with you in order to alleviate as much as possible the pangs of your heart.}

He has expressed himself so well that I have nothing to add in excuse of my negligence or idleness, influenza or distraction, or, or, or—you know I explain myself better in person; and when I escort you home to your mother's house this autumn, late at night along the boulevards, I shall try to obtain your pardon. I write to you without knowing what my pen is scribbling, because Liszt is at this moment playing my studies and transports me out of my proper senses. I should like to rob him of his way of rendering my own studies. As to your friends who are in Paris, I have seen the Leo family and their set [Footnote: Chopin's words are et qui s'en suit.' He refers, no doubt, to the Valentin family, relations of the Leos, who lived in the same house with them.] frequently this winter and spring. There have been some soirees at the houses of certain ambassadresses, and there was not one in which mention was not made of some one who is at Frankfort. Madame Eichthal sends you a thousand compliments. The whole Plater family were much grieved at your departure, and asked me to express to you their sympathy. (Madame d'Appony has quite a grudge against me for not having taken you to her house before your departure; she hopes that when you return you will remember the promise you made me. I may say as much from a certain lady who is not an ambassadress. [Footnote: This certain lady was the Countess d'Agoult.]

Do you know Chopin's wonderful studies?) They are admirable — and yet they will only last till the moment yours appear (a little bit of authorial modesty!!!). A little bit of rudeness on the part of the tutor —for, to explain the matter better to you, he corrects my orthographical mistakes (after the fashion of M. Marlet.

You will come back to us in the month of September, will you not? Try to let us know the day as we have resolved to give you a serenade (or charivari). The most distinguished artists of the capital —M. Franchomme (present), Madame Petzold, and the Abbe Bardin, the coryphees of the Rue d'Amboise (and my neighbours), Maurice Schlesinger, uncles, aunts, nephews, nieces, brothers-in-law, sisters-in-law, &c., &c.) en plan du troisieme, &c. [Footnote: I give the last words in the original French, because I am not sure of their meaning. Hiller, to whom I applied for an explanation, was unable to help me. Perhaps Chopin uses here the word plan in the pictorial sense (premier plan, foreground; second plan, middle distance).]

The responsible editors,

(F. LISZT.) F. CHOPIN. (Aug. FRANCHOMME.)

A Propos, I met Heine yesterday, who asked me to grussen you herzlich und herzlich. [Footnote: To greet you heartily and heartily.] A propos again, pardon me for all the "you's" — I beg you to forgive me them. If you have a moment to spare let us have news of you, which is very precious to us.

Paris: Rue de la Chaussee d'Antin, No. 5.

At present I occupy Franck's lodgings — he has set out for London and Berlin; I feel quite at home in the rooms which were so often our place of meeting. Berlioz embraces you. As to pere Baillot, he is in Switzerland, at Geneva, and so you will understand why I cannot send you Bach's Concerto.

June 20, 1833.

Some of the names that appear in this letter will give occasion for comment. Chopin, as Hiller informed me, went frequently to the ambassadors Appony and Von Kilmannsegge, and still more frequently to his compatriots, the Platers. At the house of the latter much good music was performed, for the countess, the Pani Kasztelanowa (the wife of the castellan), to whom Liszt devotes an eloquent encomium, "knew how to welcome so as to encourage all the talents that then promised to take their upward flight and form une lumineuse pleiade," being

> *in turn fairy, nurse, godmother, guardian angel, delicate benefactress, knowing all that threatens, divining all that saves, she was to each of us an amiable protectress, equally beloved and respected, who enlightened, warmed, and elevated his [Chopin's] inspiration, and left a blank in his life when she was no more.*

It was she who said one day to Chopin: "Si j'etais jeune et jolie, mon petit Chopin, je te prendrais pour mari, Hiller pour ami, et Liszt pour amant." And it was at her house that the interesting contention of Chopin with Liszt and Hiller took place. The Hungarian and the German having denied the assertion of the Pole that only he who was born and bred in Poland, only he who had breathed the perfume of her fields and woods, could fully comprehend with heart and mind Polish national music, the three agreed to play in turn, by way of experiment, the mazurka "Poland is not lost yet." Liszt began, Hiller followed, and Chopin came last and carried off the palm, his rivals admitting that they had not seized the true spirit of the music as he had done. Another anecdote, told me by Hiller, shows how intimate the Polish artist was with this family of compatriots, the Platers, and what strange whims he sometimes gave way to. One day Chopin came into the salon acting the part of Pierrot, and, after jumping and dancing about for an hour, left without having spoken a single word.

Abbe Bardin was a great musical amateur, at whose weekly afternoon gatherings the best artists might be seen and heard, Mendelssohn among the rest when he was in Paris in 1832-1833. In one of the many obituary notices of Chopin which appeared in French and other papers, and which are in no wise distinguished by their trustworthiness, I found the remark that the Abbe Bardin and M.M. Tilmant freres were the first to recognise Chopin's genius. The notice in question is to be found in the Chronique Musicale of November 3, 1849.

In Franck, whose lodgings Chopin had taken, the reader will recognise the "clever [geistreiche], musical Dr. Hermann Franck," the friend of many musical and other celebrities, the same with whom Mendelssohn used to play at chess during his stay in Paris. From Hiller I learned that Franck was very musical, and that his attainments in the natural sciences were considerable; but that being well-to-do he was without a profession. In the fifth decade of this century he edited for a year Brockhaus's Deutsche allgemeine Zeitung.

In the following letter which Chopin wrote to Franchomme—the latter thinks in the autumn of 1833—we meet with some new names. Dr. Hoffmann was a good friend of the composer's, and was frequently found at his rooms smoking. I take him to have been the well-known litterateur Charles Alexander Hoffmann, [Footnote: This is the usual German, French, and English spelling. The correct Polish spelling is Hofman. The forms Hoffman and Hofmann occur likewise.] the husband of Clementina Tanska, a Polish refugee who came to Paris in 1832 and continued to reside there till 1848. Maurice is of course Schlesinger the publisher. Of Smitkowski I know only that he was one of Chopin's Polish friends, whose list is pretty long and comprised among others Prince Casimir Lubomirski, Grzymala, Fontana, and Orda.

[Footnote: Of Grzymala and Fontana more will be heard in the sequel. Prince Casimir Lubomirski was a passionate lover of music, and published various compositions. Liszt writes that Orda, "who seemed to command a future," was killed at the age of twenty in Algiers. Karasowski gives the same information, omitting, however, the age. My inquiries about Orda among French musicians and Poles have had no result. Although the data do not tally with those of Liszt and Karasowski, one is tempted to identify Chopin's friend with the Napoleon Orda mentioned in Sowinski's Musiciens polonais et slaves—"A pianist-composer who had made himself known since the events of 1831. One owes to him the publication of a Polish Album devoted to the composers of this nation, published at Paris in 1838. M. Orda is the author of several elegantly-written pianoforte works." In a memoir prefixed to an edition of Chopin's mazurkas and waltzes (Boosey & Co.), J.W. Davison mentions a M. Orda (the "M." stands, I suppose, for Monsieur) and Charles Filtsch as pupils of Chopin.]

It was well for Chopin that he was so abundantly provided with friends, for, as Hiller told me, he could not do without company. But here is Chopin's letter to Franchomme:—

Begun on Saturday, the 14th, and finished on Wednesday, the 18th.

DEAR FRIEND,—It would be useless to excuse myself for my silence. If my thoughts could but go without paper to the post-office! However, you know me too well not to know that I, unfortunately, never do what I ought to do. I got here very comfortably (except for a little disagreeable episode, caused by an excessively odoriferous gentleman who went as far as Chartres—he surprised me in the night-time). I have found more occupation in Paris than I left behind me, which will, without doubt, hinder me from visiting you at Coteau. Coteau! oh Coteau! Say, my child, to the whole family at Coteau that I shall never forget my stay in Touraine—that so much kindness has made me for ever grateful. People think I am stouter and look very well, and I feel wonderfully well, thanks to the ladies that sat beside me at dinner, who

bestowed truly maternal attentions upon me. When I think of
all this the whole appears to me such an agreeable dream that
I should like to sleep again. And the peasant-girls of
Pormic! [FOOTNOTE: A village near the place where Chopin had
been staying.] and the flour! or rather your graceful nose
which you were obliged to plunge into it.

[FOOTNOTE: The remark about the "flour" and Franchomme's "nez
en forme gracieuse" is an allusion to some childish game in
which Chopin, thanks to his aquiline nose, got the better of
his friend, who as regards this feature was less liberally
endowed.]

A very interesting visit has interrupted my letter, which was
begun three days ago, and which I have not been able to
finish till to-day.

Hiller embraces you, Maurice, and everybody. I have delivered
your note to his brother, whom I did not find at home.

Paer, whom I saw a few days ago, spoke to me of your return.
Come back to us stout and in good health like me. Again a
thousand messages to the estimable Forest family. I have
neither words nor powers to express all I feel for them.
Excuse me. Shake hands with me — I pat you on the shoulder — I
hug you — I embrace you. My friend — au revoir.

Hoffmann, the stout Hoffmann, and the slim Smitkowski also,
embrace you.

[FOOTNOTE: The orthography of the French original is very
careless. Thus one finds frequent omissions and misplacements

of accents and numerous misspellings, such as trouvais

instead of trouve, engresse instead of engraisse, plonge

instead of plonger. Of course, these mistakes have to be

ascribed to negligence not to ignorance. I must mention yet

another point which the English translation does not bring

out—namely, that in addressing Franchomme Chopin makes use

of the familiar form of the second person singular.]

The last-quoted letter adds a few more touches to the portraiture of Chopin which has been in progress in the preceding pages. The insinuating affectionateness and winning playfulness had hitherto not been brought out so distinctly. There was then, and there remained to the end of his life, something of a woman and of a boy in this man. The sentimental element is almost wholly absent from Chopin's letters to his non-Polish friends. Even to Franchomme, the most intimate among these, he shows not only less of his inmost feelings and thoughts than to Titus Woyciechowski and John Matuszyriski, the friends of his youth, but also less than to others of his countrymen whose acquaintance he made later in life, and of whom Grzymala may be instanced. Ready to give everything, says Liszt, Chopin did not give himself—

his most intimate acquaintances did not penetrate into the

sacred recess where, apart from the rest of his life, dwelt

the secret spring of his soul: a recess so well concealed

that one hardly suspected its existence.

Indeed, you could as little get hold of Chopin as, to use L. Enault's expression, of the scaly back of a siren. Only after reading his letters to the few confidants to whom he freely gave his whole self do we know how little of himself he gave to the generality of his friends, whom he pays off with affectionateness and playfulness, and who, perhaps, never suspected, or only suspected, what lay beneath that smooth surface. This kind of reserve is a feature of the Slavonic character, which in Chopin's individuality was unusually developed.

The Slavonians [says Enault pithily] lend themselves, they do

not give themselves; and, as if Chopin had wished to make his

country-men pardon him the French origin of his family, he

showed himself more Polish than Poland.

Liszt makes some very interesting remarks on this point, and as they throw much light on the character of the race, and on that of the individual with whom we are especially concerned in this book, I shall quote them:—

With the Slavonians, the loyalty and frankness, the
familiarity and captivating desinvoltura of their manners, do
not in the least imply trust and effusiveness. Their feelings
reveal and conceal themselves like the coils of a serpent
convoluted upon itself; it is only by a very attentive
examination that one discovers the connection of the rings.
It would be naive to take their complimentary politeness,
their pretended modesty literally. The forms of this
politeness and this modesty belong to their manners, which
bear distinct traces of their ancient relations with the
East. Without being in the least infected by Mussulmanic
taciturnity, the Slavonians have learned from it a defiant
reserve on all subjects which touch the intimate chords of
the heart. One may be almost certain that, in speaking of
themselves, they maintain with regard to their interlocutor
some reticence which assures them over him an advantage of
intelligence or of feeling, leaving him in ignorance of some
circumstance or some secret motive by which they would be the
most admired or the least esteemed; they delight in hiding
themselves behind a cunning interrogatory smile of
imperceptible mockery. Having on every occasion a taste for
the pleasure of mystification, from the most witty and droll
to the most bitter and lugubrious kinds, one would say that
they see in this mocking deceit a form of disdain for the
superiority which they inwardly adjudge to themselves, but
which they veil with the care and cunning of the oppressed.

And now we will turn our attention once more to musical matters. In the letter to Hiller (August 2, 1832) Chopin mentioned the coming of Field and Moscheles, to which, no doubt, he looked forward with curiosity. They were the only eminent pianists whom he had not yet heard. Moscheles, however, seems not to have gone this winter to Paris; at any rate, his personal acquaintance with the Polish artist did not begin till 1839. Chopin, whose playing had so often reminded people of Field's, and who had again and again been called a pupil of his, would naturally take a particular interest in this pianist. Moreover, he esteemed him very highly as a composer. Mikuli tells us that Field's A flat Concerto and nocturnes were among those compositions which he delighted in playing (spielte mit Vorliebe). Kalkbrenner is reported [FOOTNOTE: In the Allgemeine musikalische Zeitung of April 3, 1833.] to have characterised Field's performances as quite novel and incredible; and Fetis, who speaks of them in the highest terms, relates that on hearing the pianist play a concerto of his own composition, the public manifested an indescribable enthusiasm, a real delirium. Not all accounts, however, are equally favourable.

[FOOTNOTE: In the Revue musicale of December 29, 1832. The criticism is worth reproducing:—"Quiconque n'a point entendu ce grand pianiste ne peut se faire d'idee du mecanisme admirable de ses doigts, mecanisme tel que les plus grandes difficultes semblent etre des choses fort simples, et que sa main n'a point l'air de se mouvoir. Il n'est d'ailleurs pas mains etonnant dans l'art d'attaquer la note et de varier a l'infini les diverses nuances de force, de douceur et d'accent. Un enthousiasme impossible a decrire, un veritable delire s'est manifeste dans le public a l'audition de ce concerto plein de charme rendu avec une perfection de fini, de precision, de nettete et d'expression qu'il serait impossible de surpasser et que bien peu de pianistes pourraient egaler." Of a MS. concerto played by Field at his second concert, given on February 3, 1833, Fetis says that it is "diffus, peu riche en motifs heureux, peu digne, en un mot, de la renommee de son auteur," but "la delicieuse execution de M. Field nous a tres-heureusement servi de compensation"]

Indeed, the contradictory criticisms to be met with in books and newspapers leave on the reader the impression that Field disappointed the expectations raised by his fame. The fact that the second concert he gave was less well attended than the first cannot but confirm this impression. He was probably no longer what he had been; and the reigning pianoforte style and musical taste were certainly no longer what they had been. "His elegant playing and beautiful manner of singing on the piano made people admire his talent," wrote Fetis at a later period (in his "Biographie universelle des Musiciens"), "although his execution had not the power of the pianists of the modern school." It is not at all surprising that the general public and the younger generation of artists, more especially the romanticists, were not unanimously moved to unbounded enthusiasm by "the clear limpid flow" and "almost somnolent tranquillity" of Field's playing, "the placid tenderness, graceful candour, and charming ingenuousness of his melodious reveries." This characterisation of Field's style is taken from Liszt's preface to the nocturnes. Moscheles, with whom Field dined in London shortly before the latter's visit to Paris, gives in his diary a by no means flattering account of him. Of the man, the diarist says that he is good-natured but not educated and rather droll, and that there cannot be a more glaring contrast than that between Field's nocturnes and Field's manners, which were often cynical. Of the artist, Moscheles remarks that while his touch was admirable and his legato entrancing, his playing lacked spirit and accent, light and shadow, and depth of feeling. M. Marmontel was not far wrong when, before having heard Field, he regarded him as the forerunner of Chopin, as a Chopin without his passion, sombre reveries, heart-throes, and morbidity. The opinions which the two artists had of each other and the degree of their mutual sympathy and antipathy may be easily guessed. We are, however, not put to the trouble of guessing all. Whoever has read anything about Chopin knows of course Field's criticism of him—namely, that he was "un talent de chambre de malade," which, by the by, reminds one of a remark of Auber's, who said that Chopin was dying all his life (il se meurt tonte sa vie). It is a pity that we have not, as a pendant to Field's criticism on Chopin, one of Chopin on Field. But whatever impression Chopin may have received from the artist, he cannot but have been repelled by the man. And yet the older artist's natural disposition was congenial to that of the younger one, only intemperate habits had vitiated it. Spohr saw Field in 1802-1803, and describes him as a pale, overgrown youth, whose dreamy, melancholy playing made people forget his awkward bearing and badly-fitting clothes. One who knew Field at the time of his first successes portrays him as a young man with blonde hair, blue eyes, fair complexion, and pleasing features, expressive of the mood of the moment—of child-like ingenuousness, modest good-nature, gentle roguishness, and artistic aspiration. M. Marmontel, who made his acquaintance in 1832, represents him as a worn-out, vulgar-looking man of fifty, whose outward appearance contrasted painfully with his artistic performances, and whose heavy, thick-set form in conjunction with the delicacy and dreaminess of his musical thoughts and execution called to mind Rossini's saying of a celebrated singer, "Elle a l'air d'un elephant qui aurait avale un rossignol." One can easily imagine the surprise and disillusion of the four pupils of Zimmermann—MM. Marmontel, Prudent, A. Petit, and Chollet—who, provided with a letter of introduction by their master, called on Field soon after his arrival in Paris and beheld the great pianist—

> in a room filled with tobacco smoke, sitting in an easy
> chair, an enormous pipe in his mouth, surrounded by large and
> small bottles of all sorts [entoure de chopes et bouteilles
> de toutes provenances]. His rather large head, his highly-
> coloured cheeks, his heavy features gave a Falstaff-like
> appearance to his physiognomy.

Notwithstanding his tipsiness, he received the young gentlemen kindly, and played to them two studies by Cramer and Clementi "with rare perfection, admirable finish, marvellous agility, and exquisiteness of touch." Many anecdotes might be told of Field's indolence and nonchalance; for instance, how he often fell asleep while giving his lessons, and on one occasion was asked whether he thought he was paid twenty roubles for allowing himself to be played to sleep; or, how, when his walking-stick had slipped out of his hand, he waited till some one came and picked it up; or, how, on finding his dress-boots rather tight, he put on slippers, and thus appeared in one of the first salons of Paris and was led by the mistress of the house, the Duchess Decazes, to the piano—but I have said enough of the artist who is so often named in connection with Chopin.

From placid Field to volcanic Berlioz is an enormous distance, which, however, we will clear at one leap, and do it too without hesitation or difficulty. For is not leaping the mind's natural mode of locomotion, and walking an artificially-acquired and rare accomplishment? Proceeding step by step we move only with more or less awkwardness, but aided by ever so slight an association of ideas we bound with the greatest ease from any point to any other point of infinitude. Berlioz returned to Paris in the latter part of 1832, and on the ninth of December of that year gave a concert at which he produced among other works his "Episode de la vie d'un artiste" (Part I.—"Symphonic fantastique," for the second time; Part II—"Lelio, ou le retour a la vie," for the first time), the subject of which is the history of his love for Miss Smithson. Chopin, no doubt, made Berlioz's acquaintance through Liszt, whose friendship with the great French symphonic composer dated from before the latter's departure for Italy. The characters of Chopin and Berlioz differed too much for a deep sympathy to exist between them; their connection was indeed hardly more than a pleasant social companionship. Liszt tells us that the constant intercourse with Berlioz, Hiller, and other celebrities who were in the habit of saying smart things, developed Chopin's natural talent for incisive remarks, ironical answers, and ambiguous speeches. Berlioz. I think, had more affection for Chopin than the latter for Berlioz.

But it is much more the artistic than the social attitude taken up by Chopin towards Berlioz and romanticism which interests us. Has Liszt correctly represented it? Let us see. It may be accepted as in the main true that the nocturnes of Field, [Footnote: In connection with this, however, Mikuli's remark has to be remembered.] the sonatas of Dussek, and the "noisy virtuosities and decorative expressivities" of Kalkbrenner were either insufficient for or antipathetic to Chopin; and it is plainly evident that he was one of those who most perseveringly endeavoured to free themselves from the servile formulas of the conventional style and repudiated the charlatanisms that only replace old abuses by new ones. On the other hand, it cannot be said that he joined unreservedly those who, seeing the fire of talent devour imperceptibly the old worm-eaten scaffolding, attached themselves to the school of which Berlioz was the most gifted, valiant, and daring representative, nor that, as long as the campaign of romanticism lasted, he remained invariable in his predilections and repugnances. The promptings of his genius taught Chopin that the practice of any one author or set of authors, whatever their excellence might be, ought not to be an obligatory rule for their successors. But while his individual requirements led him to disregard use and wont, his individual taste set up a very exclusive standard of his own. He adopted the maxims of the romanticists, but disapproved of almost all the works of art in which they were embodied. Or rather, he adopted their negative teaching, and like them broke and threw off the trammels of dead formulas; but at the same time he rejected their positive teaching, and walked apart from them. Chopin's repugnance was not confined only to the frantic side and the delirious excesses of romanticism as Liszt thinks. He presents to us the strange spectacle of a thoroughly romantic and emphatically unclassical composer who has no sympathy either with Berlioz and Liszt, or with Schumann and other leaders of romanticism, and the object of whose constant and ardent love and admiration was Mozart, the purest type of classicism. But the romantic, which Jean Paul Richter defined as "the beautiful without limitation, or the beautiful infinite" [das Schone ohne Begrenzung, oder das schone Unendliche], affords more scope for wide divergence, and allows greater freedom in the display of individual and national differences, than the classical.

Chopin's and Berlioz's relative positions may be compared to those of V. Hugo and Alfred de Musset, both of whom were undeniably romanticists, and yet as unlike as two authors can be. For a time Chopin was carried away by Liszt's and Killer's enthusiasm for Berlioz, but he soon retired from his championship, as Musset from the Cenacle. Franchomme thought this took place in 1833, but perhaps he antedated this change of opinion. At any rate, Chopin told him that he had expected better things from Berlioz, and declared that the latter's music justified any man in breaking off all friendship with him. Some years afterwards, when conversing with his pupil Gutmann about Berlioz, Chopin took up a pen, bent back the point of it, and then let it rebound, saying: "This is the way Berlioz composes—he sputters the ink over the pages of ruled paper, and the result is as chance wills it." Chopin did not like the works of Victor Hugo, because he felt them to be too coarse and violent. And this may also have been his opinion of

Berlioz's works. No doubt he spurned Voltaire's maxim, "Le gout n'est autre chose pour la poesie que ce qu'il est pour les ajustements des femmes," and embraced V. Hugo's countermaxim, "Le gout c'est la raison du genie"; but his delicate, beauty-loving nature could feel nothing but disgust at what has been called the rehabilitation of the ugly, at such creations, for instance, as Le Roi s'amuse and Lucrece Borgia, of which, according to their author's own declaration, this is the essence:—

> Take the most hideous, repulsive, and complete physical deformity; place it where it stands out most prominently, in the lowest, most subterraneous and despised story of the social edifice; illuminate this miserable creature on all sides by the sinister light of contrasts; and then give it a soul, and place in that soul the purest feeling which is bestowed on man, the paternal feeling. What will be the result? This sublime feeling, intensified according to certain conditions, will transform under your eyes the degraded creature; the little being will become great; the deformed being will become beautiful. —Take the most hideous, repulsive, and complete moral deformity; place it where it stands out most prominently, in the heart of a woman, with all the conditions of physical beauty and royal grandeur which give prominence to crime; and now mix with all this moral deformity a pure feeling, the purest which woman can feel, the maternal feeling; place a mother in your monster and the monster will interest you, and the monster will make you weep, and this creature which caused fear will cause pity, and this deformed soul will become almost beautiful in your eyes. Thus we have in Le Roi s'amuse paternity sanctifying physical deformity; and in Lucrece Borgia maternity purifying moral deformity. [FOOTNOTE: from Victor Hugo's preface to "Lucrece Borgia."]

In fact, Chopin assimilated nothing or infinitely little of the ideas that were surging around him. His ambition was, as he confided to his friend Hiller, to become to his countrymen as a musician what Uhland was to the Germans as a poet. Nevertheless, the intellectual activity of the French capital and its tendencies had a considerable influence on Chopin.

They strengthened the spirit of independence in him, and were potent impulses that helped to unfold his individuality in all its width and depth. The intensification of thought and feeling, and the greater fulness and compactness of his pianoforte style in his Parisian compositions, cannot escape the attentive observer. The artist who contributed the largest quotum of force to this impulse was probably Liszt, whose fiery passions, indomitable energy, soaring enthusiasm, universal tastes, and capacity of assimilation, mark him out as the very opposite of Chopin. But, although the latter was undoubtedly stimulated by Liszt's style of playing the piano and of writing for this instrument, it is not so certain as Miss L. Ramann, Liszt's biographer, thinks, that this master's influence can be discovered in many passages of Chopin's music which are distinguished by a fiery and passionate expression, and resemble rather a strong, swelling torrent than a gently-gliding rivulet. She instances Nos. 9 and 12 of "Douze Etudes," Op. 10; Nos. 11 and 12 of "Douze Etudes," Op. 25; No. 24 of "Vingt-quatre Preludes," Op. 28; "Premier Scherzo," Op. 20; "Polonaise" in A flat major, Op. 53; and the close of the "Nocturne" in A flat major, Op. 32. All these compositions, we are told, exhibit Liszt's style and mode of feeling. Now, the works composed by Chopin before he came to Paris and got acquainted with Liszt comprise not only a sonata, a trio, two concertos, variations, polonaises, waltzes, mazurkas, one or more nocturnes, &c., but also—and this is for the question under consideration of great importance—most of, if not all, the studies of Op. 10, [FOOTNOTE: Sowinski says that Chopin brought with him to Paris the MS. of the first book of his studies.] and some of Op. 25; and these works prove decisively the inconclusiveness of the lady's argument. The twelfth study of Op. 10 (composed in September, 1831) invalidates all she says about fire, passion, and rushing torrents. In fact, no cogent reason can be given why the works mentioned by her should not be the outcome of unaided development. [FOONOTE: That is to say, development not aided in the way indicated by Miss Ramann. Development can never be absolutely unaided; it always presupposes conditions— external or internal, physical or psychical, moral or intellectual—which induce and promote it. What is here said may be compared with the remarks about style and individuality.] The first Scherzo alone might make us pause and ask whether the new features that present themselves in it ought not to be fathered on Liszt. But seeing that Chopin evolved so much, why should he not also have evolved this? Moreover, we must keep in mind that Liszt had, up to 1831, composed almost nothing of what in after years was considered either by him or others of much moment, and that his pianoforte style had first to pass through the state of fermentation into which Paganini's, playing had precipitated it (in the spring of 1831) before it was formed; on the other hand, Chopin arrived in Paris with his portfolios full of masterpieces, and in possession of a style of his own, as a player of his instrument as well as a writer for it. That both learned from each other cannot be doubted; but the exact gain of each is less easily determinable. Nevertheless, I think I may venture to assert that whatever be the extent of Chopin's indebtedness to Liszt, the latter's indebtedness to the former is greater. The tracing of an influence in the works of a man of genius, who, of course, neither slavishly imitates nor flagrantly appropriates, is one of the most difficult tasks. If Miss Ramann had first noted the works produced by the two composers in question before their acquaintance began, and had carefully examined Chopin's early productions with a view to ascertain his capability of growth, she would have come to another conclusion, or, at least, have spoken less confidently. [FOOTNOTE: Schumann, who in 1839 attempted to give a history of Liszt's development (in the "Neue Zeitschrift fur Musik"), remarked that when Liszt, on the one hand, was brooding over the most gloomy fancies, and indifferent, nay, even blase, and, on the other hand, laughing and madly daring, indulged in the most extravagant virtuoso tricks, "the sight of Chopin, it seems, first brought him again to his senses."]

It was not till 1833 that Chopin became known to the musical world as a composer. For up to that time the "Variations," Op. 2, published in 1830, was the only work in circulation; the compositions previously published in Warsaw—the "Rondo," Op. 1, and the "Rondeau a la Mazur," Op. 5—may be left out of account, as they did not pass beyond the frontier of Poland till several years afterwards, when they were published elsewhere. After the publication, in December, 1832, of Op. 6, "Quatre Mazurkas," dedicated to Mdlle. la Comtesse Pauline Plater, and Op. 7, "Cinq Mazurkas," dedicated to Mr. Johns, Chopin's compositions made their appearance in quick succession. In the year 1833 were published: in January, Op. 9, "Trois Nocturnes," dedicated to Mdme. Camille Pleyel; in March, Op. 8, "Premier Trio," dedicated to M. le Prince Antoine Radziwill; in July, Op. 10, "Douze Grandes Etudes," dedicated to Mr. Fr. Liszt; and Op. 11, "Grand Concerto" (in E minor), dedicated to Mr. Fr. Kalkbrenner; and in November, Op. 12, "Variations brillantes" (in B flat major), dedicated to Mdlle. Emma Horsford. In 1834 were published: in January, Op. 15, "Trois Nocturnes," dedicated to Mr. Ferd. Hiller; in March, Op. 16, "Rondeau" (in E flat major), dedicated to Mdlle. Caroline Hartmann; in April, Op. 13, "Grande Fantaisie sur des airs polonais," dedicated to Mr. J. P. Pixis; and in May, Op. 17, "Quatre Mazurkas," dedicated to Mdme. Lina Freppa; in June, Op. 14, "Krakowiak, grand Rondeau de Concert," dedicated to Mdme. la Princesse Adam Czartoryska; and Op. 18, "Grande Valse brillante," dedicated to Mdlle. Laura Horsford; and in October, Op. 19, "Bolero" (in C major), dedicated to

Mdme. la Comtesse E. de Flahault. [FOOTNOTE: The dates given are those when the pieces, as far as I could ascertain, were first heard of as published. For further information see "List of Works" at the end of the second volume, where my sources of information are mentioned, and the divergences of the different original editions, as regards time of publication, are indicated.]

The "Allgemeine musikalische Zeitung" notices several of Chopin's compositions with great praise in the course of 1833; in the year after the notices became more frequent. But the critic who follows Chopin's publications with the greatest attention and discusses them most fully is Rellstab, the editor of the Iris. Unfortunately, he is not at all favourably inclined towards the composer. He occasionally doles out a little praise, but usually shows himself a spendthrift in censure and abuse. His most frequent complaints are that Chopin strives too much after originality, and that his music is unnecessarily difficult for the hands. A few specimens of Rellstab's criticism may not be out of place here. Of the "Mazurkas," Op. 7, he says:—

> In the dances before us the author satisfies the passion [of writing affectedly and unnaturally] to a loathsome excess. He is indefatigable, and I might say inexhaustible [sic], in his search for ear-splitting discords, forced transitions, harsh modulations, ugly distortions of melody and rhythm. Everything it is possible to think of is raked up to produce the effect of odd originality, but especially strange keys, the most unnatural positions of chords, the most perverse combinations with regard to fingering.

After some more discussion of the same nature, he concludes thus:— If Mr. Chopin had shown this composition to a master, the latter would, it is to be hoped, have torn it and thrown it at his feet, which we hereby do symbolically.

In his review of the "Trois Nocturnes," Op. 9, occurs the following pretty passage:—

> Where Field smiles, Chopin makes a grinning grimace: where Field sighs, Chopin groans; where Field shrugs his shoulders, Chopin twists his whole body; where Field puts some seasoning into the food, Chopin empties a handful of Cayenne pepper...In short, if one holds Field's charming romances before a distorting concave mirror, so that every delicate expression becomes coarse, one gets Chopin's work...We

implore Mr. Chopin to return to nature.

I shall quote one more sentence; it is from a notice of the "Douze Etudes," Op. 10:—

> *Those who have distorted fingers may put them right by practising these studies; but those who have not, should not play them, at least, not without having a surgeon at hand.*

> *[FOOTNOTE: In the number of the Iris in which this criticism appeared (No. 5 of Vol. V., 1834 Rellstab inserts the following letter, which he says he received from Leipzig:—*

> *"P. P.*

> *"You are really a very bad man, and not worthy that God's earth either knows (sic) or bears you. The King of Prussia should have imprisoned you in a fortress; in that case he would have removed from the world a rebel, a disturber of the peace, and an infamous enemy of humanity, who probably will yet be choked in his own blood. I have noticed a great number of enemies, not only in Berlin, but in all towns which I visited last summer on my artistic tour, especially very many here in Leipzig, where I inform you of this, in order—that you may in future change your disposition, and not act so uncharitably towards others. Another bad, bad trick, and you are done for! Do you understand me, you little man, you loveless and partial dog of a critic, you musical snarler [Schnurrbart], you Berlin wit-cracker [Witzenmacher], &c.*

> *"Your most obedient Servant,*

> *"CHOPIN."*

> *To this Rellstab adds: "Whether Mr. Chopin has written this letter himself, I do not know, and will not assert it, but*

print the document that he may recognise or repudiate it."
The letter was not repudiated, but I do not think that it was
written by Chopin. Had he written a letter, he surely would
have written a less childish one, although the German might
not have been much better than that of the above. But my
chief reasons for doubting its genuineness are that Chopin
made no artistic tour in Germany after 1831, and is not known
to have visited Leipzig either in 1833 or 1834.]

However, we should not be too hard upon Rellstab, seeing that one of the greatest pianists and best musicians of the time made in the same year (in 1833, and not in 1831, as we read in Karasowski's book) an entry in his diary, which expresses an opinion not very unlike his. Moscheles writes thus:—

I like to employ some free hours in the evening in making
myself acquainted with Chopin's studies and his other
compositions, and find much charm in the originality and
national colouring of their motivi; but my fingers always
stumble over certain hard, inartistic, and to me
incomprehensible modulations, and the whole is often too
sweetish for my taste, and appears too little worthy of a man
and a trained musician.

And again—

I am a sincere admirer of Chopin's originality; he has
furnished pianists with matter of the greatest novelty and
attractiveness. But personally I dislike the artificial,
often forced modulations; my fingers stumble and fall over
such passages; however much I may practise them, I cannot
execute them without tripping.

The first criticism on Chopin's publications which I met with in the French musical papers is one on the "Variations," Op. 12. It appeared in the "Revue musicale" of January 26, 1834. After this his new works are pretty regularly noticed, and always favourably. From what has been said it will be evident that Karasowski made a mistake when he wrote that Chopin's compositions began to find a wide circulation as early as the year 1832.

Much sympathy has been undeservedly bestowed on the composer by many, because they were under the impression that he had had to contend with more than the usual difficulties. Now just the reverse was the case. Most of his critics were well-disposed towards him, and his fame spread fast. In 1834 (August 13) a writer in the "Allgemeine musikalische Zeitung" remarks that Chopin had the good fortune to draw upon himself sooner than others the attention not only of the pianists, although of these particularly, but also of a number of the musicians generally. And in 1836 even Rellstab, Chopin's most adverse critic, says: "We entertain the hope of hearing a public performance of the Concerto [the second, Op. 21] in the course of the winter, for now it is a point of honour for every pianist to play Chopin." The composer, however, cannot be said to have enjoyed popularity; his works were relished only by the few, not by the many. Chopin's position as a pianist and composer at the point we have reached in the history of his life (1833-1834) is well described by a writer in the "Revue musicale" of May 15, 1834: —

> *Chopin [he says] has opened up for himself a new route, and*
> *from the first moment of his appearance on the scene he has*
> *taken so high a stand, both by his pianoforte-playing and by*
> *his compositions for this instrument, that he is to the*
> *multitude an inexplicable phenomenon which it looks on in*
> *passing with astonishment, and which stupid egoism regards*
> *with a smile of pity, while the small number of connoisseurs,*
> *led by a sure judgment, rather by an instinct of progress*
> *than by a reasoned sentiment of enjoyment, follow this artist*
> *in his efforts and in his creations, if not closely, at least*
> *at a distance, admiring him, learning from him, and trying to*
> *imitate him. For this reason Chopin has not found a critic,*
> *although his works are already known everywhere. They have*
> *either excited equivocal smiles and have been disparaged, or*
> *have provoked astonishment and an overflow of unlimited*
> *praise; but nobody has as yet come forward to say in what*
> *their peculiar character and merit consists, by what they are*
> *distinguished from so many other compositions, what assigns*
> *to them a superior rank, &c.*

No important events are to be recorded of the season 1833-1834, but that Chopin was making his way is shown by a passage from a letter which Orlowski wrote to one of his friends in Poland: —

> *Chopin [he says] is well and strong; he turns the heads of*

all the Frenchwomen, and makes the men jealous of him. He is

now the fashion, and the elegant world will soon wear gloves

a la Chopin, Only the yearning after his country consumes

him.

In the spring of 1834 Chopin took a trip to Aix-la-Chapelle, where at Whitsuntide the Lower Rhenish Music Festival was held. Handel's "Deborah," Mozart's Jupiter Symphony, and part of Beethoven's Ninth were on the programme, and the baton was in the hand of Ferdinand Ries. Hiller, who had written additional accompaniments to the oratorio and translated the English words into German, had received an invitation from the committee, and easily persuaded Chopin to accompany him. But this plan very nearly came to naught. While they were making preparations for the journey, news reached them that the festival was postponed; and when a few days later they heard that it would take place after all, poor Chopin was no longer able to go, having in the meantime spent the money put aside for travelling expenses, probably given it away to one of his needy countrymen, to whom, as Hiller says, his purse was always open. But what was to be done now? Hiller did not like to depart without his friend, and urged him to consider if he could not contrive in one way or another to procure the requisite pecuniary outfit. At last Chopin said he thought he could manage it, took the manuscript of the Waltz in E flat (Op. 18), went with it to Pleyel, and returned with 500 francs. [FOOTNOTE: I repeat Hiller's account without vouching for its literal correctness, confining myself to the statement that the work was in print on the 1st of June,1834, and published by Schlesinger, of Paris, not by Pleyel.] Thus the barrier was removed, and the friends set out for Aix-la-Chapelle. There Hiller was quartered in the house of the burgomaster, and Chopin got a room close by. They went without much delay to the rehearsal of "Deborah," where they met Mendelssohn, who describes their meeting in a letter addressed to his mother (Dusseldorf, May 23, 1834):—

On the first tier sat a man with a moustache reading the

score, and as he was coming downstairs after the rehearsal,

and I was going up, we met in the side-scenes, and Ferdinand

Hiller stumbled right into my arms, almost crushing me in his

joyful embrace. He had come from Paris to hear the oratorio,

and Chopin had left his pupils in the lurch and come with

him, and thus we met again. Now I had my full share of

pleasure in the musical festival, for we three now remained

together, got a box in the theatre (where the performances

are given) to ourselves, and as a matter of course betook
ourselves next morning to a piano, where I enjoyed myself
greatly. They have both still further developed their
execution, and Chopin is now one of the very first pianoforte-
players; he produces as novel effects as Paganini does on the
violin, and performs wonders which one would never have
imagined possible. Hiller, too, is an excellent player,
powerful and coquettish enough. Both are a little infected by
the Parisian mania for despondency and straining after
emotional vehemence [Verzweif-lungssucht und
Leidenschaftssucherei], and often lose sight of time and
repose and the really musical too much. I, on the other hand,
do so perhaps too little. Thus we made up for each other's
deficiencies, and all three, I think, learned something,
while I felt rather like a schoolmaster, and they like
mirliflores or incroyables.

After the festival the three musicians travelled together to Dusseldorf, where since the preceding October Mendelssohn was settled as musical director. They passed the morning of the day which Chopin and Hiller spent in the town at Mendelssohn's piano, and in the afternoon took a walk, at the end of which they had coffee and a game at skittles. In this walk they were accompanied by F. W. Schadow, the director of the Academy of Art and founder of the Dusseldorf School, and some of his pupils, among whom may have been one or more of its brightest stars—Lessing, Bendemann, Hildebrandt, Sohn, and Alfred Rethel. Hiller, who furnishes us with some particulars of what Mendelssohn calls "a very agreeable day passed in playing and discussing music," says that Schadow and his pupils appeared to him like a prophet surrounded by his disciples. But the dignified manner and eloquent discourse of the prophet, the humble silence of the devoutly-listening disciples, seem to have prevented Chopin from feeling quite at ease.

Chopin [writes Hiller], who was not known to any of them, and
extremely reserved, kept close to me during the walk,
observing everything and making remarks to me in a low, low
tone. For the later part of the evening we were invited to
the Schadows', who were never wanting in hospitality. We
found there some of the most eminent young painters. The

conversation soon became very animated, and all would have been right if poor Chopin had not sat there so reserved—not to say unnoticed. However, Mendelssohn and I knew that he would have his revenge, and were secretly rejoicing at the thought. At last the piano was opened; I began, Mendelssohn followed; then we asked Chopin to play, and rather doubtful looks were cast at him and us. But he had hardly played a few bars when all present, especially Schadow, looked at him with altogether different eyes. Nothing like it had ever been heard. They were all in the greatest delight, and begged for more and more. Count Almaviva had dropped his disguise, and all were speechless.

The following day Chopin and Hiller set out per steamer for Coblenz, and Mendelssohn, although Schadow had asked him what was to become of "St. Paul," at which he was working, accompanied them as far as Cologne. There, after a visit to the Apostles' church, they parted at the Rhine bridge, and, as Mendelssohn wrote to his mother, "the pleasant episode was over."

CHAPTER XVII

1834-1835.

MATUSZYNSKI SETTLES IN PARIS.—MORE ABOUT CHOPIN'S WAY OF LIFE.—OP. 25.—HE IS ADVISED TO WRITE AN OPERA.— HIS OWN IDEAS IN REGARD TO THIS, AND A DISCUSSION OF THE QUESTION.—CHOPIN'S PUBLIC APPEARANCES.—BERLIOZ'S CONCERT.—STOEPEL's CONCERT.—A CONCERT AT PLEYEL'S ROOMS.—A CONCERT AT THE THEATRE-ITALIEN FOR THE BENEFIT OF THE INDIGENT POLISH REFUGEES.—A CONCERT OF THE SOCIETE DES CONCERTS.—CHOPIN AS A PUBLIC PERFORMER.—CHOUQUET, LISZT, ETC., ON THE CHARACTER OF HIS PLAYING.—BELLINI AND HIS RELATION TO CHOPIN.—CHOPIN GOES TO CARLSBAD.—AT DRESDEN.—HIS VISIT TO LEIPZIG: E. F. WENZEL'S REMINISCENCES; MENDELSSOHN'S AND SCHUMANN'S REMARKS ON THE SAME EVENT.—CHOPIN'S STAY AT HEIDELBERG AND RETURN TO PARIS.

The coming to Paris and settlement there of his friend Matuszynski must have been very gratifying to Chopin, who felt so much the want of one with whom he could sigh. Matuszynski, who, since we heard last of him, had served as surgeon-major in the Polish insurrectionary army, and taken his doctor's degree at Tubingen in 1834, proceeded in the same year to Paris, where he was appointed professor at the Ecole de Medecine. The latter circumstance testifies to his excellent professional qualities, and Chopin's letters do not leave us in doubt concerning the nature of his qualities as a friend. Indeed, what George Sand says of his great influence over Chopin only confirms what these letters lead one to think. In 1834 Matuszynski wrote in a letter addressed to his brother-in-law:—

> *The first thing I did in Paris was to call on Chopin. I*
> *cannot tell you how great our mutual happiness was on meeting*
> *again after a separation of five years. He has grown strong*
> *and tall; I hardly recognised him. Chopin is now the first*
> *pianist here; he gives a great many lessons, but none under*
> *twenty francs. He has composed much, and his works are in*
> *great request. I live with him: Rue Chaussee d'Antin, No. 5.*

This street is indeed rather far from the Ecole de Medecine
and the hospitals; but I have weighty reasons for staying
with him—he is my all! We spend the evenings at the theatre
or pay visits; if we do not do one or the other, we enjoy
ourselves quietly at home.

Less interesting than this letter of Matuszynski's, with its glimpses of Chopin's condition and habits, are the reminiscences of a Mr. W., now or till lately a music-teacher at Posen, who visited Paris in 1834, and was introduced to Chopin by Dr. A. Hofman. [FOONOTE: See p. 257.] But, although less interesting, they are by no means without significance, for instance, with regard to the chronology of the composer's works. Being asked to play something, Mr. W. chose Kalkbrenner's variations on one of Chopin's mazurkas (the one in B major, Op. 7, No. 1). Chopin generously repaid the treat which Kalkbrenner's variations and his countryman's execution may have afforded him, by playing the studies which he afterwards published as Op. 25.

Elsner, like all Chopin's friends, was pleased with the young artist's success. The news he heard of his dear Frederick filled his heart with joy, nevertheless he was not altogether satisfied. "Excuse my sincerity," he writes, on September 14, 1834, "but what you have done hitherto I do not yet consider enough." Elsner's wish was that Chopin should compose an opera, if possible one with a Polish historical subject; and this he wished, not so much for the increase of Chopin's fame as for the advantage of the art. Knowing his pupil's talents and acquirements he was sure that what a critic pointed out in Chopin's mazurkas would be fully displayed and obtain a lasting value only in an opera. The unnamed critic referred to must be the writer in the "Gazette musicale," who on June 29, 1834, in speaking of the "Quatre Mazurkas," Op. 17, says—

Chopin has gained a quite special reputation by the clever
spirituelle and profoundly artistic manner in which he knows
how to treat the national music of Poland, a genre of music
which was to us as yet little known...here again he appears
poetical, tender, fantastic, always graceful, and always
charming, even in the moments when he abandons himself to the
most passionate inspiration.

Karasowski says that Elsner's letter made Chopin seriously think of writing an opera, and that he even addressed himself to his friend Stanislas Kozmian with the request to furnish him with a libretto, the subject of which was to be taken from Polish history. I do not question this statement. But if it is true, Chopin soon abandoned the idea. In fact, he thoroughly made up his mind, and instead of endeavouring to become a Shakespeare he contented himself with being an Uhland. The following conversations will show that Chopin acquired the rarest and most precious kind of knowledge, that is, self-knowledge. His countryman, the painter Kwiatkowski, calling one day on Chopin found him and Mickiewicz in the midst of a very excited discussion. The poet urged the composer to undertake a great work, and not to fritter away his power on trifles; the composer, on the other hand, maintained that he was not in possession of the qualities requisite for what he was advised to undertake. G. Mathias, who studied under Chopin from 1839 to 1844, remembers a conversation between his master and M. le Comte de Perthuis, one of Louis Philippe's aides-de-camp. The Count said —

"Chopin, how is it that you, who have such admirable ideas, do not compose an opera?" [Chopin, avec vos idees admirables, pourquoi ne nous faites-vous pas un opera?] "Ah, Count, let me compose nothing but music for the pianoforte; I am not learned enough to compose operas!" [Ah, Monsieur le Comte, laissez-moi ne faire que de la musique de piano; pour faire des operas je ne suis pas assez savant.]

Chopin, in fact, knew himself better than his friends and teacher knew him, and it was well for him and it is well for us that he did, for thereby he saved himself much heart-burning and disappointment, and us the loss of a rich inheritance of charming and inimitable pianoforte music. He was emphatically a Kleinmeister—i.e. a master of works of small size and minute execution. His attempts in the sonata-form were failures, although failures worth more—some of them at least—than many a clever artist's most brilliant successes. Had he attempted the dramatic form the result would in all probability have been still less happy; for this form demands not only a vigorous constructive power, but in addition to it a firm grasp of all the vocal and instrumental resources—qualities, in short, in which Chopin was undeniably deficient, owing not so much to inadequate training as to the nature of his organisation. Moreover, he was too much given to express his own emotions, too narrow in his sympathies, in short, too individual a composer, to successfully express the emotions of others, to objectively conceive and set forth the characters of men and women unlike himself. Still, the master's confidence in his pupil, though unfounded in this particular, is beautiful to contemplate; and so also is his affection for him, which even the pedantic style of his letters cannot altogether hide. Nor is it possible to admire in a less degree the reciprocation of these sentiments by the great master's greater pupil: —

> What a pity it is [are the concluding words of Elsner's
> letter of September 14, 1834] that we can no longer see each
> other and exchange our opinions! I have got so much to tell
> you. I should like also to thank you for the present, which
> is doubly precious to me. I wish I were a bird, so that I
> might visit you in your Olympian dwelling, which the
> Parisians take for a swallow's nest. Farewell, love me, as I
> do you, for I shall always remain your sincere friend and
> well-wisher.

In no musical season was Chopin heard so often in public as in that of 1834-35; but it was not only his busiest, it was also his last season as a virtuoso. After it his public appearances ceased for several years altogether, and the number of concerts at which he was subsequently heard does not much exceed half-a-dozen. The reader will be best enabled to understand the causes that led to this result if I mention those of Chopin's public performances in this season which have come under my notice. On December 7, 1834, at the third and last of a series of concerts given by Berlioz at the Conservatoire, Chopin played an "Andante" for the piano with orchestral accompaniments of his own composition, which, placed as it was among the overtures to "Les Francs-Juges" and "King Lear," the "Harold" Symphony, and other works of Berlioz, no doubt sounded at the concert as strange as it looks on the programme. The "Andante" played by Chopin was of course the middle movement of one of his concertos. [Footnote: Probably the "Larghetto" from the F minor Concerto. See Liszt's remark on p. 282.]

On December 25 of the same year, Dr. Francois Stoepel gave a matinee musicale at Pleyel's rooms, for which he had secured a number of very distinguished artists. But the reader will ask—"Who is Dr. Stoepel?" An author of several theoretical works, instruction books, and musical compositions, who came to Paris in 1829 and founded a school on Logier's system, as he had done in Berlin and other towns, but was as unsuccessful in the French capital as elsewhere. Disappointed and consumptive he died in 1836 at the age of forty-two; his income, although the proceeds of teaching were supplemented by the remuneration for contributions to the "Gazette musicale," having from first to last been scanty. Among the artists who took part in this matinee musicale were Chopin, Liszt, the violinist Ernst, and the singers Mdlle. Heinefetter, Madame Degli-Antoni, and M. Richelmi. The programme comprised also an improvisation on the orgue expressif (harmonium) by Madame de la Hye, a grand-niece of J.J. Rousseau's. Liszt and Chopin opened the matinee with a performance of Moscheles' "Grand duo a quatre mains," of which the reporter of the "Gazette musicale" writes as follows:—

> We consider it superfluous to say that this piece, one of the
> masterworks of the composer, was executed with a rare
> perfection of talent by the two greatest pianoforte-virtuosos
> of our epoch. Brilliancy of execution combined with perfect
> delicacy, sustained elevation, and the contrast of the most
> spirited vivacity and calmest serenity, of the most graceful
> lightness and gravest seriousness—the clever blending of all
> the nuances can only be expected from two artists of the same
> eminence and equally endowed with deep artistic feeling. The
> most enthusiastic applause showed MM. Liszt and Chopin better
> than we can do by our words how much they charmed the
> audience, which they electrified a second time by a Duo for
> two pianos composed by Liszt.

This work of Liszt's was no doubt the Duo for two pianos on a theme of Mendelssohn's which, according to Miss Ramann, was composed in 1834 but never published, and is now lost.

The "Menestrel" of March 22, 1835, contains a report of a concert at Pleyel's rooms, without, however, mentioning the concert-giver, who was probably the proprietor himself:—

> The last concert at Pleyel's rooms was very brilliant. Men of
> fashion, litterateurs, and artists had given each other
> rendez-vous there to hear our musical celebrities—MM. Herz,
> Chopin, Osborne, Hiller, Reicha, Mesdames Camille Lambert and
> Leroy, and M. Hamati [read Stamati], a young pianist who had
> not yet made a public appearance in our salons. These artists
> performed various pieces which won the approval of all.

And now mark the dying fall of this vague report: "Kalkbrenner's Variations on the cavatina 'Di tanti palpiti' were especially applauded."

We come now to the so much talked-of concert at the Italian Opera, which became so fateful in Chopin's career as a virtuoso. It is generally spoken of as a concert given by Chopin, and Karasowski says it took place in February, 1834. I have, however, been unable to find any trace of a concert given by Chopin in 1834. On the other hand, Chopin played on April 5, 1835, at a concert which in all particulars except that of date answers to the description of the one mentioned by Karasowski. The "Journal des Debats" of April 4, 1835, draws the public's attention to it by the following short and curious article:—

> The concert for the benefit of the indigent Poles [i.e.,
>
> indigent Polish refugees] will take place to-morrow,
>
> Saturday, at the Theatre-Italien, at eight o'clock in the
>
> evening. Mdlle. Falcon and Nourrit, MM. Ernst, Dorus, Schopin
>
> [sic], Litz [sic], and Pantaleoni, will do the honours of
>
> this soiree, which will be brilliant. Among other things
>
> there will be heard the overtures to "Oberon" and "Guillaume
>
> Tell," the duet from the latter opera, sung by Mdlle. Falcon
>
> and Nourrit, and romances by M. Schubert, sung by Nourrit and
>
> accompanied by Litz, &c.

To this galaxy of artistic talent I have yet to add Habeneck, who conducted the orchestra. Chopin played with the orchestra his E minor Concerto and with Liszt a duet for two pianos by Hiller.

> As you may suppose [says a writer of a notice in the "Gazette
>
> musicale"] M. Chopin was not a stranger to the composition of
>
> the programme of this soiree in behalf of his unhappy
>
> countrymen. Accordingly the fete was brilliant.

In the same notice may also be read the following:—

> Chopin's Concerto, so original, of so brilliant a style, so
>
> full of ingenious details, so fresh in its melodies, obtained
>
> a very great success. It is very difficult not to be
>
> monotonous in a pianoforte concerto; and the amateurs could
>
> not but thank Chopin for the pleasure he had procured them,
>
> while the artists admired the talent which enabled him to do
>
> so [i.e., to avoid monotony], and at the same time to
>
> rejuvenate so antiquated a form.

The remark on the agedness of the concerto-form and the difficulty of not being monotonous is naive and amusing enough to be quoted for its own sake, but what concerns us here is the correctness of the report. Although the expressions of praise contained in it are by no means enthusiastic, nay, are not even straightforward, they do not tally with what we learn from other accounts. This discrepancy may be thus explained. Maurice Schlesinger, the founder and publisher of the "Gazette musicale," was on friendly terms with Chopin and had already published some of his compositions. What more natural, therefore, than that, if the artist's feelings were hurt, he should take care that they should not be further tortured by unpleasant remarks in his paper. Indeed, in connection with all the Chopin notices and criticisms in the "Gazette musicale" we must keep in mind the relations between the publisher and composer, and the fact that several of the writers in the paper were Chopin's intimate friends, and many of them were of the clique, or party, to which he also belonged. Sowinski, a countryman and acquaintance of Chopin's, says of this concert that the theatre was crowded and all went well, but that Chopin's expectations were disappointed, the E minor Concerto not producing the desired effect. The account in Larousse's "Grand Dictionnaire" is so graphic that it makes one's flesh creep. After remarking that Chopin obtained only a demi-success, the writer of the article proceeds thus: "The bravos of his friends and a few connoisseurs alone disturbed the cold and somewhat bewildered attitude of the majority of the audience." According to Sowinski and others Chopin's repugnance to play in public dates from this concert; but this repugnance was not the outcome of one but of many experiences. The concert at the Theatre-Italien may, however, have brought it to the culminating point. Liszt told me that Chopin was most deeply hurt by the cold reception he got at a concert at the Conservatoire, where he played the Larghetto from the F minor Concerto. This must have been at Berlioz's concert, which I mentioned on one of the foregoing pages of this chapter.

Shortly after the concert at the Theatre-Italien, Chopin ventured once more to face that terrible monster, the public. On Sunday, April 26, 1835, he played at a benefit concert of Habeneck's, which is notable as the only concert of the Societe des Concerts du Conservatoire in which he took part. The programme was as follows:—1. The "Pastoral Symphony," by Beethoven; 2. "The Erl-King," by Schubert, sung by M. Ad. Nourrit; 3. Scherzo from the "Choral Symphony," by Beethoven; 4. "Polonaise avec introduction" [i.e., "Polonaise brillante precedee d'un Andante spianato"], composed and played by M. Chopin; 5. Scena, by Beethoven, sung by Mdlle. Falcon; 6. Finale from the C minor Symphony, by Beethoven. The writer of the article Chopin in Larousse's "Grand Dictionnaire" says that Chopin had no reason to repent of having taken part in the concert, and others confirm this statement. In Elwart's "Histoire des Concerts du Conservatoire" we read:—"Le compositeur reveur, l'elegiaque pianiste, produisit a ce concert un effet delicieux." To the author of the "Histoire dramatique en France" and late curator of the Musee du Conservatoire I am indebted for some precious communications. M. Gustave Chouquet, who at the time we are speaking of was a youth and still at the College, informed me in a charming letter that he was present at this concert at which Chopin played, and also at the preceding one (on Good Friday) at which Liszt played Weber's "Concertstuck," and that he remembered very well "the fiery playing of Liszt and the ineffable poetry of Chopin's style." In another letter M. Chouquet gave a striking resume of the vivid reminiscences of his first impressions:—

> Liszt, in 1835 [he wrote], represented a merveilleux the
> prototype of the virtuoso; while in my opinion Chopin
> personified the poet. The first aimed at effect and posed as
> the Paganini of the piano; Chopin, on the other hand, seemed
> never to concern himself [se preuccuper] about the public,
> and to listen only to the inner voices. He was unequal; but
> when inspiration took hold of him [s'emparait de hit] he made
> the keyboard sing in an ineffable manner. I owe him some
> poetic hours which I shall never forget.

One of the facts safely deducible from the often doubtful and contradictory testimonies relative to Chopin's public performances is, that when he appeared before a large and mixed audience he failed to call forth general enthusiasm. He who wishes to carry the multitude away with him must have in him a force akin to the broad sweep of a full river. Chopin, however, was not a Demosthenes, Cicero, Mirabeau, or Pitt. Unless he addressed himself to select conventicles of sympathetic minds, the best of his subtle art remained uncomprehended. How well Chopin knew this may be gathered from what he said to Liszt:—

> I am not at all fit for giving concerts, the crowd
> intimidates me, its breath suffocates me, I feel paralysed by
> its curious look, and the unknown faces make me dumb. But you
> are destined for it, for when you do not win your public, you
> have the power to overwhelm it.

Opposition and indifference, which stimulate more vigorous natures, affected Chopin as touch does the mimosa pudica, the sensitive plant—they made him shrink and wither. Liszt observes correctly that the concerts did not so much fatigue Chopin's physical constitution as provoke his irritability as a poet; that, in fact, his delicate constitution was less a reason than a pretext for abstention, he wishing to avoid being again and again made the subject of debate. But it is more difficult for one in similar circumstances not to feel as Chopin did than for a successful virtuoso like Liszt to say:—

If Chopin suffered on account of his not being able to take
part in those public and solemn jousts where popular
acclamation salutes the victor; if he felt depressed at
seeing himself excluded from them, it was because he did not
esteem highly enough what he had, to do gaily without what he
had not.

To be sure, the admiration of the best men of his time ought to have consoled him for the indifference of the dull crowd. But do we not all rather yearn for what we have not than enjoy what we have? Nay, do we not even often bewail the unattainableness of vain bubbles when it would be more seasonable to rejoice in the solid possessions with which we are blessed? Chopin's discontent, however, was caused by the unattainableness not of a vain bubble, but of a precious crown. There are artists who pretend to despise the great public, but their abuse of it when it withholds its applause shows their real feeling. No artist can at heart be fully satisfied with the approval of a small minority; Chopin, at any rate, was not such a one. Nature, who had richly endowed him with the qualities that make a virtuoso, had denied him one, perhaps the meanest of all, certainly the least dispensable, the want of which balked him of the fulfilment of the promise with which the others had flattered him, of the most brilliant reward of his striving. In the lists where men much below his worth won laurels and gold in abundance he failed to obtain a fair share of the popular acclamation. This was one of the disappointments which, like malignant cancers, cruelly tortured and slowly consumed his life.

The first performance of Bellini's "I Puritani" at the Theatre-Italien (January 24, 1835), which as well as that of Halevy's "La Juive" at the Academie (February 23, 1835), and of Auber's "Le cheval de bronze" at the Opera-Comique (March 23, 1835), was one of the chief musico-dramatic events of the season 1834-1835, reminds me that I ought to say a few words about the relation which existed between the Italian and the Polish composer. Most readers will have heard of Chopin's touching request to be buried by the side of Bellini. Loath though I am to discredit so charming a story, duty compels me to state that it is wholly fictitious. Chopin's liking for Bellini and his music, how ever, was true and real enough. Hiller relates that he rarely saw him so deeply moved as at a performance of Norma, which they attended together, and that in the finale of the second act, in which Rubini seemed to sing tears, Chopin had tears in his eyes. A liking for the Italian operatic music of the time, a liking which was not confined to Bellini's works, but, as Franchomme, Wolff, and others informed me, included also those of Rossini, appears at first sight rather strange in a musician of

Chopin's complexion; the prevalent musical taste at Warsaw, and a kindred trait in the national characters of the Poles and Italians, however, account for it. With regard to Bellini, Chopin's sympathy was strengthened by the congeniality of their individual temperaments. Many besides Leon Escudier may have found in the genius of Chopin points of resemblance with Bellini as well as with Raphael—two artists who, it is needless to say, were heaven-wide apart in the mastery of the craft of their arts, and in the width, height, and depth of their conceptions. The soft, rounded Italian contours and sweet sonorousness of some of Chopin's cantilene cannot escape the notice of the observer. Indeed, Chopin's Italicisms have often been pointed out. Let me remind the reader here only of some remarks of Schumann's, made apropos of the Sonata in B flat minor, Op. 35:—

It is known that Bellini and Chopin were friends, and that
they, who often made each other acquainted with their
compositions, may perhaps have had some artistic influence on
each other. But, as has been said, there is [on the part of
Chopin] only a slight leaning to the southern manner; as soon
as the cantilena is at an end the Sarmatian flashes out
again.

To understand Chopin's sympathy we have but to picture to ourselves Bellini's personality—the perfectly well-proportioned, slender figure, the head with its high forehead and scanty blonde hair, the well-formed nose, the honest, bright look, the expressive mouth; and within this pleasing exterior, the amiable, modest disposition, the heart that felt deeply, the mind that thought acutely. M. Charles Maurice relates a characteristic conversation in his "Histoire anecdotique du Theatre." Speaking to Bellini about "La Sonnambula," he had remarked that there was soul in his music. This expression pleased the composer immensely. "Oui, n'est-ce pas? De l'ame!" he exclaimed in his soft Italian manner of speaking, "C'est ce que je veux...De L'ame! Oh! je suis sensible! Merci!...C'est que l'ame, c'est toute la musique!" "And he pressed my hands," says Charles Maurice, "as if I had discovered a new merit in his rare talent." This specimen of Bellini's conversation is sufficient to show that his linguistic accomplishments were very limited. Indeed, as a good Sicilian he spoke Italian badly, and his French was according to Heine worse than bad, it was frightful, apt to make people's hair stand on end.

When one was in the same salon with him, his vicinity inspired one with a certain anxiety mingled with the fascination of terror which repelled and attracted at the same time. His puns were not always of an amusing kind. Hiller also mentions Bellini's bad grammar and pronunciation, but he adds that the contrast between what he said and the way he said it gave to his gibberish a charm which is often absent from the irreproachable language of trained orators. It is impossible to conjecture what Bellini might have become as a musician if, instead of dying before the completion of his thirty-third year (September 24, 1835), he had lived up to the age of fifty or sixty; thus much, however, is certain, that there was still in him a vast amount of undeveloped capability. Since his arrival in Paris he had watched attentively the new musical phenomena that came there within his ken, and the "Puritani" proves that he had not done so without profit. This sweet singer from sensuous Italy was not insensible even to the depth and grandeur of German music. After hearing Beethoven's Pastoral Symphony, for instance, he said to Hiller, his eyes glistening as if he had himself done a great deed: "E bel comme la nature!" [Footnote: I give the words literally as they are printed in Hiller's Kimmerleben. The mixture of Italian and French was no doubt intended, but hardly the spelling.] In short, Bellini was a true artist, and therefore a meet companion for a true artist like Chopin, of whose music it can be said with greater force than of that of most composers that "it is all soul." Chopin, who of course met Bellini here and there in the salons of the aristocracy, came also in closer contact with him amidst less fashionable but more congenial surroundings. I shall now let Hiller, the pleasant story-teller, speak, who, after remarking that Bellini took a great interest in piano-forte music, even though it was not played by a Chopin, proceeds thus:—

> *I can never forget some evenings which I spent with him*
> *[Bellini] and Chopin and a few other guests at Madame*
> *Freppa's. Madame Freppa, an accomplished and exceedingly*
> *musical woman, born at Naples, but of French extraction, had,*
> *in order to escape from painful family circumstances, settled*
> *in Paris, where she taught singing in the most distinguished*
> *circles. She had an exceedingly sonorous though not powerful*
> *voice, and an excellent method, and by her rendering of*
> *Italian folk-songs and other simple vocal compositions of the*
> *older masters charmed even the spoiled frequenters of the*
> *Italian Opera. We cordially esteemed her, and sometimes went*
> *together to visit her at the extreme end of the Faubourg St.*
> *Germain, where she lived with her mother on a troisieme au*
> *dessus de l'entresol, high above all the noise and tumult of*

the ever-bustling city. There music was discussed, sung, and
played, and then again discussed, played, and sung. Chopin
and Madame Freppa seated themselves by turns at the
pianoforte; I, too, did my best; Bellini made remarks, and
accompanied himself in one or other of his cantilene, rather
in illustration of what he had been saying than for the
purpose of giving a performance of them. He knew how to sing
better than any German composer whom I have met, and had a
voice less full of sound than of feeling. His pianoforte-
playing sufficed for the reproduction of his orchestra,
which, indeed, is not saying much. But he knew very well what
he wanted, and was far from being a kind of natural poet, as
some may imagine him to have been.

In the summer of 1835, towards the end of July, Chopin journeyed to Carlsbad, whither his father had been sent by the Warsaw physicians. The meeting of the parents and their now famous son after a separation of nearly five years was no doubt a very joyous one; but as no accounts have come down to us of Chopin's doings and feelings during his sojourn in the Bohemian watering-place, I shall make no attempt to fill up the gap by a gushing description of what may have been, evolved out of the omniscience of my inner consciousness, although this would be an insignificant feat compared with those of a recent biographer whose imaginativeness enabled her to describe the appearance of the sky and the state of the weather in the night when her hero became a free citizen of this planet, and to analyse minutely the characters of private individuals whose lives were passed in retirement, whom she had never seen, and who had left neither works nor letters by which they might be judged.

From Carlsbad Chopin went to Dresden. His doings there were of great importance to him, and are of great interest to us. In fact, a new love-romance was in progress. But the story had better be told consecutively, for which reason I postpone my account of his stay in the Saxon capital till the next chapter.

Frederick Wieck, the father and teacher of Clara, who a few years later became the wife of Robert Schumann, sent the following budget of Leipzig news to Nauenburg, a teacher of music in Halle, in the autumn of 1835:—

The first subscription concert will take place under the
direction of Mendelssohn on October 4, the second on October

4. *To-morrow or the day after to-morrow Chopin will arrive*
here from Dresden, but will probably not give a concert, for
he is very lazy. He could stay here for some time, if false
friends (especially a dog of a Pole) did not prevent him from
making himself acquainted with the musical side of Leipzig.
But Mendelssohn, who is a good friend of mine and Schumann's,
will oppose this. Chopin does not believe, judging from a
remark he made to a colleague in Dresden, that there is any
lady in Germany who can play his compositions—we will see
what Clara can do.

The Neue Zeitschrift fur Musik, Schumann's paper, of September 29,
1835, contained the following announcement:—

Leipzig will soon be able to show a Kalisz [Footnote: An
allusion to the encampment of Russian and Prussian troops and
friendly meeting of princes which took place there in 1835.]
as regards musical crowned heads. Herr Mendelssohn has
already arrived. Herr Moscheles comes this week; and besides
him there will be Chopin, and later, Pixis and Franzilla.
[Footnote: Franzilla (or Francilla) Pixis, the adopted
daughter of Peter Pixis, whose acquaintance the reader made
in one of the preceding chapters (p. 245).]

The details of the account of Chopin's visit to Leipzig which I am now
going to give, were communicated to me by Ernst Ferdinand Wenzel, the
well-known professor of pianoforte-playing at the Leipzig Conservatorium,
who died in 1880.

In the middle of the year 1835 the words "Chopin is coming" were
passing from mouth to mouth, and caused much stir in the musical circles
of Leipzig. Shortly after this my informant saw Mendelssohn in the street
walking arm in arm with a young man, and he knew at once that the Polish
musician had arrived, for this young man could be no other than Chopin.
From the direction in which the two friends were going, he guessed whither
their steps were tending. He, therefore, ran as fast as his legs would carry him
to his master Wieck, to tell him that Chopin would be with him in another
moment. The visit had been expected, and a little party was assembled,
every one of which was anxious to see and hear the distinguished artist.
Besides Wieck, his wife, daughter, and sister-in-law, there were present
Robert Schumann and Wieck's pupils Wenzel, Louis Rakemann, and Ulex.

But the irascible pedagogue, who felt offended because Chopin had not come first to him, who had made such efforts for the propagation of his music, would not stay and welcome his visitor, but withdrew sulkily into the inner apartments. Wieck had scarcely left the room when Mendelssohn and Chopin entered. The former, who had some engagement, said, "Here is Chopin!" and then left, rightly thinking this laconic introduction sufficient. Thus the three most distinguished composers of their time were at least for a moment brought together in the narrow space of a room. [Footnote: This dictum, like all superlatives and sweeping assertions, will no doubt raise objectors; but, I think, it may be maintained, and easily maintained with the saving clause "apart from the stage."] Chopin was in figure not unlike Mendelssohn, but the former was more lightly built and more graceful in his movements. He spoke German fluently, although with a foreign accent. The primary object of Chopin's visit was to make the acquaintance of Clara Wieck, who had already acquired a high reputation as a pianist. She played to him among other things the then new and not yet published Sonata in F sharp minor (Op. 11) by Schumann, which she had lately been studying. The gentlemen dared not ask Chopin to play because of the piano, the touch of which was heavy and which consequently would not suit him. But the ladies were bolder, and did not cease entreating him till he sat down and played his Nocturne in E flat (Op. 9, No. 2). After the lapse of forty-two years Wenzel was still in raptures about the wonderful, fairy-like lightness and delicacy of Chopin's touch and style. The conversation seems to have turned on Schubert, one of Schumann's great favourites, for Chopin, in illustration of something he said, played the commencement of Schubert's Alexander March. Meanwhile Wieck was sorely tried by his curiosity when Chopin was playing, and could not resist the temptation of listening in the adjoining room, and even peeping through the door that stood slightly ajar. When the visit came to a close; Schumann conducted Chopin to the house of his friend Henrietta Voigt, a pupil of Louis Berger's, and Wenzel, who accompanied them to the door, heard Schumann say to Chopin: "Let us go in here where we shall find a thorough, intelligent pianist and a good piano." They then entered the house, and Chopin played and also stayed for dinner. No sooner had he left, than the lady, who up to that time had been exceedingly orthodox in her musical opinions and tastes, sent to Kistner's music-shop, and got all the compositions by Chopin which were in stock.

The letter of Mendelssohn which I shall quote presently and an entry in Henrietta Voigt's diary of the year 1836, which will be quoted in the next chapter, throw some doubt on the latter part of Herr Wenzel's reminiscences. Indeed, on being further questioned on the subject, he modified his original information to this, that he showed Chopin, unaccompanied by Schumann, the way to the lady's house, and left him at the door. As to the general credibility of the above account, I may say that I have added nothing to my informant's communications, and that in my intercourse with him I found him to be a man of acute observation and tenacious memory. What, however, I do not know, is the extent to which the mythopoeic faculty was developed in him.

[Footnote: Richard Pohl gave incidentally a characterisation of this exceedingly interesting personality in the Signale of September, 1886, No. 48. Having been personally acquainted with Wenzel and many of his friends and pupils, I can vouch for its truthfulness. He was "one of the best and most amiable men I have known," writes R. Pohl, "full of enthusiasm for all that is beautiful, obliging, unselfish, thoroughly kind, and at the same time so clever, so cultured, and so many-sided as—excuse me, gentlemen—I have rarely found a pianoforte-teacher. He gave pianoforte lessons at the Conservatorium and in many private houses; he worked day after day, year after year, from morning till night, and with no other outcome as far as he himself was concerned than that all his pupils—especially his female pupils—loved him enthusiastically. He was a pupil of Friedrich Wieck and a friend of Schumann."]

In a letter dated October 6, 1835, and addressed to his family, Mendelssohn describes another part of Chopin's sojourn in Leipzig and gives us his opinion of the Polish artist's compositions and playing:—

> The day after I accompanied the Hensels to Delitzsch, Chopin
> was here; he intended to remain only one day, so we spent
> this entirely together and had a great deal of music. I
> cannot deny, dear Fanny, that I have lately found that you do
> not do him justice in your judgment [of his talents]; perhaps
> he was not in a right humour for playing when you heard him,
> which may not unfrequently be the case with him. But his
> playing has enchanted me anew, and I am persuaded that if you
> and my father had heard some of his better pieces played as
> he played them to me, you would say the same. There is
> something thoroughly original and at the same time so very
> masterly in his piano-forte-playing that he may be called a
> really perfect virtuoso; and as every kind of perfection is
> welcome and gratifying to me, that day was a most pleasant
> one, although so entirely different from the previous ones
> spent with you Hensels.

I was glad to be once more with a thorough musician, not with
those half-virtuosos and half-classics who would gladly
combine in music les honneurs de la vertu et les plaisirs du
vice, but with one who has his perfect and well-defined genre
[Richtung]. To whatever extent it may differ from mine, I can
get on with it famously; but not with those half-men. The
Sunday evening was really curious when Chopin made me play
over my oratorio to him, while curious Leipzigers stole into
the room to see him, and how between the first and second
parts he dashed off his new Etudes and a new Concerto, to the
astonishment of the Leipzigers, and I afterwards resumed my
St. Paul, just as if a Cherokee and a Kaffir had met and
conversed. He has such a pretty new notturno, several parts
of which I have retained in my memory for the purpose of
playing it for Paul's amusement. Thus we passed the time
pleasantly together, and he promised seriously to return in
the course of the winter if I would compose a new symphony
and perform it in honour of him. We vowed these things in the
presence of three witnesses, and we shall see whether we both
keep our word. My works of Handel [Footnote: A present from
the Committee of the Cologne Musical Festival of 1835.]
arrived before Chopin's departure, and were a source of quite
childish delight to him; but they are really so beautiful
that I cannot sufficiently rejoice in their possession.

Although Mendelssohn never played any of Chopin's compositions in public, he made his piano pupils practise some of them. Karasowski is wrong in saying that Mendelssohn had no such pupils; he had not many, it is true, but he had a few. A remark which Mendelssohn once made in his peculiar naive manner is very characteristic of him and his opinion of Chopin. What he said was this: "Sometimes one really does not know whether Chopin's music is right or wrong." On the whole, however, if one of the two had to complain of the other's judgment, it was not Chopin but Mendelssohn, as we shall see farther on.

To learn what impression Chopin made on Schumann, we must once more turn to the Neue Zeitschrift fur Musik, where we find the Polish artist's visit to Leipzig twice mentioned:—

October 6, 1835. Chopin was here, but only for a few hours, which he passed in private circles. He played just as he composes, that is, uniquely.

The second mention is in the P.S. of a transcendental Schwarmerbrief addressed by Eusebius (the personification of the gentle, dreamy side of Schumann's character) to Chiara (Clara Wieck):—

October 20, 1835. Chopin was here. Florestan [the personification of the strong, passionate side of Schumann's character] rushed to him. I saw them arm in arm glide rather than walk. I did not speak with him, was quite startled at the thought.

On his way to Paris, Chopin stopped also at Heidelberg, where he visited the father of his pupil Adolph Gutmann, who treated him, as one of his daughters remarked, not like a prince or even a king, but like somebody far superior to either. The children were taught to look up to Chopin as one who had no equal in his line. And the daughter already referred to wrote more than thirty years afterwards that Chopin still stood out in her memory as the most poetical remembrance of her childhood and youth.

Chopin must have been back in Paris in the first half or about the middle of October, for the Gazette musicale of the 18th of that month contains the following paragraph:—

One of the most eminent pianists of our epoch, M. Chopin, has returned to Paris, after having made a tour in Germany which has been for him a real ovation. Everywhere his admirable talent obtained the most flattering reception and excited enthusiasm. It was, indeed, as if he had not left our capital at all.

CHAPTER XVIII

1835—1837.

PUBLICATIONS IN 1835 AND 1836.—FIRST PERFORMANCE OF LES HUGUENOTS.— GUSIKOW, LIPINSKI, THALBERG.—CHOPIN'S IMPRESSIONABLENESS AND FICKLENESS IN REGARD TO THE FAIR SEX.—THE FAMILY WODZINSKI.—CHOPIN'S LOVE FOR MARIA WODZINSKA (DRESDEN, 1835; MARIENBAD, 1836).—ANOTHER VISIT TO LEIPZIG (1836).—CHARACTER OF THE CHIEF EVENTS IN 1837.— MENTION OF HIS FIRST MEETING WITH GEORGE SAND.—HIS VISIT TO LONDON.—NEWSPAPER ANNOUNCEMENT OF ANOTHER VISIT TO MARIENBAD.—STATE OF HIS HEALTH IN 1837.

IF we leave out of account his playing in the salons, Chopin's artistic activity during the period comprised in this chapter was confined to teaching and composition. [Footnote: A Paris correspondent wrote in the Neue Zeitschrift fur Musik of May 17, 1836, that Chopin had not been heard at all that winter, meaning, of course, that he had not been heard in public.] The publication of his works enables us to form an approximate idea of how he was occupied as a creative musician. In the year 1835 were published: in February, Op. 20, Premier Scherzo (in B minor), dedicated to Mr. T. Albrecht, and in November, Op. 24, Quatre Mazurkas, dedicated to M. le Comte de Perthuis. In 1836 appeared: in April, Op. 21, Second Concerto (in F minor), dedicated to Madame la Comtesse Delphine Potocka: in May, Op. 27, Deux Nocturnes (in C sharp minor and D flat major), dedicated to Madame la Comtesse d'Appony; in June, Op. 23, Ballade (in G minor), dedicated to M. le Baron de Stockhausen; in July, Op. 22, Grande Polonaise brillante (E flat major) precedee d'un Andante spianato for pianoforte and orchestra, dedicated to Madame la Baronne d'Est; and Op. 26, Deux Polonaises (in C sharp minor and E flat minor), dedicated to Mr. J. Dessauer. It is hardly necessary to point out that the opus numbers do not indicate the order of succession in which the works were composed. The Concerto belongs to the year 1830; the above notes show that Op. 24 and 27 were sooner in print than Op. 23 and 26; and Op. 25, although we hear of its being played by the composer in 1834 and 1835, was not published till 1837.

The indubitably most important musical event of the season 1835-1836, was the production of Meyerbeer's Les Huguenots, which took place on February 29, 1836, and had an extraordinary success. The concert-rooms, however, concern us more than the opera-houses. This year brought to Paris two Polish musicians: Lipinski, the violinist, and Gusikow, the virtuoso on the Strohfiedel, [FOOTNOTE: "Straw-fiddle," Gigelira, or Xylophone, an instrument consisting of a graduated series of bars of wood that lie on cords of twisted straw and are struck with sticks.] whom Mendelssohn called "a true genius," and another contemporary pointed out as one of the three great stars (Paganini and Malibran were the two others) at that time shining in the musical heavens. The story goes that Lipinski asked Chopin to prepare the ground for him in Paris. The latter promised to do all in his power if Lipinski would give a concert for the benefit of the Polish refugees. The violinist at first expressed his willingness to do so, but afterwards drew back, giving as his reason that if he played for the Polish refugees he would spoil his prospects in Russia, where he intended shortly to make an artistic tour. Enraged at this refusal, Chopin declined to do anything to further his countryman's plans in Paris. But whether the story is true or not, Lipinski's concert at the Hotel de Ville, on March 3, was one of the most brilliant and best-attended of the season. [FOOTNOTE: Revue et Gazette musicale of March 13, 1836. Mainzer had a report to the same effect in the Neue Zeitschrift fur Musik.]

The virtuoso, however, whose appearance caused the greatest sensation was Thalberg. The Gazette musicale announced his arrival on November 8, 1835. He was first heard at M. Zimmermann's; Madame Viardot-Garcia, Duprez, and De Beriot being the other artists that took active parts in the soiree. The enthusiasm which Thalberg on this occasion as well as subsequently excited was immense. The Menestrel expressed the all but unanimous opinion when, on March 13, 1836, it said: "Thalberg is not only the first pianist in the world, but he is also a most distinguished composer." His novel effects astonished and delighted his hearers. The pianists showed their appreciation by adopting their confrere's manipulations and treatment of the piano as soon as these ceased to puzzle them; the great majority of the rising Parisian pianists became followers of Thalberg, nor were some of the older ones slow in profiting by his example. The most taking of the effects which Thalberg brought into vogue was the device of placing the melody in the middle—i.e., the most sonorous part of the instrument—and dividing it so between the hands that they could at the same time accompany it with full chords and brilliant figures. Even if he borrowed the idea from the harpist Parish-Alvars, or from the pianist Francesco G. Pollini, there remains to him the honour of having improved the invention of his forerunners and applied it with superior ability. His greatness, however, does not solely or even mainly rest on this or any other ingeniously-contrived and cleverly-performed trick. The secret of his success lay in the aristocratic nature of his artistic personality, in which exquisite elegance and calm self-possession reigned supreme. In accordance with this fundamental disposition were all the details of his style of playing. His execution was polished to the highest degree; the evenness of his scales and the clearness of his passages and embellishments could not be surpassed. If sensuous beauty is the sole end of music, his touch must be pronounced the ideal of perfection, for it extracted the essence of beauty. Strange as the expression "unctuous sonorousness" may sound, it describes felicitously a quality of a style of playing from which roughness, harshness, turbulence, and impetuosity were altogether absent. Thalberg has been accused of want of animation, passion, in short, of soul; but as Ambros remarked with great acuteness—

> *Thalberg's compositions and playing had soul, a salon soul to*
> *be sure, somewhat like that of a very elegant woman of the*
> *world, who, nevertheless, has really a beautiful disposition*
> *[Gemueth], which, however, is prevented from fully showing*
> *itself by the superexquisiteness of her manners.*

This simile reminds me of a remark of Heine's, who thought that Thalberg distinguished himself favourably from other pianists by what he (Heine) felt inclined to call "his musical conduct [Betragen]." Here are some more of the poet-critic's remarks on the same subject:—

> *As in life so also in art, Thalberg manifests innate tact;*
> *his execution is so gentlemanlike, so opulent, so decorous,*
> *so entirely without grimace, so entirely without forced*
> *affectation of genius [forcirtes Genialthun], so entirely*
> *without that boastful boorishness which badly conceals the*
> *inner pusillanimity...He enchants by balsamic euphony, by*
> *sobriety and gentleness....There is only one I prefer. That*
> *is Chopin.*

As a curiosity I must quote a passage from a letter dated July 10, 1836, and addressed by George Sand to the Comtesse d'Agoult. Feelings of friendship, and, in one case at least, of more than friendship, made these ladies partial to another prince of the keyboard:—

> *I have heard Thalberg in Paris. He made on me the impression*
> *of a good little child, very nice and very well-behaved.*

There are hours when Franz [Liszt], while amusing himself,

trifles [badine], like him, on some notes in order to let the

furious elements afterwards loose on this gentle breeze.

Liszt, who was at the time of Thalberg's visit to Paris in Switzerland, doubted the correctness of the accounts which reached him of this virtuoso's achievements. Like Thomas he would trust only his own senses; and as his curiosity left him no rest, he betook himself in March, 1836, to Paris. But, unfortunately, he arrived too late, Thalberg having quitted the capital on the preceding day. The enthusiastic praises which were everywhere the answer to his inquiries about Thalberg irritated Liszt, and seemed to him exaggerations based on delusions. To challenge criticism and practically refute the prevalent opinion, he gave two private soirees, one at Pleyel's and another at Erard's, both of which were crowded, the latter being attended by more than four hundred people. The result was a brilliant victory, and henceforth there were two camps. The admiration and stupefaction of those who heard him were extraordinary; for since his last appearance Liszt had again made such enormous progress as to astonish even his most intimate friends. In answer to those who had declared that with Thalberg a new era began, Berlioz, pointing to Liszt's Fantasia on I Pirati and that on themes from La Juive, now made the counter-declaration that "this was the new school of pianoforte-playing." Indeed, Liszt was only now attaining to the fulness of his power as a pianist and composer for his instrument; and when after another sojourn in Switzerland he returned in December, 1836, to Paris, and in the course of the season entered the lists with Thalberg, it was a spectacle for the gods. "Thalberg," writes Leon Escudier, "est la grace, comme Liszt la force; le jeu de l'un est blond, celui de l'autre est brun." A lady who heard the two pianists at a concert for the Italian poor, given in the salons of the Princess Belgiojoso, exclaimed: "Thalberg est le premier pianiste du monde."—"Et Liszt?" asked the person to whom the words were addressed—"Liszt! Liszt—c'est le seul!" was the reply. This is the spirit in which great artists should be judged. It is oftener narrowness of sympathy than acuteness of discrimination which makes people exalt one artist and disparage another who differs from him. In the wide realm of art there are to be found many kinds of excellence; one man cannot possess them all and in the highest degree. Some of these excellences are indeed irreconcilable and exclude each other; most of them can only be combined by a compromise. Hence, of two artists who differ from each other, one is not necessarily superior to the other; and he who is the greater on the whole may in some respects be inferior to the lesser. Perhaps the reader will say that these are truisms. To be sure they are. And yet if he considers only the judgments which are every day pronounced, he may easily be led to believe that these truisms are most recondite truths now for the first time revealed. When Liszt after his first return from Switzerland did not find Thalberg himself, he tried to satisfy his curiosity by a careful examination of that pianist's compositions. The conclusions he came to be set forth in a criticism of Thalberg's Grande Fantaisie, Op. 22, and the Caprices, Op. 15 and 19, which in 1837 made its appearance in the Gazette musicale, accompanied by an editorial foot-note expressing dissent. I called Liszt's article a criticism, but "lampoon" or "libel" would have been a more appropriate designation. In the introductory part Liszt sneers at Thalberg's title of "Pianist to His Majesty the Emperor of Austria," and alludes to his rival's distant (i.e., illegitimate) relationship to a noble family, ascribing his success to a great extent to these two circumstances. The personalities and abusiveness of the criticism remind one somewhat of the manner in which the scholars of earlier centuries, more especially of the sixteenth and seventeenth, dealt critically with each other. Liszt declares that love of truth, not jealousy, urged him to write; but he deceived himself. Nor did his special knowledge and experience as a musician and virtuoso qualify him, as he pretended, above others for the task he had undertaken; he forgot that no man can be a good judge in his own cause. No wonder, therefore, that Fetis, enraged at this unprovoked attack of one artist on a brother-artist, took up his pen in defence of the injured party. Unfortunately, his retort was a lengthy and pedantic dissertation, which along with some true statements contained many questionable, not to say silly, ones. In nothing, however, was he so far off the mark as in his comparative estimate of Liszt and Thalberg. The sentences in which he sums up the whole of his reasoning show this clearly: "You are the pre-eminent man of the school which is effete and which has nothing more to do, but you are not the man of a new school! Thalberg is this man—herein lies the whole difference between you two." Who can help smiling at this combination of pompous authoritativeness and wretched short-sightedness? It has been truly observed by Ambros that there is between Thalberg and Liszt all the difference that exists between a man of talent and a man of genius; indeed, the former introduced but a new fashion, whereas the latter founded really a new school. The one originated a few new effects, the other revolutionised the whole style of writing for the pianoforte. Thalberg was perfect in his genre, but he cannot be compared to an artist of the breadth, universality, and, above all, intellectual and emotional power of Liszt. It is possible to describe the former, but the latter, Proteus-like, is apt to elude the grasp of him who endeavours to catch hold of him. The Thalberg controversy did not end with Fetis's article. Liszt wrote a rejoinder in which he failed to justify himself, but succeeded in giving the poor savant some hard hits. I do not think Liszt would have approved of the republication of these literary escapades if he had taken the trouble to re-read them. It is very instructive to compare his criticism of Thalberg's compositions with what Schumann—who in this case is by no means partial—said of them. In the opinion of the one the Fantaisie sur Les Huguenots is not only one of the most empty and mediocre works, but it is also so supremely monotonous that it produces extreme weariness. In the opinion of the other the Fantaisie deserves the general enthusiasm which it has called forth, because the composer proves himself master of his language and thoughts, conducts himself like a man of the world, binds and loosens the threads with so much ease that it seems quite unintentional, and draws the audience with him wherever he wishes without either over-exciting or wearying it. The truth, no doubt, is rather with Schumann than with Liszt. Although Thalberg's compositions cannot be ranked with the great works of ideal art, they are superior to the morceaux of Czerny, Herz, and hoc genus omne, their appearance marking indeed an improvement in the style of salon music.

But what did Chopin think of Thalberg? He shared the opinion of Liszt, whose side he took. In fact, Edouard Wolff told me that Chopin absolutely despised Thalberg. To M. Mathias I owe the following communication, which throws much light on Chopin's attitude:—

> I saw Chopin with George Sand at the house of Louis Viardot, before the marriage of the latter with Pauline Garcia. I was very young, being only twelve years old, but I remember it as though it had been yesterday. Thalberg was there, and had played his second fantasia on Don Giovanni (Op. 42), and upon my word Chopin complimented him most highly and with great gravity; nevertheless, God knows what Chopin thought of it in his heart, for he had a horror of Thalberg's arrangements, which I have seen and heard him parody in the most droll and amusing manner, for Chopin had the sense of parody and ridicule in a high degree.

Thalberg had not much intercourse with Chopin, nor did he exercise the faintest shadow of an influence over him; but as one of the foremost pianist-composers—indeed, one of the most characteristic phenomena of the age—he could not be passed by in silence. Moreover, the noisy careers of Liszt and Thalberg serve as a set-off to the noiseless one of Chopin.

I suspect that Chopin was one of that race of artists and poets "qui font de la passion un instrument de l'art et de la poesie, et dont l'esprit n'a d'activite qu'autant qu'il est mis en mouvement par les forces motrices du coeur." At any rate, the tender passion was a necessary of his existence. That his disappointed first love did not harden his heart and make him insensible to the charms of the fair sex is apparent from some remarks of George Sand, who says that although his heart was ardent and devoted, it was not continuously so to any one person, but surrendered itself alternately to five or six affections, each of which, as they struggled within it, got by turns the mastery over all the others. He would passionately love three women in the course of one evening party and forget them as soon as he had turned his back, while each of them imagined that she had exclusively charmed him. In short, Chopin was of a very impressionable nature: beauty and grace, nay, even a mere smile, kindled his enthusiasm at first sight, and an awkward word or equivocal glance was enough to disenchant him. But although he was not at all exclusive in his own affections, he was so in a high degree with regard to those which he demanded from others. In illustration of how easily Chopin took a dislike to anyone, and how little he measured what he accorded of his heart with what he exacted from that of others, George Sand relates a story which she got from himself. In order to avoid misrepresenting her, I shall translate her own words:—

> He had taken a great fancy to the granddaughter of a
> celebrated master. He thought of asking her in marriage at
> the same time that he entertained the idea of another
> marriage in Poland—his loyalty being engaged nowhere, and
> his fickle heart floating from one passion to the other. The
> young Parisian received him very kindly, and all went as well
> as could be till on going to visit her one day in company
> with another musician, who was of more note in Paris than he
> at that time, she offered a chair to this gentleman before
> thinking of inviting Chopin to be seated. He never called on
> her again, and forgot her immediately.

The same story was told me by other intimate friends of Chopin's, who evidently believed in its genuineness; their version differed from that of George Sand only in this, that there was no allusion to a lady-love in Poland. Indeed, true as George Sand's observations are in the main, we must make allowance for the novelist's habit of fashioning and exaggerating, and the woman's endeavour to paint her dismissed and aggrieved lover as black as possible. Chopin may have indulged in innumerable amorous fancies, but the story of his life furnishes at least one instance of his having loved faithfully as well as deeply. Nor will it be denied that Chopin's love for Constantia Gladkowska was a serious affair, whether the fatal end be attributable to him or her, or both. And now I have to give an account of another love-affair which deserves likewise the epithet "serious."

As a boy Chopin contracted a friendship with the brothers Wodzinski, who were boarders at his father's establishment. With them he went repeatedly to Sluzewo, the property of their father, and thus became also acquainted with the rest of the family. The nature of the relation in which Chopin and they stood to each other is shown by a letter written by the former on July 18, 1834, to one of the brothers who with his mother and other members of the family was at that time staying at Geneva, whither they had gone after the Polish revolution of 1830-31, in which the three brothers—Anthony, Casimir, and Felix—had taken part:—

> *My dear Felix,—Very likely you thought "Fred must be moping that he does not answer my letter!" But you will remember that it was always my habit to do everything too late. Thus I went also too late to Miss Fanche, and consequently was obliged to wait till honest Wolf had departed. Were it not that I have only recently come back from the banks of the Rhine and have an engagement from which I cannot free myself just now, I would immediately set out for Geneva to thank your esteemed mamma and at the same time accept her kind invitation. But cruel fate—in one word, it cannot be done. Your sister was so good as to send me her composition. It gives me the greatest pleasure, and happening to improvise the veryevening of its arrival in one of our salons, I took for my subject the pretty theme by a certain Maria with whom in times gone by I played at hide and seek in the house of Mr. Pszenny...To-day! Je prends la liberte d'envoyer a mon estimable collegue Mile Marie une petite valse que je viens de publier. May it afford her a hundredth part of the pleasure which I felt on receiving her variations. In conclusion, I once more thank your mamma most sincerely for kindly remembering her old and faithful servant in whose veins also there run some drops of Cujavian blood.*
> *[Footnote: Cujavia is the name of a Polish district.]*

F. CHOPIN.

P.S.—Embrace Anthony, stifle Casimir with caresses if you can; as for Miss Maria make her a graceful and respectful bow. Be surprised and say in a whisper, "Dear me, how tall she has grown!"

The Wodzinskis, with the exception of Anthony, returned in the summer of 1835 to Poland, making on their way thither a stay at Dresden. Anthony, who was then in Paris and in constant intercourse with Chopin, kept the latter informed of his people's movements and his people of Chopin's. Thus it came about that they met at Dresden in September, 1835, whither the composer went after his meeting with his parents at Carlsbad, mentioned in the preceding chapter (p. 288). Count Wodzinski says in his Les trois Romans de Frederic Chopin that Chopin had spoken to his father about his project of marrying Maria Wodzinska, and that this idea had sprung up in his soul by the mere force of recollections. The young lady was then nineteen years of age, and, according to the writer just mentioned, tall and slender in figure, and light and graceful in gait. The features, he tells us, were distinguished neither by regularity nor classical beauty, but had an indefinable charm. Her black eyes were full of sweetness, reverie, and restrained fire; a smile of ineffable voluptuousness played around her lips; and her magnificent hair was as dark as ebony and long enough to serve her as a mantle. Chopin and Maria saw each other every evening at the house of her uncle, the Palatine Wodzinski. The latter concluded from their frequent tete-a-tete at the piano and in corners that some love-making was going on between them. When he found that his monitory coughs and looks produced no effect on his niece, he warned his sister-in-law. She, however, took the matter lightly, saying that it was an amitie d'enfance, that Maria was fond of music, and that, moreover, there would soon be an end to all this—their ways lying in opposite directions, hers eastward to Poland, his westward to France. And thus things were allowed to go on as they had begun, Chopin passing all his evenings with the Wodzinskis and joining them in all their walks. At last the time of parting came, the clock of the Frauenkirche struck the hour of ten, the carriage was waiting at the door, Maria gave Chopin a rose from a bouquet on the table, and he improvised a waltz which he afterwards sent her from Paris, and which she called L'Adieu. Whatever we may think of the details of this scene of parting, the waltz composed for Maria at Dresden is an undeniable fact. Facsimiles may be seen in Szulc's Fryderyk Chopin and Count Wodziriski's Les trois Romans de Frederic Chopin. The manuscript bears the superscription: "Tempo de Valse" on the left, and "pour Mlle. Marie" on the right; and the subscription: "F. Chopin, Drezno [Dresden],

September, 1835." [FOOTNOTE: It is Op. 69, No. 1, one of the posthumous works published by Julius Fontana.]

The two met again in the following summer, this time at Marienbad, where he knew she and her mother were going. They resumed their walks, music, and conversations. She drew also his portrait. And then one day Chopin proposed. Her answer was that she could not run counter to her parents' wishes, nor could she hope to be able to bend their will; but she would always preserve for him in her heart a grateful remembrance. [FOOTNOTE: Count Wodzinski relates on p. 255 of his book that at a subsequent period of her life the lady confided to him the above-quoted answer.] This happened in August, 1836; and two days after mother and daughter left Marienbad. Maria Wodzinska married the next year a son of Chopin's godfather, Count Frederick Skarbek. The marriage turned but an unhappy one, and was dissolved. Subsequently the Countess married a Polish gentleman of the name of Orpiszewski, who died some years ago in Florence. She, I think, is still alive.

Karasowski relates the affair very differently. He says Chopin, who knew the brothers Wodzinski in Poland, met them again in Paris, and through them made the acquaintance of their sister Maria, whose beauty and amiability inspired him at once with an interest which soon became ardent love. But that Chopin had known her in Poland may be gathered from the above letter to Felix Wodzinski, quite apart from the distinct statements of the author of Les trois Romans that Chopin was a frequent visitor at Sluzewo, and a great friend of Maria's. Further, Karasowski, who does not mention at all the meeting of Chopin and the Wodzinskis at Dresden in 1835, says that Chopin went in the middle of July, 1836, to Marienbad, where he knew he would find Maria and her mother, and that there he discovered that she whom he loved reciprocated his affection, the consequence being an engagement approved of by her relations. When the sojourn in Marienbad came to an end, the whole party betook itself to Dresden, where they remained together for some weeks, which they spent most pleasantly.

[FOOTNOTE: Karasowski relates that Chopin was at the zenith of happiness. His good humour was irresistible. He imitated the most famous pianists, and played his dreamy mazurkas in the manner much in favour with Warsaw amateurs—i.e., strictly in time and with the strongly-accented rhythm of common dance-tunes. And his friends reminded him of the tricks which, as a boy, he had played on his visits to the country, and how he took away his sisters' kid gloves when he was going to an evening-party, and could not buy himself new ones, promising to send them dozens as soon as he had gained a good position in Paris. Count Wodzinski, too, bears witness to Chopin's good humour while in the company of the Wodzinskis. In the course of his account of the sojourn at Marienbad, this writer speaks of Chopin's polichinades: "He imitated then this or that famous artist, the playing of certain pupils or compatriots, belabouring the keyboard with extravagant gestures, a wild [echevele] and romantic manner, which he called aller a la chasse aux pigeons."]

Unless Chopin was twice with the Wodzinskis in Dresden, Karasowski must be mistaken. That Chopin sojourned for some time at Dresden in 1835 is evidenced by Wieck's letter, quoted on p. 288, and by the above-mentioned waltz. The latter seems also to confirm what Count Wodzinski says about the presence of the Wodzinskis at Dresden in that year. On the other hand, we have no such documents to prove the presence at Dresden in 1836 either of Chopin or the Wodzinskis. According to Karasowski, the engagement made at Marienbad remained in force till the middle of 1837, when Chopin received at Paris the news that the lady withdrew from it. [FOOTNOTE: In explanation of the breaking-off of this supposed engagement, it has also been said that the latter was favoured by the mother, but opposed by the father.] The same authority informs us that before this catastrophe Chopin had thoughts of settling with his future wife in the neighbourhood of Warsaw, near his beloved parents and sisters. There he would cultivate his art in retirement, and found schools for the people. How, without a fortune of his own, and with a wife who, although belonging to a fairly wealthy family, would not come into the possession of her portion till after the death of her parents, he could have realised these dreams, I am at a loss to conjecture.

[FOONOTE: To enable his readers to measure the social distance that separated Chopin from his beloved one, Count Wodzinski mentions among other details that her father possessed a domain of about 50,000 acres (20,000 hectares). It is hardly necessary to add that this large acreage, which we will suppose to be correctly stated, is much less a measure of the possessor's wealth than of his social rank.]

Chopin's letters, which testify so conclusively to the cordial friendship existing between him and the Wodzinskis, unfortunately contain nothing which throws light on his connection with the young lady, although her name occurs in them several times. On April 2, 1837, Chopin wrote to Madame Wodzinska as follows:—

I take advantage of Madame Nakwaska's permission and enclose

a few words. I expect news from Anthony's own hand, and shall

send you a letter even more full of details than the one

which contained Vincent's enclosure. I beg of you to keep

your mind easy about him. As yet all are in the town. I am
not in possession of any details, because the correspondents
only give accounts of themselves. My letter of the same date
must certainly be in Sluzewo; and, as far as is possible, it
will set your mind at rest with regard to this Spaniard who
must, must write me a few words. I am not going to use many
words in expressing the sorrow I felt on learning the news of
your mother's death — not for her sake whom I did not know,
but for your sake whom I do know. (This is a matter of
course!) I have to confess, Madam, that I have had an attack
like the one I had in Marienbad; I sit before Miss Maria's
book, and were I to sit a hundred years I should be unable to
write anything in it. For there are days when I am out of
sorts. To-day I would prefer being in Sluzewo to writing to
Sluzewo. Then would I tell you more than I have now written.
My respects to Mr. Wodzinski and my kind regards to Miss
Maria, Casimir, Theresa, and Felix.

The object of another letter, dated May 14, 1837, is likewise to give news of Anthony Wodzinski, who was fighting in Spain. Miss Maria is mentioned in the P.S. and urged to write a few words to her brother.

After a careful weighing of the evidence before us, it appears to me that—notwithstanding the novelistic tricking-out of Les trois Romans de Frederic Chopin—we cannot but accept as the true account the author's statement as to Chopin's proposal of marriage and Miss Wodzinska's rejection at Marienbad in 1836. The testimony of a relation with direct information from one of the two chief actors in the drama deserves more credit than that of a stranger with, at best, second-hand information; unless we prefer to believe that the lady misrepresented the facts in order to show herself to the world in a more dignified and amiable character than that of a jilt. The letters can hardly be quoted in support of the engagement, for the rejection would still admit of the continuation of the old friendship, and their tone does not indicate the greater intimacy of a closer relationship.

Subsequent to his stay at Marienbad Chopin again visited Leipzig. But the promises which Mendelssohn and Chopin had so solemnly made to each other in the preceding year had not been kept; the latter did not go in the course of the winter to Leipzig, and if he had gone, the former could not have performed a new symphony of his in honour of the guest. Several passages in letters written by Schumann in the early part of 1836 show, however, that Chopin was not forgotten by his Leipzig friends, with whom he seems to have been in correspondence. On March 8, 1836, Schumann wrote to Moscheles:—

Mendelssohn sends you his hearty greetings. He has finished
his oratorio, and will conduct it himself at the Dusseldorf
Musical Festival. Perhaps I shall go there too, perhaps also
Chopin, to whom we shall write about it.

The first performance of Mendelssohn's St. Paul took place at Dusseldorf on May 22, and was a great success. But neither Schumann nor Chopin was there. The latter was, no doubt, already planning his excursion to Marienbad, and could not allow himself the luxury of two holidays within so short a time.

Here is another scrap from a letter of Schumann's, dated August 28, 1836, and addressed to his brother Edward and his sister-in-law Theresa:—

I have just written to Chopin, who is said to be in
Marienbad, in order to learn whether he is really there. In
any case, I should visit you again in autumn. But if Chopin
answers my letter at once, I shall start sooner, and go to
Marienbad by way of Carlsbad. Theresa, what do you think! you
must come with me! Read first Chopin's answer, and then we
will fully discuss the rest.

Chopin either had left or was about to leave Marienbad when he received Schumann's letter. Had he received it sooner, his answer would not have been very encouraging. For in his circumstances he could not but have felt even the most highly-esteemed confrere, the most charming of companions, in the way.[FOOTNOTE: Mendelscohn's sister, Rebecka Dirichlet, found him completely absorbed in his Polish Countess. (See The Mendelssohn Family, Vol. II, p. 15.)] But although the two musicians did not meet at Marienbad, they saw each other at Leipzig. How much one of them enjoyed the visit may be seen in the following extract from a letter which Schumann wrote to Heinrich Dorn on September 14, 1836:—

The day before yesterday, just after I had received your
letter and was going to answer it, who should enter? —Chopin.
This was a great pleasure. We passed a very happy day
together, in honour of which I made yesterday a holiday...I
have a new ballade by Chopin. It appears to me his

*genialischstes (not genialstes) work; and I told him that I
liked it best of all.*

*[FOOTNOTE: "Sein genialischstes (nicht genialstes) Werk." I
take Schumann to mean that the ballade in question (the one
in G minor) is Chopin's most spirited, most daring work, but
not his most genial—i.e., the one fullest of genius.
Schumann's remark, in a criticism of Op. 37, 38, and 42, that
this ballade is the "wildest and most original" of Chopin's
compositions, confirms my conjecture.]*

*After a long meditative pause he said with great emphasis: "I
am glad of that, it is the one which I too like best." He
played besides a number of new etudes, nocturnes, and
mazurkas—everything incomparable. You would like him very
much. But Clara [Wieck] is greater as a virtuoso, and gives
almost more meaning to his compositions than he himself.
Imagine the perfection, a mastery which seems to be quite
unconscious of itself!*

Besides the announcement of September 16, 1836, that Chopin had been
a day in Leipzig, that he had brought with him among other things new
"heavenly" etudes, nocturnes, mazurkas, and a new ballade, and that he
played much and "very incomparably," there occur in Schumann's writings
in the Neue Zeitschrift fur Musik unmistakable reminiscences of this visit of
the Polish musician. Thus, for instance, in a review of dance-music, which
appeared in the following year, and to which he gave the fantastic form of
a "Report to Jeanquirit in Augsburg of the editor's last artistico-historical
ball," the writer relates a conversation he had with his partner Beda:—

*I turned the conversation adroitly on Chopin. Scarcely had
she heard the name than she for the first time fully looked
at me with her large, kindly eyes. "And you know him?" I
answered in the affirmative. "And you have heard him?" Her
form became more and more sublime. "And have heard him
speak?" And when I told her that it was a never-to-be-
forgotten picture to see him sitting at the piano like a*

dreaming seer, and how in listening to his playing one seemed
to one's self like the dream he created, and how he had the
dreadful habit of passing, at the end of each piece, one
finger quickly over the whizzing keyboard, as if to get rid
of his dream by force, and how he had to take care of his
delicate health—she clung to me with ever-increasing
timorous delight, and wished to know more and more about him.

Very interesting is Schumann's description of how Chopin played some etudes from his Op. 25; it is to be found in another criticism of the same year (1837):—

As regards these etudes, I have the advantage of having heard
most of them played by Chopin himself, and, as Florestan
whispered in my ear at the time, "He plays them very much a
la Chopin." Imagine an AEolian harp that had all the scales,
and that these were jumbled together by the hand of an artist
into all sorts of fantastic ornaments, but in such a manner
that a deeper fundamental tone and a softly-singing higher
part were always audible, and you have an approximate idea of
his playing. No wonder that we have become fondest of those
pieces which we heard him play himself, and therefore we
shall mention first of all the first one in A flat, which is
rather a poem than an etude. It would be a mistake, however,
to suppose that he brought out every one of the little notes
with distinctness; it was more like a billowing of the A flat
major chord, swelled anew here and there by means of the
pedal; but through the harmonies were heard the sustained
tones of a wondrous melody, and only in the middle of it did
a tenor part once come into greater prominence amid the
chords along with that principal cantilena. After listening
to the study one feels as one does after a blissful vision,
seen in a dream, which, already half awake, one would fain
bring back. He soon came to the one in F minor, the second in
the book, likewise one which impresses one indelibly with his

originality; it is so charming, dreamy, and soft, somewhat
like the singing of a child in its sleep. Beautiful also,
although less new in character than in the figure, was the
following one in F major; here the object was more to exhibit
bravura, the most charming bravura, and we could not but
praise the master highly for it....But of what use are
descriptive words?

This time we cannot cite a letter of Mendelssohn's; he was elsewhere similarly occupied as Chopin in Marienbad. After falling in love with a Frankfort lady, Miss Jeanrenaud, he had gone to Scheweningen to see whether his love would stand the test of absence from the beloved object. It stood the test admirably, and on September 9, a few days before Chopin's arrival in Leipzig, Mendelssohn's engagement to the lady who became his wife on March 28, 1837, took place.

But another person who has been mentioned in connection with Chopin's first visit to Leipzig, Henrietta Voigt, [FOOTNOTE: The editor of "Acht Briefe und ein Facsimile van Felix Mendelssohn-Bartholdy" speaks of her as "the artistic wife of a Leipzig merchant, whose house stood open to musicians living in and passing through Leipzig."] has left us an account of the impression made upon her. An entry in her diary on September 13, 1836, runs thus:—

Yesterday Chopin was here and played an hour on my piano—a
fantasia and new etude of his—interesting man and still more
interesting playing; he moved me strangely. The over-
excitement of his fantastic manner is imparted to the keen-
eared; it made me hold my breath. Wonderful is the ease with
which his velvet fingers glide, I might almost say fly, over
the keys. He has enraptured me—I cannot deny it—in a way
which hitherto had been unknown to me. What delighted me was
the childlike, natural manner which he showed in his
demeanour and in his playing.

After this short break of his journey at Leipzig, which he did not leave without placing a wreath of flowers on the monument of Prince Joseph Poniatowski, who in 1812 met here with an early death, being drowned in the river Elster, Chopin proceeded on his homeward journey, that is toward Paris, probably tarrying again for a day or two at Heidelberg.

The non-artistic events of this period are of a more stirring nature than the artistic ones. First in time and importance comes Chopin's meeting with George Sand, which more than any other event marks an epoch in the composer's life. But as this subject has to be discussed fully and at some length we shall leave it for another chapter, and conclude this with an account of some other matters.

Mendelssohn, who arrived in London on August 24, 1837, wrote on September 1 to Hiller:—

> Chopin is said to have suddenly turned up here a fortnight
> ago; but he visited nobody and made no acquaintances. He
> played one evening most beautifully at Broadwood's, and then
> hurried away again. I hear he is still suffering very much.

Chopin accompanied by Camille Pleyel and Stanislas Kozmian, the elder, came to London on the 11th of July and stayed till the 22nd. Pleyel introduced him under the name of M. Fritz to his friend James Broadwood, who invited them to dine with him at his house in Bryanston Square. The incognito, however, could only be preserved as long as Chopin kept his hands off the piano. When after dinner he sat down to play, the ladies of the family suspected, and, suspicion being aroused, soon extracted a confession of the truth.

Moscheles in alluding in his diary to this visit to London adds an item or two to its history:—

> Chopin, who passed a few days in London, was the only one of
> the foreign artists who visited nobody and also did not wish
> to be visited, as every conversation aggravates his chest-
> complaint. He went to some concerts and disappeared.

Particularly interesting are the reminiscences of the writer of an enthusiastic review [Footnote: Probably J. W. Davison.]of some of Chopin's nocturnes and a scherzo in the "Musical World" of February 23, 1838:—

> Were he [Chopin] not the most retiring and unambitious of all
> living musicians, he would before this time have been
> celebrated as the inventor of a new style, or school, of
> pianoforte composition. During his short visit to the
> metropolis last season, but few had the high gratification of
> hearing his extemporaneous performance. Those who experienced
> this will not readily lose its remembrance. He is, perhaps,

par eminence, the most delightful of pianists in the drawing-
room. The animation of his style is so subdued, its
tenderness so refined, its melancholy so gentle, its niceties
so studied and systematic, the tout-ensemble so perfect, and
evidently the result of an accurate judgment and most
finished taste, that when exhibited in the large concert-
room, or the thronged saloon, it fails to impress itself on
the mass. The "Neue Zeitschrift fur Musik" of September 8,
1837, brought the piece of news that Chopin was then at a
Bohemian watering-place. I doubt the correctness of this
statement; at any rate, no other information to that effect
has come to my knowledge, and the ascertained facts do not
favour the assumption of its truth.

Never robust, Chopin had yet hitherto been free from any serious illness. Now, however, the time of his troubles begins. In a letter, undated, but very probably written in the summer of 1837, which he addressed to Anthony Wodzinski, who had been wounded in Spain, where civil war was then raging, occur remarks confirmatory of Mendelssohn's and Moscheles' statements:—

My dearest life! Wounded! Far from us—and I can send you
nothing....Your friends are thinking only of you. For mercy's
sake recover as soon as possible and return. The newspaper
accounts say that your legion is completely annihilated.
Don't enter the Spanish army....Remember that your blood may
serve a better purpose....Titus [Woyciechowski] wrote to ask
me if I could not meet him somewhere in Germany. During the
winter I was again ill with influenza. They wanted to send me
to Ems. Up to the present, however, I have no thought of
going, as I am unable to move. I write and prepare
manuscript. I think far more of you than you imagine, and
love you as much as ever.

F. C.

Believe me, you and Titus are enshrined in my memory.

On the margin, Chopin writes—

I may perhaps go for a few days to George Sand's, but keep
your mind easy, this will not interfere with the forwarding
of your money, for I shall leave instructions with Johnnie
[Matuszynski].

With regard to this and to the two preceding letters to members of the
Wodzinski family, I have yet to state that I found them in M. A. Szulc's
"Fryderyk Chopin."

CHAPTER XIX

GEORGE SAND: HER EARLY LIFE (1804—1836); AND HER CHARACTER AS A WOMAN, THINKER, AND LITERARY ARTIST.

It is now necessary that the reader should be made acquainted with Madame Dudevant, better known by her literary name, George Sand, whose coming on the scene has already been announced in the preceding chapter. The character of this lady is so much a matter of controversy, and a correct estimate of it so essential for the right understanding of the important part she plays in the remaining portion of Chopin's life, that this long chapter— an intermezzo, a biography in a biography—will not be regarded as out of place or too lengthy. If I begin far off, as it were before the beginning, I do so because the pedigree has in this case a peculiar significance.

The mother of George Sand's father was the daughter of the Marschal de Saxe (Count Maurice of Saxony, natural son of August the Strong, King of Poland and Elector of Saxony, and the Countess Maria Aurora von Konigsmark) and the dame de l'opera, Mdlle. de Verrieres, whose real name was Madame de la Riviere, nee Marie Rinteau. This daughter, Marie Aurore, married at the age of fifteen Comte de Home, a natural son of Louis XV., who died soon after; and fifteen years later she condescended to accept the hand of M. Dupin de Francueil, receveur general, who, although of an old and well-connected family, did not belong to the high nobility. The curious may read about Mdlle. de Verrieres in the "Memoires" of Marmontel, who was one of her many lovers, and about M. Dupin, his father, mother-in-law, first wife &c., in Rousseau's "Confessions," where, however, he is always called De Francueil. Notwithstanding the disparity of age, the husband being twice as old as his wife, the marriage of M. Dupin and the Comtesse de Home proved to be a very happy one. They had one child, a son, Maurice Francois Elisabeth Dupin. He entered the army in 1798, and two years later, in the course of the Italian campaign, became first lieutenant and then aide-de-camp to General Dupont.

In Italy and about the same time Maurice Dupin saw and fell in love with Sophie Victoire Antoinette Delaborde, the daughter of a Paris bird-seller, who had been a supernumerary at some small theatre, and whose youth, as George Sand delicately expresses it, "had by the force of circumstances been exposed to the most frightful hazards." Sacrificing all the advantages she was then enjoying, she followed Maurice Dupin to France. From this liaison sprang several children, all of whom, however, except one, died very young. A month before the birth of her in whom our interest centres, Maurice Dupin married Sophie Delaborde. The marriage was a civil one and contracted without the knowledge of his mother, who was opposed to this union less on account of Sophie's plebeian origin than of her doubtful antecedents.

It was on July 5, 1804, that Amantine Lucile Aurore Dupin, who under the name of George Sand became famous all the world over, saw for the first time the light of day. The baby, which by a stratagem was placed in the arms of her grandmother, mollified the feelings of the old lady, whom the clandestine marriage had put in a great rage, so effectually that she forgave her son, received his wife, and tried to accommodate herself to the irremediable. After the Spanish campaign, during which he acted as aide-de-camp to Murat, Maurice Dupin and his family came to Nohant, his mother's chateau in Berry. There little Aurora lost her father when she was only four years old. Returning home one evening from La Chatre, a neighbouring town, he was thrown off his horse, and died almost instantly.

This was an event that seriously affected the future of the child, for only the deceased could keep in check the antagonism of two such dissimilar characters as those of Aurora's mother and grandmother. The mother was "dark-complexioned, pale, ardent, awkward and timid in fashionable society, but always ready to explode when the storm was growling too strongly within"; her temperament was that "of a Spaniard—jealous, passionate, choleric, and weak, perverse and kindly at the same time." Abbe Beaumont (a natural son of Mdlle. de Verrieres and the Prince de Turenne, Duke de Bouillon, and consequently grand-uncle of Aurora) said of her that she had a bad head but a good heart. She was quite uneducated, but had good natural parts, sang charmingly, and was clever with her hands. The grandmother, on the other hand, was "light-complexioned, blonde, grave, calm, and dignified in her manners, a veritable Saxon of noble race, with an imposing demeanour full of ease and patronising goodness." She had been an assiduous student of the eighteenth century philosophers, and on the whole was a lady of considerable culture. For about two years these two women managed to live together, not, however, without a feeling of discord which was not always successfully suppressed, and sometimes broke out into open dissension. At last they came to an arrangement according to which the child was to be left in the keeping of the grandmother, who promised her daughter-in-law a yearly allowance which would enable her to take up her abode in Paris. This arrangement had the advantage for the younger

Madame Dupin that she could henceforth devote herself to the bringing-up of another daughter, born before her acquaintance with Aurora's father.

From her mother Aurora received her first instruction in reading and writing. The taste for literary composition seems to have been innate in her, for already at the age of five she wrote letters to her grandmother and half-brother (a natural son of her father's). When she was seven, Deschartres, her grandmother's steward, who had been Maurice Dupin's tutor, began to teach her French grammar and versification, Latin, arithmetic, botany, and a little Greek. But she had no liking for any of these studies. The dry classifications of plants and words were distasteful to her; arithmetic she could not get into her head; and poetry was not her language. History, on the other hand, was a source of great enjoyment to her; but she read it like a romance, and did not trouble herself about dates and other unpleasant details. She was also fond of music; at least she was so as long as her grandmother taught her, for the mechanical drilling she got from the organist of La Chatre turned her fondness into indifference. That subject of education, however, which is generally regarded as the foundation of all education—I mean religion—was never even mentioned to her. The Holy Scriptures were, indeed, given into the child's hands, but she was left to believe or reject whatever she liked. Her grandmother, who was a deist, hated not only the pious, but piety itself, and, above all, Roman Catholicism. Christ was in her opinion an estimable man, the gospel an excellent philosophy, but she regretted that truth was enveloped in ridiculous fables. The little of religion which the girl imbibed she owed to her mother, by whose side she was made to kneel and say her prayers. "My mother," writes George Sand in her "Histoire de ma Vie," from which these details are taken, "carried poetry into her religious feeling, and I stood in need of poetry." Aurora's craving for religion and poetry was not to remain unallayed. One night there appeared to her in a dream a phantom, Corambe by name. The dream-created being took hold of her waking imagination, and became the divinity of her religion and the title and central figure of her childish, unwritten romance. Corambe, who was of no sex, or rather of either sex just as occasion might require—for it underwent numberless metamorphoses—had "all the attributes of physical and moral beauty, the gift of eloquence, and the all-powerful charm of the arts, especially the magic of musical improvisation," being in fact an abstract of all the sacred and secular histories with which she had got acquainted.

The jarrings between her mother and grandmother continued; for of course their intercourse did not entirely cease. The former visited her relations at Nohant, and the latter and her grandchildren occasionally passed some weeks in Paris. Aurora, who loved both, her mother even passionately, was much harassed by their jealousy, which vented itself in complaints, taunts, and reproaches. Once she determined to go to Paris and live with her mother, and was only deterred from doing so by the most cruel means imaginable—namely, by her grandmother telling her of the dissolute life which her mother had led before marrying her father.

I owe my first socialistic and democratic instincts to the

singularity of my position, to my birth a cheval so to speak

on two classes—to my love for my mother thwarted and broken

by prejudices which made me suffer before I could comprehend

them. I owe them also to my education, which was by turns

philosophical and religious, and to all the contrasts which

my own life has presented to me from my earliest years.

At the age of thirteen Aurora was sent to the convent of English Augustines in Paris, the only surviving one of the three or four institutions of the kind that were founded during the time of Cromwell. There she remained for the next three years. Her knowledge when she entered this educational as well as religious establishment was not of the sort that enables its possessor to pass examinations; consequently she was placed in the lowest class, although in discussion she could have held her own even against her teachers. Much learning could not be acquired in the convent, but the intercourse with other children, many of them belonging, like the nuns, to English-speaking nations, was not without effect on the development of her character. There were three classes of pupils, the diables, betes, and devotes (the devils, blockheads, and devout). Aurora soon joined the first, and became one of their ringleaders. But all of a sudden a change came over her. From one extreme she fell into the other. From being the wildest of the wild she became the most devout of the devout: "There was nothing strong in me but passion, and when that of religion began to break out, it devoured everything in my heart; and nothing in my brain opposed it." The acuteness of this attack of religious mania gradually diminished; still she harboured for some time the project of taking the veil, and perhaps would have done so if she had been left to herself.

After her return-to Nohant her half-brother Hippolyte, who had recently entered the army, gave her riding lessons, and already at the end of a week she and her mare Colette might be seen leaping ditches and hedges, crossing deep waters, and climbing steep inclines. "And I, the eau dormante of the convent, had become rather more daring than a hussar and more robust than a peasant." The languor which had weighed upon her so long had all of once given way to boisterous activity. When she was seventeen she also began seriously to think of self-improvement; and as her grandmother was now paralytic and mentally much weakened, Aurora had almost no other guidance than that of chance and her own instinct. Thomas a Kempis' "Imitation of Christ," which had been her guide since her religious awakening, was now superseded, not, however, without some struggles, by Chateaubriand's "Le Genie du Christianisme." The book was lent her by her confessor with a view to the strengthening of her faith, but it produced quite the reverse effect, detaching her from it for ever. After reading and enjoying Chateaubriand's book she set to work on the philosophers and essayists Mably, Locke, Condillac, Montesquieu, Bacon, Bossuet, Aristotle, Leibnitz, Pascal, Montaigne, and then turned to the poets and moralists La Bruyere, Pope, Milton, Dante, Virgil, Shakespeare, &c. But she was not a metaphysician; the tendencies of her mind did not impel her to seek for scientific solutions of the great mysteries. "J'etais," she says, "un etre de sentiment, et le sentiment seul tranchait pour moi les questions a man usage, qui toute experience faite, devinrent bientot les seules questions a ma, portee." This "le sentiment seul tranchait pour moi les questions" is another self-revelation, or instance of self-knowledge, which it will be useful to remember. What more natural than that this "being of sentiment" should prefer the poets to the philosophers, and be attracted, not by the cold reasoners, but by Rousseau, "the man of passion and sentiment." It is impossible to describe here the various experiences and doings of Aurora. Without enlarging on the effects produced upon her by Byron's poetry, Shakespeare's "Hamlet," and Chateaubriand's "Rene"; on her suicidal mania; on the long rides which, clad in male attire, she took with Deschartres; on the death of her grandmother, whose fortune she inherited; on her life in Paris with her extravagantly-capricious mother; on her rupture with her father's family, her aristocratic relations, because she would not give up her mother—I say, without enlarging on all this we will at once pass on to her marriage, about which there has been so much fabling.

Aurore Dupin married Casimir Dudevant in September, 1822, and did so of her own free will. Nor was her husband, as the story went, a bald-headed, grey-moustached old colonel, with a look that made all his dependents quake. On the contrary, Casimir Dudevant, a natural son of Colonel Dudevant (an officer of the legion of honour and a baron of the Empire), was, according to George Sand's own description, "a slender, and rather elegant young man, with a gay countenance and a military manner." Besides good looks and youth—he was twenty-seven—he must also have possessed some education, for, although he did not follow any profession, he had been at a military school, served in the army as sub-lieutenant, and on leaving the army had read for the bar and been admitted a barrister.

There was nothing romantic in the courtship, but at the same time it was far from commonplace.

> He did not speak to me of love [writes George Sand], and
> owned that he was little inclined to sudden passion, to
> enthusiasm, and in any case no adept in expressing it in an
> attractive manner. He spoke of a friendship that would stand
> any test, and compared the tranquil happiness of our hosts
> [she was then staying with some friends] to that which he
> believed he could swear to procure me.

She found sincerity not only in his words, but also in his whole conduct; indeed, what lady could question a suitor's sincerity after hearing him say that he had been struck at first sight by her good-natured and sensible look, but that he had not thought her either beautiful or pretty?

Shortly after their marriage the young couple proceeded to Nohant, where they spent the winter. In June, 1823, they went to Paris, and there their son Maurice was born. Their only other offspring, the daughter Solange, did not come into the world till fiveyears later. The discrepancies of the husband and wife's character, which became soon apparent, made themselves gradually more and more felt. His was a practical, hers a poetic nature. Under his management Nohant assumed an altogether different aspect—there was now order, neatness, and economy, where there was previously confusion, untidiness, and waste. She admitted that the change was for the better, but could not help regretting the state of matters that had been—the old dog Phanor taking possession of the fire-place and putting his muddy paws upon the carpet; the old peacock eating the strawberries in the garden; and the wild neglected nooks, where as a child she had so often played and dreamed. Both loved the country, but they loved it for different reasons. He was especially fond of hunting, a consequence of which was that he left his wife much alone. And when he was at home his society may not always have been very entertaining, for what liveliness he had seems to have been rather in his legs than in his brain. Writing to her mother on April i, 1828, Madame Dudevant says: "Vous savez comme il est paresseux de l'esprit et enrage des jambes." On the other hand, her temper, which was anything but uniformly serene, must have been trying to her husband. Occasionally she had fits of weeping without any immediate cause, and one day at luncheon she surprised her husband by a sudden burst of tears which she was unable to account for. As M. Dudevant attributed his wife's condition to the dulness of Nohant, the recent death of her grandmother, and the air of the country, he proposed a change of scene, which he did the more readily as he himself did not in the least like Berry. The pleasant and numerous company they found in the house of the friends with whom they went to stay at once revived her spirits, and she became us frolicsome as she had before been melancholy. George Sand describes her character as continually alternating between "contemplative solitude and complete giddiness in conditions of primitive innocence." It is hardly to be wondered at that one who exhibited such glaring and unaccountable contrasts of character was considered by some people whimsical (bizarre) and by her husband an idiot. She herself admits the possibility that he may not have been wrong. At any rate, little by little he succeeded in making her feel the superiority of reason and intelligence so thoroughly that for a long time she was quite crushed and stupefied in company. Afraid of finding themselves alone at Nohant, the ill-matched pair continued their migration on leaving their friends. Madame Dudevant made great efforts to see through her husband's eyes and to think and act as he wished, but no sooner did she accord with him than she ceased to accord with her own instincts. Whatever they undertook, wherever they went, that sadness "without aim and name" would from time to time come over her. Thinking that the decline of her religiousness was the cause of her lowness of spirits, she took counsel with her old confessor, the Jesuit Abbe de Premord, and even passed, with her husband's consent, some days in the retirement of the English convent. After staying during the spring of 1825 at Nohant, M. and Madame Dudevant set out for the south of France on July 5, the twenty-first anniversary of the latter's birthday. In what George Sand calls the "History of my Life," she inserted some excerpts from a diary kept by her at this time, which throw much light on the relation that existed between wife and husband. If only we could be sure that it is not like so much in the book the outcome of her powerful imagination! Besides repeated complaints about her husband's ill-humour and frequent absences, we meet with the following ominous reflections on marriage:—

Marriage is beautiful for lovers and useful for saints.

Besides saints and lovers there are a great many ordinary minds and placid hearts that do not know love and cannot attain to sanctity.

Marriage is the supreme aim of love. When love has left it, or never entered it, sacrifice remains. This is very well for those who understand sacrifice. The latter presupposes a

measure of heart and a degree of intelligence which are not
frequently to be met with.

For sacrifice there are compensations which the vulgar mind
can appreciate. The approbation of the world, the routine
sweetness of custom, a feeble, tranquil, and sensible
devotion that is not bent on rapturous exaltation, or money,
that is to say baubles, dress, luxury—in short, a thousand
little things which make one forget that one is deprived of
happiness.

The following extracts give us some glimpses which enable us to realise the situation:—

I left rather sad. ____ said hard things to me, having been told
by a Madame ____ that I was wrong in making excursions
without
my husband. I do not think that this is the case, seeing that
my husband goes first, and I go where he intends to go.

My husband is one of the most intrepid of men. He goes
everywhere, and I follow him. He turns round and rebukes me.
He says that I affect singularity. I'll be hanged if I think
of it. I turn round, and I see Zoe following me. I tell her
that she affects singularity. My husband is angry because Zoe
laughs.

...We quickly leave the guides and the caravan behind us.
We ride over the most fantastic roads at a gallop. Zoe is mad
with courage. This intoxicates me, and I at once am her
equal.

In addition to the above, we must read a remark suggested by certain entries in the diary:—

Aimee was an accomplished person of an exquisite distinction.
She loved everything that in any way is elegant and ornate in
society: names, manners, talents, titles. Madcap as I

assuredly was, I looked upon all this as vanity, and went in

quest of intimacy and simplicity combined with poesy. Thanks

to God, I found them in Zoe, who was really a person of

merit, and, moreover, a woman with a heart as eager for

affection as my own.

M. and Madame Dudevant spent the greater part of autumn and the whole winter at Guillery, the chateau of Colonel Dudevant. Had the latter not died at this time, he might perhaps have saved the young people from those troubles towards which they were drifting, at least so his daughter-in-law afterwards thought. In the summer of 1826 the ill-matched couple returned to Nohant, where they continued to live, a few short absences excepted, till 1831. Hitherto their mutual relation had left much to be desired, henceforth it became worse and worse every day. It would, however, be a mistake to account for this state of matters solely by the dissimilarity of their temperaments—the poetic tendency on the one side, the prosaic on the other—for although it precluded an ideal matrimonial union, it by no means rendered an endurable and even pleasant companionship impossible. The real cause of the gathering clouds and imminent storm is to be sought elsewhere. Madame Dudevant was endowed with great vitality; she was, as it were, charged with an enormous amount of energy, which, unless it found an outlet, oppressed her and made her miserable. Now, in her then position, all channels were closed up. The management of household affairs, which, if her statement may be trusted, she neither considered beneath her dignity nor disliked, might have served as a safety-valve; but her administration came to an untimely end. When, after the first year of their married life, her husband examined the accounts, he discovered that she had spent 14,000 francs instead of 10,000, and found himself constrained to declare that their purse was too light for her liberality. Not having anything else to do, and her uselessness vexing her, she took to doctoring the poor and concocting medicines. Hers, however, was not the spirit that allows itself to be fettered by the triple vow of obedience, silence, and poverty. No wonder, therefore, that her life, which she compared to that of a nun, was not to her taste. She did not complain so much of her husband, who did not interfere with her reading and brewing of juleps, and was in no way a tyrant, as of being the slave of a given situation from which he could not set her free. The total lack of ready money was felt by her to constitute in our altogether factitious society an intolerable situation, frightful misery or absolute powerlessness. What she missed was some means of which she might dispose, without compunction and uncontrolled, for an artistic treat, a beautiful book, a week's travelling, a present to a poor friend, a charity to a deserving person, and such like trifles, which, although not indispensable, make life pleasant.

"Irresponsibility is a state of servitude; it is something like the disgrace of the interdict." But servitude and disgrace are galling yokes, and it was not likely that so strong a character would long and meekly submit to them. We have, however, not yet exhausted the grievances of Madame Dudevant. Her brother Hippolyte, after mismanaging his own property, came and lived for the sake of economy at Nohant. His intemperance and that of a friend proved contagious to her husband, and the consequence was not only much rioting till late into the night, but occasionally also filthy conversations. She began, therefore, to consider how the requisite means might be obtained— which would enable her to get away from such undesirable surroundings, and to withdraw her children from these evil influences. For four years she endeavoured to discover an employment by which she could gain her livelihood. A milliner's business was out of the question without capital to begin with; by needlework no more than ten sous a day could be earned; she was too conscientious to make translation pay; her crayon and water-colour portraits were pretty good likenesses, but lacked originality; and in the painting of flowers and birds on cigar-cases, work-boxes, fans, &c., which promised to be more successful, she was soon discouraged by a change of fashion.

At last Madame Dudevant made up her mind to go to Paris and try her luck in literature. She had no ambition whatever, and merely hoped to be able to eke out in this way her slender resources. As regards the capital of knowledge she was possessed of she wrote: "I had read history and novels; I had deciphered scores; I had thrown an inattentive eye over the newspapers....Monsieur Neraud [the Malgache of the "Lettres d'un Voyageur"] had tried to teach me botany. According to the "Histoire de ma Vie" this new departure was brought about by an amicable arrangement; her letters, as in so many cases, tell, however, a very different tale. Especially important is a letter written, on December 3, 1830, to Jules Boucoiran, who had lately been tutor to her children, and whom, after the relation of what had taken place, she asks to resume these duties for her sake now that she will be away from Nohant and her children part of the year. Boucoiran, it should be noted, was a young man of about twenty, who was a total stranger to her on September 2, 1829, but whom she addressed on November 30 of that year as "Mon cher Jules." Well, she tells him in the letter in question that when looking for something in her husband's writing-desk she came on a packet addressed to her, and on which were further written by his hand the words "Do not open it till after my death." Piqued by curiosity, she did open the packet, and found in it nothing but curses upon herself. "He had gathered up in it," she says, "all his ill-humour and anger against me, all his reflections on my perversity." This was too much for her; she had allowed herself to be humiliated for eight years, now she would speak out.

> *Without waiting a day longer, still feeble and ill, I*
> *declared my will and mentioned my motives with an aplomb and*
> *coolness which petrified him. He hardly expected to see a*
> *being like me rise to its full height in order to face him.*
> *He growled, disputed, beseeched. I remained immovable. I want*
> *an allowance, I shall go to Paris, my children will remain at*
> *Nohant.*

She feigned intractability on all these points, but after some time relented and consented to return to Nohant if her conditions were accepted. From the "Histoire de ma Vie" we learn what these conditions were. She demanded her daughter, permission to pass twice three months every year in Paris, and an allowance of 250 francs per month during the time of her absence from Nohant. Her letters, however, show that her daughter was not with her during her first three months at Paris.

Madame Dudevant proceeded to Paris at the beginning of 1831. Her establishment there was of the simplest. It consisted of three little rooms on the fifth story (a mansarde) in a house on the Quai Saint-Michel. She did the washing and ironing herself, the portiere assisting her in the rest of the household work. The meals came from a restaurant, and cost two francs a day. And thus she managed to keep within her allowance. I make these and the following statements on her own authority. As she found her woman's attire too expensive, little suited for facing mud and rain, and in other respects inconvenient, she provided herself with a coat (redingote-guerite), trousers, and waistcoat of coarse grey cloth, a hat of the same colour, a large necktie, and boots with little iron heels. This latter part of her outfit especially gave her much pleasure. Having often worn man's clothes when riding and hunting at Nohant, and remembering that her mother used to go in the same guise with her father to the theatre during their residence in Paris, she felt quite at home in these habiliments and saw nothing shocking in donning them. Now began what she called her literary school-boy life (vie d'ecolier litteraire), her vie de gamin. She trotted through the streets of Paris at all times and in all weathers, went to garrets, studios, clubs, theatres, coffee-houses, in fact, everywhere except to salons. The arts, politics, the romance of society and living humanity, were the studies which she passionately pursued. But she gives those the lie who said of her that she had the "curiosite du vice."

The literary men with whom she had constant intercourse, and with whom she was most closely connected, came, like herself, from Berry. Henri de Latouche (or Delatouche, as George Sand writes), a native of La Chatre, who was editor of the Figaro, enrolled her among the contributors to this journal. But she had no talent for this kind of work, and at the end of the month her payment amounted to perhaps from twelve to fifteen francs. Madame Dudevant and the two other Berrichons, Jules Sandeau and Felix Pyat, were, so to speak, the literary apprentices of Delatouche, who not only was much older than they, having been born in 1785, but had long ago established his reputation as a journalist, novelist, and dramatic writer. The first work which Madame Dudevant produced was the novel "Rose et Blanche"; she wrote it in collaboration with Jules Sandeau, whose relation to her is generally believed to have been not only of a literary nature. The novel, which appeared in 1831, was so successful that the publishers asked the authors to write them another. Madame Dudevant thereupon wrote "Indiana", but without the assistance of Jules Sandeau. She was going to have it published under the nom de plume Jules Sand, which they had assumed on the occasion of "Rose et Blanche." But Jules Sandeau objected to this, saying that as she had done all the work, she ought to have all the honour. To satisfy both, Jules Sandeau, who would not adorn himself with another's plumes, and the publishers, who preferred a known to an unknown name, Delatouche gave Madame Dudevant the name of George Sand, under which henceforth all her works were published, and by which she was best known in society, and generally called among her friends. "Valentine" appeared, like "Indiana," in 1832, and was followed in 1833 by Lelia. For the first two of these novels she received 3,000 francs. When Buloz bought the Revue des deux Mondes, she became one of the contributors to that journal. This shows that a great improvement had taken place in her circumstances, and that the fight she had to fight was not a very hard one. Indeed, in the course of two years she had attained fame, and was now a much-praised and much-abused celebrity.

All this time George Sand had, according to agreement, spent alternately three months in Paris and three months at Nohant. A letter written by M. Dudevant to his wife in 1831 furnishes a curious illustration of the relation that existed between husband and wife. The accommodating spirit which pervades it is most charming:—

> I shall go to Paris; I shall not put up at your lodgings, for
> I do not wish to inconvenience you any more than I wish you
> to inconvenience me (parceque je ne veux pas vous gener, pas
> plus que je ne veux que vous me geniez).

In August, 1833, George Sand and Alfred de Musset met for the first time at a dinner which the editor Buloz gave to the contributors to the Revue des deux Mondes. The two sat beside each other. Musset called on George Sand soon after, called again and again, and before long was passionately in love with her. She reciprocated his devotion. But the serene blissfulness of the first days of their liaison was of short duration. Already in the following month they fled from the Parisian surroundings and gossipings, which they regarded as the disturbers of their harmony. After visiting Genoa, Florence, and Pisa, they settled at Venice. Italy, however, did not afford them the hoped-for peace and contentment. It was evident that the days of "adoration, ecstasy, and worship" were things of the past. Unpleasant scenes became more and more frequent. How, indeed, could a lasting concord be maintained by two such disparate characters? The woman's strength and determination contrasted with the man's weakness and vacillation; her reasoning imperturbation, prudent foresight, and love of order and activity, with his excessive irritability and sensitiveness, wanton carelessness, and unconquerable propensity to idleness and every kind of irregularity. While George Sand sat at her writing-table engaged on some work which was to bring her money and fame, Musset trifled away his time among the female singers and dancers of the noiseless city. In April, 1834, before the poet had quite recovered from the effects of a severe attack of typhoid fever, which confined him to his bed for several weeks, he left George Sand after a violent quarrel and took his departure from Venice. This, however, was not yet the end of their connection. Once more, in spite of all that had happened, they came together; but it was only for a fortnight (at Paris, in the autumn of 1834), and then they parted for ever.

It is impossible, at any rate I shall not attempt, to sift the true from the false in the various accounts which have been published of this love-drama. George Sand's version may be read in her Lettres d'un Voyageur and in Elle et Lui; Alfred de Musset's version in his brother Paul's book Lui et Elle. Neither of these versions, however, is a plain, unvarnished tale. Paul de Musset seems to keep on the whole nearer the truth, but he too cannot be altogether acquitted of the charge of exaggeration. Rather than believe that by the bedside of her lover, whom she thought unconscious and all but dead, George Sand dallied with the physician, sat on his knees, retained him to sup with her, and drank out of one glass with him, one gives credence to her statement that what Alfred de Musset imagined to be reality was but the illusion of a feverish dream. In addition to George Sand's and Paul de Musset's versions, Louise Colet has furnished a third in her Lui, a publication which bears the stamp of insincerity on almost every page, and which has been described, I think by Maxime du Camp, as worse than a lying invention—namely, as a systematic perversion of the truth. A passage from George Sand's Elle et Lui, in which Therese and Laurent, both artists, are the representatives of the novelist and poet, will indicate how she wishes the story to be read:—

> Therese had no weakness for Laurent in the mocking and
> libertine sense that one gives to this word in love. It was
> by an act of her will, after nights of sorrowful meditation,
> that she said to him—"I wish what thou wishest, because we
> have come to that point where the fault to be committed is
> the inevitable reparation of a series of committed faults. I
> have been guilty towards thee in not having the egotistical
> prudence to shun thee; it is better that I should be guilty
> towards myself in remaining thy companion and consolation at
> the expense of my peace and of my pride."..."Listen," she
> added, holding his hand in both of hers with all the strength
> she possessed, "never draw back this hand from me, and,
> whatever happens, preserve so much honour and courage as not
> to forget that before being thy mistress I was thy
> FRIEND....I ask of thee only, if thou growest weary of my
> Jove as thou now art of my friendship, to recollect that it
> was not a moment of delirium that threw me into thy arms, but
> a sudden impulse of my heart, and a more tender and more
> lasting feeling than the intoxication of voluptuousness."

I shall not continue the quotation, the discussion becomes too nauseous. One cannot help sympathising with Alfred de Musset's impatient interruption of George Sand's unctuous lecturing reported in his brother's book—"My dear, you speak so often of chastity that it becomes indecent." Or this other interruption reported by Louise Colet:—

> When one gives the world what the world calls the scandale of
> love, one must have at least the courage of one's passion. In
> this respect the women of the eighteenth century are better
> than you: they did not subtilise love in metaphysics [elles
> n'alambiquaient pas l'amour dans la metaphysique].

It is hardly necessary to say that George Sand had much intercourse with men of intellect. Several litterateurs of some distinction have already been mentioned. Sainte-Beuve and Balzac were two of the earliest of her literary friends, among whom she numbered also Heine. With Lamartine and other cultivators of the belles-lettres she was likewise acquainted. Three of her friends, men of an altogether different type and calibre, have, however, a greater claim on the attention of the student of George Sand's personality than any of those just named, because their speculations and teachings gave powerful impulses to her mind, determined the direction of her thoughts, and widened the sphere of her intellectual activity. The influences of these three men—the advocate Michel of Bourges, an earnest politician; the philosopher and political economist: Pierre Leroux, one of the founders of the "Encyclopedie Nouvelle," and author of "De l'humanite, de son principe et de son avenir"; and the Abbe Lamennais, the author of the "Essai sur l'indifference en matiere de religion," "Paroles d'un Croyant," &c.—are clearly traceable in the "Lettres a Marcie, Spiridion," "Les sept Cordes de la Lyre," "Les Compagnons du tour de France," "Consuelo," "La Comtesse de Rudolstadt," "Le Peche de M. Antoine," "Le Meunier d'Angibault," &c. George Sand made the acquaintance of Pierre Leroux and the Abbe Lammenais in 1835. The latter was introduced to her by her friend Liszt, who knew all the distinguished men of the day, and seems to have often done her similar services. George Sand's friendship with Michel of Bourges, the Everard of her "Lettres d'un Voyageur," dates farther back than 1835.

During George Sand's stay in Venice M. Dudevant had continued to write to her in an amicable and satisfied tone. On returning in the summer of 1834 to France she therefore resumed her periodical sojourns at Nohant; but the pleasure of seeing her home and children was as short-lived as it was sweet, for she soon discovered that neither the former nor the latter, "morally speaking," belonged to her. M. Dudevant's ideas of how they ought to be managed differed entirely from those of his wife, and altogether things had become very uncongenial to her. George Sand, whose view of the circumstances I am giving, speaks mysteriously of abnormal and dangerous influences to which the domestic hearth was exposed, and of her inability to find in her will, adverse as it was to daily struggles and family quarrels, the force to master the situation. From the vague and exceedingly brief indications of facts which are scattered here and there between eloquent and lengthy dissertations on marriage in all its aspects, on the proper pride of woman, and more of the same nature, we gather, however, thus much: she wished to be more independent than she had been hitherto, and above all to get a larger share of her revenues, which amounted to about 15,000 francs, and out of which her husband allowed her and her daughter only 3,000 francs. M. Dudevant, it must be noted, had all along been living on his wife's income, having himself only expectations which would not be realised till after his stepmother's death. By the remonstrances of his wife and the advice of her brother he was several times prevailed upon to agree to a more equitable settlement. But no sooner had he given a promise or signed a contract than he revoked what he had done. According to one of these agreements George Sand and her daughter were to have a yearly allowance of 6,000 francs; according to another M. Dudevant was to have a yearly allowance of 7,000 francs and leave Nohant and the remainder of the revenues to his wife. The terms of the latter of these agreements were finally accepted by both parties, but not till after more than a year's quarrelling and three lawsuits. George Sand sued for a divorce, and the Court of La Chatre gave judgment in her favour on February 16, 1836. This judgment was confirmed after a second trial by the same Court on May 11, 1836.

[Footnote: What George Sand calls her "matrimonial biography" can be read in "Le Droit" ("Journal des Tribunaux") of May 18, 1836. The account there given, no doubt inspired by her advocate if not directly by herself, contains some interesting items, but leaves others unmentioned. One would have liked to learn something more of the husband's pleadings.

The proceedings began on October 30, 1835, when "Madame D——- a forme centre son mari une demande en separation de corps. Cette demande etait fondee sur les injures graves, sevices et mauvais traitements dont elle se plaignait de la part de son mari."

The following is a passage from Michel of Bourges, her advocate's defence: "Des 1824, la vie intime etait devenue difficile; les egards auxquels toute femme a droit furent oublies, des actes d'emportement et de violence revelerent de la part de M. D——- un caractere peu facile, peu capable d'apprecier le devouement et la delicatesse qu'on lui avail temoignes. Les mauvais traitements furent d'abord plus rares que les mauvais precedes, ainsi les imputations d'imbecillite, de stupidite, furent prodiguees a Madame D——- le droit de raisonner, de prendre l'art a la conversation lui fut interdit... des relations avec d'autres femmes furent connues de l'epouse,et vers le mois de Decembre, 1828, toute cohabitation intime cessa.

"Les enfants eux-memes eurent quelque part dans les mauvais traitements."]

M. Dudevant then appealed to the Court of Cassation at Bourges, where the case was tried on July 25; but he withdrew his appeal before judgment was given. The insinuations and revelations made in the course of these lawsuits were anything but edifying. George Sand says that she confined herself to furnishing the proofs strictly demanded by the law, and revealed only such facts as were absolutely necessary. But these facts and proofs must have been of a very damaging nature, for M. Dudevant answered them by imputations to merit one hundred-thousandth part of which would have made her tremble. "His attorney refused to read a libel. The judges would have refused to listen to it." Of a deposition presented by M. Dudevant to the Court, his wife remarks that it was "dictated, one might have said, drawn up," by two servants whom she had dismissed. She maintains that she did not deserve this treatment, as she betrayed of her husband's conduct only what he himself was wont to boast of.

George Sand's letters [Footnote: George Sand: Correspondence 1812-1876; Six volumes (Paris: Calman Levy).] seem to me to show conclusively that her chief motives for seeking a divorce were a desire for greater independence and above all for more money. Complaints of ill-treatment are not heard of till they serve to justify an action or to attain a purpose. And the exaggeration of her varying statements must be obvious to all but the most careless observer. George Sand is slow in making up her mind; but having made it up she acts with fierce promptitude, obstinate vigour, and inconsiderate unscrupulousness, in one word, with that concentration of self which sees nothing but its own desires. On the whole, I should say that M. Dudevant was more sinned against than sinning. George Sand, even as she represents herself in the Histoire de ma Vie and in her letters, was far from being an exemplary wife, or indeed a woman with whom even the most angelic of husbands would have found it easy to live in peace and happiness.

From the letters, which reveal so strikingly the ungentlewomanlikeness (not merely in a conventional sense) of her manners and her numerous and curious intimacies with men of all ages, more especially with young men, I shall now cull a few characteristic passages in proof of what I have said.

One must have a passion in life. I feel ennui for the want of
one. The agitated and often even rather needy life I am
leading here drives spleen far away. I am very well, and you
will see me in the best of humours. [To her friend A. M.
Duteil. Paris, February 15, 1831.]

I have an object, a task, let me say the word, a passion. The
profession of writing is a violent and almost indestructible
one. [To Jules Boucoiran. Paris, March 4, 1831.]

I cannot bear the shadow of a constraint, this is my
principal fault. Everything that is imposed upon me as a duty
becomes hateful to me.

After saying that she leaves her husband full liberty to do what he likes—"qu'il a des maitresses ou n'en a pas, suivant son appetit,"—and speaking highly of his management of their affairs, she writes in the same letter as follows:—

Moreover, it is only just that this great liberty which my
husband enjoys should be reciprocal; otherwise, he would
become to me odious and contemptible; that is what he does
not wish to be. I am therefore quite independent; I go to bed
when he rises, I go to La Chatre or to Rome, I come in at
midnight or at six o'clock; all this is my business. Those
who do not approve of this, and disparage me to you, judge
them with your reason and your mother's heart; the one and
the other ought to be with me. [To her mother. Nohant, May
31, 1831.]

Marriage is a state so contrary to every kind of union and
happiness that I have good reason to fear for you. [To Jules
Boucoiran, who had thoughts of getting married. Paris, March
6, 1833.]

You load me with very heavy reproaches, my dear child... you
reproach me with my numerous liaisons, my frivolous
friendships. I never undertake to clear myself from the
accusations which bear on my character. I can explain facts
and actions; but never defects of the mind or perversities of
the heart. [To Jules Boucoiran. Paris, January 18, 1833.]

Thou hast pardoned me when I committed follies which the
world calls faults. [To her friend Charles Duvernet. Paris,

October 15, 1834.]

But I claim to possess, now and for ever, the proud and
entire independence which you believe you alone have the
right to enjoy. I shall not advise it to everyone; but I
shall not suffer that, so far as I am concerned, any love
whatever shall in the least fetter it. I hope to make my
conditions so hard and so clear that no man will be bold and
vile enough to accept them. [To her friend Adolphe Gueroult.
Paris, May 6, 1835.]

Nothing shall prevent me from doing what I ought to and what
I will do. I am the daughter of my father, and I care not for
prejudices when my heart enjoins justice and courage. [To her
mother. Nohant, October 25, 1835.]

Opinion is a prostitute which must be sent about her business
with kicks when one is in the right. [To her friend Adolphe
Gueroult. La Chatre, November 9, 1835.]

The materials made use of in the foregoing sketch of George Sand's
life up to 1836 consist to a very considerable extent of her own DATA, and
in part even of her own words. From this fact, however, it ought not to be
inferred that her statements can always be safely accepted without previous
examination, or at any time be taken au pied de la lettre. Indeed, the writer of
the Histoire de ma Vie reveals her character indirectly rather than directly,
unawares rather than intentionally. This so-called "history" of her life
contains some truth, although not all the truth; but it contains it implicitly,
not explicitly. What strikes the observant reader of the four-volumed work
most forcibly, is the attitude of serene self-admiration and self-satisfaction
which the autobiographer maintains throughout. She describes her nature
as pre-eminently "confiding and tender," and affirms that in spite of the
great and many wrongs she was made to suffer, she never wronged anyone
in all her life. Hence the perfect tranquillity of conscience she always
enjoyed. Once or twice, it is true, she admits that she may not be an angel,
and that she as well as her husband may have had faults. Such humble

words, however, ought not to be regarded as penitent confessions of a sinful heart, but as generous concessions of a charitable mind. In short, a thorough belief in her own virtuousness and superior excellence was the key-note of her character. The Pharisaical tendency to thank God for not having made her like other people pervades every page of her autobiography, of which Charles Mazade justly says that it is—

a kind of orgy of a personality intoxicated with itself, an

abuse of intimate secrets in which she slashes her friends,

her reminiscences, and—truth.

George Sand declares again and again that she abstains from speaking of certain matters out of regard for the feelings or memories of other persons, whereas in reality she speaks recklessly of everybody as long as she can do so without compromising herself. What virtuous motives can have prompted her to publish her mother's shame? What necessity was there to expatiate on her brother's drunkenness? And if she was the wronged and yet pitiful woman she pretended to be, why, instead of burying her husband's, Musset's, and others' sins in silence, does she throw out against them those artful insinuations and mysterious hints which are worse than open accusations? Probably her artistic instincts suggested that a dark background would set off more effectively her own glorious luminousness. However, I do not think that her indiscretions and misrepresentations deserve always to be stigmatised as intentional malice and conscious falsehood. On the contrary, I firmly believe that she not only tried to deceive others, but that she actually deceived herself. The habit of self-adoration had given her a moral squint, a defect which was aggravated by a powerful imagination and excellent reasoning faculties. For, swayed as these were by her sentiments and desires, they proved themselves most fertile in generating flattering illusions and artful sophisms. George Sand was indeed a great sophist. She had always in readiness an inexhaustible store of interpretations and subterfuges with which to palliate, excuse, or even metamorphose into their contraries the most odious of her words and actions. It is not likely that any one ever equalled, much less surpassed, her expertness in hiding ugly facts or making innocent things look suspicious. To judge by her writings and conversations she never acted spontaneously, but reasoned on all matters and on all occasions.

At no time whatever [writes Paul Lindau in his "Alfred de

Musset"] is there to be discovered in George Sand a trace of

a passion and inconsiderateness, she possesses an

imperturbable calmness. Love sans phrase does not exist for
her. That her frivolity may be frivolity, she never will
confess. She calculates the gifts of love, and administers
them in mild, well-measured doses. She piques herself upon
not being impelled by the senses. She considers it more
meritorious if out of charity and compassion she suffers
herself to be loved. She could not be a Gretchen [a Faust's
Margaret], she would not be a Magdalen, and she became a Lady
Tartuffe.

George Sand's three great words were "maternity," "chastity," and
"pride." She uses them ad nauseam, and thereby proves that she did not
possess the genuine qualities. No doubt, her conceptions of the words
differed from those generally accepted: by "pride" (orgueil), for instance,
she seems to have meant a kind of womanly self-respect debased by a
supercilious haughtiness and self-idolatry. But, as I have said already,
she was a victim to self-deception. So much is certain, the world, with an
approach to unanimity rarely attained, not only does not credit her with the
virtues which she boasts of, but even accuses her of the very opposite vices.
None of the writers I have consulted arrives, in discussing George Sand's
character, at conclusions which tally with her own estimate; and every
person, in Paris and elsewhere, with whom I have conversed on the subject
condemned her conduct most unequivocally. Indeed, a Parisian—who, if
he had not seen much of her, had seen much of many who had known her
well—did not hesitate to describe her to me as a female Don Juan, and added
that people would by-and-by speak more freely of her adventures. Madame
Audley (see "Frederic Chopin, sa vie et ses oeuvres," p. 127) seems to me to
echo pretty exactly the general opinion in summing up her strictures thus:—

A woman of genius, but a woman with sensual appetites, with

insatiable desires, accustomed to satisfy them at any price,

should she even have to break the cup after draining it,

equally wanting in balance, wisdom, and purity of mind, and

in decorum, reserve, and dignity of conduct.

Many of the current rumours about her doings were no doubt inventions
of idle gossips and malicious enemies, but the number of well-ascertained
facts go far to justify the worst accusations. And even though the evidence
of deeds were wanting, have we not that of her words and opinions as set

forth in her works? I cannot help thinking that George Sand's fondness for the portraiture of sensual passion, sometimes even of sensual passion in its most brutal manifestations, is irreconcilable with true chastity. Many a page in her novels exhibits indeed a surprising knowledge of the physiology of love, a knowledge which presupposes an extensive practical acquaintance with as wellas attentive study of the subject. That she depicts the most repulsive situations with a delicacy of touch which veils the repulsiveness and deceives the unwary rather aggravates the guilt. Now, though the purity of a work of art is no proof of the purity of the artist (who may reveal only the better part of his nature, or give expression to his aspirations), the impurity of a work of art always testifies indubitably to the presence of impurity in the artist, of impurity in thought, if not in deed. It is, therefore, not an unwarranted assumption to say that the works of George Sand prove conclusively that she was not the pure, loving, devoted, harmless being she represents herself in the "Histoire de ma Vie." Chateaubriand said truly that: "le talent de George Sand a quelque ratine dans la corruption, elle deviendrait commune en devenant timoree." Alfred Nettement, who, in his "Histoire de la litterature franqaise sous le gouvernement de Juillet," calls George Sand a "painter of fallen and defiled natures," remarks that—

> most of her romances are dazzling rehabilitations of
> adultery, and in reading their burning pages it would seem
> that there remains only one thing to be done—namely, to break
> the social chains in order that the Lelias and Sylvias may go
> in quest of their ideal without being stopped by morality and
> the laws, those importune customs lines which religion and
> the institutions have opposed to individual whim and
> inconstancy.

Perhaps it will be objected to this that the moral extravagances and audacious sophistries to be met with in "Lelia," in "Leoni," and other novels of hers, belong to the characters represented, and not to the author. Unfortunately this argument is untenable after the publication of George Sand's letters, for there she identifies herself with Lelia, and develops views identical with those that shocked us in Leoni and elsewhere.

[Footnote: On May 26, 1833, she writes to her friend Francois Rollinat with regard to this book: "It is an eternal chat between us. We are the gravest personages in it." Three years later, writing to the Comtesse d'Agoult, her account differs somewhat: "I am adding a volume to 'Lelia.' This occupies me more than any other novel has as yet done. Lelia is not myself, je suis meilleure enfant; but she is my ideal."—Correspondance, vol. I., pp. 248 and 372.]

These letters, moreover, contain much that is damaging to her claim to chastity. Indeed, one sentence in a letter written in June, 1835 (Correspondance, vol. I., p. 307), disposes of this claim decisively. The unnecessarily graphic manner in which she here deals with an indelicate subject would be revolting in a man addressing a woman, in a woman addressing a man it is simply monstrous.

As a thinker, George Sand never attained to maturity; she always remained the slave of her strong passions and vitiated principles. She never wrote a truer word than when she confessed that she judged everything by sympathy. Indeed, what she said of her childhood applies also to her womanhood: "Il n'y avait de fort en moi que la passion... rien dans man cerveau fit obstacle." George Sand often lays her finger on sore places, fails, however, not only to prescribe the right remedy, but even to recognise the true cause of the disease. She makes now and then acute observations, but has not sufficient strength to grapple successfully with the great social, philosophical, and religious problems which she so boldly takes up. In fact, reasoning unreasonableness was a very frequent condition of George Sand's mind. That the unreasonableness of her reasoning remains unseen by many, did so at any rate in her time, is due to the marvellous beauty and eloquence of her language. The best that can be said of her subversive theories was said by a French critic—namely, that they were in reality only "le temoignage d'aspirations genereuses et de nobles illusions." But even this is saying too much, for her aspirations and illusions are far from being always generous and noble. If we wish to see George Sand at her best we must seek her out in her quiet moods, when she contents herself with being an artist, and unfolds before us the beauties of nature and the secrets of the human heart. Indeed, unless we do this, we cannot form a true idea of her character. Not all the roots of her talent were imbedded in corruption. She who wrote Lelia wrote also Andre, she who wrote Lucrezia Floriani wrote also La petite Fadette. And in remembering her faults and shortcomings justice demands that we should not forget her family history, with its dissensions and examples of libertinism, and her education without system, continuity, completeness, and proper guidance.

The most precious judgment pronounced on George Sand is by one who was at once a true woman and a great poet. Mrs. Elizabeth Barrett Browning saw in her the "large-brained woman and large-hearted man... whose soul, amid the lions of her tumultuous senses, moans defiance and answers roar for roar, as spirits can"; but who lacked "the angel's grace of a pure genius sanctified from blame." This is from the sonnet to George Sand, entitled "A Desire." In another sonnet, likewise addressed to George Sand and entitled "A Recognition," she tells her how vain it was to deny with a manly scorn the woman's nature... while before

> *The world thou burnest in a poet-fire,*
> *We see thy woman-heart beat evermore*
> *Through the large flame. Beat purer, heart, and higher,*
> *Till God unsex thee on the heavenly shore*
> *Where unincarnate spirits purely aspire!*

9789359321103